Women Fielding Danger

Women Fielding Danger

Negotiating Ethnographic Identities in Field Research

Edited by Martha K. Huggins
and Marie-Louise Glebbeek

ROWMAN & LITTLEFIELD PUBLISHERS, INC.
Lanham • Boulder • New York • Toronto • Plymouth, UK

ROWMAN & LITTLEFIELD PUBLISHERS, INC.

Published in the United States of America
by Rowman & Littlefield Publishers, Inc.
A wholly owned subsidiary of The Rowman & Littlefield Publishing Group, Inc.
4501 Forbes Boulevard, Suite 200, Lanham, Maryland 20706
www.rowmanlittlefield.com

Estover Road
Plymouth PL6 7PY
United Kingdom

British Library Cataloguing in Publication Information Available

Library of Congress Cataloging-in-Publication Data

Women fielding danger : negotiating ethnographic identities in field research /
edited by Martha K. Huggins and Marie-Louise Glebbeek.
    p. cm.
  Includes bibliographical references.
  ISBN-13: 978-0-7425-4119-1 (cloth : alk. paper)
  ISBN-10: 0-7425-4119-3 (cloth : alk. paper)
  ISBN-13: 978-0-7425-4120-7 (pbk. : alk. paper)
  ISBN-10: 0-7425-4120-7 (pbk. : alk. paper)
  eISBN-13: 978-0-7425-5756-7
  eISBN-10: 0-7425-5756-1
  1. Social sciences—Fieldwork. 2. Women in the social sciences. I. Huggins,
Martha Knisely, 1944– II. Glebbeek, Marie-Louise, 1971–
  H62.W64 2009
  300.72—dc22   2008030484

Printed in the United States of America

♾ ™ The paper used in this publication meets the minimum requirements of
American National Standard for Information Sciences—Permanence of Paper
for Printed Library Materials, ANSI/NISO Z39.48-1992.

To those lost "when the levees broke," to those who struggle to return, to outsiders who rebuild a city forgotten by government, and to those who continue struggling for justice.

—Martha K. Huggins, New Orleans, Louisiana

To the most important men in my life, Richard and Joost van der Wal, who make me a happy woman every single day, and to my father, who taught me to fight for important things but who lost his own struggle for life a few months before this book's publication.

—Marie-Louise Glebbeek, Utrecht, Netherlands

Contents

Acknowledgments

We could not have assembled this volume without the excellent research of the scholars published in *Women Fielding Danger*. We have learned much more from them than can be communicated in the volume's academic introduction.

Martha Huggins wishes to thank Marie-Louise Glebbeek for providing a model for understanding the importance of subjective material in cross-gender research on police, something that, after decades of her own research, had not been seriously considered and was only reluctantly entertained as a serious undertaking.

We have been inspired by so many who have written about field research, but certainly among the most important is Carolyn Nordstrom and Antonius Robben's *Fieldwork Under Fire: Contemporary Studies of Violence and Survival* (University of California Press, 1996). We also give appreciation to the scholars who supported *Women Fielding Danger* throughout its preparation, including Lori Marso, Melinda Gouldner, and Cynthia Enloe.

This volume would not have been possible without early support from the University of Wisconsin's Women and Gender Studies and World Studies programs. Having these scholars express enthusiasm for the "Women Fielding Danger Project," in the form of a 2003 conference, provided the intellectual and moral support to complete *Women Fielding Danger*. We are especially indebted to Leigh Payne of the University of Wisconsin's Political Science Department for seeking internal funding and for organizing the 2003 University of Wisconsin conference. The scholars there will never know how important their support was for Martha Huggins in the dark first two years after Hurricane Katrina, when she was balancing university and city recovery with some very dark moments of her own. Equally important, of course, was the patience and support of the women whose research is in this volume: They kept the light burning.

We extend our thanks to Carolyn Micklas, the Webmaster for our *Women Fielding Danger* Web site (www.womenfieldingdanger.com). Our patient former editor at Rowman & Littlefield, Jessica Gribble, was supportive throughout the far too many years encompassing this project's initiation and development. Our new editor, Carrie Broadwell-Tkach, and our production editor, Catherine Forrest Getzie, carried us to publication with skill and care.

Finally, we give thanks to our families: Marie-Louise, for the love and joy given her by Richard, her husband, and by Joost, her young son; and Martha, for the love of her husband, Malcolm.

Introduction

Similarities among Differences

Martha K. Huggins and Marie-Louise Glebbeek

Anticipating the methodological discoveries that could emerge from research by fifteen academic women from five different disciplines researching a variety of topics in twelve different world regions, we assumed that their methodological problems and strategies would vary greatly. Instead, they revealed more similarities than differences. We expected physical dangers would be their greatest fieldwork threat. Instead, we discovered the researchers' greatest concern to be "gender incredibility"—their interlocutors' persistent assumption that the statuses of "female" and "researcher" are incongruent—e.g., "status inconsistent." This was true whether the researcher was interacting with a woman or man.

Even during her sometimes physically dangerous research in the early 1990s in postwar Albania and Kosovo, Stephanie Schwandner-Sievers recognized that, although

> [l]oved ones worried that conducting research in regions experiencing great political and social turmoil . . . could surely result in violence against me—even in my death . . . , I increasingly discovered as a woman working on my own that the greatest threat was not the violence toward me, but rather not being taken seriously as a researcher.

After gender incredibility, another formidable research hurdle was juggling multiple research challenges. Failing to work out a balance among simultaneous field difficulties could derail a research interaction. In the midst of this dynamic, researchers found themselves confronted by yet another pressing danger: emergent ethical concerns. The moral guidelines they brought with them had lost some of their viability in fast-paced

1

researcher-interlocutor interactions, making research ethics another "dangerous" undertaking.

These emergent dangers—gender incredibility, avoiding physical danger itself, juggling multiple research interactions, upholding research ethics—have set the four themes discussed in this introduction: gender's preeminence, varied field dangers, negotiating research identities, and addressing ethics in situ.

A CURIOSITY OF THEMES

The four themes derived from the research reported in *Women Fielding Danger* emerge to varying degrees among articles from different world regions and countries—Africa (Zanzibar), Asia (East Timor, Burma, and India), Central and South America (Brazil, El Salvador, Guatemala, Nicaragua), Europe (Albania and Kosovo), the Middle East (Lebanon), and the United States (the Louisiana Bayou, Pennsylvania, and Tennessee). The authors represent five academic specialties: six anthropologists (Demovic, Glebbeek, Goldstein, Sanford, Schwanders-Sievers, and Skidmore), five sociologists (Bickham-Mendez, Rito, Sehgal, Subramaniam, and Viterna), two criminologist-sociologists (Huggins and Presser), one political scientist (Fredriksson), and one specialist in Asian and Near Eastern languages and literature and international and area studies (Shaery-Eisenlohr). Nevertheless, in spite of the differences in field site political geography, substantive focus, and disciplinary approaches to epistemology and methods, there turned out to be more similarities than differences in the field experiences of the researchers represented here.

By design, of course, much will be left out of our introduction. Readers will consult each of the volume's lively chapters for additional themes. You might contribute your own field experiences and other relevant materials to our Web site, womenfieldingdanger.com—a resource for researchers to share methodological issues and field strategies with one another. An important objective of this book and of our Web site is to elevate the research *process* to more than an appendix or footnote in researchers' articles or books. We are encouraged too often by teachers, advisers, colleagues, article or book referees, or our editors to leave "subjective matter" out of research methods discussions—"such material is not objective"; "it is 'highly subjective' and could spoil appreciation of research outcomes"; "it adds too many 'nonessential' pages to the length of your book or article"; or "at most include a very brief summary in your book's appendix." However, as *Women Fielding Danger* illustrates, it is precisely in the context of such "subjective matter" that scholars obtain serendipitous research findings and demonstrate a range of gendered roadblocks and opportunities, and, in spite of these, secure most of the material they sought in the first place, albeit through unexpected and often frustrating routes of inquiry.

THEME 1: FIELD DANGERS—VARIED AND UBIQUITOUS

Researcher Vulnerability

While physical danger is not among the dangers most mentioned by researchers in this volume, physical violence—whether real or threatened—was ubiquitous in their field sites. However, as several researchers explain, just because danger exists does not mean that it will be perceived as threatening. For example, finding herself confronting multiple dangers simultaneously in post-9/11 Swahili Muslim Zanzibar, Angela Demovic asks, "How do we understand danger?" Her answer: "We can't always objectively know when we are in danger, but instead rely on a number of heuristic devices to constantly (and unconsciously) evaluate our risk in any given situation." Speaking to such "heuristic devices," Monique Skidmore calls attention to "affective field sites," explaining that these exist where "normal geographic familiarity is overlaid by a topography of *emotionally experienced* locations." Within affective field sites, "the familiar routines and assumptions about personal safety are revealed to be comforting fictions."

Lynn Fredriksson's academic advisers feared and discouraged her carrying out research in East Timor, seen as a perilous conflict zone. Fredriksson, determined to continue her research there, argued that "it is at the intersection of gender and risk from which some of our most brilliant social science research and theory derive." Knowing full well the dangers that awaited her—since she had conducted human rights advocacy research in East Timor during the nation's Indonesian military occupation and immediately thereafter—Fredriksson explained to her academic advisers that "the more isolated and dangerous the field situation, the greater the need for research." This was a hard sell. Why? Because university academics are overly cautions with students? Because universities fear lawsuits? Because Frederiksson and her advisers assessed "the field" from different generational standpoints?

Pointing to the latter, Skidmore—a skilled researcher of military-controlled Burma (Myanmar)—explains that her own evaluations of "acceptable" and "unacceptable" risk changed across her own life cycle:

> At the beginning of my academic research career, there were some potentially dangerous risks that I was willing to take. As a childless doctoral student living in Rangoon, I reasoned that research activities that might land me in jail temporarily or lead to my deportation—for example, discussing politics with Burmese people—were "acceptable risks" for conducting research about the Burmese government's war against its own people.

As the years rolled on, and my personal life as well, what had once been an "acceptable" level of fieldwork risk became "unacceptable." . . . [As] a mother of two, I can no longer enter Burma without defining safety and danger in terms of my children. They need their mother and I have a responsibility to conduct research in a manner that doesn't endanger me.

Informant Vulnerability

Researchers in this volume express frequent concern about their research placing their interlocutors in danger. Jennifer Bickham Mendez feared doing this due to the wide variety of research actors and organizations with whom she interacted—namely, the local immigrant community, whether legally or illegally in the United States; the organization assisting "legal" immigrants and the organization's funders; and the U.S. Immigration Service. Simply put, Bickham Mendez gained access to information about immigrants that could have harmed them; if she assisted the "illegals" among this group, because of her association with the immigrant assistance organization, the organization's funders might cut support. Bickham Mendez had to balance her accountability to the social service organization's immigrant clients while being bound to the social service organization's own "rules, laws, and policies." This meant balancing such concerns within an "increasingly hostile, anti-immigrant climate" in the United States.

Skidmore discusses informant vulnerability in her research on military-ruled Burma: How could she, an international in a country suspicious of foreigners, carry out research on locals without making them vulnerable to arrest? "[S]ince first beginning research in Rangoon in 1994," she writes, "I have relied successfully on my network of urban friends and acquaintances, a network painstakingly created and maintained." However, Skidmore's local network was "continually threatened by the heavy tension created . . . by fear and the vulnerability that comes from . . . knowing [a foreigner], and knowing that military agents know of these taboo associations."

One strategy was to "hide in the open," involving "taking a walk [with an interlocutor] in an open space, or meeting, supposedly by chance, in busy open places such as markets." Presumably, open public areas are less likely to be perceived by military officials and informants as places where "espionage" would take place, thus making interactions between nationals and foreigners less threatening for these participants.

Emotional Blowback

Painfully and compellingly, Sanford explains that after taking more than four hundred testimonies from Maya survivors of Guatemalan army massacres and then writing about them, she came back from Guatemala with *susto*. What is *susto*, you ask. The direct translation is scare or fright. But *susto* is really something deeper and far more profound. It is a malady understood in Maya communities and pondered by anthropologists and those who study "folklore." But *susto* is real . . . [it happens when] the individual body and soul . . . cannot bear the weight of fear and sorrow in the physical and spiritual realms.

For Sanford, "*susto* was physical and spiritual . . . [a kind of] secondary trauma or post-traumatic stress disorder."

Having spent a long period in military Burma's "affective field," Skidmore discovered that even after she returned home to the United States, it took more than a year for her to stop sliding her eyes toward street corners to see if any danger was lurking and to stop covering her mouth with her hands when she spoke. Skidmore found that "even to think of writing about [her] field experiences caused [her] fear." Likewise, Meera Sehgal, who had carried out undercover research among women in India's violent Hindu nationalist movement, delayed publishing her book out of "a combination of fear and . . . ethics."

The myriad dangers experienced by researchers in this volume will continue to be identified in "gender's preeminence."

THEME 2: GENDER'S PREEMINENCE

Women Fielding Danger illustrates that whether studying women or men, and whether a researcher defined herself as feminist or not, being a woman profoundly shaped the researchers' interactions with interviewees and associated actors. For example, attempts to transform the researcher into a particular culture's notion of a "good" wife, mother, sister, or daughter—or into a "sex object"—resulted in the researcher's being excluded from the status of "research scientist." (See Glebbeek in Huggins and Glebbeek, Presser, Shaery-Eisenlohr, Rito, Schwandner-Sievers, and Viterna.) Roschanack Shaery-Eisenlohr, a Shiite woman conducting research among male Shiites in Lebanon, found that soon after she introduced herself to a prospective interlocutor, her gender became the focus of the research interaction. The interlocutor would ask, "Are you married?" After receiving a "yes," the interlocutor would then ask, "How many children do you have?" Responding that she had none, the interviewee would then ask, "Why are you *still* childless—*considering your age*?" Seeing the confusion and disappointment in her interlocutors' faces and voices, Shaery-Eisenlohr explained, "My studies are important . . . and . . . having children now could put an end to my research." Recognizing an interlocutor's continued disappointment, Shaery-Eisenlohr added that she was "planning to have children later on," which was often followed by the interviewee's well-meaning recommendation of a doctor who could help with the "medical problems" that were causing her "childlessness." Such exchanges made Shaery-Eisenlohr feel "that [she] was not taken seriously as a researcher."

Several researchers in this volume reported that being seen as a "woman" rather than as a "research professional" kept them from obtaining information needed for their research. Schwandner-Sievers remembers that "as a female 'associate' of a Western male research team," she was excluded from male-only spaces of Albanian homes, which had implications for what Schwandner-Sievers could learn about "certain aspects of village life and customs." For Demovic, being a woman—even more than being American in post-9/11 Swahili Muslim Zanzibar—excluded her from information about Zanzibar Island's political climate. Jocelyn Viterna encountered difficulties obtaining interviews with village women in El Salvador until she joined the women in making the day's tortillas. Kat Rito, conducting research on land rights and conflicts in southern Louisiana's Atchafalaya Basin, found that every question about land rights or conflict was responded to by questions about her academic program or romantic life. Rito's curiosity about such gendered preliminaries was answered when one interviewee, twenty minutes into their discussion, stopped talking and asked when "the researcher" would arrive. He had assumed that Rito was a research assistant and was waiting until the *real* researcher arrived to answer questions.

On the other hand, Fredriksson found that being a female provided a kind of "cultural disguise": "Being [a woman] often led to . . . being perceived as less threatening, thus increasing interviewees' feelings of safety." Skidmore recognized that "being short, plump, and female [was] an advantage for . . . a foreign researcher in Burma":

> My build makes it less likely that, to Burmese, I appear menacing or particularly shifty. Indeed, Burmese people say that I look like the "idyllic version" of a respectable, middle-class married Burmese woman. Coupled with my Burmese language skills and knowledge of Burmese habits and customs, I have repeatedly gained permission from the Burmese regime to conduct in-country fieldwork.

In Skidmore's words, "By Burmese women identifying with my multiple roles of mother, professional, advocate for social justice, wife, and co-manager of a busy household, I might have [gained] 'respectability' and 'approachability,' which might provide some measure of safety in the process."

Schwandner-Sievers argues that being a woman enhanced her research freedom and her personal safety in Albania, but only after she had been absorbed into Albanian patriarchal customs. For her part, Skidmore decided that being female in military Burma ultimately limited her freedom to be in war zones: "I decided very early in my research career that the systematic rape of minority women, girl children, and infants in Burma's eastern war zones made these areas too risky for me, since this deliberate war strategy has been reserved largely for women." Schwandner-Sievers, as a "woman in need of patriarchal protection," found herself excluded from certain household locations and certain kinds of ritualized processes. On the other hand, as "an 'honored foreign guest,' . . . [she] gained the respect allocated to a short-term 'guest,'" which resulted in her being less controlled in her research. However, as a *female* honored guest, she suspects that she was still more controlled than if she had been a male guest.

By pointing to gender's preeminence in interactions among researchers and interlocutors, we do not suggest that other ascribed and achieved statuses did not also structure research processes and outcomes. Fredriksson believes that her non-Asian nationality "nurture[d] a kind of 'cultural trust'" among Timorese because "[n]on-Indonesian Asians were often mistaken [by Timorese] for Indonesians and considered potential military collaborators." Fredriksson adds that being a non-Asian Anglo *and* a women helped to diminish "interviewees' feelings of fear, skepticism, and mistrust." Bickham Mendez, Goldstein, Huggins, and Sanford each found that being "from the United States" facilitated obtaining interviews, created a trust-facilitating climate, and helped in obtaining certain "lifestyle" privileges. For example, Goldstein believes that being a North American carrying out research in a Brazilian slum gave her opportunities for safety that locals did not have: She could "leave [the poor community] and sleep in a comparatively secure middle-class neighborhood whenever . . . there was a potential for violence." A version of this was noted by Sanford and Viterna, as well.

Martha Huggins discovered that as an American academic she was facilitated in obtaining torturers' testimonies: Being a foreigner meant that she would leave the country with their information; being an academic meant that she was considered "objective." "Journalists," Huggins's police interviewees told her, "are biased, and academics are not" (Huggins et al. 2002). Schwandner-Sievers reports that she benefited in the immediate postwar Balkans from what she calls the "White Jeep factor": Having a visible relationship with a Western organization, something that was communicated when Schwandner-Sievers arrived in a community in a white jeep with its United Nations flag, enhanced her professional status. However, on the downside of being a female international, various researchers—for example, Glebbeek and Viterna—report having to strategically manage being seen by both men and women as sexually "loose": Research locations were sexualized; researchers were seen by men as potential romantic conquests and by local women as romantic competitors. One strategy for negotiating these designations was for a researcher to "play into" a prevalent patriarchy.

This was as important for gaining women's trust as it was when interacting with the men. Viterna explains this in her research in rural El Salvador:

> Given that earning the women's trust was most important for my research, I decided I would have to behave in a manner that did not promote a promiscuous image, even if it meant distancing myself from the male interviewees. . . . I . . . kept my distance from men in the villages except when interviewing them. At community gatherings, I would stand with the women and away from the men. When I attended a community dance, I only danced with young children. I always wore conservative slacks and shirts in the villages. On those occasions where I would need to bathe in a relatively public place (a fairly common occurrence in El Salvador, where water supplies are publicly shared), I would bathe while wearing a t-shirt and shorts.

Bickham Mendez and Viterna both found that being an international—particularly from the United States or Europe—led interlocutor nationals in Nicaragua and El Salvador, respectively, to request their assistance in grant writing and/or obtaining international aid for their local community or nongovernmental organization. Carrying out such administrative activities while simultaneously observing the interlocutors was a formidable research challenge.

Just as sometimes a researcher was challenged by gender, (international) nationality, ethnicity, and/or caste or class, she also often benefited from one or another of these. However, such benefits often brought issues of their own, the biggest one being the researcher's privileges at the "cost" of interlocutors. Bickham Mendez saw that being White and "from the United States" gave her unwanted power and influence over the female interviewees she hoped to engage in "collaborate advocacy research." Huggins and Goldstein each found that they "benefited" from the Brazilian cultural preference for whiteness over blackness: Where light skin and associated physical characteristics are valued over darker ones, privilege was derived from their positively esteemed phenotype. Lois Presser, in U.S. research on male convicts, some "marginalized by class and race," felt compromised in that her research safety was based on "the state's project of controlling those marginalized by class and race."

In the end, we cannot say whether it was gender or race/ethnicity or nationality acting alone or in combination that most influenced research interactions. We do know that relationships between interlocutor and researcher were initially unequal in one important respect: Most researchers are European or U.S. Anglos—with the exception of Seghal, Shaery-Eisenlohr, and Subramaniam—and most interviewees were (usually poor) people of color—Asian, African/African Diasporic, Ibero/Brazilian, Latino/as. The research in this volume will show that these and other factors interacted in both different and similar ways in each interaction to produce research opportunities and challenges. A researcher's strategy for influencing outcomes was to employ research reflexivity, which resulted in identity negotiations and some kind of identity approximation, as the next section explains.

THEME 3: NEGOTIATING IDENTITIES

We would argue that the most important research contribution of *Women Fielding Danger* is researchers' illustrating how fieldwork identity dynamics facilitated and/or inhibited the research process, researchers' and interlocutors' safety, and researchers' ethical choices and outcomes. Within field sites fraught with difficult choices at every turn, each researcher sought and eventually discovered strategies for negotiating within, around, and through the research challenges associated with gender, danger, identity interactions, and ethics. Their methodological "toolbox" for accomplishing this included research reflexivity, identity negotiations and approximations, and ethical outcomes. Through these strategies, field researchers navigated a field site's political geography (for example, a country under military control, a prison, a paramilitary training camp, a rural village); "gender incredibility"; physical, emotional, and organizational dangers; and ethical perils.

Speaking about *research reflexivity*, Audrey Kleinsasser (2000) defines it as: "(a) the process of critical self-reflection on one's biases, theoretical predispositions, preferences; (b) an acknowledgement of the inquirer's place in the setting, context, or social phenomenon he or she seeks to understand and a means for a critical examination of the entire research process." The researchers in this volume demonstrate that research reflexivity was their most important methodological tool in sorting through field research challenges.

Identity negotiation as a process begins with Myfanwy Franks's three static "ethnographic positionalities"—ascribed (given), selective (chosen and worked out), and enforced. Sehgal defines positionality as "a researcher's location within existing hierarchies of power and the ways in which the researcher's identity and affiliations are positioned among and by others." That is, an identity assertion or positionality is presented by the researcher and then either fully accepted or rejected by an interlocutor—if not, then the two actors renegotiate and reshape their relative positionalities. Such outcomes occur within a field site's political geography, interactive systems of power, and cultural norms and expectations. Pointing to the complicated and dynamic nature of ethnographic identities, Subramaniam argues that identities are "*dynamic* and *multiple*, rather than . . . role-set *static opposites*." In interviews with Brazilian torturers, Huggins discovered that the identities in play—hers and theirs—were in part real, in part fictional, and always shifting: "[A]n interviewer cannot express all that she really feels and expect an interviewee to give up what she needs. . . . [I]nterviewees cannot disclose everything that they are and still protect their . . . secrets."

As readers will see, identity negotiations often proceed by trial and error—according to Subramaniam, "renegotiated within each changing field setting." One outcome is what we label *identity approximation*: the coming together—at least temporarily within each trial-and-error, give-and-take identity negotiation—of researcher and interlocutor positionalities. Each actor in an interaction goes as far as she can and will go in creating and accepting her own and the others' selective positionalities. For example, some researchers in this book decided to accept certain aspects of a culturally defined ascribed gender positionality in order to craft a status that would produce a safe space for researcher and researched, enhance research outcomes (i.e., data collection), and protect research ethics. How Franks's three ethnographic positionalities interacted within any one research performance—for example, a researcher's sexuality or ethnic-religious positionality being back-staged, or the status of "honored guest" front-staged relative to other positionalities—shapes a researcher's "field persona"—"an amalgamation of who, by local cultural norms, [the researcher] *should be* and who [she *is*], according to [her] own and [her] discipline's expectations." Schwandner-Sievers learned to see herself in the field "as one actor among a range of other cultural actors, [where] all 'performers' switched between back- and front-stage positions during a research interaction." (See also Schippers 2002, 2008.)

Negotiating into Positionality

Rito, consistently faced with an inability to get Louisiana Cajun men to accept her interviewing them inside a Louisiana bayou—a region historically marked as *men's* hunting territory—had to invite her father into the field with her. As a young woman in the bayou, Rito was then "appropriately" represented and "protected" by a male family member, an expectation that required Rito's back-staging her vision of herself and her identity claim as a "professional researcher." Donna Goldstein elected not to disclose to poor Brazilian slum dwellers that she is a lesbian, recognizing that within the gendered dimensions of Brazilian poverty, her sexuality could nevertheless structure research outcomes and personal safety. Goldstein thus performed the selective ethnographic positionality of "heterosexual" by talking to interviewees about being "in a relationship"—that is, having a boyfriend—even though she was not. Pointing to the two-way nature of this selective positionality, as to whether and how it was received by others in her research site, Goldstein's interlocutor, Glória, "knew . . . that there was probably a good chance that [Goldstein] was a lesbian . . . , but was always careful to ask [her] about [her] 'boyfriend.'" Goldstein assumed that Glória knew "'the truth,' but was choosing to ignore it for various reasons." Through their unspoken understanding, Goldstein and her informant entered into an implicit agreement about what could and would be a part of their jointly worked-out identity performances. This identity approximation included their silently agreeing to keep "veiled"[1] aspects of Goldstein's identity.

Schwandner-Sievers discovered in Albania that she could garner protections for herself and facilitate obtaining research information by becoming a household's "fictive cousin," a selective positionality that required the larger community's support to make it work. The Albanian cultural practice of being silent about information that could reduce a household's respect in the community facilitated the identity approximations between Schwandner-Sievers and the larger community. Everyone in the community knew that Schwandner-Sievers

> was not a "real cousin," yet they were still perfectly willing to enter into this social role relationship with [her], while fully recognizing that [she] was "really" an outsider. . . . [She] benefited from the cultural practice . . . of . . . *not speaking* publicly about incongruent or culturally embarrassing information.

Sehgal points to a case in her research where a two-way identity approximation was based on an assumed quid pro quo:

> I began to see that my own covertness was matched by that of the Hindu nationalist interlocutors. . . . [E]ach of us was subtly and covertly "bargaining" for our interests on the basis of what we perceived to be the identity and social location of the other. Within such a dynamic, I discovered that the Hindu nationalists and myself each held assumptions about, and goals for, the other that were not always totally true and usually not fully explicit.

Sehgal and Indian nationalist interlocutors came together within a fragile and fictitious identity approximation: Nationalist movement "leaders . . . hoped to use 'the me' that they 'saw' to expand their movement into the United States. . . . [L]eaders assumed that, as a Hindu doctoral student in sociology at a prominent, public American university, I could be used to spread and strengthen the movement inside the United States." Indicating neither that she would "do so, nor . . . that [she] would not" helped Sehgal to gain entry into a Nationalist paramilitary camp.

In an important, nuanced discovery about ethnographic positionalities, several contributors (see especially Brickham Mendez and Subramaniam) illustrate how organizational settings shaped positionality negotiation possibilities and "identity approximation" outcomes. In some Indian field sites—especially those closest to national power and in a formal organization—Subramaniam found research subjects focusing on her assumed "connections to Indian government bureaucrats." This led state- and district-level functionaries to see Subramaniam as having higher status and power—a designation that could enhance positionality negotiations in her favor and facilitate obtaining interviewees.[2] On the other hand, when Subramaniam was seen by bureaucrats in those same organizations as merely "a woman and a researcher," she was "rendered . . . more subordinate and . . . less prestigious and powerful." At yet another Indian field site, this time a much less formal organizational setting—"the collectives of poor rural [Indian] women"—Subramanian found it difficult to even "make [her] 'real' status, as a 'graduate student conducting research,'" understood to interlocutors. Within these settings, Subramaniam's acceptance "was based upon . . . being a young woman, like the women's daughter or sister." Subramaniam concluded that "a researcher takes into the field a variety of roles that make possible multiple field-level identities; research subjects may accept or reject one or more of these, taking those aspects of a researcher's 'real' and 'presented' identities that have salience within the research subjects' social, cultural, and organizational milieu."

The Veiled Researcher

As Sehgal discovered in her research on Hindu women of the violent Indian nationalist movement, where disclosure would be dangerous, aspects of a researcher's identity must be totally hidden. For example, if she is "studying dangerous groups that have more power than she does . . . [and the researcher's status and/or political beliefs would go against those she is studying, then] aspects of her identity must be 'veiled.'" Pointing to Kathleen Blee's fieldwork (1998) on women in U.S. racist groups (the Ku Klux Klan, Christian Identity groups, neo-Nazi skinheads), Sehgal argues that "as social actors as well as researchers, we ourselves are always partial: We perform and present contradictory and shifting identities that are culturally contextualized and circumscribed by the power dynamics within a particular setting."

Fredriksson needed to conceal her being a human rights advocate in East Timor under military rule: "Some might say that I was in disguise the day I arrived in Dilli. I wondered whether my subterfuge was any different from wearing a ring to feign marriage? Or growing a mustache or dying one's hair as partial disguise? I believed that I was simply playing a role necessary to guard my safety and gain access to crucial and vulnerable sources." Glebbeek "tried to be as honest as possible" about her research on Guatemalan police, but "still felt manipulative" because in order to gain trust and establish rapport, she had to be sensitive to the interviewee's expectations:

> When I noticed that an interviewee liked to display his knowledge, as if he were a teacher speaking to a young student, I became an eager pupil. When

I recognized that an interviewee was probing my academic knowledge of policing, I adopted the role of an expert, showing that I had good academic knowledge about police institutions. When an interviewee was authoritarian, I became subordinate.

Demovic, like Schwandner-Sievers, skillfully balanced her own multi-layered research identities with local cultural expectations for her as an American in Zanzibar. For example, Demovic struggled in Zanzibar to effectively and respectfully position herself—a non-Muslim woman—vis-à-vis the island's Swahili Muslim population: Should she wear any head covering? Should she use the traditional *kanga* head covering? Should she adopt a Westernized version of the *kanga*? Demovic discovered that her range of "selective positionality" options was constrained by culturally "enforced positionality" expectations. Resolving to use a head covering to signal her "purity" and respect for Muslim customs, Demovic was initially discouraged from doing so by local women: As a non-Muslim Swahili, they argued, she should not use the traditional *kanga* head covering—presumably because it signified her membership in "their culture." In response, Demovic "began experimenting with other ways to signal [her] purity" that balanced Swahili Muslim culture's expectations for "good" women with what Demovic, a Western feminist, could live with and would be acceptable to her interlocutors. In Demovic's words, "my wearing a common scarf—a 'Westernization' of the veil—allowed me to expropriate one of the culture's own gendered identity markers while still retaining some of my own Western independence."

Negotiating Identities: Serendipitous Research Benefits

Ultimately, several researchers in *Women Fielding Danger* reflected on whether, in the process of "veiling" different sides of their own identities, they had lost who they really are. As Schwandner-Sievers explains, "As my time in the field progressed and I mulled over my emerging research persona, I realized that it was unquestionably being shaped by patriarchy—a fact that was nonetheless greatly facilitating my research in northern Albanian and Kosovar villages." Many researchers in *Women Fielding Danger* came to see that "playing into" patriarchal definitions of a "woman" often facilitated their research even though they initially saw it as placing barriers on themselves. Shaery Eisenlohr was frustrated that male Shiite interviewees considered Lebanese politics, religion, and national identity unacceptable subjects for her—a woman—to study. It complicated matters even more that by conducting research she was "positioned," especially by Hezbollah male Shiites, as a Westernized, "fallen-away" Shiite. Her gender, religion, and layered nationalities seemed an endless distraction from the real topics of Shaery-Eisenlohr's research: Iranian Shiite "identity—nationally, politically, ideologically, and religiously." Over time, and through much reflection, Shaery-Eisenlohr came to realize that she was learning seren-dipitously, through interlocutors' essentialist treatment of her, just how various Lebanese Shiite groups—Hezbollah and AMAL Party members, for example—each conceptualized their own politico-religious and national identities. When Hezbollah interlocutors chided her for not wearing a veil, she was learning how "Hezbollah constructs religious authenticity and dif-ferentiates out its political opponents." When AMAL Party Shiite interlocu-tors explained Shaery-Eisenlohr's lack of head covering as positively distanc-ing herself from the ruling circles of Iran's Islamic Republic—precisely what Hezbollah did not accept—Shaery-Eisenlohr discovered subtle differences between the Huzbullah and AMAL national, international, and political world views. However, even more than this—and not initially a subject of Shaery-Eisenlohr's Lebanese research—Shaery-Eisenlohr discovered that be-ing "an Iranian woman triggered discussions about the differences between Iranian and Lebanese Shiite women."

Crafting Safe Spaces

Before a researcher crafts a safe research space, she has to know its kinds and types of dangers. Recognizing that research dangers in field sites consti-tute much more than physical danger, this section is nevertheless devoted to how the researchers negotiated physical violence and its threats. Most began crafting a safe research space by seeking cultural insider ("emic") information about danger and security. However, as Demovic illustrates, Swahili male insiders were not always willing to share their assessments with a female outsider. Sehgal's research on the Hindu nationalist move-ment demonstrates that cultural insiders' understanding can even raise rather than alleviate a researcher's fears. In a suggested response to this, Sanford recommends that

> [f]or the outsider seeking to understand La Violencia, the trick is to assume nothing. One must accept the survivor as the guide through the labyrinth of terror. Embrace the path of the memory and allow the survivor to carry it to closure. Even if the path to closure is far beyond the untested limits of one's imagination.

Fredriksson and Skidmore, however, point out how receiving some kinds of information from a cultural insider can create and enhance dan-ger for researcher and interlocutor alike. The complicated relationship between insider and outsider knowledge points to the researcher's ethical responsibility to protect such information and the interlocutors who pass it on to them.

If increased danger can be one outcome of entering the insider lives of those we are studying, how did the researchers in *Women Fielding Danger* address simultaneously their own and their interlocutors' safety? The range of mechanisms they employed included "negotiating 'safe spaces'" (Schwandner-Sievers); surviving "poisonous knowledge" (Sanford); negotiating an "affective field" as a "coconspirator/activist-by-proxy" (Skidmore); "hiding in the open" (Skidmore); researching in "transnational spaces" (Bickham Mendez and Viterna); employing "strategic essentialism" (Sehgal, Shaery-Eisenlohr, Viterna); negotiating "situationally salient field identities" (Subramaniam); managing "studying up" and "studying down" (Sehgal and Huggins; Bickham Mendez, Presser, and Viterna, respectively); negotiating "research seduction" (Huggins, Haritos-Fatouros, and Zimbardo 2002, see also Robben 1995); "deposing atrocity" (Huggins); navigating where "no neutrals are allowed" (Fredriksson, Glebbeek, Goldstein, Sanford, Schwandner-Sievers, and Sehgal); and balancing ideological "sides" (Presser, Fredriksson, and Huggins). Each of these strategies, as the researchers in *Women Fielding Danger* illustrate, requires multilayered positionality negotiations and produces unexpected ethical dilemmas.

Several of these strategies offer a window into the others. Speaking about military Burma's urban "geographies of danger," Skidmore argues that

> geographic division of space for each individual or group . . . is overlaid by a continually shifting map of emotionally dangerous places. Buildings that house the apparatus of the state and its military hardware (and spyware) are tacitly avoided by pedestrians. When arriving at and leaving the psychiatric hospital, one of my field sites, it was necessary to pass a major military installation. . . . At times of unrest, several tanks would line its entranceway. Near these kinds of places, civilian traffic is sparse and hurried and I was almost completely unaware of the many such sites that I avoided.

Speaking about navigating such sites, Skidmore points out that "[w]herever and whenever terror, political violence, and propaganda are at work and fear is thus pervasive," her strategy was to pay "constant attention to how [to] negotiate danger and fear." In order to protect interlocutors, Skidmore not only selected interview locations as devoid as possible of their affectively negative imagery and painful memories, but also adopted the strategy of "hiding in the open." Counterintuitively, in a society shot through with military repression, fear, and secrecy, rather than carrying out interviews in a secret place—where secrecy itself might call attention to a foreigner talking to a national—Skidmore asked her interviewees to select a public place in which interaction would not be as likely to cause such suspicion.

Personal Impact of Negotiated Identity

Several researchers in *Women Fielding Danger* feigned accepting an inter-locutor's opinions—or at least did not challenge them—in order to keep from jeopardizing the research. For example, Lois Presser, in interviews with men convicted of serious crimes, was troubled that her interviewees' self-presentations and discourse "effectively reproduced binary distinctions between men and women, victims and offenders, and good and evil." Be-lieving that "such constructed differences lay the basis for social injustice, violence and inequality and that [they] threaten safety," Presser just the same participated in interviewees' "'difference-making' . . . [because] it . . . seemed to *ensure* my safety [among] . . . men [who thought that they] were 'doing goodness' with me in the interviews."

Huggins felt compromised by fostering torturer interviewees' fictionally positive self-presentations. "Bruno," a former prison warden on a human rights group's list of known torturers, was vehement that he had never tor-tured anyone. Huggins knew this was untrue, but did not contradict him. However, by not challenging Bruno's positive presentation of himself, wasn't Huggins validating this known torturer's positive image? Was this man's tes-timony sufficiently important to warrant Huggins's becoming part of—and therefore promoting, albeit temporarily—Bruno's fictional identity?

Sanford employed research reflexivity to manage "poisonous knowl-edge"—interlocutors' accounts that bring a researcher to "a naked encoun-ter with humanity's dark side." Through field research and human rights advocacy, Sanford has been able to transform hearing interlocutors' "dark side" into

a spiritual experience . . . where the disciplined "normal" becomes out of place and thus challenges the anthropologist (or anyone else in the field) to begin to peel the onion— . . . to . . . make sense of one's own self and the many daily acts and interpretations that customarily guide one through daily life. Fieldwork displaces structures of understanding and disorients trajectories of meaning.

THEME 4: RESEARCH ETHICS—SHAPED BY FIELD DYNAMICS

The fourth theme of *Women Fielding Danger*, ethics shaped in the field by a dialectic that included a field site's political geography, identity negotia-tions, and the ongoing results of these, disclosed eight relatively persistent ethical challenges: ethics in motion, navigating "conduct codes" data out of place, fear and pain, unloved groups, no neutrals allowed, veiled re-searcher, doing public relations, approximating the enemy. All researchers in this volume were guided by the ethical premise that even though they may put themselves in danger to carry out research, they were duty-bound to keep from endangering informants. The researchers did so by balancing research performances and identity approximations within a field site's political geography.

Ethics in Motion

Fredriksson found that ethical challenges changed as her own biography— human rights advocate; advanced graduate student—intersected with the type of research she was conducting—human rights advocacy; academic—during different phases of East Timor's own national status—military occupied; newly unoccupied; independent nation. Having begun her career in military-occupied East Timor as a human rights advocacy researcher, Fredriksson reasoned that when "[p]eople were suffering and dying in a small country under occupation, should I even worry about a little subterfuge [necessary] to carry out my human rights mission?" One ethical line beyond which Fredriksson would not go was that "[a]s a nonviolent activist I feigned no semblance of [accepting] . . . violence."

Then, as a human rights advocacy researcher in East Timor's immediate postoccupation period, Frederikkson struggled greatly with "whose side" she was on—new "sides" had emerged, and some formerly collaborative groups had become disaffected with one another. Fredriksson saw as her goal to "obtain the information necessary to inform the American public of human rights abuses in East Timor." And although Fredriksson knew whose "side [she] was on," once the "sides" had changed and/or become blurred, it was more difficult to assess "the truth" and separate "perpetrators" from "victims."

After East Timor's formal independence from Indonesia, Fredriksson began research as a doctoral student on a new issue that emerged: "By 2002 when I returned to East Timor to carry out academic research, . . . I was coping with the effects of my own and my informants' unhealed physical and psychological wounds," an ethical situation discussed by Huggins, Sanford, and Skidmore as well.

"Conduct Codes"

All researchers in *Women Fielding Danger* experienced ethical challenges around what we call "conduct codes." Such challenges involved a researcher's making an ethical determination about "right" and "wrong" as these designations were applied locally to her conduct—an ethical conundrum that was complicated by a researcher's being part of a culture, organizational system, "transnational space" that varied in its norms from her own sociopolitical and gender norms. A researcher's decisions about the "correct" conduct codes therefore required balancing her own cultural, political, and gender standards with those of the culture, organization, and people she was studying. For example, Demovic elected to

> [a]ssum[e] . . . roles considered appropriate by Muslim men for their women, a set of conditions that [she], as an American feminist and a young professor of women's studies, could not help but question. [She] struggled for some time trying to discover the balance between "appropriate" clothing for [her]— assuming that there were no "cultural exceptions" to modesty if [she] wanted to be seen as a "good" woman and a serious researcher—while still avoiding encroachment on [her] own cultural identity.

Goldstein had to discover how to balance being a lesbian and Jewish in a Brazilian community were negative meanings are attached to those statuses. Goldstein explains:

> Early on in my fieldwork I had made a decision not to discuss two important aspects of my personal identity that were meaningful to me in the United States: my cultural/religious background and my sexual orientation. . . . [B]ecause my fieldwork was one of immersion and long-term engagement, I had to be at peace with denying [these] particular aspect[s] of my identity, even among people who were extremely curious about my life.

Subramaniam faced challenges related to Indian caste proscriptions, requiring her to balance her own beliefs with some Indian conduct codes with which she disagreed. Subramaniam explains her dilemma as follows:

> An Indian woman from an upper-middle-class and upper-caste Indian family, I was studying poor *dalit* [untouchable] women in small rural villages. Such differences between myself [and] . . . my research subjects, *might have* been easier to negotiate in a more urban research setting. However, where the researcher is in a small traditional village, focusing on the lives of lower-caste women—where caste differences very strongly proscribed where I could stay, with whom I could associate, and what and with whom I could eat—the mere act of *navigating* caste was complicated. . . . While I could not fully ignore such norms and rules, I made conscious attempts to convey that I did not believe in and did not want to adhere to them.

Data Out of Place

How does a researcher protect what Bickham Mendez calls "dangerous pieces of information" from falling into the wrong hands? The ultimate answer is to destroy it—as Frederiksson did after she was arrested by Indonesian police. Or to return "dangerous pieces of information" to an interlocutor—as Skidmore did in the case of a previous interviewee to prevent its falling into the hands of Burma's vigilant military. Strategies with less drastic consequences for research include taking precautions to make "dangerous information" difficult to discover. Huggins, in her study of Brazilian torturers—fearing that her tape-recorded data might be seized either in Brazil or as she left the country—sent some of her translated cassettes home with a friend, kept a set for her departure from Brazil, and left a set with a friend in Brazil. Skidmore "made it clear to . . . [Burmese] villagers . . . that I would go away and take my questions with me if that is what they wanted." Fredriksson, keenly aware of the need to retain and protect interlocutor secrecy, anticipated being arrested by Indonesian officials, so she "alter[ed her] already illegible handwriting to the point where even [her] frustrated colleague, and onlooker interlocutors, could not decipher what [she] was writing [in her journal]." The phone number of an interviewee was flushed down a hotel toilet to keep Indonesian officials from confiscating it.

The need to protect "dangerous pieces of information" did not end for researchers when they left the field. Several (Fredriksson, Glebbeek, and Huggins, as well as Bickham Mendez) reported returning "several times to the narrative to ensure that the information in it did not harm the various actors included in my research." In writing her findings, Sehgal "changed names of people, places, dates, and identifying characteristics that might connect specific individuals to [her] work," then—like Huggins and Sanford as well—"held off publishing [her] work for a while." Sanford waited more than a decade to share with readers aspects of the testimony of a former Kaibil—a member of the Guatemalan army's elite fighting forces—who had participated in civilian massacres and committed a range of other atrocities.

Fear and Pain

Various researchers confronted ethical issues related to fear and pain. How does a researcher conduct a study ethically within a climate of fear—in what Skidmore calls an "affective field site"? Will the researcher inevitably increase an interlocutor's level of fear and/or psychological pain? There is no easy answer to these questions. Glebbeek explains (as do Sanford and Viterna) that she "strategically delayed exploring sensitive information in order to secure such information later." Glebbeek decided that "[a]n important interview strategy was being sensitive to what I was 'supposed' to know and when I was 'supposed' to know it." Viterna struggled with the ethics of "probing into interviewees' experiences with violence[: What might be the impact on] their lives, especially given that poverty left them with few if any resources for effectively dealing with trauma." Viterna's response was to "seek to uncover reports of past violence, [while] . . . only push[ing] for the most basic outline of an occurrence. [She] would leave additional details to the interviewees' discretion."

Huggins discovered that asking sensitive questions even in a respectful and informed way did not always leave an interviewee unscathed. In an interview with Bruno, a man on a Brazilian human rights list[3] for brutality against prisoners during the country's military period, Huggins learned that the day after Bruno's interview that he suffered an anxiety attack. When Huggins recounted this story to U.S. criminal justice scholars and students, some expressed moral outrage about the ethics of conducting research that so deeply upset an interviewee—"even if he was a torturer." Conversely, when Huggins described Bruno's breakdown to Latin American faculty and students—whether or not they have been or have had a family member victimized by security force abuse—their response was exactly the opposite: "Such a man gave so much misery to others that he deserves whatever he gets."

Just the same, being upset that she might have caused Bruno's emotional crisis, Huggins asked his colleagues, "How is Bruno enjoying retirement from police work?" Their reply was, "[N]ot well. Bruno has been in therapy for some time for alcoholism and anxiety problems" (Huggins et al 2001). Rather than resolving whether research that could uncover an interviewee's painful memories should be carried out in the first place, Huggins ended up introducing an additional ethical dilemma: Given that some ethical challenges have place in existing emotional scars, how can a researcher find out what these might be before entering the field? While Huggins's experience with torturers might suggest that it is better to avoid research on even the perpetrators of atrocities, this generalization would then have to be extended to victims of atrocity, who also carry enormous emotional scars. Obviously the wealth of important research on atrocity survivors suggests that researchers have discovered ways to conduct such research that avoids unnecessary pain for survivors.

But what about the emotional "blowback" for those who conduct research on "unloved" groups? Remembering when she was in Guatemala in 1996 and 1997, conducting research on massacres, Sanford explains,

> I used to flee from the villages because I felt I could not bear the weight of one more story. "Aren't you overwhelmed?" I asked Julia, my translator, after the fourteenth testimony on a particularly cold, damp day in Nebaj as I looked out at the line of survivors still waiting to give testimony. "Of course, Victoria," she responded. "But they want to talk and who else will listen?"

Reasoning that it is a researcher's *responsibility* to bear witness to atrocity, Sanford employs Trinh Minh-ha's (1992) argument that "[t]he witnesses go on living to bear witness to the unbearable." But does such an insight really apply to "unloved groups" (see Fielding 1993)?

Unloved Groups

Several researchers in this volume would answer, "Yes." Huggins found in research on Brazilian torturers that, in sharp contrast to the permissibility of research on survivors of atrocity—where an interviewer can morally accept taking simultaneously the role of interviewer, observer, and victim (see Gunn 1997; Campbell 2001) and be morally transformed by this (Frank 1995; Gunn 1997, 3)—the researcher who "deposes atrocity" must solicit the accounts of morally indefensible violence perpetrators. Objectively telling their stories can make a researcher appear to be taking the wrong "moral side." Clearly, a researcher must decide how she will explain research on "unloved" groups, as much to herself as to others. Sehgal believes that an important ethical reason for studying violent Hindu nationalist women is founded in feminist *activist ideology*:

> I wanted to produce knowledge for resisting an Indian variant of fascism, discovering the contradictory spaces and fissures that could crack open the fundamentalist facade of imagined Hindu unity, and identify the potential for dissent and resistance within the ranks of the movement. [I knew that feminist activism would] provide me with an effective route toward achieving these research outcomes[, recognizing that the research process would involve negotiations over power].

The ethical concerns related to studying "unloved" groups are often predicated upon a researcher's being able to distinguish "bad guys" from "good guys." However, as Fredriksson discovered in research on independent East Timor:

> [W]e, as interviewers, were finding it difficult to differentiate Timorese victims from perpetrators—the indicators and indications of each had been conflated by independence. It had become easier to see former perpetrators as victims. We learned of their forced recruitment, of threats they received from both sides of the conflict to ensure loyalty. Their accounts blurred the categories of "perpetrator" and "victim." . . . I was caught in a spider web of perspectives.

Huggins and her colleagues also found that dichotomizing "perpetrators" and "victims" was an intellectual dead-end. The police "violence workers," who had been full-time torturers across many years, had become "burned out" by their violent deeds (Huggins et al. 2002), a phenomenon manifested by Bruno's needing therapy and medication for anxiety and alcoholism. Bruno had become a "victim" of state-sanctioned violence against "terrorist" Brazilians.

Huggins's approach to interviewing an "unloved" group was to become an "an 'onlooker witness' deposing atrocity. She mediated between each of two pairs of research approaches—listening without moral acceptance, empathizing without condoning—a process that began when an interviewee account raised questions about [Huggins's] own values and identity. "Fredriksson, reflecting on the meaning of "objectivity" for a person soliciting the narratives of "unloved" Indonesian military occupiers of East Timor, states that

> when . . . [she] entered the world of Timorese sympathetic to, or cooperating with, Indonesian authorities, or the spaces of those authorities themselves, [she knew that she] had to narrate their stories to the outside world as well. But how was [she] to do this? Could [she] be objective? What was objectivity for a human rights advocate monitoring egregious violations in East Timor?

Glebbeek discovered that the challenges associated with researching "unloved" Guatemalan police would continue to plague her, "even far away in the Netherlands, writing about Guatemalan police illegalities." Glebbeek remembers feeling as if she "were betraying police informants' trust—an irrational way of thinking that illustrates the conflicts inherent in adopting 'progression to friendship' in research on violence perpetrators." Glebbeek had to continually ask herself "how someone studying a police institution with a long history of violence and repression could become in any way partial to that institution."

No Neutrals Allowed

Particularly when studying "unloved" groups, although not exclusively with them alone, critical ethical questions can arise about ideologically divided field sites. Sehgal illustrates in her research on women in the violent Hindu nationalist movement that "when conducting ethnographic research in communities involved in political conflict and violence[,] '[w]hether or not you take sides, those actively involved in the situation are going to define whose side they think you are on. They will act toward you on the basis of this definition, regardless of your professions of neutrality'" (see Sluka 1995: 287). Clearly, such enforced positionality has implications for one's ethical choices and research outcomes.

As Sehgal learned, especially when a field is politically divided, there is pressure on a researcher to "prove" her allegiances. Attending a Hindu nationalist rally that was being video taped by the movement's TV station, Sehgal was spotted by the event's speaker, "an impassioned popular female ascetic whom [Sehgal] had interviewed earlier." As this woman was starting her speech, she invited Sehgal to join her onstage. Sitting on stage with Hindu nationalist dignitaries and organizers, the speaker urged the audience to raise their fists and chant various Hindu nationalist slogans. As the speaker and audience were chanting, this former interviewee looked over at Sehgal "to check if I was participating in a sufficiently impassioned manner." Her own participation in the rally gave Sehgal "nightmarish visions of being broadcast on the Hindu nationalist cable channel—'outed' as an apparent Hindu nationalist to the Indian progressives monitoring the movement."

Doing Public Relations

What would other researchers do if placed in the position of Sehgal? In fact, as several researchers in this volume demonstrate, they were challenged in various ways to do public relations for organizations they were studying, albeit of a lesser intensity than required of Sehgal. Bickham Mendez ideologically supported the Nicaraguan women's organization that she was studying and collaborating with, yet she still felt uncomfortable with members' using her cultural capital—an educated, bilingual academic from the United States—to achieve organizational goals. Bickham Mendez explains that leaders of the Nicaraguan women's organization invited her to attend important meetings "because of the power and influence ('transnational social capital') that [her] U.S. 'outsider' status signified," certainly a symbolic form of public relations for their organization. On one occasion, Bickham Mendez was asked to accompany the organization's coordinator in a meeting with representatives of the U.S. Agency for International Development (USAID). Bickham Mendez learned that "one reason for such invitations was that, when the encounters among leaders became controversial, a foreigner's presence would inhibit or temper heated discussions." Another reason, of course, was that Bickham Mendez brought convincing cultural capital to meetings with representatives of the U.S. government.

Approximating the Enemy

When researches are studying groups that they respect and admire, they do not have to worry about their interactions leading to their coming to "approximate the enemy." For those who study "unloved" groups, this is an ever-present threat. Huggins consciously shut down emotionally during an interview with a torturer in order to protect herself from what she was hearing. This led her to question whether she was engaging in the same kind of psychological numbing that had made it possible for violence workers to maim and kill their victims. Was she becoming an emotionless machine in order to continue to hear the objectionable content of torturers' narratives?

Fredriksson also developed rules for coping with the danger and violence she saw and learned of as a human rights advocate in East Timor. By compartmentalizing her emotions and responses, Fredriksson could better

> cope with and record raw brutality, usually falling back on "comparing atrocities," willing [her]self not to cry, and recognizing that at times [she] would still break [her] own "coping" rules, usually waiting until [she] was alone. Within such a framework of recognized vulnerability [she] came increasingly to see the utility of compartmentalizing [her] responses to human tragedy into front- and back-stage reactions.

Glebbeek struggled to develop an insider understanding of another person's world—only to recognize that through this process, she had come to identify with (e.g., "approximate") unloved Guatemalan police:

> I had not anticipated that objectivity itself—that is, seeing interviewees as people first and listening openly to their accounts—would pull me into the interviewee's point of view. If, as researchers, we could simply objectify and demonize the violent police we study—as they have done to their victims—this would certainly provide a check on developing feelings of humanity toward them. But, of course, demonizing and objectifying those we study would violate the most basic rules of research and ethical practice.

Sehgal discovered that

> After two weeks of veiled participant observation at the Samiti paramilitary camp, I had unwittingly internalized elements of the Hindu nationalist worldview that required considerable time and energy to neutralize once I had left the field. . . . I had come to believe that the "self-defense" techniques being taught at the paramilitary camps were empowering for women. I was indignant about the seeming organizational inability of Indian feminist groups to reach women and girls to teach them self-defense. I felt that the Hindu nationalist movement genuinely filled the vacuum in a highly contested political arena by providing services sorely needed by urban middle-class Indian women.
> It took many hours of post-camp discussions in my parents' home with my feminist secular historian husband to shake off the Samiti's camp indoctrination. . . . We examined together the reports by Indian civil liberties groups of human rights violations by the Hindu right. By the end of this process I began to see how deep the movement's hook had lodged within me. Having regained reflexive balance, I could begin rereading my field notes from the ideological indoctrination sessions at the Samiti's paramilitary camp.

Coming to see that she was developing empathy with some of her violent interviewees, Sanford came to see that interviewees "defied the neat categories of victim and victimizer."

The soldier, who had been forcibly recruited into an elite squad of the Guatemalan army and brutalized in the process just the same generated in Sanford "a revulsion and gut reaction" as he talked about the atrocities that he had committed. However, in the process of her research Sanford had come "[to feel] pity for him":

> He was my friend. Each time he came to my house, he would spend a few minutes with my ninety-seven-year-old grandmother. He was a gentle man with aspirations of being an artist. He was also a key activist in the Guatemalan refugee community who would be absolutely ostracized if I shared this particular story with anyone.

Sanford "vomited when he left [her] house." She felt "wasted . . . empty, emotionally spent" after hours of hearing about atrocities. She "would shower and often weep under the flow of warm water" after an interviewee had left. Huggins often did the same after a long interview with a torturer. The shower seemed a safe place to wash away a torturer's poisonous words. Ironically, Huggins did not even recognize her own pollution-cleansing ritual until she interviewed an assassin who said that after a "kill" he would return home, drop his clothes inside the back door, and go to the shower to "cleanse away the *necessary* violence of his job."

READING *WOMEN FIELDING DANGER*

Our introduction has identified four themes among research in this volume—gender's preeminence, danger's many forms, negotiating identities, and ethics in situ. As readers will quickly recognize, it was difficult to locate chapters that, taken as a set, neatly illustrate each of the volume's four themes. Rather, each of the contributors illustrates to varying degrees all of the four themes. However, in the interest of this volume's readability, we have separated the research into sections featuring each of the volume's four themes.

Readers are invited to discover new themes, seek illustrations of identity positionality and approximations as the latter were employed to negotiate around, through, and within gender, danger, and as mechanics for guarding research ethics. We invite readers to contribute to our *Women Fielding Danger* Web site (www.womenfieldingdanger.com), particularly their own lessons from the field. We hope that making connections with other researchers will help to mitigate field dangers in all of their forms.[4] Readers are encouraged to elevate the qualitative experience of research to a visible place within their various disciplines.

NOTES

1. This excellent concept was suggested by Meera Sehgal in this volume. Demovic and Shaery-Eisenlohr demonstrate in their chapters the role and impacts of the use—or not—of head coverings by a researcher in Muslim societies. Sehgal shows that "veiling" takes many other forms—for example, from a researcher's being fully open with interlocutors about her identity "facts" to being totally covert about them.

2. In contrast, having Latin American interviewees see a researcher as a U.S. government "insider" could have a negative impact upon the researcher's being seen as trustworthy (see Bickham Mendez, Sanford, and Viterna).

3. While the tactic of human rights groups of placing a known brutalizer on a public list of people to be tried and/or punished for gross human rights violations can be one tool for accomplishing restorative justice, in fact, we often forget that not only the human rights violator is punished by such action. His or her family—in the Brazilian case—often including grandchildren as well, also pay a heavy price for the sins of their parent.

4. We especially invite undergraduate and graduate field research methods classes to join us in discussing what they are leaning as a way of contributing to the "Women Fielding Danger Project."

REFERENCES

Blee, Kathleen M. (1998). "White Knuckle Research: Emotional Dynamics in feildwork with Racist Activists." *Qualitative Sociology* 21, no. 4.

———. (2002). *Inside Organized Racism: Women in the Hate Movement*. Berkeley and Los Angeles: University of California Press.

Campbell, Rebecca. (2001). *Emotionally Involved: The Impact of Researching Rape*. New York: Routledge.

Fielding, Nigel. (1993). "Mediating the Message: Affinity and Hostility in Research on Sensitive Topics." In *Researching Sensitive Topics*, edited by Claire M. Renzetti and Raymond M. Lee. Newbury Park, CA: Sage.

Frank, Arthur W. (1995). *The Wounded Storyteller: Body, Illness, and Ethics*. Chicago: University of Chicago Press.

Franks, Myfanwy. (2002). "Feminisms and Cross-Ideological Feminist Social Research: Standpoint, Situatedness and Positionality—Developing Cross-Ideological Feminist Research." *Journal of International Women's Studies* 3, no. 2. Bridgewater, MA: Bridgewater State College.

Goffman, Erving. (1959). *The Presentation of Self in Everyday Life*. Garden City, NY: Doubleday.

Gunn, Janet Varner. (1997). "Autobiography in the 'Emergency Zone': Reading as Witnessing." Paper presented at the Modern Languages Association Conference, Toronto, ON, December 29.

Hill-Collins, Patricia. (1986). "Learning from the Outsider Within: The Sociological Significance of Black Feminist Thought." *Social Problems* 33, 514–32.

Huggins, Martha K., and Myriam Mesquita. (2000). "Civic Invisibility, Marginality, and Moral Exclusion: The Murders of Street Youth in Brazil." In *Children on the Streets of the Americas: Globalization, Homelessness and Education in the United States, Brazil, and Cuba*, edited by Roslyn A. Mickelson. New York: Routledge.

Huggins, Martha K., Mika Haritos-Fatouros, and Philip Zimbardo. (2002). *Violence Workers: Torturers and Murderers Reconstruct Brazilian Atrocities*. Berkeley and Los Angeles: University of California Press.

Kleinsasser, Audrey M. (2000). "Researchers, Reflexivity, and Good Data: Writing to Unlearn." *Theory into Practice* 39, no. 3 (Summer), 155–62

Mitchell, Richard G., Jr. (1993). "Secrecy and Fieldwork." In *Qualitative Research Methods*, vol. 29. Newbury Park, NJ: Sage.

Pierce, Jennifer. (1995). *Gender Trials: Emotional Lives in Contemporary Law Firms*. Berkeley and Los Angeles: University of California Press.

Robben, Antonius C. G. M. (1995). "The Politics of Truth and Emotion among Victims and Perpetrators of Violence." In *Fieldwork Under Fire: Contemporary Studies of Violence and Survival*, edited by Carolyn Nordstrum and Antonius Robben, 81–103. Berkeley and Los Angeles: University of California Press.

Sanford, Victoria. (2004). *Buried Secrets: Truth and Human Rights in Guatemala*. New York: Palgrave/Macmillan.

Schippers, Mimi. (2002). *Rockin' out of the Box: Gender Maneuvering in Alternative Hard Rock*. New Brunswick, NJ: Rutgers University Press.

———. (2008). "Doing Power/Doing Difference: Negotiations of Race and Gender in a Mentoring Program." *Symbolic Interaction* 31, no. 1, 77–98.

Sluka, Jeffery A. (1995). "Reflections on Managing Danger in Fieldwork: Dangerous Anthropology in Belfast." In *Fieldwork under Fire: Contemporary Violence and Survival*, edited by Carolyn Nordstrum and Antonius Robben, 276–94. Berkeley and Los Angeles: University of California Press.

Trinh Minh-ha. (1992). *Framer Framed*. New York: Routledge.

———. (1997). *Framer Framed*. In *Interpretative Ethnography: Ethnographic Practices for the Twentieth Century*, edited by Norman K. Denzin, 72–75. Thousand Oaks, CA: Sage.

Ulysse, Gina. (2004). "Mediating Stigma: Gendering Class and Color Codes in Jamaica." Lecture Presented at the Department of Anthropology Colloquium Series at the University of Colorado–Boulder, March 12.

I

GENDER'S FRONT STAGE: INSIDERS AND OUTSIDERS

1

Fixing and Negotiating Identities in the Field: The Case of Lebanese Shiites

Roschanack Shaery-Eisenlohr

POLITICAL IDENTITIES AND IDENTITY DESIGNATIONS: A PROJECT IN MOTION

The larger study for which this research was conducted[1] explored the variety of ways that dominant Lebanese Shiite political parties and groups have constructed their national and political identities and positioned themselves in terms of the Lebanese nation, all within the context of the varying relationships of these groups with Iran since the 1970s. As a Western-educated secular Shiite woman of Iranian parentage, I quickly discovered that during thirteen months of field research in Beirut, Lebanon, exploring the larger issue of Lebanese male politico-religious and national identity involved taking account of how my interlocutors' identities, and their perceptions of what seemed to them to be my identities, interacted with my own definitions and presentations of these. In the process of conducting this research, I began to realize that how differently politically situated interlocutors made sense of me and my background revealed much information relevant to my research. First, a male Lebanese Shiite interlocutor's positioning of my identity—politically, ideologically, religiously, and according to gender—suggested ways that Lebanese Shiites of various political shadings conceptualized their own politico-religious and national belonging. Second, by positioning me in various ways in terms of past and present Iranian politics, Lebanese Shiite interlocutors often quite clearly indicated how they defined their own relations with Iran in both political and cultural terms.

This chapter, which focuses on the research dynamics that grew out of the interactions between self-defined and ascribed identities, will illustrate that what could have been perceived as a stumbling block to the

successful unfolding of an interview, in fact, disclosed much about "transnationalism, Shi'ism, and the Lebanese State. Of course, such knowledge
was not always obtained in the manner that I initially expected. I was not
quite prepared for much that happened during an interview, particularly
having an interlocutor's *assumptions* about my identity and the political
allegiances they saw as associated with that assumed identity intrude
into the research process. Especially at the beginning of my research, my
impression management—which, according to Erving Goffman, inescap-
ably shapes interpersonal interaction in both research as well as everyday
life[2]—was informed by worries that certain identity subtexts were negatively shaping and complicating my conversations and interviews with
male Lebanese interlocutors.

Undaunted, I began my research on the roles of national and transnational contexts in shaping Lebanese Shiite identity constructions with the
objective of describing Lebanon's politico-religious terrain, especially in its
relationship to modern Iranian politics. This meant understanding Lebanon's two important Shiite movements-turned–political parties and their
relationships to the Iranian state. Each of these politico-religious groups—
AMAL and Hezbollah—has a markedly different relationship to Islam and
to Iranian politics, with implications for how they position themselves in
Lebanon—politically, religiously, and socially.

This chapter, which focuses on identity building and dynamics in the
interview phase of my research, is divided into six parts and a conclusion.
The first part introduces the main Shiite actors in Lebanon's political landscape; their ideas and politico-religious beliefs became part of our interview
identity dynamics. In the second and third sections, I lay out my own biography and its impact on locating interlocutors. The chapter's next three
parts describe the dynamics of interviewing and negotiating self-defined
and ascribed identities. In the conclusion, I explore the outcomes of shifting identities within my Lebanese research setting.

THE POLITICAL PARTIES

The Afwaj al-Muqawama al-Lubnaniyya (AMAL) political party, currently
led by the speaker of the Lebanese parliament Nabih Berri, was organized
in 1974 by Musa Sadr, the Iranian-born Lebanese Shiite leader. Founded
just one year before the 1975 Lebanese civil war, AMAL was the first Lebanese Shiite militia organization. After the success of the Iranian revolution
in Iran, AMAL members rejected Ayatollah Khomeini's concept of the jur-
isprudential model of political rule (*wilayat al-faqih*); Khomeini's objective
was to establish an Iranian-based hegemony over Shiites the world over. In
1982, Lebanon's AMAL Party broke off relations with the Iranian govern-

ment, with this policy holding until the mid-1990s and resuming officially after the election of Iranian president Muhammad Khatami in 1997. The new president wanted state-to-state relations between Iran and Lebanon, and improved relations with all religious groups in Lebanon.

The second Lebanese Shiite political party, Hezbollah, established in 1982, emerged out of groups disaffected with AMAL politics. Those who formed Hezbollah favored the Shiite Islamist politics of postrevolutionary Iran; their political position to confront the occupying Israeli army by military means was particularly enhanced after the 1982 Israeli invasion of Lebanon. Through ideological and financial support from the Iranian ruling religious elite, Hezbollah is currently competing with AMAL over leadership of Lebanon's Shiite community. Hezbollah maintains close ties with Iran's religious elite, which the Western media often refers to as the Iranian government's conservative wing. Hezbollah and the religious elite in Iran place major importance on the Palestinian cause, defining themselves as staunch supporters of the Palestinians, especially those affiliated with Hamas, the Palestinian Islamist party. Lebanon's Hezbollah considers itself as "the guardian of authentic Shi'ism," excluding the AMAL party just the same from its "circle of Islamists." AMAL, often dubbed by Western media as a "secular" Shiite party, is religious in its outlook but imagines its politics as more moderate and thus fitting more into the realities of multisectarian Lebanon. AMAL does not maintain close ties to the religious elite in Iran.

Another set of important Lebanese actors, although not a political party, is the Lebanese Shiite followers of Sayyid Muhammad Husayn Fadlallah (b. 1936), a Lebanese Shiite religious scholar who considers himself a "source of emulation" (*mut'a*) for Shiite Muslims the world over. Fadlallah was widely considered the spiritual leader of Hezbollah until relations between Sayyid Fadlallah and the Iranian ruling elite darkened in 1995 as a result of power struggles over Fadlallah's claim that he ranked among the Islamic world's supreme Shiite leaders (*mut'a*). Such a claim placed Fadlallah in direct conflict with Iran's ruling religious elite.

SITUATING RESEARCHER'S BIOGRAPHY

Because my own background played a major role in the research process, it requires further explanation. Born in Germany into an Iranian family, I lived in Germany until I was three years old. In 1974 my family moved back to Iran, a few years before the 1978 Iranian revolution. Our family again returned to Germany in 1986, in the middle of the Iran-Iraq War. After receiving my master's degree in Germany, where I am a citizen, and marrying a German national, I left Germany in 1995 with my husband for the United States. There I began graduate studies in Near Eastern languages and civilizations at the University of Chicago. During the twelve years that I have lived in the United States, I have traveled to Lebanon for research, maintaining the United States as my residence.

I grew up in an upper-middle-class Iranian family, where Shiite religiosity played a minor role. Shiite practice was characteristic of my father's family, while being largely absent among relatives on my mother's side. Having spent most of my life outside of Iran, I define myself as a diasporic Iranian, an Iranian living outside of Iran who nonetheless feels a deep commitment toward Iran and maintains ties to that country. I acknowledge that the years spent in Germany and the United States have shaped my identity such that it would be difficult to call myself "an Iranian" without further explaining the ways in which I see myself as Iranian. The importance of this for my fieldwork is that, during my research in Lebanon, my hyphenated Iranian background seemed often unacceptable to my Lebanese interlocutors.

LOCATING INTERLOCUTORS

My research included both ethnographic work—participant observation and semistructured interviews—and archival research. This chapter focuses on the ethnographic dimensions of my research in Beirut, Lebanon, during the period from April 2002 to May 2003.

I conducted more than fifty interviews with various Lebanese and Iranian Shiite ethnic leaders in Lebanon and took part in Shiite rituals and visited Shiite-run schools. The research objectives of this fieldwork were twofold: to study the tensions between official political representations of Shiite identity production and Iran's role in such productions and to document the "unofficial" everyday ways that Shiites position themselves within the Lebanese national context and vis-à-vis the Iranian government.

My interviewees in Lebanon were primarily men above forty, many of whom had been in the Lebanese AMAL and Hezbollah militia during Lebanon's 1975–1990 civil war and who had not only participated in combat against other Lebanese sectarian groups but also against other Lebanese Shiite groups. In particular, Hezbollah and AMAL had fought intensely for two years, from 1988 to 1990, over leadership of the Lebanese Shiite community and over Iran's role in Lebanon and in the Lebanese Shiite community. Many of my interlocutors had done battle for access to and control of Lebanese state institutions.

My principal research associate during fieldwork was a Lebanese Shiite woman who had spent three years in Iran and also spoke Persian fluently. Her father, among the first group of Shiites to leave Lebanon for Iran after the 1979 revolution, was well connected politically in Lebanon. Furthermore, my research associate's husband—also well connected politically—

was a high-ranking member of Lebanon's AMAL political party. Due to the important political background of my research associate's father and husband, and because of her own activities in the AMAL movement, my research partner was invaluable to the success of my project. I expected that her connections to a wide range of Shiite personalities in Lebanon would result in a steady stream of interviewees, and I was not disappointed. Unsurprisingly, the research questions that I hoped to pursue with interlocutors—such as transnational relations between Iranians and Lebanese—was a sensitive topic to many Shiites. As in the United States, transnational connections between Iranians and Lebanese are generally designated as "terrorist networks." It increased the reluctance of Lebanese Shiites to discuss Iranian Lebanese relations with me that I was affiliated with an educational institution inside the United States: Some potential interlocutors assumed that I was carrying out intelligence work. Given this background, I found the generosity and eagerness of my research associate to help me with the research absolutely striking. Asking about her enthusiasm for the research project, my research associate set aside politics and relied on our intersecting personal biographies: "I lived in Iran and I like Iranians a lot, and then [it is also because] you are Shiite. I felt close to you the first time I saw you; the questions in your research have been central to my life, I lived in the middle of it all."

PERFORMING AND NEGOTIATING IDENTITIES

In the first few months of research in Lebanon, while my research associate and I were still primarily establishing contacts, I noticed that one interlocutor would introduce me to another one as a *Bahitha Iraniyya*—a female Iranian researcher. Such an introduction conveyed the impression that I had come to Lebanon *from Iran* to conduct research. However, before describing the research itself to a potential interviewee, I would explain my ethnic and national background: that I am of Iranian parentage and have lived in Germany and the United States, and am now affiliated with the University of Chicago. This introduction complete, I was immediately struck by how little interest prospective interlocutors showed in my "German" or "American" background and how much they focused on my "Iranianness." I recognized very early that presenting my complex and layered identities made little sense to most of my interlocutors. In the eyes of Lebanese Shiites, I was an "upper-class Iranian woman," a designation that had emerged from two facts about my biography: I was studying in the West and I did not observe *hijab*—the latter, a cultural and religious expectation about modest dress that includes using a head scarf to cover the head and neck.

The combination of these two visible realities of my identity was interpreted by most interlocutors as a sign of my political opposition to the current Iranian regime, a position often associated with the wealthy "Iranian royalists" now living in the United States. These two assumed facts about my personal, political, and social identities influenced the dynamics of my research in major ways. Most important, I felt that what I believed to be the subtleties of my identity were back-staged and stereotyped: I was seen as "an Iranian woman," not as I saw myself, a German or American woman. If I presented myself as "a German Iranian," many interlocutors assumed that I was "ashamed" of my Iranian Muslim parentage. In the end, due to my national and cross-national background, and because of my being an unveiled Shiite women, I could not escape being associated, at best, with Iran's reformists and, at worst, with the U.S. government—presumably one of its spies. In either case, I could count on interviews sometimes becoming overtly politicized.

For example, after interviewing several Hezbollah members, I noticed that our conversations had resembled the debates in Iran between conservative and reformist political camps. My interview questions—such as "What book do you use in your [Hezbollah] schools?" or "Why have you chosen these books and not others?"—were usually interpreted as attacks on politically and religiously conservative Iranian ideologies. Such interpretations often resulted in my interlocutors' expounding at length about what they viewed as the faults of the Iranian reformist movement associated with President Khatami. When visiting one Hezbollah-run educational institution in Beirut, I asked about the number of their schools in other parts of Lebanon; the school director responded: "Are you upset that Iran sends money to Lebanon? If Iranians like you get to power in Iran, there will be no support for other Muslims outside of Iran because your identity is not based on religion but on secular values." The school director was assuming that I was a supporter of the reformist movement in Iran, which he labeled negatively as "holding secular values"—equating secularism with "godlessness." In the school director's mind, this favored "nationalist" ideologies that would create an obstacle for pan-Islamic mobilization.

I had to address the dynamic of distrust that was sometimes created by some of my interlocutors' assumptions about my political and social identities if an interview was to proceed. In the case of the previous interlocutor, I responded that I did not think of Iranian reformists as "secularists," explaining that I had not lived in Iran for a long time and did not associate with any political group inside or outside of Iran. Sometimes this explanation eased tensions, while other interviewees still could not imagine that I did not maintain ties to the Iranian government, considering how important Lebanese Shiites were to Iran's foreign policy. With the motives for my research in question, along with the disconnect between interlocutors' assumptions about my identity and my own self-assumed identities, I tried other strategies for getting around interlocutors' skepticism, some of which I will describe in the section "Mediating Stumbling Blocks." Yet, however, it remained a distinct challenge to interview those Hezbollah members who had strongly negative views about diasporic Iranians. Those holding such views are generally suspicious of Iranians from "the West," and particularly of a Shiite woman who does not respect *hijab*.

Yet another source of suspicion about me and my research grew out of the circumstance that Lebanese Shiites very rarely get to know Iranian nationals personally. Daily encounters with Shiite taxi drivers (*servis*) underscored this fact: When the drivers asked me where I was from, and I replied, "I am an Iranian (*iraniyya*)," many of these taxi drivers assuming that I had said, "I am an Armenian (*armaniyya*)." This confusion of identities most certainly was not solely the result of my accented Arabic; it is equally probable that Lebanese cab drivers had difficulties imaging an Iranian woman without the *hijab*, thus assuming that she must be an Armenian Christian. Because I was violating the taxi drivers' images of Iranian women's "proper" dress, they "heard" me say, "I am an Armenian," since an Iranian woman would not be in public without a head covering. The background of this is that most Lebanese derive their knowledge about Iran and Iranians from television, mainly from the Hezbollah television station al-Manar. This station's reporting is highly selective, presenting Iran as a successful Islamic government, where all women observe full *hijab* voluntarily. Al-Manar omits the struggles and diversity in Iranian views on religion and *hijab*. In any case, a day rarely passed without someone—on a Beirut street, in a social situation, during research—commenting about my identity. Some Lebanese Shiites speculated that I was an Armenian Iranian, others thought that I was an Iranian Zoroastrian or Baha'i. An unveiled Iranian Shiite woman was a conundrum to those whose primary knowledge of Iranian Shiites, and of Iranian Shiite women, had come from one-dimensional television news and feature film portrayals.

As for research among members of Lebanon's AMAL political party, these actors portrayed their activities in Lebanon as "moderate," explaining that they are "just like" the reformist movement in Iran. AMAL interlocutors took me for an upper-class "L.A. royalist"—a large proportion of Iranians in the United States reside in the greater Los Angeles area. AMAL members interpreted my "diasporic background" as evidence that their own critical views of postrevolutionary Iranian politics—which they began to share with me after a while—had been right. Assuming that my family had left Iran after the revolution because of the disagreeable political atmosphere there meant that their party's policy toward the Iranian government and their own judgment about its faults had been right. Being critical of Iranian religious conservatives, the AMAL interlocutors felt quite comfortable criticizing Iran and expressing their frustrations about what they saw as "Iran's hegemonic attempts in Lebanon."

However, some AMAL interlocutors associated me with Iran's 1980s military involvement in Lebanon. Their frustrations with the Iranian government were couched in pointed comments targeted at me: "*You* killed many of us during the war," referring to the fighting between AMAL and Hezbollah in the final stages of the 1988–1990 Lebanese civil war. Still attempting to locate me politically, after many meetings with AMAL interlocutors, they began to ask whether I was related to any members of the Iranian liberation movement—an Iranian anti-shah opposition movement active in the 1970s that operated mainly outside of Iran. Some of this movement's activists had been based in Lebanon. These questions became a turning point in my interviews with AMAL interlocutors, who generally became more open to my questions after locating me politically in a manner that squared my identity and past with their own and with their party's political worldview.

My meetings and interviews with AMAL members helped my research immensely: I became able to glimpse beyond official party rhetoric—that AMAL and the Iranian government have reestablished good relations— and understand how AMAL members construct their differences with Iranian Shiites and create a Lebanese Shiite religious "authenticity" that is directly connected to the history of Iranian–AMAL relations. My research associate, who arranged many of these meetings and attended some of them as well, was of immense help. She participated in some interviews and would introduce, from the position of an AMAL party member herself, her impressions of Iranians. The ensuing dialogue between my associate and an interviewee often enabled me to understand the ideas and practices through which AMAL members construct a Lebanese Shiite identity and see Iran through that lens.

BEING SHIITE AND FEMALE

I discovered in the process of research that interlocutors had two principal reactions to what they perceived as my gendered identities. On one hand, there were those pro-Iranian ruling clerical elite Shiites for whom my gender came before all else, shaping the interview process and their responses. These interlocutors saw me as a woman first and, based on what this meant to them, had trouble recognizing me as a professional researcher and scholar. This included primarily (but not exclusively) Hezbollah interlocutors. On the other hand, some interviewees placed my nationality and ethnicity above gender, resulting in their seeing my being in Lebanon as an opportunity for them to give voice to their frustrations about Iran's political intentions and projects in Lebanon. Many AMAL interlocutors acted along these lines.

No matter what the political stripe of a Shiite interviewee, these interlocutors had questions about my marital status. I cannot recollect one interview, whether formal or a more informal extended conversation, in which the issue of my martial status did not come up. On the one hand, while many interlocutors seemed reassured when I told them that I was married, just as many were visibly troubled by the fact that my husband—at least those who believed I actually had one—was not with me during most of my fieldwork in Lebanon. Shiite women would show two kinds of reactions toward me, both related to my most important role as wife and mother: I was asked whether I was not worried that—considering that I did not have a child at the time—my husband would leave me and marry another woman[3]; or whether my work was worth the trouble that living far away from one's spouse could cause. At the same time, some Shiite women actually compared their lives unfavorably to mine, saying how much they would have enjoyed studying or researching, if only their husbands had allowed it. They thought I was lucky to be married to a European who was supportive of what was important to me. In their view, no Lebanese husband would have allowed me to conduct research in a foreign country, mostly on my own.

That I did not have children at an age many considered "overripe," and that I was in the field alone, and that my husband was European, seemed to make it acceptable for some male interlocutors to flirt with me. For example, one male Shiite interlocutor remarked: "You have beautiful Persian eyes," in response to an interview question I had just asked him. Another interlocutor—being interviewed about Iranian politics and the Lebanese AMAL Party—responded: "We won the war against Iran in 1990, [but] I am not sure I will win against you." Such sexualizing comments also occurred in response to my questions about an interlocutor's family background, to which one interviewee responded: "Why don't *you* have children at your age, and how come your husband allows you to come to Lebanon?"

Being childless and in the field without my European husband also increased interlocutors' suspicions about the political motives behind my research. Distrust was in their faces and expressed directly. Some of them would ask, "Who gave you this research topic?" "Who has given you these questions to ask?" "Why are you interested in this topic?" "Who is your adviser?" "Why are you doing research in Lebanon?" and "Is your husband Lebanese?" Interestingly, such interlocutors' questions—besides indicating suspicion about the ends to which my research might be put—also questioned my research competence: What kind of researcher cannot come up with a research topic, develop acceptable research questions, and have sophisticated research interests? I presumably needed a strong other—an adviser, for example—to imagine, plan, and carry out research.

In another focus on my gender over my researcher status, almost as frequently as interlocutors asked about my marital status, they questioned me about children. For example, within the first five minutes after I introduced myself and explained my research project to a prospective interlocutor, once the interviewee had gotten beyond my marital status, he would then ask if I had children—more specifically, "How many children do you have?" After saying that I had no children, this person would then question why I was *still* childless, "considering your age"; this would be followed by a question about "the number of years that you have been married." Seeing the confusion and disappointment in these interlocutors' faces and in their tone of voice, I then explained that "my studies are important to me" and that having children now could put an end to my research and to my education. I then assured interviewees that I was "planning to have children later on." Unsatisfied with this explanation, some interlocutors recommended a doctor who could help me with the "medical problems" that were causing my "childlessness." Some would even suggest that I divorce my husband and marry a Lebanese Shiite man because, as they explained, Lebanese Shiite men were the most virile (fertile) among all Lebanese men. These interlocutors often had either themselves or a relative in mind who would guarantee my having children.

Perhaps because of interlocutors' insistent focus on aspects of my gender identity that seemed unrelated, at least in my mind, to my research project, I often felt that I was not taken seriously as a researcher. Would these questions have been so common if I had been a Shiite man? I often recognized that my interviewees, who were mainly middle-aged men, seemed amused when I interviewed them political questions. To these interlocutors, a "young Iranian woman" asking about powerful issues that had crucially shaped their identities and were important to their political lives seemed like entertainment. Politics, I realized from these interlocutors' responses (or nonresponses), was not an acceptable domain for a young woman. In Lebanon, women have rarely held political posts, and, as politicians' wives, women mainly carry out charity activities. Within such a gendered framework, it is highly uncommon for a young Shiite women from the Middle East to study Lebanese-Iranian politics. There is no easy category into which interlocutors can place such a woman.

Without doubt, ethnic and religious markers profoundly shaped my interactions with interlocutors. In particular, being an Iranian Shiite established many Lebanese Shiites, expectations about me as a woman, especially among Hezbollah members, whose idealized image of Iran's Islamic Republic led them to conceive all Iranians as practicing Muslims. By necessity, Muslims had an obligation to be a moral and religious example to Shiites around the world. Accordingly, therefore, my appearance as an Iranian woman without the *hijab* raised serious questions. Among some Hezbollah my failure to wear *hijab* dominated interviews and led to discussions about my political sympathies regarding Iran—which they assumed were with the religious reformists there.

Even Lebanese Shiites not associated with Hezbollah were surprised that a woman with an Iranian background did not wear *hijab*, had a secular outlook, and was married to a European. However, at the same time, one aspect of my image was clear: An Iranian Shiite by background, I could not be correctly classified as a foreigner, yet at the same time I did not fit stereotyped expectations for a Shiite woman. I continued to ask myself throughout the field research whether this was an asset or an obstacle: Did it help or hinder my research that I was an "outsider"? The answer to this question certainly had implications for my research. Surely, my cultural knowledge of Shiism, which made many interviewees view me as an "insider," was an asset, since it triggered discussions about how certain Shiite rituals are performed in Lebanon and how they differ in Iran. These conversations were part of most of my informal meetings with Lebanese Shiites, and, while not "officially" about the topic of my research, such discussions helped establish rapport with interlocutors, but also enabled me to learn more about the role of everyday practices in marking the differences between Lebanese and Iranian Shiites.

By engaging in informal conversations that revealed my cultural knowledge of Shiism, I began to discover issues directly related to the subject of my research. Although my research was not initially about gender and its relationship to constructions of nationalism, I was pleasantly surprised that my being an Iranian woman triggered discussions about the differences between Iranian and Lebanese Shiite women. Most of the Lebanese male interlocutors explained that Iranian women were "dominant and aggressive" and Iranian men "submissive" to their wives. The interlocutors usually then added that, in contrast, Lebanese women are feminine—"more feminine" than Iranian women.

It also complicated my research that interlocutors wanted to be sure that I write "positively" about Shiism and Lebanese Shiites. Their message, whether direct or indirect, was that, as a Shiite woman, it was my obligation to stand by my community and defend it against hostile Western stereotyping. They would advise me at length about subjects they thought important for me to include in my dissertation. As a woman culturally familiar with the politeness codes, I sat silently and listened to interlocutors' expositions. I knew that any overt move to return to what I judged to be my research interests would likely have been considered rude and evidence of a lack of respect for their concerns and for "my religious community." In a few cases, I interrupted an interlocutor as politely as I could to ask for more details or moved too quickly to the next question. Interlocutors' reactions to this were mixed. Some insisted that what they were telling me was more important than the questions I wanted to ask. Others answered the next question that I asked and then quickly returned to what they had been saying before the interruption. In those cases where I listened silently throughout an interview, I felt ill at ease: Some interlocutors gave me the impression that, as they saw it, I knew nothing about Lebanese Shiite politics, especially as a woman, and was in need of an education and lengthy lectures. In fact, what they shared with me is common knowledge among scholars of Shiism and of Lebanese Shiites. At the same time, sitting silently as an interlocutor answered a series of questions made me wonder if the interlocutor thought that I agreed with his political opinions and ideologies. Often I did not, but in only a few cases did I voice my opinion.

Especially after interviews with Hezbollah interlocutors, I was conflicted about whether I had conducted a successful interview. I had made a decision at the beginning of my research to cover my hair out of respect for religious figures or when going to Hezbollah or AMAL institutions. I decided not to cover my head when conducting interviews outside the setting of such institutions, except in encounters with religious dignitaries. Yet I could not help but wonder, had I worn the *hijab* for the sake of an interview, would the interview have been more productive? The fact that interviews with Hezbollah members usually became polemical—a fact in part influenced by these interlocutors' interpretation of my politics as contrary to theirs, and in part due to my being a Muslim woman without *hijab*—made me continually question my not having covered my head for research. I was also troubled by doubts about whether it had been a waste of time for me to discuss and try to rectify with Hezbollah interlocutors the erroneous images that they had about my politics. I must admit that before every interview—and up to the end of my research—such questions continued to dog me.

MEDIATING STUMBLING BLOCKS

In the process of conducting research, one of my best strategies seemed to be to establish a joking relationship with interviewees. This seemed to neutralize somewhat a research terrain that could easily become a minefield due to the assumed and real politics between Iran and Lebanon, and between Iranian and Lebanese Shiites, and as a result of Lebanese Shiite perceptions of me as a woman, of my politics relative to theirs, of my religious identifications, and of my politics in relation to Iran's Islamic Republic. For example, when interlocutors explicitly associated me negatively with the Iranian reformist movement or with the exiled Iranian "royalists," I would jokingly say that I planned to become the next president in Iran and would make sure to keep their politico-religious interests in mind if they helped me with my project. Sometimes jokes helped to create the desired impression that I was interested in collecting material for my dissertation and without any political project of my own.

However, humor was not always positive in an interview. In one case, an interviewee turned a serious question of mine into a joke, which threatened to derail the interview. I was interested in the debates about temporary marriage (*muta'*) in Lebanon, a permissible practice according to Shiite jurisprudence. I wanted to know whether this practice had changed since the Iranian revolution. When I brought up this subject, interlocutors had two reactions: One was for interlocutors to respond to questions about "temporary marriage" as if my question reflected a desire on my part: "Why are you interested in this topic? Are you interested in such an arrangement?" Although these interlocutors presented their response as a joke, their response in fact created an uncomfortable atmosphere that needed to be reoriented. I often found it impossible to reorient the discussion after such a "humorous" frame break by a male interlocutor. A situation had been created with the capacity to shut down any real discussion about temporary marriage and potentially even produce an embarrassing break in the interview itself. In another set of reactions to my questions about "temporary marriage," some interlocutors saw my questions as patently unacceptable: "You should not write about this since it gives a bad impression of Shiites." Such interlocutors refused to respond to questions about "temporary marriage."

Most commonly, the religious and ethnic markers of my identity created tensions during research, with interlocutors often slipping between being too familiar, based on their readings of my questionable "insider" female status—"You have beautiful Persian eyes"—or too distant, based on their designations of my somewhat-more-questionable "outsider" status—"Why do you sit like a European woman?" or "Why are you so aggressive?" Both sets of interlocutor responses were more likely to occur after questions asked "too directly" or when I "pushed" an interlocutor "too hard" about something that he seemed to want to avoid answering. For example, once when I tried to edge a particular interlocutor toward a specific topic that he did not consider relevant or was simply unwilling to talk about, my behavior was labeled "pushy and aggressive." In such cases, the sense of solidarity that was based on shared religion suddenly disappeared, and I became "like a European." My interlocutors often considered me "one of them" if I agreed to let them direct the topics and steer our conversation without interrupting.

I came to see that the borders were quite fluid between what an interlocutor was willing or not willing to reveal. In one case, I was struck by how generously one person shared details about topics that he considered secret, while another time, that same person would behave suspiciously and distance himself from a question dealing with things that were already well known. For example, one Hezbollah interlocutor denied that Iran had played any role in the creation of the Hezbollah Party, even though Iran's involvement in the founding of Hezbollah is well known. Then, to my surprise, during a subsequent interview this interlocutor spoke very freely and critically about the Iranian government and offered his negative impressions of Iran.

CONCLUSION

At the beginning of my research I was sometimes disappointed that inter-locutors had, as I then felt, disclosed relatively little about Iranian-Lebanese Shiite relations. As interviews progressed, I began to realize that the ways my own background was interpreted by an interlocutor enabled me to learn much about the two central and interrelated objectives of my larger research project. First, the positioning of my identity and nationally, politi-cally, ideologically, and religiously by Lebanese Shiite interlocutors, helped me understand how various Lebanese Shiite groups conceptualized their own politico-religious and national identities. For example, Hezbollah's association with Iran's religious ruling elite and Hezbollah assumptions that Iranian reformists were secular and as such were undermining politico-religious Shia traditions and political objectives, showed how Hezbollah constructs religious authenticity and differentiates out its political oppo-nents. For them, as a woman, I had a particular duty to give an exemplary moral image of the nation I was seen to represent. For Hezbollah associates, this was inseparable from the wearing of proper *hijab*, while for AMAL sup-porters my lack of *hijab* was read as a distancing from the ruling circles of the Islamic Republic, and therefore a sign of moral superiority in itself.

Second, by positioning me in terms of past and present Iranian politics, each set of actors (e.g., Hezbollah and AMAL) among the Lebanese Shiite interlocutors expressed how they imagined the dynamics of such transna-tional networks with Iran. For example, many Lebanese Shiites asked me about my views on the Iranian revolution, on Iranian president Muham-mad Khatami, and how I defined my own identity as an Iranian. With respect to the latter question, when I responded that my many years in Germany, and later in the United States, had shaped my sense of "national belonging" and my politics, I was sometimes interrupted with, "Why are you ashamed of being a Shiite and an Iranian?" I tried to explain that seeing myself as a secular Shiite woman with ties to several countries did not mean that I was ashamed of either the Iranian or the Shiite side of myself. Linking my apparent neglect of religious identity to the idea that I was ashamed of it was directly related to these Lebanese Shiite interlocutors' experience in

Lebanon, where Shiites are labeled as low-class, backward, and often excessively religious. Shame was not a category that I associated with my Shiite identity. The distinction in the Iranian context while I was growing up there was between secular and religious Shiites, not between backward Shiites and modern non-Shiites.

However, most of my interlocutors rejected this explanation, reaffirming that my sense of "belonging"—my identity—had to be defined in terms of my (rigidly prescribed) political and religious loyalties. Rather than seeing a person's identity as layered, flexible, and changing, most interlocutors tended to understand identity as categorical and fixed in ways that positioned a person as either congruent with their identity or in stark opposition to it, a way of positioning of identities that was specifically related to how sectarian identities in Lebanon are powerfully institutionalized, leaving very little room for public negotiation of ethno-religious belonging. This is illustrated by the questions of a Lebanese Shiite friend, followed by my responses to her, and her interpretations of those responses:

My friend asked:

——"What is the name of your father?"

——"Where was he born?"

——"What is his religion?"

I replied:

——"My father's name is Muhammad Mehdi."

——"He was born in Iran."

——"He is a Shiite."

My friend responded:

——"So that is who you are [an Iranian Shiite]. What is then all this fuss (*fawda*) about your German and your American identity?"

This exchange suggests that, for this Shiite friend, in any ranking of my possible identities, my categorical status as Iranian and Shiite trumps all other possible images of myself, including my gender and my roots in the West.[4] It also shows the importance of patrilinear genealogy. For example, in Lebanon, citizenship is transmitted through the father's line of descent and mediated through the religious community. In other words, as a Lebanese living in Lebanon, one is identified with the religious community of the father and obtains citizenship though him. While such ascriptions of belonging, in their various forms, often complicated my conversations and interviews, especially because my background as an Iranian Shiite provoked doubts about my ultimate research motives, as I have said, such doubts also provoked discussions about Iran's role in Lebanon and therefore helped me understand interlocutors' images of Iran. In the end, a question about how Lebanese Shiites imagined Iran, which was not initially included among the foci of my research, emerged as a serendipitous, valuable finding. I embraced the opportunity to write about the intersections between religious and national identities and how these, in case of Iranian-Lebanese networks, played out in one research setting. Thus, the very thing that I had initially considered least important to the success or failure of my research—interlocutors' designations of my layered identities and my own definition of self—opened an important page for me in an often unelaborated aspect of field research methods.

NOTES

1. Shaery Eisenlohr 2008.
2. See Goffman 1995 [1959].
3. For a somewhat similar experience and type of questions regarding marital status and children during fieldwork, see Fawzi El-Solh 1995.
4. This is evocative of Lila Abu-Lughod's (1986) report of how her fieldwork was crucially supported by her Arab father's personal introduction to the Bedouin community she studied, as subsequently her Egyptian Bedouin interlocutors preferred to highlight her Arab descent and identity over the American dimensions of her background during her research and residence among them.

REFERENCES

Abu-Lughod, Lila. (1986). *Veiled Sentiments: Honor and Poetry in a Bedouin Society.* Berkeley and Los Angeles: University of California Press.

Fawzi El-Solh, Camillia. (1988). "Gender, Class, and Origin: Aspects of Role During Fieldwork in Arab Society." In *Arab Women in the Field: Studying Your Own Society*, edited by Soraya Altorki and Camillia Fawzi El-Solh, 91–114. Syracuse, NY: Syracuse University Press, 1988.

Goffman, Erving. (1995 [1959]). "On Face-Work: An Analysis of Ritual Elements in Social Interaction." In *Language, Culture and Society*, edited by Ben Blount. Prospect Heights, IL: Waveland Press.

Shaery-Eisenlohr, Roschanack. (2008). *Shiite Lebanon: Transnational Religion and the Making of National Identities.* New York: Columbia University Press.

2

Studying Environmental Rights and Land Usage: Undergraduate Researcher Gets "Gendered In"

Kat Rito

In the summer of 2002, I received a grant from the Regional Deep South Humanities Center at Tulane University to study environmental and property conflicts in Louisiana's Atchafalaya Basin. The basin, which includes the largest swamp in the United States, is situated in south-central Louisiana and combines wetlands and a river delta area created by the confluence of the Atchafalaya River and the Gulf of Mexico. The main goal of my research in the Atchafalaya Basin was to learn which of the conflicting management policy suggestions for the region was the most environmentally sound. To answer this question, I would execute a three-month ethnographic study that would include interviewing members of the three social groups involved in the dispute: Cajun[1] landowners, employees of the United States Army Corps of Engineers (USACOE), and of the Louisiana State Department of Tourism.

While studying the Atchafalaya Basin's Cajun community, I discovered the centrality of gender, even over my young age, on male Cajuns' participation in an interview. This led me to think about the gender- and age-related methodological issues associated with carrying out and completing such a research project—the subject of this chapter's eight substantive sections. Beginning with an overview of Cajuns and their land, I then identify the various actors in the dispute over Atchafalaya Basin land rights and usage. Focusing in the next six sections exclusively on the Atchafalaya Basin's Cajun community, I elaborate different aspects of my experiences carrying out research with people who have traditionally resisted being studied. I identify the challenges I faced conducting field research and the strategies I used to negotiate and mediate these challenges. In the chapter's conclusion, I discuss several methodological insights from my research; most important among these is that if I'm going to insinuate myself into someone else's life, it's only fair that, on some level, I allow the same in return.

CAJUNS AND THEIR LAND

The Cajun landowners were the primary focus of my study, and they are the sole focus of this chapter. The ancestors of the Cajuns I interviewed first settled the Louisiana swamplands in the late 1700s, and they still maintain claims to the founding families' original properties. The ancestral Cajuns ultimately landed in southern Louisiana because it was one place where they were free of persecution—mainly because no one else wanted to live there. Because of their ability to cooperate and adapt to the environment, they were able to survive the harsh swamp conditions. Further, because the region was secluded from the rest of the United States, the Cajuns received little cultural influence from other groups. This makes the culture especially unique because it has maintained its heritage over the centuries: Cajun French is still spoken, and traditional community social events such as *fais do-do* (outdoor community dances) and *boucheries* (a traditional community meal) are still commonplace today.

Cajuns still use their Atchafalaya Basin land for traditional purposes; it is kept in the families and used for hunting, fishing, and other activities that maintain the close bonds between family members. For this Cajun community, the land is an integral part of their culture; it is not simply seen as "nature," or the environment in which they happen to live. For many, the Atchafalaya Basin *is* their culture—any changes in the environment will cause changes in the unique, defining structures of their cultural community. Thus, the increased interest of outside organizations in the Atchafalaya Basin would significantly affect both the basin's environment and the Cajun culture.

As the federal and Louisiana state governments have become more interested in the Atchafalaya Basin, Cajuns have experienced increased pressure to sell their land—and a correlating desire to protect it. Cajuns who are not active land users are selling their properties for economic gain. If the governments succeed in land buyouts, within fifteen years they will hold almost all land acreage in the Atchafalaya Basin. In response to this, several Cajun families actively using their land have mobilized to encourage others not to sell their land to anyone outside their own community.

ACTORS IN CONFLICT

My initial observations suggested that, for Cajuns, "nature" is synonymous with "culture." I modified my research question to include both concepts, for it seemed impossible for "the environment" to exist without "culture." What cultural consequences would there be, I asked, if changes in state and national land policies constricted Cajuns' right to land usage in the Atchafalaya Basin? To understand the extent to which this culture—including its environment—is threatened by new policies, I had to gain an understanding of the two main organizations that could have the greatest impact on the basin: the USACOE and the state of Louisiana.

The USACOE gauges the environmental heath of the Atchafalaya Basin. The basin is the nation's largest old-growth hardwood swamp, and is vital in maintaining Louisiana's environmental stability. It prevents erosion, diverts floodwater from the Mississippi River, and is home to thousands of plant and animal species. The USACOE's decades-long campaign to buy a majority of the land in the basin for environmental purposes has caused many landowners to stop supporting the USACOE's presence in the basin. Some Cajuns believe it is a puppet of political and corporate interests and do not trust that the USACOE's interests are aligned with environmental preservation.

The regional office of the USACOE, which is in economic competition with the other Corps districts, must constantly find ways to secure funding for its own projects. The basin, with its atypically good environmental health and ecological significance, is a prime candidate for bringing national funding into the region. Thus the USACOE has a good deal to gain politically from increasing its hold in the basin. With greater control over the basin, the USACOE could request increased federal funding for local projects, potentially turning the basin into a living laboratory to test new procedures for manipulating the environment. Some Cajuns worry that experimental procedures will cause irreversible ecological damage to the basin, and thus work to prevent increased federal control over the territory.

Some alleged the USACOE is using scare tactics to encourage other landowners to cede their holdings out of "environmental necessity." While no members of the USACOE would directly clarify this issue for me, they have sent letters to landowners stating that the USACOE may need ownership of basin property to increase environmental protection, offering a bid to purchase the land at market value. Because privately held property deeds gave the USACOE the right to alter land for environmental purposes anyway, landowners were wary of the USACOE's stated need for a greater percentage of land ownership. The Cajuns also contended the basin is environmentally healthy and overall ecologically sound. They worried that any tampering with the physical environment could prove disastrous to one of the nation's most viable ecosystems.

But the USACOE is not the only government organization whose policies impact land usage in the Atchafalaya Basin. Louisiana state government is also interested in increasing its basin holdings. Ecological tourism has become popular in recent years, and Louisiana has worked to showcase the Atchafalaya region as an "ecotourism" destination. Thus, the third group I studied was the Louisiana State Department of Tourism. It has worked to increase tourist traffic in the basin area with a national campaign of Louisiana as a family-oriented and ecological destination. With its historic culture and strong grounding in religion and family-friendly activities, "Acadiana culture" is one of the central features of this campaign. To bolster this, Louisiana began property acquisitions to expand its park systems, which theoretically make the environment accessible for this purpose. The state claims that increased public land means everyone can enjoy using it—tourists and locals alike. But the situation is more complex; increased state ownership means increased regulation and restriction of overall land use. Some Cajun families are concerned this will actually decrease their ability to use and enjoy their ancestral land.

Controversies over sporting rights are a prime example of this issue. Hunting and fishing is a system of ritual and tradition for local families. Hunting is a year-round event, even when a season is not open. Cajun men spend the entire year preparing for hunting seasons, building stands and blinds, training dogs, and teaching these skills to the younger generations. Fishing is the same way; large nets and boats must be constructed and maintained, and enough fish are often caught in a single outing to feed an entire extended family. The men and children bring their catches home, the women help prepare them, and a single meal becomes a family reunion. Such activities reinforce family tradition and solidarity and, therefore, are crucial to the preservation of local culture.

It may be argued that increasing open land allows non-property-owning families greater participation in these activities, which would ultimately preserve local culture. But actual state policies on land use sometimes have the opposite effect. For example, the state may auction "hunting leases" to specific tracts of land. Wealthier out-of-state hunting clubs can outbid local families and clubs, therefore securing exclusive rights to prime hunting locations. Thus, the end result may be that, in some regions, locals are effectively barred from traditional use of their land.

In addition to limiting patterns of traditional land use, changes in the state's ecotourism policies may also harm the environment. Increased human presence in the basin may have detrimental effects on its environment. Visitors trespass onto private land, littering and damaging property on some of the islands. Because most Cajuns no longer live in the basin, they are not present to protect their property from such invasions. The wildlife is impacted by an influx of tourism as well. Increased boat traffic may result in overfishing or destruction of nesting grounds, and the increased noise and human visibility makes other forms of wildlife scarce as well.

LEARNING AND CHANGING

As I learned more about the land conflicts in the Atchafalaya Basin, my research came to cover more than the issue of land autonomy, or whose ownership and policy ideas would best protect the region. The viability of the Atchafalaya Basin is more than a question of environmental protection; the region is tied to several levels of economics and politics, and simultaneously preserves local history and culture. My original research question, "Who best speaks for nature?" seemed too simple. As I studied the regional history, I lost my understanding of what "nature" even is. Everyone had his or her own definition of it. Unless I learned the viewpoints of all three groups acting within the basin, I could not hope to answer my research questions. I had assumed that my research would begin by determining who best protected the region and its "nature." However, I actually had to take several steps backward in the research design, and first formulate a definition of "nature." Doing so was crucial; if I didn't, my own thoughts would get lost in the turmoil of so many conflicting—and charged— viewpoints. And, as my calendar constantly reminded me, my research had to be completed in three months if I were to present my findings at the grant symposium that fall!

I altered my research plan to study the three groups not only through their actions, but also through how they framed concepts of "nature" and of "environmental protection." Despite my intense efforts, my findings ended up being compelling but inconclusive at best. Due to the anticipated constraints of time—and unanticipated problems such as institution affiliation, age, and gender—executing this project was impossible. Yet in my attempt, I gained invaluable insight in the nature of doing field research, including an unexpected respect for the feminist perspective in the social sciences. In dealing with all three groups, my role as a researcher was challenged and undermined in unique ways. Even the most basic tasks required cleverness, luck, and a lot of self-confidence—a fact rarely mentioned in any of my research methodology textbooks.

GETTING INTO THE FIELD

Time Lacking; Networking Required

The greatest constraint on the project was my three-month time limitation—I had given myself only the span of my summer break to conduct field research. I applied for a research grant early in the spring semester, but they would not be awarded until April, immediately before semester final exams. I also knew that with the courses I planned to take in the upcoming fall semester, I simply would not have time to continue field research once classes resumed. Initially I felt prepared for this limit. Before the project even got off the ground, my adviser and I discussed exactly how I would work within a three-month time line. In these formative stages, it was clear that if I got the grant for summer research, I had no time for "extensive preliminaries"—from day one I would be in the field, arranging and conducting interviews. After submitting my grant proposal for the Atchafalaya Basin research project, I casually asked members of my home community—my parents lived in the Acadiana region—not only how they felt about the land rights controversies, but also if they felt the issue was worthy of academic study. The response was very enthusiastic, and several offered to serve as gatekeepers if I secured the research grant.

Consulting Literature

In addition to preliminary networking, I reviewed any and all literature I could find on the basin. I requested all of the information available from both the USACOE and the Louisiana Department of Tourism (one of the nice things about studying government institutions, I found, is that reprints of most data are free), including press statements, maps, geological time lines, and anything else to help understand their "official" explanations for becoming more involved in the region. I spent hours at libraries at local universities, scouring the literature for studies done on Cajun culture and its history.

In the end, this literature did little more than familiarize me with the history of the Cajun people; most cultural studies done on this group appeared to state basic stereotypes about them and then explain why the stereotypes might be true. The literature explained that Cajuns are a very difficult culture to study, historically close-knit and geographically removed from the rest of the country—and thus from the eye of sociology. I was oblivious to the obvious foreshadowing this had on my own research. I already fancied myself an "insider," having attended school in the region as a child and because some landowners already offered to participate in my research. I'd researched extensively. I'd mapped out the issues and key figures—everything my adviser told me to do. All I had to do was show up, talk to people and review my findings in light of those I'd gathered on the USACOE and Louisiana Department of Tourism. I was confident I could execute the fieldwork leg of the study in three months.

NEGOTIATING FIELD HURDLES

Academic Preparation

As soon as university classes ended in May, I returned to my family's home in the Atchafalaya region[2] and renewed contact with my promised gatekeepers. However, it was not until August—on the eve of my return to school—that I finally accessed information on the "Cajun" side of this conflict, the one group I'd been confident in my ability to study. Notwithstanding my careful preparation, several unexpected factors hindered the project and each had to be resolved if I had any hopes of completing the project.

Institutional Support

Institutional support was my smallest issue, but at the outset it did catch me off guard. I learned in research design class that being sanctioned by a university is an asset—it shows that a researcher is relatively unbiased, implying that you are interested in the region for academic purposes as opposed to economic data collection. But this was not to be. Coming from a private university proved a significant initial hurdle to beginning the research process.

According to some of my initial gatekeepers, researchers are from, or are assumed to come from, state universities. Members of the Cajun community were often curious as to why Tulane would be interested in issues affecting their community. This curiosity lead to increased distrust. I spent a lot of time explaining that *I* was interested in the culture—Tulane just happened to be funding me. After a few unsuccessful conversations, I stopped introducing myself as "Kat Rito, a researcher from Tulane University," and just stuck with my name. Once they agreed to an interview, seeing Tulane's name on top of the release forms did not concern them as much as when they heard the institutional name outright. I'd realized that in this instance it was better to draw the focus away from my institutional support and onto the research itself. But before I could convince the Cajuns to participate in my study, I had to overcome yet another set of related issues: my outsider, gender, and age statuses.

"Outsider" Status

The Cajuns I met had all the traits that prior literature told me to expect—Cajuns had a humble demeanor and patriarchal families, and were distrustful of outsiders. These characteristics seriously complicated the pace of my research, particularly given my three-month time line. Many would not trust anyone from outside their communities, especially someone asking questions about an ongoing legal battle between themselves and the state and federal governments. Believe it or not, people just are not comfortable sharing confidential legal information with someone they only superficially know.

Others refused to share information with me because they felt that they were "wasting my time"—they could not understand why anyone would want to study their problems. Obviously, if I remained a peripheral member of the community they would not be willing to share personal documents, such as legal orders/property sale offers by the state and the USACOE. If my project were to succeed, I had to gain entry into the community and then prove to potential interviewees that I was sincerely interested in both the Cajun culture and its issues. This often meant first convincing Cajuns that these issues were important enough to talk about.

Gender and Age

While advance planning and careful phrasing of conversations helped me to navigate some research problems, the greatest barriers to my research were the unavoidable facts of my age and gender. I was almost twenty when the study began, and I was a woman attempting to study a patriarchal culture. Perhaps it was because I did not see myself as a true "outsider" to the culture—after all, my parents lived there and I'd attended a local high school. Or perhaps it was because I was new to research and just failed to appreciate how I would appear to my research subjects as a researcher— because some Cajuns supported my research in theory, maybe I wrongly assumed they would cooperate without hesitation. Whatever the reason, I did not plan that I would be ascribed "outsider" status, or that it would hinder my research. But when I attempted to enter into an academic research relationship with the Cajun community, I was anything but welcome. I was someone horning my way into their private lives, and I was a girl/woman challenging traditional gender barriers. To the Cajuns, my research was not always, or actually, about Atchafalaya Basin and land rights—it was about someone who had decided to enter specific realms where women were not allowed. I was perceived as a threat to privileged realms of Cajun cultural and social behavior.

Had my project been on a "feminine" issue within Cajun culture, gaining entry might have been much easier. However, because I was researching a "male" issue—land rights—primarily in the "out-of-doors," I had entered a strictly male environment. It is the men who typically maintain the property and engage in sporting activities. Also, since most families who own Atchafalaya Basin property now live elsewhere, few females are actually in the area. As a consequence, Cajuns of both genders felt that there was simply no reason for women to be there.

My study took me into a geographical no-woman's land. The Atchafalaya Basin spans over eight hundred thousand acres. Physical entry requires a boat and an extensive knowledge of the terrain. It is very easy to become lost in the vast maze of canals, marshes, and islands that make up the Atchafalaya ecosystem. Lacking this knowledge, and also the ability to use a motorboat, I could not locate the Atchafalaya Basin's Cajun social networks without at least one gatekeeper to bring me into a group. Because my presence there would not be passive, the men had little incentive to invite me into their private culture. To gain entry, I needed to prove my trustworthiness as a researcher and ultimately that I was worthy of being allowed into this region of Cajun men's culture.

But before I could convince anyone to let me into the Atchafalaya Basin, I had to meet them personally, not as myself but as a researcher. Introductory discussions and associated interviews that took place by phone or e-mail were never problematic. In contrast, the in-person interviews were a great challenge. Most face-to-face interviews invariably began in the same manner: An astonished look, with the person protesting, "But you . . . you're so *young.*" If this happened, I felt fortunate. It meant that a participant actually recognized that I was a researcher. In the obverse case, where my age and gender trumped my researcher status, every time I mentioned land rights conflicts in the Atchafalaya Basin, an interviewee would talk over me by asking polite questions about me—usually about school or my romantic life.

I thought that perhaps this were some sort of test; southern cultures can be maddeningly polite. Maybe, I reasoned, the interviewee is going to judge how much he is willing to share with me by my manners. But the interviewee's idle questions were typically endless. This was problematic for two reasons. First, they took time away from substantive discussions on land issues in the basin. Second, they impeded my ability to conduct an in-person interview because they removed the focus of discussions from the land and placed it on me. Losing control of these interviews was, honestly, terrifying, because I had no clue how to control them, and they were critically important.

The interviews were vital for two reasons. First, they would establish good rapport between the male interviewee and myself. No man would take me to the Atchafalaya Basin, a culturally honored and considered a sacred region, unless he trusted me. Likewise, because the basin is a dangerous, secluded place, I would not go unless I had a trustworthy guide. Second, I needed to gain an idea of what to look for when I made my first trips into the basin. I had expected preliminary interviews would yield a basic understanding of how Cajun men conceptualized the environment and the problems surrounding it.

Faced with continuing personal questions during interviews, I racked my brain for ways to regain control of the conversations. After an interviewee asked a question, I would fire one right back—I thought that through these exchanges, I might direct the conversation to land issues without anyone realizing it. But to no avail. About twenty minutes into this conversational ping-pong, one of the men commented that my adviser was late, and perhaps I should call to check up on him. At that point, I realized that the interviewees were not dodging my questions because of some southern conversation ritual—they simply did not want to begin the interview until the "real" researcher had arrived. I could not believe they did not think I was *the* researcher, when over the phone and on paper I had stressed that I would be conducting the interviews. I had distributed my adviser's contact data as I was instructed by my adviser to do—but always reinforcing that he would not be present at any time. Of course, as surprised as I was by the male interviewees' reactions, the interviewees seemed even more shocked that someone of my age would be conducting serious social research unaccompanied by an "adult professional."

Along with the common assumption that I was a research assistant, I was often treated as though I were in high school. My project was repeatedly referred to as a "book report." A handful of informants asked whether I would be starting college in the fall—never mind that the introductory letters I had sent them told of my affiliation with Tulane. Similar comments directed at my youth manifested in interviewees' responses to my interview questions. For example, if I asked an interviewee a complex question about historical legal conflicts in the basis, I was rebuked with a response like, "I think that might be a little above your head." The undermining of my researcher role did not end at the close of an interview. When an interview was completed, participants offered me a ride home or asked if I needed to borrow their cell phone to call my parents for a ride. This was my first solo research project, and to be honest, I had not seriously expected to land the research grant; I'd taken only two or three social science courses. I knew I was nervous at the start of the interview process, and I assumed that I had created the image of a young, unprepared, high school girl. I blamed myself for interviewees' infantilizing me.

STRATEGIZING GENDER AND "CHILD" STATUS

Even after my initial nervousness had worn off, thus eliminating my first theory about why I was not taken seriously by participants, interviewees still met my serious interview questions with seemingly irrelevant personal questions. Interviews became frustrating, and I took it personally. I had worked so hard to learn the correct research questions and issues, and I was denied access to the answers because I was seen as "too young" for such matters. After a few failures, the unfairness of this designation hit me hard. I had no control over my age, and it was a controlling factor in the research process. To counter this, I prepared myself even more carefully for upcoming interviews, employing several tactics which I hoped would offset the fact that I was a woman, albeit still between twenty and forty years younger than those I interviewed, but nonetheless grown-up and mature enough to discuss these matters.

I tried to prove my maturity by using an especially large vocabulary and dressing in a more professional manner. Both tactics backfired spectacularly and only further complicated the relationship between my subjects and myself. The large vocabulary only reinforced for some that I was a "private school snob," a fact that was merely off-putting to some and very intimidating to others. Indeed, some contacts who had known me before I moved to New Orleans for college considered the fact that I had not gone to a state university something of a social slight, and my actions made them revisit that sentiment.

Dressing professionally—even if that only meant a skirt or nice pair of slacks—also caused its problems. Upon seeing me, many subjects felt as though they had underdressed for the meeting. I had unwittingly shamed some interviewees, which certainly did nothing to encourage a dialogue between us. Some interviewees who had known me previously couldn't help but comment on how "grown up" or "adorable" I looked. While enduring trips down memory lane did help put few of these interviewees at ease, for the most part it only seemed to underscore my age—again. It was as though they knew that I was dressing up to compensate for my age. Cajun culture is informal, and I think we all knew there was no real reason for me to dress in a professional manner at all, save to ensure my own peace of mind.

While it was difficult to separate interviewees' reactions to my young age from their reactions to my gender, or from the interaction of these two ascribed status categories, it now seems that my gender was by far the greatest trial during the field research project. Another unintended consequence of dressing nicely was that it caused some male subjects to think that my interest in the interview was more than academic. After an interview, I often received a call from a male interviewee asking if I were free that night, or to call him again if I "wanted to do some advanced research." As a result, I found myself spending more time setting up boundaries between myself and my respondents and proving my worth as an individual rather than doing any actual research.

Formal interviews, for example, were almost always held over lunch. Male participants often tried to pay for the meal, typically leading to a struggle over the check. In the end, if I prevailed, it was by insisting that since the project was grant-funded, Tulane University was actually paying for the lunch—neither of us was really paying for the meal. It was personally frustrating to have to lean on my institution in order to maintain control over a gender-marked situation. Explaining that according to academic protocol, I, as the researcher, should assume expenses because the subjects ought to receive some reimbursement for their time and participation seemed like gender-protective deception. But just because I was successful in paying for a meal, I was by no means guaranteed that the interviewee took the research process seriously. When I reminded an interviewee that the expenses were "on Tulane University," several informants seemed to construct my research as a game or joke. In some instances it was apparent the interviewee was not interested in furthering the research; they only played along for a free meal.

Yet, while paying for meals may seem trivial outside ethical issues, the symbolic meaning of a male interviewee's doing this had enormous implications for the study. If subjects succeeded in paying a meal check, I ran the risk of being seen as more of a "date" than an interviewer. But in some instances, there was an unexpected positive outcome when an interviewee succeeded in paying for lunch—he was sometimes more willing to talk again later. When I "behaved" and stayed within my expected gender role by allowing the gentleman at the table to cover the bill, I came across as slightly less threatening. I lost a small amount of situational control in that I was forbidden to pay, but the tradeoff was that this encouraged some male interviewees to talk more freely, making my self-perceived decrease in researcher status more tolerable. Once I started conforming to their expectations of me, interviewees finally participated in the research and shared information on their land and heritage with me.

CHALLENGES NEVER END

I didn't expect further problems after I finally interviewed the key landowners. I had assumed that if they agreed to speak with me, they implicitly agreed to participate further in the project. But, to my surprise, not a single interviewee was willing to serve as a gatekeeper into to Atchafalaya Basin itself. My requests were ignored, dates were rescheduled indefinitely, and initial invitations were revoked outright. If I pressed too far, participants would tell me that the topic was simply "too masculine" and suggest I study something else. Although initially enthusiastic about the project, when it was time for me to enter the Atchafalaya Basin, several hunting groups and landowners—the same men who initially refused to take me seriously—now felt threatened by my presence. These interviewees made promises to me they had no intention of keeping.

A woman wanting to spend her summer in a Louisiana swamp was unheard of. The heat and humidity is sweltering; the basin is teeming with snakes, alligators, and leeches; there are no lines of communication, and no hospitals or stores for miles. These factors understandably serve as a barrier to anyone who might want to visit the Atchafalaya Basin. The environment is neither inviting nor easily tolerable, and anyone doing so commands a good deal of respect. The ability to survive in these conditions is linked to strength and, ultimately, masculine superiority. The men who frequented the basin clearly did not want that badge undermined by the presence of a young woman. At this point, I was halfway through the project time frame and, cultural-gender implications be damned, I was determined to find a way into the basin.

One night I complained to my father about how surprisingly impossible it was to access the basin.[3] He tried explaining that women just don't go to the basin in general, and that I was asking a lot by wanting to invade this male space. Time was running out. My frustration was at a breaking point and I was in no mood to respect whatever secret male rituals took place in the basin. Had I realized exactly how crucial the following dialogue would be, I would have recorded it for the sake of this paper. But it went something like this: "Daddy! When I did the initial research, I had informants who promised to help me, and now they won't! I did all this work and got the grant and the one thing I need—to get into the Atchafalaya Basin—is *not* happening! And it's just *not fair!*"

My father said nothing, and left the room. Ten minutes later he returned and said gruffly, "Be ready bright and early Saturday morning for a trip into the basin." I should have allied myself with my father earlier in the project. As a close friend of several of the local hunting families, my father has long been a participant in whatever goes on in the Atchafalaya Basin. I would finally get my chance to experience the basin's unique culture firsthand. But as with so much of the research project up to that point, my gender identity was implicated in the process. If asked his general opinion of female presence in the basin, my father would echo that of the other men. My father would not have called in that favor for me as a social researcher, but he was willing to break the rules for me—his little girl. I finally found my way into the vast social network of the Atchafalaya Basin, but what would become of me as a researcher in the process? Would I be seen as a professional? Would I become a mere tag-along daughter? Would my father simply take the researcher role himself?

And so it went that on my very first trip into the field as a sociologist, my father came to oversee the entire affair. During the ride to the boat landing, I sat in the back seat of our guide's truck and wrestled with the gender implications of having my father as my escort. There was an obvious geography in the guide's truck that delivered a clear message to me as to my place in the basin. The two men sat in the front seat, chatting with one another, and I sat alone, excluded in the back seat. Would my dependence on two men prove to the others—already skeptical of my project—that a woman cannot do things on her own? Surely my inability to enter the field without my father's arrangements would reinforce the men's notion that a woman had no right to be outside of her predetermined social realms. Likewise, my Italian father is hardly sympathetic to feminist issues. Would this trip be as unproductive as my early interviews, where I was treated as though I were working on a high school book report or playing some kind of intellectual make-believe?

At the outset, it seemed my fears were justified. Rather than delving into the issues I wanted to discuss, I was taken on a tourist's boat ride through the Atchafalaya Basin. I was shown eagle's nests, alligators, and some of the better fishing spots. It wasn't at all what I wanted. To make matters worse, my answers elicited only minimal responses from my guide, and I was learning nothing. Frustrated, I finally gave up and just listened to my guide talk. At one point, I asked a question to my father about the natural gas lines crossing the canals. He did not know the answer, and so asked his friend, our guide. To my surprise, I was given a detailed answer explaining not only the mechanics of the system, but why our guide feared for the environment because of it! A multistep system of information gathering developed: I addressed my question to my father, he then asked our guide, and the guide then responded to my father as if I were not there. I received answers to my questions by listening to the conversation between the two men. It was an unexpected interview process, but ultimately secured some invaluable information.

As the day wore on and the three of us grew comfortable together, the trip became more relaxed. While my specific questions about land rights and the environment had been answered earlier in the day, I still wanted to learn exactly what "land" meant as a social construct to those who lived in the Basin. Clearly, asking, "What does the land mean to you?" was not going to work. I knew an outright question so broad would not get an accurate answer. So I sat quietly in the boat and listened to the guide and my father gossip about local residents and their problems. To illustrate his points, our guide often brought us to the location of such stories—a particular island, oil rig, or houseboat—and then discuss his point further.

Being a female and a nonresident, I had no role in these conversations, and my presence was virtually ignored. At first I worried about my inability to control the conversations directly, but there was something to be said about being a fly on the boat wall that day. And from this passive position, I gleaned many key ideas about the environment as a cultural framework for Cajun men.

FITTING GENDER INTO AN ATCHAFALAYA SWAMP

Whatever my initial misgivings were, I could not have asked for a better gatekeeper than my father. As a practical matter, I could trust him with my personal safety. I was about nineteen—barely twenty at most—when I entered the field in this mini-ethnography. In hindsight, it takes a foolish girl to agree to go deep into the wilderness with strange men she barely knows, with no viable safety plan to prevent any physical harm. But it's certainly something I would have done at the time for academia's sake. With two years' hindsight, I am very thankful I had the luxury of having my father around so that safety—aside from the perils of the environment—was of little concern. It was also of practical benefit for the men I observed; with my father there, if anything happened to me, it would be his problem and not theirs. Relief from full responsibility for me made them more tolerable of my presence.

But there was also a symbolic value that came from my father's presence, which increased my credibility with the men I hoped to observe. Cajun culture is family oriented; having my father act as a gatekeeper, and deferring to his authority, showed that I was not above following social conventions and hierarchy. But being allowed to witness the culture from inside the environment did not mean I was welcome to participate in it. Regardless of any developments that occurred in my favor, I was still a woman in a man's territory. The men's behavior toward me, and my responsive actions, constantly reminded me I was not given full credibility in this group.

For example, while traveling in the basin, I was never without at least one trusted male escort. This made intuitive sense, given the hazards of the environment, but it still frustrated me. Certain areas of the Atchafalaya Basin were familiar to me from occasional camping trips during my childhood. When I was younger and visited the basin for recreational purposes, I was allowed to roam unsupervised in certain areas, traveling by foot or all-terrain vehicle. This is allowed for a child supervised by her parents in a general enclosed setting, but this independence was not granted to an adult female outsider, and the men imposed several restrictions on me. I was in their territory, a man's domain. As a woman researcher, I was a threat to male Cajun culture, because they were not quite sure what I was looking for, or what I would do with whatever information I gathered. And, because I was a woman, they felt obligated to protect me. In either role, I was a burden to their activities in this environment. If I was going to learn anything there, I had to overcome these burdens.

To combat gender bias in the Atchafalaya Basin field site, I negotiated my appearance by choosing layered, loose-fitting clothing that covered as much of my body as possible, making it impossible for men to sexualize my gender. I had clearly not learned any lessons from the primary interview sessions on potential drawbacks to compensating for appearance. This clothing made it almost impossible to navigate the dense underbrush. I was constantly snagged by thorns and vines, and weighed down easily in the boggy mud. I fell behind the group often and constantly needed "saving" from these obstacles. Rather than hiding my gender, it only reinforced the notion that I was a hopeless, helpless woman. My inability to walk became a running joke, and I worried I would never be taken seriously.

I needed to find a way to prove myself to the group in order to gain acceptance and therefore be allowed to spend more time with them. I tried my best to keep up with the men and earn some level of respect, and I eventually succeeded in this regard. The men I encountered tested my knowledge and gumption regularly, though certain tests were more severe than others. In one instance I was crossing a canal with one participant, who instructed me to step on a log to keep from getting wet. I refused, pointing out to him that the "log" was actually a large alligator. Another participant suggested I use a clearing as a shortcut to a hunting cabin; I again refused, because the "shortcut" was overrun with poison ivy. In yet another instance, I was urged to jump out of our boat to chase and catch a large speckled king snake—I was unsuccessful, but applauded for my efforts. These tests were unrelenting at first; in fact, my father—my protector—even initiated many of them. He later explained to me that he did this to demonstrate my wilderness savvy to the others. I eventually proved to the men I studied that I belonged, at least for the short term, and they accepted my presence in the swamp.

But "fitting in" did not solve all my problems. My success at the men's tests suggested that something was wrong with me as a woman. If I possessed such masculine qualities, then it followed that I was somewhere lacking in feminine qualities. Despite my gradual admission into the group, my gender identity remained under a microscope. I was often asked what my boyfriend thought of the project. I truthfully responded that I did not have one, but if I did, his opinion would have no impact on the study. As a result, either I was told, "With an attitude like that, no wonder you're single!" or someone would promise to introduce me to a son or a nephew. All I could do was laugh off the comments. Any defensiveness on my part might have alienated me from this group of which I wanted so desperately to be a part. If the Cajun men were going to allow me to access this portion of their world, I needed them to like me regardless of the slights I would have to endure.

After some time, I was taken to stay at a particular hunting camp. We docked at the island and I moved to climb out of the boat—after the men, of course. But I was stopped and instructed to wait until given permission to depart the boat. Apparently some other men who used the camp were spending the weekend there, and my guide would not bring me there without their permission. (I later learned that my guide wanted to make sure they were "clothed decent enough" to be seen by a woman.) Moments like this made me appreciate what a leap it was for them to bring a woman to stay in the Atchafalaya Basin—some behavioral rituals simply were not established with women in mind. Virtually every event in the basin went similarly; men who I had not yet met had to grant me permission to join their activities.

But being "the girl" wasn't all bad. My gender did confer one advantage—being a female made it less difficult to learn from Cajun women, who ultimately proved key to my study. The men I interviewed spent the most time in the basin, but the women—their wives, sisters, mothers, and daughters—were the most knowledgeable about actual laws and policies affecting the basin. As the keepers of the family, the women closely monitored the status of the family property. I needed to spend time with the men to understand the cultural implications of land use in the basin, and also to learn that I would need to meet Cajun women if I were to understand how these legal battles were playing out.

Like my forays into the Atchafalaya Basin, my initial interviews with Cajun women took place in the presence of male chaperones. I thought my father's need to keep watch over me in the basin was a function of my age and gender, but at this point I began to think it was merely a function gender alone. The first woman I interviewed, significantly older than I, would not agree to speak with me unless accompanied by her brothers. At the interview I directed my questions specifically toward her. She would deflect the question to her brothers, who would then refer the question back to her because she knew the answer. At this point, she would finally answer the question. As with my father and our male guides in the basin, this interview process was mediated through gender hierarchies. In the case of this one particular woman—which was not atypical—she was genuinely uncomfortable possessing expertise of a "wilderness issue" over her brothers. Presumably, by allowing her brothers to mediate the questions, she drew them into the interview process in a manner that pulled the focus away from her actual expertise. Eventually, she began speaking confidently about the issue, and she invited me to her house for further discussion on the matter.

My gender again played a role in gathering information from the Cajun women, my second set of research participants. In this instance, rather than downplaying my gender, I had to learn to use it to my advantage in the study. Many women would simply defer to their husbands as "experts" in the area of property rights and usage. This was frustrating and confusing to me, because when I asked specific questions about legal conflicts in the field, the men avoided the questions, telling me the women in their families were "keeping track of that legal stuff." The men I befriended in the field encouraged the women they knew to speak with me, but the women did not cooperate immediately. It took a lot of general gossip and discussing things "woman to woman"—eventually becoming friends—before the women opened up and shared their personal legal information with me. Finally, I gained the information needed to address my research questions. But by then it was nearing September, and I had to return to school.

It was unfortunate that I could not speak to the women in the beginning. Instead, it took weeks of cultivating the friendship and respect of the men I studied before I even learned that the women would be best situated to discuss legal and policy issues I sought to study. If I had spoken to the Cajun women first, I might have been able to collect enough data to answer at least part of my research question within my three-month time frame.

CONCLUDING THOUGHTS

To answer my very narrow research question about legal issues of land ownership, I needed only to speak to the women I interviewed, and not the men. In the end, I was left with a nagging question: To answer my research question—"Whose land policies best protect nature?"—was it necessary to gain entry into the basin system itself, or did I waste valuable research time on a red herring? What did I gain from spending so much time in the basin and focusing on Cajun men? I wondered what I could have done to make my research design more efficient, but in hindsight, there is still nothing I would have done differently. Indeed, there is little I could have done, because in an ethnographic study you cannot control your research subjects. The channels I took were the only way I could have accessed the data I needed for the study. My only methodological regret was the three-month time constraint. As soon as I'd gained significant entry into the basin's Cajun community, it was time to wrap up the project and prepare for the new academic semester.

After the project officially ended, I was given the chance to extend the study and work toward a publication of my findings. But at the time I was too exhausted and frustrated, and was still concerned that I could not generate enough data to make the project worthwhile. I received permission to defer the decision to continue the project until I had time to objectively distance myself from it. The demands of my semester's coursework made reentry into the Cajun community too impractical to pursue. But I'll be honest—the unexpected stress and difficulties of the research process were the greatest factor in my decision to discontinue it. Juggling the roles of "young woman" and "social researcher" was not easy, and no one warned me I'd have to do so. For all my academic preparation, I did not emotionally prepare myself to conduct an ethnography. Trying to establish and maintain my researcher role—rather than being seen as a woman, girl, or tourist—led to some drawn-out power struggles between myself and the participants.

I am a consummate perfectionist; when I submitted my findings, I was certain I hadn't produced anything of sociological significance. I had learned what "nature" meant to the subsection of the Cajun culture I studied, but I had little evidence to answer my primary research question,

"Which local actor in the Atchafalaya Basin really speaks for nature?" I returned to Tulane with scraped arms, a terrible sunburn, a face swollen (and now, scarred) from insect bites, and a notebook more telling of my efforts to negotiate my way through the research process than anything pertinent to land rights and usage in the Atchafalaya Basin.

For a year I asked myself, "What did I learn in the Basin?" It took me a while to come up with the answer: "I learned a lot." I learned some about land rights and its intersection with local culture, but I took away some invaluable lessons on social research in general. Before undertaking this study, I think I had taken two sociology classes, in which I had critiqued someone else's ethnographic studies and methodology from the sterile confines of a classroom. It was another thing entirely to conduct my own ethnography, in a boat miles from anywhere, far from the experience and reassurances of my academic adviser. All things considered, I think the work I accomplished was impressive given only three months and my gross inexperience. If I had to report the findings of my project today, it would not be the fact that I failed to gain sufficient data to answer my primary research questions; it would be that ethnographic field research is not a passive, one-way process—there is no all-powerful researcher soliciting information from his subjects.

The latter hold control over the situation, and to some extent the researcher is only along for the ride. But even that statement oversimplifies the reality, for I was not there as just a researcher. Whether I liked it or not, I was in the field in my personal capacity as well. I naively assumed my role as a researcher would transcend my other social identities, particularly that as a woman. Until I revisited this project from a reflective methodological perspective, I never fully appreciated the impact personal identity would have on a study. I had to balance how my personal factors would influence the outcome of all my research activities. If I were seen as a young girl, no one would take me seriously; if I were seen as a woman researcher, I would be a threat to the status quo. For my research to be even remotely successful, I had to learn to navigate the participants' gender and age-biased stereotypes about me. And to do that, I had to allow them to know me personally.

It was difficult to allow my research subjects to examine me on the personal levels upon which I examined them; hypocritical, I know, but in the context of the study, from their perspective I envisioned myself only as a researcher—not a person. And that limited understanding of my place in the group had implications for the project—and for me. I did not enter the field expecting the experience to be glamorous or easy. But I didn't expect it to be so hard, either. Executing the research was alienating, lonely, and, at times, a blow to my sense of self—something my social research textbooks glossed over. I had learned that being a researcher meant eradicating all traces of my personality. The books I read ignored complicated issues of trust building between researchers and their subjects. In contrast, through-out the duration of this project I had to allow others to see more of myself as a person than I would have ordinarily tolerated.

I'm reserved by nature; I was not comfortable answering questions about my personal life, and even more uncomfortable allowing strangers to make judgmental observations about me and how I lived my life. My subjects were researching me as I researched them. I wanted a perspective on their personal interest and investment in the land, and they, in turn, wanted a perspective on why I was motivated to care about it. In the end, the greatest sociological lesson I learned from field research in the Atchafalaya Basin was one of equity—I cannot fairly expect to insinuate myself into someone else's life unless, on some level, I allow them the same privileges in return.

NOTES

1. According to the Acadian/Cajun Genealogy and History Web site,

The Acadians were French . . . who settled the area (now known as Nova Scotia) in the 1600's. In the mid 18th century, they were exiled [from there] by the British. Over the following 30 years, several thousand of the exiled Acadians made their way to south Louisiana. Over the next 100+ years, the Acadians became the dominant culture in cer-tain areas of south Louisiana. They retained much of their culture, and absorbed some of the other cultural influences. The German, Spanish, French, English, Indian and other cultures added to the Acadian culture to produce the Cajun culture. The word "Cajun" comes from the word "Acadian." (www.acadian-cajun.com/index.htm)

2. I lived at my parents' home that summer to decrease the percentage of my grant that would be consumed by living costs. A direct outcome of this arrangement was that my family was subject to the daily trials and triumphs of my project.

3. Located in south-central Louisiana, the Atchafalaya Basin, covering 595,000 acres, is the largest swamp wetlands in the United States.

3

Globalizing Feminist Research

Jennifer Bickham Mendez

The power of a feminist method grows out of the fact that it enables us to connect everyday life with an analysis of the social institutions which shape that life. Feminism as a mode of analysis relies on the idea that we come to know the world, to change it and be changed by it, through our everyday experiences.

—Hartsock 1998, 36

Research takes on a political dimension when it gives voice to the muffled, silenced voices of the oppressed and the exploited in defining the injustice created by globalization and in describing or analyzing the process of its deconstruction.

—Lindio-McGovern 2005, 343

This chapter discusses the challenge that globalization poses for social science researchers to shift the locus of research from geographically conceived "places" to social, political, and economic processes that transcend geographic localities and even national borders. Globalization's delinking of the spatial and social has led to a rethinking of a number of important social science concepts; for example, "community" and "place" are newly understood as integrated into global economic structures and infused by transnational social relations. The gendered dimensions of globalization also present a particular challenge to feminist researchers who have long debated and criticized traditional social science methods and epistemologies. Although feminists have devoted considerable attention to theorizing the ways in which globalization works in tandem with gendered power structures, they have not focused sufficiently on the employment of feminist methods within globalized contexts (see Mendez and Wolf 2007).

In this chapter I take up the question of how an approach that emphasizes the synergies between global and local processes can inform and address the contradictions, dilemmas, and possibilities of feminist research. In line with others who have worked to rethink ethnographic methodologies under globalization (Gille and Ó Riain 2002; Albrow 1997; Marcus 1995), I argue for the reconceptualization of the "research site" as a "transnational space"[1]—a politically produced field of social activity in which global social, economic, and political processes interact with and shape localized social dynamics. By drawing attention to the unfolding of globalization "on the ground" as well as the interconnections of social processes across multiple places and scales, a global approach offers possibilities for the expansion and refinement of feminist methods and intensifies and complicates existing challenges and dilemmas associated with feminist research—in particular, accountability and power.

After providing a brief introduction to the challenges that globalization poses to social science research methods and an overview of the some of the key debates about feminist methods, I discuss two research projects in which I worked with organizations situated in very distinct "local" settings but for which global processes were extremely relevant: a working and unemployed women's organization in Nicaragua—the Working and Unemployed Women's Movement, María Elena Cuadra (MEC)—and a community health organization that targets low-income families in Williamsburg, Virginia—the Program for Integral Community Health (PICH).[2] I analyze my experiences as a politically engaged feminist researcher in order to identify three sets of challenges to feminist research that a global approach has presented, complicated, or intensified: "power differentials," "researcher as insider/outsider," and the "dangers" of "accountability and ethical" issues.

I argue that globalizing feminist research methods must involve a critical evaluation of the ways in which research processes and relationships are situated within intersecting global/local relations of power and how locally unfolding global processes complicate social membership in nations, communities, groups and organizations. Despite the influence of globalization, "place" and "location" continue to "matter"; my research experiences illustrate how the specifics of history, geopolitics, and local social and economic conditions shape the ways in which global processes play themselves out in "transnational spaces." Concepts and principles drawn from feminism—such as a feminist conceptualization of power, an attention to process, a reliance on research reflexivity, and an emphasis on personal research relationships, with an understanding that all of these are deeply political—are a foundation for confronting the dilemmas and contradictions of conducting research in "transnational spaces."

GLOBALIZATION

To say that the term "globalization" has been ubiquitous in the social science literature, especially since the 1990s, is an understatement. Despite important endeavors to refine the term's conceptual specificity (Sassen 2006; Glick Schiller 1999), "globalization" continues to come dangerously close to meaning all things to all people. For the sake of conceptual clarity, in this chapter globalization refers to the historical, economic process through which individuals, groups, and institutions are increasingly interconnected on a worldwide scale. The scope of global processes largely, although certainly not completely or evenly, reaches across the globe without specific reference to national territories or/and geographic localities (Glick Schiller 1999).

As globalization disassociates social, political, cultural, and economic processes from geographic places, it also calls into question a long-standing social science assumption that "nation-states" are the appropriate locus for examining social relations. It challenges social science researchers to reexamine how the "social" should be defined, so as to make understandable the ways in which social relations occur across local settings, and in de-territorialized space (Gille and Ó Riain 2002; Albrow 1995; Giddens 1991). Scholars have developed different analytical techniques for studying the contradictory processes associated with globalization. Some have focused attention on the interconnections and interplay among the global, national, and subnational settings, such as "global cities," allowing for a better understanding of the concrete, localized processes through which globalization operates (Sassen 2001; Guidry, Kennedy, and Zald 2000). Transnational studies ground the abstract notion of globalization by centering analysis on the ways in which everyday people react to, engage with, and even re-create and influence global processes—often in unanticipated ways (Glick Schiller 1999; Smith and Guarnizo 1998; Basch, Glick Schiller, and Blanc 1994). Responding to the challenges posed by globalization, ethnographers have shifted their units of analysis to flows of cultural products, people, and commodities across national borders and spaces, including the social relations that transcend borders, and the politically produced and contested "places" or place-making projects (Gille and Ó Riain 2002, 274–77; see also Burawoy et al. 2000; Freeman 2000).

Gender is integral to globalization, and gender ideologies and power structures make up a kind of foundation upon which the global economy rests.

Under the global hegemony of neoliberalism and the worldwide shrinking of public services, women shoulder the burden of meeting the needs of their families and increasingly take on breadwinner roles in ways that both draw on and undermine traditional gender roles (Peterson and Runyan 1999, 130–47). In search of an ever cheaper, more docile workforce, transnational corporations target young women for employment in factories—often referred to as *maquiladoras* or, colloquially, *maquilas*—where light manufacturing goods are assembled for the global market. Conditions in developing countries that arise from the implementation of neoliberal policies and the opening of local markets to the global economy have spurred international migration, with women ("transnational mothers") leaving their children behind in order to work in industrialized countries. These women are among the ranks of migrants who send home remittances to support their families (Hondagneu-Sotelo 2001; Parreñas 2001). A generation of feminist research has explored and raised questions about the economic, social, and cultural impacts of globalization on women of different races and ethnicities and from different localities (cf. Pyle and Ward 2003, 463), as well as what globalization has meant for gendered ideologies, practices, and political organizing (Mendez 2005; Eschle 2001). The gendered dimensions of globalization bring urgency to how to develop feminist research methods that both contribute to understanding gender and globalization and to the transformation of global gender inequalities.

FEMINIST RESEARCH

Just as there are multiple ways to be or act feminist, there is no single feminist research methodology. Despite this diversity of perspectives, feminists' commitment to transformative politics and placing women's everyday experiences at the center of critical inquiry has led them to experiment with new methodological approaches and forms of representation that seek to decenter the interpretative authority of the researcher and generate polyvocal texts through which the "researched" present their perspectives (Wolf 1996b). Feminist researchers have interrogated and analyzed how hierarchies of power and authority shape the research process and relationships between researcher and those studied, revealing how the privilege of the powerful to speak and be heard can be reproduced in scholarship (Gordon 1995; Bell, Caplan, and Karim 1993).

Rather than claiming the position of the "objective observer," whose presence goes unexamined, feminist researchers analyze their own social locations and the ways in which power differentials can reinforce and reproduce inequalities. Feminist epistemologies challenge the assumptions of positivism, in which the researcher observes phenomena from a detached position of value-free political neutrality, testing hypotheses and drawing causal relationships between variables in order to discover "the truth" (Hesse-Biber 2007, 7). Instead, feminist theorists and methodologists highlight how the universalism underlying the scientific method privileges a dominant perspective and excludes other voices and subjugated ways of knowing (Harding 2005; Hesse-Biber and Yaiser 2004; Collins 2000; Haraway 1988).

Feminists of color and "third world" feminists have been some of the most vocal critics of the ways in which research (often carried out by white female academics) "on" third world women has reproduced racialized colonial systems of power, reinforcing dominant representations of marginalized women from the developing world (Bhavnani 2004, 68; Ong 1995; Mohanty 1991). Some feminists have called for research to be rooted in transformative struggles and for methodologies that emphasize political engagement and action, all leading to the development of collaborative research models in which researcher and researched devise and implement projects together (Maguire 1987, 2001; Mies 2007). Where such types of projects have been carried out (Rappaport 2007; Richards 2006; Thayer 2004), collaboration has taken many shapes and involved varied levels of working together to accomplish such tasks as formulating research questions, developing interview or survey questions, interpreting "data," and even writing final research "products" (cf. Wolf 1996a, 27).

Feminist research methods present a number of exciting possibilities, but also some thorny dilemmas. Feminists have debated whether reducing power differentials between researcher and researched is ever fully possible (Patai 1991). Among the many risks and "dangers" associated with collaborative feminist research is the very real possibility that even the best-intentioned researchers will assume the maternalistic position of "helping" to raise the consciousness and awareness of "needy" women, further reinscribing structures of power and inequality. As Judith Stacey (1991) has pointed out, close personal relationships between the ethnographic researcher and her respondents might actually lead to increased potential for exploitation as personal information shared with the researcher is transformed into "data." Collaborative projects are "time consuming, demanding and troublesome" (Maguire 1987, 37), and few if any projects have achieved collaboration at all stages of the research and writing process.

Like other feminist scholars (cf. Mies 2007), my own political orientation and vision of social change have led me to engage in projects that integrate research into action. My methodological training in qualitative sociology provided the basis for my initial research designs, for close working relationships with those I studied—which my projects have all involved—and in shaping the direction and activities of my research. I am reminded that in decisions about research processes the "personal" is "political." In other words, the research strategies I describe here are grounded in "experiential knowledge" of the people whose lives and struggles I have entered into as a researcher. Although I made unilateral decisions about many aspects of my research, my overall role within each organization, as well as many of the specific activities in which I engaged, emerged out of a dialogue with people in "the field." Nonetheless, I was intensely aware of how global relations of power structured and shaped social relations during my fieldwork. Power dynamics operated very differently in my research in Nicaragua and in my current "local" project in Williamsburg. My interest here is to analyze each research site as a transnational space of interaction in order to delineate the ways in which place-specific dynamics articulate with global economic processes, geopolitics, and relations of power.

WORKING AND UNEMPLOYED WOMEN'S MOVEMENT, MARÍA ELENA CUADRA

For my dissertation and subsequent book, *From the Revolution to the Maquiladoras* (2005), I conducted sixteen months of collaborative ethnographic research in the mid-1990s with a Nicaraguan working women's organization—the Working and Unemployed Women's Movement, María Elena Cuadra (MEC). Named after a union organizer who was killed by a drunk driver, MEC was born in 1994 when it emerged as an autonomous, women-only organization from a deep-seated crisis within the Sandinista Workers' Central (CST), at that time the largest trade union confederation in Nicaragua. The CST had been founded as a mass organization of the revolutionary party, the Frente Sandinista de Liberación Nacional (FSLN), which held state power in the Central American country of Nicaragua from 1979 to 1990.

MEC's birth as an independent organization signified its split not only from the Nicaraguan labor movement, but also from the Sandinista party and its organizations, where MEC founders had received their political socialization as revolutionaries. Joining the ranks of the larger autonomous women's movement in Nicaragua, MEC directed its efforts toward organizing women workers and improving conditions in *maquiladora* factories—the assembly factories that operate in the country's free trade zones (FTZs)[3] and manufacture exports (primarily garments) almost entirely for the U.S. market. Unlike other countries in Central America whose economies had been structured around export production for a much longer time period, the *maquila* industry has only had a significant presence in Nicaragua since the early 1990s. In 1990 the socialist-oriented FSLN lost election to the U.S.-supported coalition of opposition parties, the National Opposition Union

(UNO). A new neoliberal regime, headed by President Violeta Chamorro, took power and ushered in a new postrevolutionary era in Nicaragua. The Chamorro government implemented neoliberal reforms to attract foreign investment and reinsert Nicaragua into the global economy. The Sandinista government's consumer subsidies, its system of agricultural and workers' cooperatives, and its emphasis on public welfare gave way to the privatization of state-owned enterprises and a dramatic reduction of public spending. In 1992 the Chamorro government's first state-owned FTZ, dubbed "La Zona Franca Las Mercedes," opened with eight factories (Renzi 1996).

As in FTZs all over the world, *maquila* workers in Nicaragua (today numbering eighty-five thousand, 90 percent of whom are estimated to be women) labor long hours at below-subsistence wages and suffer routine violations of their labor rights in the form of forced overtime and a lack of social security and other such worker benefits—foreign companies are often "exempted" from paying these benefits.[4] The illegal firing of women workers when they become pregnant or miss work to care for sick children, as well as sexual harassment, shop floor violence, and verbal and psychological abuse are among the many issues facing the predominantly young, female labor force who are often the sole providers for large extended families.

In the 1990s, Nicaragua's Working and Unemployed Women's Movement (MEC), organizers struggled to raise national, regional, and international public awareness about working conditions in the *maquilas* and organize and support workers in understanding and defending their rights. The organization launched internationally supported campaigns to lobby for pressure on factory owners to uphold workers' human rights and comply with local labor laws. MEC developed and offered educational programs for female factory workers and unemployed women, sensitizing women about such gender issues as domestic violence and reproductive health, while providing training on leadership skills and human and labor rights. Other programs provided job training, scholarships, and income-generating opportunities, such as microcredit to start small microenterprises and make housing improvements.

MEC's organizational structure included a national organizing team of six or seven women and various regional organizers who ran programs out of the offices in the different regions of the country. In addition, various *promotoras* linked the MEC organization with its social base. For example, *promotoras* in *maquila* factories served as immediate contacts on the shop floor, recruiting interested program participants, circulating information about MEC's activities to other workers, and bringing workers who had experienced rights violations to the MEC office to receive legal counseling. Health *promotoras* supported women in local neighborhoods and brought interested women to MEC offices for assistance in obtaining health or legal services. Finally, program participants made up MEC's social base of *maquila* workers and women who were unemployed or marginally employed in the informal sector, all of whom resided in poor communities and took part in the programs, activities, meetings, and events that MEC organized.

During my field research in the mid-1990s, I occupied the position of *cooperante*, a role that had been carved out during the Cold War of the 1980s when the Central American solidarity movement in the United States, Canada, and Europe supported the Sandinista government as it defended the country from the Reagan-sponsored *contra* war that included, besides overt and covert military action against the Sandinista government, suspending multilateral aid and a U.S. trade embargo. Progressive organizations from the north organized brigades of international volunteers to work in solidarity with the Sandinista government and the sectoral organizations that represented the link between the state and *el pueblo* (the people). Such mass organizations were charged with defending the interest of each sector of society (e.g., women, agricultural workers, youth, and grassroots communities) and implementing the FSLN's "revolutionary project" of building a new socialist society (Vanden and Prevost 1993, 51).

Simultaneously occupying the position of *cooperante* and ethnographer, I collaborated with MEC as part of the organization's "collective" or "working team," as MEC leaders referred to its core group of leaders and organizers. During my three research stints, I worked nearly every day in MEC's Managua office and less regularly in the regional offices, where I wrote funding proposals and collaborated with MEC organizers in facilitating workshops on gender issues and rights training and in developing strategies for organizing and lobbying for improved working conditions inside *maquila* factories. I also drafted project reports and collaborated in the design of diagnostic studies to support MEC's lobbying efforts. As a researcher, I conducted participant-observation at MEC meetings and workshops, and at venues organized for MEC's constituents. Finally, I carried out intensive interviews with MEC participants, organizers, and leaders.

The role of *cooperante* is based on notions of solidarity and *compañerismo*—concepts that were foundational to *Sandinismo*, the New Left ideology heavily influenced by Marxist-Leninism that formed the intellectual underpinnings of the Sandinista revolutionary project. My historically constituted role of *cooperante* provided a set of preestablished norms and guidelines for expected activities that helped structure my research collaboration with MEC organizers and participants; it also provided a blue print for integrating my research into the MEC's mission to combat the injustices facing poor women in Nicaragua. *Cooperante* was, by definition, an "international" role, having grown, as I have explained, out of political relationships of solidarity forged in the 1980s between Nicaraguan revolutionaries and their northern allies. My role as a *cooperante* meant that I was yet another knot in the transnational web of individuals and organizations that supported MEC and its programs, campaigns, and political strategies, as MEC participated and continues to participate in a *transnational* arena of political action and interorganizational relations. That is, within a context of neoliberal state downsizing, MEC depends on financial and political support from its transnational linkages with nongovernmental organizations (NGOs) and solidarity groups in Europe and North America. In addition, the organization maintains transnational relations with a wide range of international NGOs and individuals who work with MEC to launch public awareness and carry out lobbying campaigns, to provide technical expertise, and to pressure for improved conditions in FTZ assembly plants. As a *cooperante*, my role included efforts to connect MEC with funding sources for specific projects and to serve as a link between MEC and individuals and organizations in the North.

WILLIAMSBURG, VIRGINIA: PROGRAM FOR INTEGRAL COMMUNITY HEALTH (PICH)

While my research in the mid-1990s with MEC had dealt with the effects of capital mobility on the lives of Nicaraguan women and their political organizing around gender and labor issues, my current project in Williamsburg, Virginia, explores issues of labor mobility within a rapidly developing geographical area of the Unites States, the "Nuevo 'New' South" (Fink 2003). Like other cities and small towns in the South Atlantic states, Williamsburg has experienced strong population growth and rapid suburbanization. The influx of affluent retirees and professionals from cities in the northern states who are drawn to Williamsburg for its low taxes, scenic beauty, colonial history, and high "quality of life," as well as its booming housing market, have fueled the expansion of entry-level service-sector jobs—one of the main factors attracting immigrants from Mexico and Central America[5] to the Williamsburg region.

Williamsburg has a bifurcated economy with a cluster of professional jobs mainly associated with the College of William and Mary, the Colonial Williamsburg Foundation, health care, and real estate, and a large cluster of service sector jobs with low wages and poor or no worker benefits. A large concentration of the immigrants to Williamsburg, who are often either undocumented or on guest worker visas, work in the service sector—in the hotel and restaurant industry, as commercial groundskeepers, and in construction. These workers, who are often paid "under the table," face numerous obstacles related to their "undocumented" status and poor English skills. On top of this, many of such émigrés are women, who are assigned the cultural role of caretakers of the family. They face the challenges of meeting the needs of their households and families in low-paid work with high job insecurity. They have difficulties accessing medical care and securing affordable housing and reliable transportation. Economic dependence on male partners and reliance on them for transportation and housing increases the isolation of such women with small children, making them susceptible to depression and vulnerable to domestic violence and sexual abuse. Such women also face difficulties managing the care and education of their children due to the shortage of educational professionals and health-care providers who speak Spanish.

In 2003 I began a collaboration with PICH, a community organization whose mission is to "partner with communities to strengthen families with young children, to improve community health and to increase family self-sufficiency" (PICH brochure, note 3). Part of a statewide network, the organization receives state and county funds as well as support from local foundations and private donations and works to improve low-income families' access to public services and medical care. By conducting in-home visits and accompanying families on doctors' visits and to other social service appointments, PICH takes a family-centered approach to addressing issues such as housing, nutrition, education, employment, and transportation.

Although both Nicaragua's MEC and Williamsburg's PICH could be considered nongovernmental organizations that facilitate poor women's access to resources and services, they clearly are situated in very different national and political contexts, and their orientations, structures, and visions diverge considerably. Simply put, having emerged from the mass organizations of the Nicaraguan revolution, MEC is an NGO that acts as a social movement organization with a social justice agenda. It is, therefore, a political organization at heart. In contrast, PICH of Williamsburg is a "professional" nonprofit organization, complete with a paid staff of "family consultants" whose job it is to provide services to the organization's "clients." Although, certainly there are political implications to ensuring equal access to social services, PICH's orientation and objectives are less explicitly oriented to social change and justice.

MEC's history of close ties to the Nicaraguan Sandinista FSLN and this organization's emergence from the labor movement brings an adherence to revolutionary principles of social change. MEC's organizing structure involves leaders selecting and grooming *promotoras* (like cadres) who are drawn from the ranks of the *compañeras*, their social base of women who participate in MEC programs and activities. In contrast, PICH has a bureaucratic hierarchy and the statewide network of sites, all governed by a board of directors. A program director oversees a team of outreach workers ("family consultants") and registered nurses who work directly with the low-income "client" families at each site. At the Williamsburg PICH, the program director reports to other administrators within an umbrella nonprofit organization that coordinates all early childhood services in the Williamsburg area.

Despite such significant differences between MEC and PICH, one important similarity between them is their mission to improve conditions for women whose lives are directly and negatively impacted by economic globalization and neoliberalism. And in both cases the work of these two organizations takes on significant transnational dimensions. For PICH, the effects of globalization are reflected in a demographic shift in the people who receive services, including a large proportion of non-English-speaking immigrants. This change has posed an array of challenges, beginning with language and other cultural differences that require the PICH organization to broaden its understandings of the new "clientele."

PICH staff has had to learn about and adapt to the needs of immigrant families who struggle economically because they send a large percentage of their income as remittances to support children left in home communities. Some of these parents also face the difficulty of lacking documented immigration status and having to seek medical care and services for themselves and/or for children who are U.S. citizens and entitled to such public services as food stamps and Medicaid. A shortage of affordable housing is a problem faced by all low-income Williamsburg residents, but undocumented immigrants face an added burden of lacking proper identification and documentation that qualify them as renters. Finally, immigrants and organizations that seek to support them must contend with growing local and national anti-immigrant public sentiments and policies.

My partnership with PICH began when the program director asked me to organize and facilitate a support group for Spanish-speaking families; this would then serve as a network of immigrant families to interview about their experiences in Williamsburg. This group, which usually included between fifteen and twenty-two parents, was a space for immigrants to meet and share stories and information in their own language, building a sense of solidarity as they reflected on their lives as parents and recent immigrants. My collaborations with PICH also involved accompanying outreach workers on home visits and providing linguistic and cultural support for Spanish-speaking immigrants at their doctor and social service appointments. I also engaged in a wide variety of community activities that addressed immigration issues—from sitting on boards of community organizations, to presenting information and giving presentations on immigration issues at community forums, to volunteering as an interpreter for local organizations or collaborating to organize community events.

In association with PICH and participants of its parent group, I initiated a community-based research project focusing on Latin immigrants' experiences of exclusion, economic survival, and integration. Through intensive interviews with recent immigrants, using interview questions that had grown out of parent group meetings and from my participant observation with immigrants, I learned about these immigrants' experiences from their own narratives. One of the goals of this project was to identify barriers that immigrants face and the strategies that they develop as they seek to meet the needs of their families within a community under transition. I have endeavored to convey this information to community organizations in Williamsburg in order to contribute to making visible immigrants' obstacles to inclusion, including the misconceptions and negative representations of immigrants.

As in my Nicaraguan project, my role in the Williamsburg study has involved blending political commitments and research. Also, like my work with Nicaragua's MEC, the Williamsburg research involved an ethnographic approach and analytical focus centered on the economic and social relationships that link people and places in the global economy. By maintaining social, economic, and cultural ties with their families and communities "back home," through telephone and e-mail contact, the circulation of remittances and the exchange of cultural products and practices, Latino/a immigrants participate within transnational social fields that anchor and define their daily realities (Levitt 2001). Facilitated by members of the parent support group, I made two research trips to Central Mexico to visit immigrants' home communities and interview their family members and community leaders, allowing me to explore the view of migration to Williamsburg from "south of the border."

RESEARCH IN "TRANSNATIONAL SPACES"

In this section I will cover the three central themes of this chapter: power differentials in research; the feminist researcher as insider/outsider; and accountability and ethical "dangers." I will analyze my position within social dynamics in the field, which included differences of nationality, race, and class status, and how these interfaced and collided with one another in the field research process.

Power Differentials

According to Diane Wolf (1996b, 2), "the most central dilemma for contemporary feminists in fieldwork . . . is power and the unequal hierarchies or levels of control that are often maintained, perpetuated, created and re-created during and after field research." In my research collaborations I found it impossible to ignore the power dynamics associated with differences in national origin, race, and class that constantly lurked under the surface, resulting in complex and varied political terrain for collaborative research in "transnational spaces." Like all organizations, PICH and MEC were not monolithic entities, but were crosscut by differences of perspective, authority, and status. Such differences were articulated within global and local relations of power to shape the research process and my position vis-à-vis the individuals with whom I worked. Sometimes such articulations created opportunities for solidarity and mutual understanding, and at other times they generated tensions.

At MEC

In my interactions with MEC's program participants, I endeavored to adopt a complicated dual position of being "just another member of the working team" as well as a researcher with an independent, although related, agenda to the organization's own. The contradictions that sometimes emerged between these roles, as well as the images associated with my nationality and race/class, clearly generated mixed understandings about me and my position within the MEC organization. As much as I would insist, "I am not in charge [in MEC]," MEC participants would still ask me to intercede on their behalf in accessing the organization's programs: Could I help obtain admission into a particular MEC program? Could I get a "scholarship" for a family member (MEC's job training programs often came in the form of scholarships)? Could I arrange preferential admittance into MEC microcredit programs? Such requests suggested the participants' perception that I had influence and authority within MEC.

Some of these perceptions were rooted in my symbolizing, by virtue of my race and nationality, MEC's international legitimacy and "transnational social capital."[6] The *promotoras* and some organizers would make reference to my involvement in their organization as an indication of international support for MEC's lobbying campaigns and organizing efforts, which was seen as an indication of the effectiveness and international recognition of MEC's programs and strategies. Of course, my whiteness and position as a *gringa* also brought with them the assumption of my greater access to wealth and other resources. MEC program participants would pull me aside and ask for financial assistance, medicine, clothing, or employment assistance—did I know of an organization that would employ their partners or family members? In most cases I found the differences in real and perceived status and power suggested by MEC members to be almost impossible to bridge. To my dismay, MEC program participants showed deference to me in ways that dispelled any illusions that I might have held that I could be just another *compañera* in the MEC organization.

My relationships with MEC organizers must be understood within a context of larger global and national political processes, specifically, southern

NGOs' dependency on resources from foundations, international NGOs, and individual donors. MEC organizers constantly struggled to court new funders and report to current ones, while not compromising their ability to create and structure programs and projects according to the needs of their participants and their organization's mission and vision. MEC's relationship with solidarity organizations and other funders from the north was distinctly ambivalent. Struggling as it was to reconcile its newfound autonomy from the male-dominated trade union confederation, MEC needed to maintain good relations with international donors. However, MEC's love/hate relationship with international solidarity organizations and their representatives created tensions, which at times were played out in my relationships with MEC organizers. As both a *chela*—white woman—and a foreigner, I could easily be seen as representing the "eyes of the north." And even though I made it clear to MEC leaders and participants that I worked neither for an international NGO nor for the U.S. government, my affiliation with the U.S. Embassy through my Fulbright Fellowship connected me to powerful institutions and potentially to new resources.

I was simultaneously an "outsider"—foreigner and *chela* with connections to international organizations—and a *cooperante* who had been allowed by the MEC working team into its "insider" spaces. As a rule, MEC organizers did not like airing the movement's "dirty laundry" in front of *los cheles*—a fact that may have been behind the organizers' sending me out of the meeting that I had organized. I remember that in my daily presence at the MEC office, organizers were quite conscientious of how a particular practice might look to me, and then potentially to other northerners, which added a level of surveillance and impression management to their daily activities, which I am sure they found draining.

At PICH

One of the most visible ways that inequalities between myself and the Latino/a immigrants receiving services from PICH manifested themselves was through dramatic asymmetries in cultural and social capital—cultural knowledge, English, and how and what social institutions could be tapped for economic and social resources. My advocacy work with immigrants included my accompanying them as an interpreter on doctor's visits and appointments with social services and connecting them to legal services and to English as a second language (ESL) resources. As an advocate, I spoke on their behalf to insurance companies, banks, and officials at the local courts. Such advocacy work reflected my class privileges as well as my cultural knowledge of "the system." Despite my own feminist political orientation that sees personal empowerment of women as integral to wider structural social change, my collaborations with PICH placed me in the position of a "service provider" with the potential to be seen as someone who "does for"—not "with"—another person. I was constantly aware of the danger that, at best, I was perceived as a powerful ally and at worst a powerful "patron" (matron?) who could be called upon for favors.

Despite my sustained attempts to discourage and overcome these and other inequalities, the subtle and not so subtle politics of deference were evidenced in my work with Williamsburg's PICH clients in multiple ways. To give just one example, one Guatemalan woman and longtime participant in the monthly parent group answered for several months to my calling her "Claudia," without correcting that this was not her name at all. When—in utter embarrassment—I realized that Claudia was not her name and apologized profusely for the error, she shrugged the issue off as "not important."

Although my research was unavoidably rooted within an inequitable distribution of power that structured its progress and my continuing relationship with PICH clients, the ways in which my advocacy work with Latino/a immigrants in Williamsburg was interwoven with my research served utilitarian purposes that allowed the research to progress (like increasing my snowball sample of interviewees and opening doors for my transnational research in Mexico). But my work as an interpreter and advocate also enriched the research by allowing cultivation of a deeper understanding of immigrants' lives (cf. Pessar 2003, 29) and providing a means for poor, (often) undocumented immigrant women *not* simply to passively receive "help" but actively reciprocate by contributing to the research project as "knowledgeable, empowered participants in the research process" (Hale 2007, 5). Although it may be true that some immigrants felt socially obligated to agree to be interviewed, most expressed great willingness to participate and did so with a great deal of candor and openness.

As the organizer and facilitator of the parent support group, I drew from my experiences as a teacher and activist to cultivate an environment conducive to participants' building solidarity with one another as women, as immigrants, and as mothers seeking ways to work together to improve their situations. At meetings participants would share victories, sorrows, and disappointments. They might tearfully describe the pain of leaving children in their home countries, the daily fear and insecurity that comes with undocumented status, and the anxieties associated with a spouse's injury on the job, resulting in no household income and no way to pay expensive medical bills.

At these meetings I was not a detached facilitator or meeting "leader"— as a mother of two small children I also participated by sharing my own experiences. My preschool-aged daughter would play along with the children of the immigrants while the other parents and I gathered to talk. The parent group had formed shortly after I began an extremely painful separation from my children's father. On more than one occasion the tears at support group meetings were also mine, and it was the immigrant mothers who held *me* up, telling me, "You have to value yourself and stay strong for your children."

I certainly would not argue that such interactions equalized or overcame all power differentials between my research respondent/collaborators and myself, but such moments of human connection established an ongoing dialogic encounter with participants based on mutual understanding and solidarity. This process and its outcomes also enriched my research in important ways. As I begin to analyze and write up the results of my research, this sense of solidarity contributes to my aim not to "objectify" those represented in my work, but rather for the analysis to be the vehicle for "meaningfully engag[ing] the world and collectively act[ing] within it . . . in order to name the world and transform it" (De Genova 2005, 25).

FEMINIST RESEARCHER AS INSIDER/OUTSIDER

Not surprisingly, the dynamics of power that underlay my collaborations— whether at the level of MEC organizers and PICH's professional staff, or at the level of MEC participants and PICH "clients"—varied considerably in ways that illustrate the research's embeddedness in different national and cultural contexts as well as within different and intersecting global and local power structures.

At MEC

As a researcher/*cooperante* in Nicaragua in the 1990s, the differences of national origin and race between myself and MEC organizers took on place-based, historically specific meanings that were linked to U.S. military, political, and economic intervention and imperialist foreign policy, but also to political solidarity between the left in the United States and Europe and the FSLN and its mass organizations (Eade 2004). My position in MEC was contextualized within a dialectic of imperialist interventions, reconfigured under globalization to include economic domination through the neoliberal agenda on the one hand and changing relations of international and transnational solidarity with opposition to U.S. empire on the other. Thus, due to my nationality and race, I represented the "international community" of NGOs upon which organizations like MEC relied for funding and other forms of support, as organizations in civil society and their international NGO supporters now fill the role of the state in working to ensure the social welfare of citizens. My nationality and race also signified my position within global economic relations between the

United States and Nicaragua, as I hailed from the "consumer side" of the global production of goods.

Local and global power differentials shaped my relationship with MEC, giving rise to a complicated position that would shift between "insider/ *cooperante*" and "outsider/foreigner." My position within the organization was also shaped by my very real dependency on MEC leaders and participants for access to their organization and its activities, in order to complete my research. MEC organizers employed their agency in claiming ownership of their daily experiences and personal histories, and they, as political actors, decided if and how to share their narratives with me. I continually negotiated with MEC organizers the scope and expectations associated with my dual role as researcher/*cooperante* as we struggled to carve out a relationship and establish the degree and scope of my autonomy but also MEC organizers' authority over me. In the process of this dynamic, several questions came to the fore.

As a *cooperante* who acted in many senses like the other members of the MEC core "collective," could MEC leaders require that I work the same number of hours as organizers who received compensation from NGO funds for their role in implementing MEC programs? Which meetings would I be allowed to attend? How were MEC organizers to assess whether my performance as a *cooperante* met their expectations? How would they ensure my accountability to the goals of the movement? Were my interviews with MEC organizers and participants a waste of their time and energy? Could my time be spent in ways that better served the MEC organization and movement? The negotiations in which I engaged around these questions revealed that MEC leaders and participants were not merely the "objects" of my research, but actors with agency who exerted control over various aspects of their relationship with me, whether in my role as a researcher or an international collaborator (*cooperante*; Kondo 1986, 80). At one point I observed MEC organizers send another U.S. *cooperante* packing when they felt she had not demonstrated sufficient commitment to the organization. "This isn't a hotel," commented one organizer after her departure. "One can't come and go as one pleases."

My daily ethnographic presence permitted my research to be highly collaborative, while always requiring constant, sometime tense, negotiations, with some resulting in conflict and misunderstandings. MEC leaders often embraced my presence at their meetings and events because of the power and influence ("transnational social capital") that my U.S. "outsider" status signified. For example, I was asked to accompany MEC's coordinator and a member of the core collective to a meeting with representatives of the U.S. Agency for International Development (USAID) to explore the possibility of receiving its funding for certain MEC programs. At other times MEC leaders invited me to attend internal meetings of the MEC leadership. I learned that one reason for such invitations was that when the encounters among leaders became controversial, a foreigner's presence would inhibit or temper heated discussions. These examples illustrate the overlapping and shifting nature of my local and transnational, insider and outsider, role within the MEC. Sometimes, as the next example illustrates, I was simply an outsider, with no "wiggle-room" for changing this designation.

For instance, several months into my fieldwork when MEC was granted a meeting with the Human Rights Commission of the Nicaraguan National Assembly, I grabbed my notepad and prepared to accompany MEC leaders to the meeting, as I usually did when organizers attended external meetings or forums. MEC organizers exchanged glances, and "Sara," MEC's coordinator, informed me that I was not permitted to attend this activity, since it was for "Nicaraguans to meet with *their* National Assembly delegates." Although I understood Sara's rationale, I was admittedly disappointed. The reason MEC organizers had given me for not permitting my presence at the meeting—that an international outsider would be out of place at a National Assembly meeting of the country's Human Rights Commission—glossed the transnational complexities of the situation. It was only after considerable internationally supported lobbying efforts—to which I contributed at least to some degree—that pressured government officials were willing to hear the testimonies of MEC organizers and the *maquila* workers they represented. It added to my frustration that a German researcher who had provided MEC with technical assistance was allowed to attend this human rights forum.

On one occasion an organizer asked me to leave a meeting—I never found out exactly why, although I left immediately, as requested. I was particularly perplexed because MEC's coordinator had specifically assigned me the responsibility of organizing that very meeting. Later, two of the *compañeras* confided to me that the MEC coordinator had sharply admonished the organizer for dismissing me; the MEC coordinator is said to have perceived my dismissal from the meeting as "inappropriate treatment of a *compañera* who has been *solidaria* [in solidarity] with the movement." The MEC coordinator's defense of my presence at this particular meeting highlights some of the relations of power that underlay my position as a researcher. My connection to the north, symbolized by my whiteness, and position as a foreigner contributed to organizers' feeling obligated to put up with my presence, and indeed, nosiness (being a *metiche*).

At PICH

At the Williamsburg PICH, power differentials also resulted in a complex terrain that I navigated as agency officials, their clients, and I negotiated the scope and dimensions of my involvement. My multiple real and perceived roles as "volunteer," "researcher," "community member," and "expert on Latin America"—and the tensions between these complimentary and conflicting roles—flavored my interactions and collaborations with PICH's professional staff. As a Spanish speaker who had traveled and conducted research extensively in Latin America, and who had studied the political and economic processes that give rise to immigration, I was considered an asset to PICH—especially since I worked on a volunteer basis. I quickly came to realize that my experiences as both an academic and as someone who had married into a Nicaraguan family, and whose children were being raised bilingual and bicultural, contributed to my quickly gaining a level of understanding and rapport with PICH's "clients." My connection with clients often surpassed that of program directors and administrators who did not speak Spanish or engage in direct service interactions with PICH clients. Like the organization's outreach workers, at the bottom of the organizational hierarchy, I could immediately relate the official discussions of clients to their faces, personal stories, and needs. In a sense, I came to possess greater cultural and experiential understanding of the daily realities of PICH's immigrant clients than the PICH program directors, who did not provide direct services.

This grounded knowledge and connection to immigrants' stories and experiences was enriched by two research trips to Mexico, where I interviewed and stayed with family members of PICH's clients. Unlike many members of PICH's staff and administrators, I came to understand many of their clients' lives from a transnational perspective, having explored and observed the social ties that linked them to their families and communities across the U.S. border. This has enhanced my research, allowing me to situate immigrants' experiences within a global analytical framework, and has also allowed me to develop a more in-depth understanding of immigrants' lives and communities.

In my interactions with PICH and its clients, I occupied a complicated set of positions within which I navigated levels of hierarchy that included administrators, program directors, outreach workers, and the Latino/a immigrant clients who receive the organization's services. My role in PICH was unique in that the multiple positions that I occupied—as an academic professional, Spanish-speaker, researcher, and volunteer—allowed me to cross borders of hierarchy, status, and culture, although not always with total success. At times my occupying of multiple and overlapping roles generated uncomfortable situations: I had to use care not to ally myself "too much" with administrators, lest this block me from establishing and maintaining working relations with administrators' subordinates, the outreach workers. At the same time, a close working relationship with the administrators was essential: My initial and ongoing collaboration with PICH was made possible by an administrator's endorsing my initial and continued involvement with the PICH. However, in my role as a "community partner" to PICH, I was sometimes asked by licensing bodies and funders to participate in program assessment and the evaluation of administrators' professional performance.

An ever-present reality of the power differentials that underlay my research collaborations with PICH, as with MEC, emanated from the dependence of both organizations on dwindling sources of funding. PICH administrators struggled to court new funders and report to current ones. PICH staff saw me as representing the "larger community," on which it was highly dependent for "community partnerships," which provided funding, resources, volunteers, and expertise. Thus, my status as an academic, an "expert" (despite my efforts to minimize or negate this designation), and a community member could not help but nurture the assumption that I was surveilling PICH activities, however unintended on my part.

As in the case of MEC, my position with PICH vacillated between "insider," a community partner and ally, and an "outsider," potentially a rule enforcer or whistle blower. The administration frequently recognized my involvement with PICH, featuring my work in the parent group and as an advocate in its reports and highlighting my attendance at community meetings. Program directors have written letters of support for grant proposals that have funded some elements of my research on migration. On the other hand, PICH program directors and administrators could deny or restrict my involvement, if they perceived it to be inappropriate or not in keeping with the organization's policies or mission.

In the end, an important lesson from my research has been recognizing the limits of a bipolar construction of "insider" and "outsider." As Naples (2004, 373) has pointed out, "insiderness and outsiderness are not fixed or static positions, rather, they are ever-shifting and permeable social locations that are differentially experienced and expressed by community members." Thus, the ethnographer constantly negotiates and renegotiates her "insiderness" and "outsiderness" in different contexts, and such renegotiations take on added complexities when positioned within global relations of power and occurring in research situations in which transnational processes come into play. In such cases differences of culture, nationality, and place-based identities shape definitions of social membership.

ACCOUNTABILITY AND ETHICAL DANGERS

If the goals of globalized feminist research include empowering women to equalize the power relations embedded within knowledge production and to increase social justice, then researchers must be accountable to their "respondents" in ever more meaningful ways. It could be argued that such goals, and the accountability required to achieve them, are challenged in complicated ways when feminist methods are employed within a global-ized context. With the transnational circulation of information and an increasingly transnational public sphere that includes the participation of NGOs and social movements coming together around increased pressures for funding, these factors produce real challenges to research. One such outcome can be interlocutors' silences about issues and situations that could cast their organization in a negative light. There is pressure on those being researched to maintain strict control over their narratives. At the very least, what they say could jeopardize an organization's relationships with potential donors or political allies (Thayer 2004; see also Mendez 2005). At the worst, particularly in the case of those women's organizations whose clients' immigration status is "undocumented," what these women "say" could result in their incarceration and/or deportation.

Given the contradictory and complex research terrain that globalization presents, there is no single homogenous community to which the researcher is accountable, but rather multiple groups, communities, organizational and international levels, and conflicting interests. It is within these often intersecting and sometimes conflicting communities that the researcher and those she is studying must negotiate mechanisms of accountability. For example, my accountability to PICH outreach workers involved being sensitive to their positions as workers with little decision-making authority over their organization's policies and activities. I had to be constantly aware that they could suffer repercussions from appearing to be criticizing the organization that employs them. For their part, PICH administrators and staff were also reluctant to criticize other local or community organizations or government social service providers. PICH's work with clients required good working relationships with community social service personnel and health-care providers. Thus, often when PICH outreach workers have wanted to communicate information that was critical of a community or-ganization, the task was passed on to me. A PICH staff member called me before a meeting of a network of community organization requesting that I indicate that some educational and health-care providers lacked translators for the immigrant families seeking their services. As one outreach worker explained to me, "They will listen to you, Jennifer; we can't say these things." Of course, this placed me in a position of potentially alienating important community organizations.

My research not only placed me in an intermediary position between the PICH and other community organizations, but it also placed me in that position relative to the conflicting sets of interests between immigrants and PICH staff and administrators. Like other service-providing agencies, PICH is governed by rules, laws, and policies to which it is accountable. There is a high level of preoccupation with documenting and reporting events and participation rates in order to satisfy organizational policies and state and other funding agency mandates. In particular, in an increasingly hostile, anti-immigrant climate, PICH must demonstrate that the organization is providing services to those who are *legally entitled* to them. Accountability to PICH entails a commitment to following the bureaucratic rules and policies of the organization, including eligibility requirements for social services, confidentiality regarding client information, and even personnel policies. My research should not cast the PICH organization in a light that could jeopardize its relationship with the "wider community" or with potential donors.

Accountability to PICH's clients and the other immigrants of my study entails taking into consideration varying sets of concerns. One of the immigrant mothers' main concerns was securing the economic well-being of their families, both in the United States and in their countries of origin. Due to the criminalization of immigrants who lack documented immigration status, these actors have great difficulties trying to meet the daily needs of their households and families. This often requires, as I learned from my position as a meeting facilitator and advocate for such women, their "bending" the law or representing themselves in such a way as to maximize eligibility for acquiring housing, food, or other resources. My close relationship with the immigrants resulted in my being privy to information that respondents may not have wanted to reveal to those in "the system." Such "dangerous pieces of information" varied greatly, some seemingly innocuous and some clearly potentially damaging: In the former category, the actual ages of a client's children and other information about household composition and the relationships among household members; in the latter category, the falsification of birth certificates or other documents, a purchased social security number, how they had acquired a driver's license. Accountability to the organization's immigrants meant having an awareness of their vulnerability as (often) criminalized "others." Within such an "accountability framework," the ethical question becomes: To whom am I ultimately accountable? How do I balance conflicting interests and accountability?

Despite the ethical and accountability complications brought by my research within global processes, the specifics of locality and place also impacted upon accountability. For example, I am more immediately accountable for the results and consequences of my PICH research than I was for the Nicaraguan research. When my fellowship ended, I left Nicaragua to return to the United States, while I continue to live and work in Williamsburg, Virginia. In Nicaragua I was the "foreigner" and my research stay was always understood as temporary. Further, the majority of the Nicaraguans with whom I worked did not read or speak English and, although I presented preliminary results of my research to them, time and resources did not permit translating all of my dissertation findings for them. On the other hand, in Williamsburg I move within the same professional and social circles as the PICH staff; they have ample opportunities to engage with my work and have a vested interest in making sure that their organization is not negatively represented in it. In the case of PICH clients, I am able to see on a daily basis the potentially negative outcomes of information getting into the "wrong" hands. Indeed, in writing this chapter, I returned several times to the narrative to ensure that the information in it did not harm the various actors included my research.

CONCLUSION

What do these research experiences tell us about utilizing feminist methods in an increasingly complicated, contradictory, and interconnected world? In the first place, there are multiple feminisms, and globalized feminist research must take varied forms of feminist methods for these to be effective tools for generating knowledge about globalization and contributing to social transformation (Lather 1991). The development of global, feminist methods is not so much a process of delineating a predetermined set of methods, but rather building a continually evolving *strategy* out of engagement with social actors on the ground; constant attention must be directed to the dialectical relationship between global and local processes—how globalization unfolds in locally specific ways and how local social processes are shaped by global forces. (DeVault 2004, 227). An important step in this regard is to approach the research "site" as a "transnational space."

Feminism itself provides tools and building blocks for confronting the challenges involved in devising research methods that capture local manifestations of globalization while embodying feminist principles. Arguably, one of feminism's most significant theoretical contributions is a conceptualization of power, not as "zero-sum," but as intersectional and multidimensional. A feminist conceptualization of power helps us recognize it in its multiple forms, not just as an "external" force present in broad economic or institutional structures, but also as constituted within communities, organizations, and small groups. Designing and implementing a global feminist research method should involve strategic awareness that there are "multiple global structures and relations of power, which intersect in complex, context-specific and contingent ways" to affect the intersubjective relations and micro-level dynamics involved in research (Eschle 2005, 30).

Second, although issues of accountability and ethics are evermore complex, it is important to remember that globalization presents a new frontier for politically engaged feminist research. There are new possibilities for yet unimagined global linkages and connections as well as for creative interweavings of resources, organization, strategies, and perspectives. Feminist-inspired attention to process and reflexivity and an openness to "othered" ways of knowing can assist the researcher in facing each specific situation. Global feminist research must have an eye to constructing creative mechanisms for ensuring accountability where there are diverse, sometime conflicting, interests, as I found to be so common within "transnational spaces" of interaction that I studied and participated in.

Finally, the second-wave feminist idea that the personal is political provides a guiding principle for developing globalized feminist research strategies. As others have noted (Richards 2006), collaborative feminist research requires relating to those being studied in different ways. Research "collaborators" are not simply "informants," but actors who bring "expertise" to the research process. Collaborations may involve the emergence of unexpected and changing relationships between researcher and collaborator that defy the categorical expectations and distinctions that social scientists may have learned in traditional methodological training. Humility and willingness to inhabit uncomfortable roles, learn new vocabularies, work on different time schedules, and establish relationships with unexpected collaborators, allies, and partners are crucial ingredients for the development of this kind of method.

Through these and other insights about the multiple ways to engage in feminist research, and by combining this information with what we know about how global processes are lived in the grounded, gendered experiences of men and women, we can confront the challenges that will emerge in the growing area of globalization research. We cannot expect to know how to "do feminism" or for that matter "feminist research" in the abstract—that is, disconnected from grounded situations and relationships with real people. If we embrace feminist principles, we will remain open to dialogues about and to the future imaginings of what engaged research could look like in the global era.

NOTES

1. I thank Martha Huggins for suggesting that I develop this theoretical concept in this chapter.

2. All references to individuals in this chapter are pseudonyms. Although MEC is the actual name of the Nicaraguan organization that is the subject of my 2005 book, PICH is a pseudonym. I deliberated long and painfully over the admittedly imperfect decisions of how to represent these organizations. I made them in very different times and contexts, and they reflect my different positions within and relationships with PICH and MEC as discussed above. My collaborations with MEC took place in the 1990s, when I was a graduate student, while my research with PICH is ongoing. At the time of my research in Nicaragua, MEC coordinators were much more directive about the ways in which I represented myself and MEC in my daily activities in

the organization and within the community of NGOs in Nicaragua and abroad than with written representations in English directed at a U.S. audience. My attempts to consult them about editorial decisions and my ethnographic accounts were in most cases waved off, given the constraints of time and energy devoted to day-to-day struggles, and I simply did not have the resources to translate all of my work. Thus, decisions of how to represent the organization in my analysis were largely left up to me, which I considered a weighty responsibility (see Mendez 2005, chap. 1). As my analysis progressed and deepened, it became clear that given the detailed discussion of its history and practices, the use of a pseudonym for MEC would serve little purpose. The unique nature of the organization and the small community of NGOs in Managua made it easily identifiable to anyone who cared to investigate. I did, however, opt to use pseudonyms and composite identities of specific individuals in MEC. Although I recognize and have wrestled with the political implications of a white woman from the north representing the words and perspectives of Nicaraguan women, I found some level of reassurance in remembering the last words MEC's coordinator said to me as I left Nicaragua for the last time: "No matter what anyone says, we value you and your work, Jennifer." On the other hand, my use of the pseudonym PICH perhaps reflects the heightened politics of accountability required of me, a local professional, by an organization in the north with which I continue to work and which is located in the community where I live (see above for a discussion of this). These examples of ethical decisions facing a politically engaged feminist researcher demonstrate differing rules of engagement and collaboration that are shaped by intersecting global and local structures of power.

3. Free trade zones, also referred to as export-processing zones (EPZs), are important components of the globalization of capital. Governments of developing countries often establish these zones to attract foreign investment and encourage transnational corporations to locate production within their borders. Import duties, customs fees, and taxes as well as local environmental and labor laws are often suspended for corporations willing to locate production within these zones. In addition, corporations are often given considerable breaks on the cost of utilities, and infrastructure is often improved in the areas surrounding these zones, thereby granting corporations access to airports and modern roads.

4. By 2001, five other FTZs were gradually established in various departments throughout the country. Over the next ten years the number of workers employed in export-processing plants grew exponentially from a little over a thousand in 1992 (*Observador Económico* 2002, 1) to nearly forty thousand in 2002 (Comisión Nacional de Zonas Francas 2002), about 90 percent of whom were women (International Labor Organization 2003, 9). According to the Comisión Nacional de Zonas Francas' Web site (2006), today there are ninety-five plants in operation in the thirty-four free trade zones in the country, employing approximately eighty-five thousand workers.

5. Though the 2000 U.S. Census (U.S. Census Bureau 2003) indicates that 2.3 percent of the greater Williamsburg area is nonwhite Hispanic, these numbers almost certainly underreport the presence of Latino/a migrants, particularly those who lack legal immigration status.

6. The concept of social capital is widely used in sociology and political science. French sociologist Pierre Bourdieu defines it as "the sum of the resources, actual or virtual, that accrue to an individual or group by virtue of possessing a durable

network of more or less institutionalized relationships of mutual acquaintance and recognition" (Bourdieu and Wacquant 1992, 119). Here I use the adjective "transnational" to refer to those social relationships that transcend national borders.

REFERENCES

Albrow, M. (1995). *The Global Age: State and Society beyond Modernity.* Cambridge: Polity.

——. (1997). "Traveling beyond Local Cultures: Socioscapes in a Global City." In *Living the Global City: Globalization as Local Process,* edited by J. Eade, 20–36. New York: Routledge.

Basch, Linda, Nina Glick Schiller, and Cristina Szanton Blanc, eds. (1994). *Nations Unbound: Transnational Projects, Postcolonial Predicaments and Deterritorialized Nation-States.* Langhorne, PA: Gordon & Breach.

Bell, D., P. Caplan, and W. J. Karim, eds. (1993). *Gendered Fields: Women, Men and Ethnography.* London: Routledge.

Bhavnani, Kum-Kum. (2004). "Tracing the Contours: Feminist Research and Feminist Objectivity." In *Feminist Perspectives on Social Research,* edited by Sharlene Nagy Hesse-Biber and Michelle L. Yaiser, 65–77. New York: Oxford University Press.

Bourdieu, Pierre, and Loïc J. D. Wacquant. (1992). *An invitation to reflexive sociology.* Chicago: University of Chicago Press.

Burawoy, Michael, Joseph A. Blum, Sheba George, Zsuzsa Gille, Teresa Gowan, Lynne Haney, et al. (2000). *Global Ethnography: Forces, Connections and Imaginations in a Transnational World.* Berkeley and Los Angeles: University of California Press.

Collins, Patricia Hill. (2000). *Black Feminist Thought.* London: HarperCollins Academic.

Comisión Nacional de Zonas Francas. (2002). Web site. www.cnzf.gob.ni/ (accessed November 23, 2004).

——. (2006). Web site. www.cnzf.gob.ni/ (accessed December 30, 2006).

De Genova, Nicholas. (2005). *Working the Boundaries: Race, Space, and "Illegality" in Mexican Chicago.* Durham, NC: Duke University Press.

DeVault, Marjorie L. (2004). "Talking and Listening from Women's Standpoint: Feminist Strategies for Interviewing and Analysis." In *Feminist Perspectives on Social Research,* edited by Sharlene Nagy Hesse-Bibler and Michelle L. Yaiser, 227–50. New York: Oxford University Press.

Eade, Deborah. (2004). "International NGOs and Unions in the South: Worlds Apart or Allies in the Struggle?" *Development in Practice* 14, no. 1–2, 71–84.

Eschle, Catherine. (2001). *Global Democracy, Social Movements, and Feminism.* Boulder, CO: Westview Press.

——. (2005). "Constructing 'the Anti-Globalisation Movement.'" In *Critical Theories, International Relations, and "the Anti-Globalisation Movement": The Politics of Global Resistance,* edited by Catherine Eschle and Bice Maiguashca, 25–56. New York: Routledge.

Fink, Leon. (2003). *The Maya of Morganton: Work and Community in the Nuevo New South*. Chapel Hill: University of North Carolina Press.

Freeman, Carla. (2000). *High Tech and High Heels in the Global Economy: Women, Work and Pink-Collar Identities in the Caribbean*. Durham, NC: Duke University Press.

Giddens, Anthony. (1991). *The Consequences of Modernity*. Cambridge: Cambridge University Press.

Gille, Zsuzsa, and Seán Ó Riain. (2002). "Global Ethnography." *Annual Review of Sociology* 28, 271–95.

Glick Schiller, Nina. (1999). "Transmigrants and Nation-States: Something Old and Something New in the U.S. Immigrant Experience." In *The Handbook of International Migration: The American Experience*, edited by Charles Hirschman, Philip Kasinitz, and Josh Dewind, 94–119. New York: Russell Sage Foundation.

Gordon, D. (1995). "Conclusion: Culture Writing Women: Inscribing Feminist Anthropology." In *Women Writing Culture*, edited by R. Behar and E. Gordon, 429–42. Berkeley and Los Angeles: University of California Press.

Guidry, John A., Michael D. Kennedy, and Mayer N. Zald. (2000). "Globalizations and Social Movements." In *Globalizations and Social Movements: Culture, Power, and the Transnational Public Sphere*, edited by John A. Guidry, Michael D. Kennedy, and Mayer N. Zald, 1–32. Ann Arbor: University of Michigan Press.

Hale, Charles R. (2007). "Introduction." In *Engaging Contradictions: Theory, Politics and Methods of Activist Scholarship*, edited by Charles R. Hale. Berkeley and Los Angeles: UCIAS Press.

Haraway, Donna. (1988). "Situated Knowledges: The Science Question in Feminism and the Privilege of Partial Perspective." *Feminist Studies* 14, no. 3, 575–99.

Harding, Sandra. (2005). "Negotiating with the Positivist Legacy: New Social Justice Movements and a Standpoint Politics of Method." In *The Politics of Method in the Human Sciences*, edited by G. Steinmetz, 346–66. Durham, NC: Duke University Press.

Hartsock, Nancy. (1998). "Fundamental Feminism: Process and Perspective." In *The Feminist Standpoint Revisited and Other Essays*, edited by Nancy Hartsock, 32–43. Boulder, CO: Westview Press.

Hesse-Biber, Sharlene Nagy. (2007). "Feminist Research: Exploring the Interconnections of Epistemology, Methodology, and Method." In *Handbook of Feminist Research: Theory and Praxis*, edited by Sharlene Nagy Hesse-Biber, 1–26. Thousand Oaks, CA: Sage.

Hesse-Biber, Sharlene Nagy, and Michelle L. Yaiser, eds. (2004). *Feminist Perspectives on Social Research*. New York: Oxford University Press.

Hondagneu-Sotelo, Pierrette. (2001). *Doméstica: Immigrant Workers Cleaning and Caring in the Shadows of Affluence*. Berkeley and Los Angeles: University of California Press.

Hondagneu-Sotelo, Pierrette, and Ernestine Avila. (1997). "'I'm Here, but I'm There': The Meanings of Latina Transnational Motherhood." *Gender & Society* 11, no. 5, 548–71.

International Labor Organization. (2003). "ILO Database on Export Processing Zones." Geneva: International Labor Organization. Available at www.ilo.org/public/english/dialogue/sector/themes/epz/epz-db.pdf.

Kondo, Dorinne K. (1986). "Dissolution and Reconstitution of Self: Implications for Anthropological Epistemology." *Cultural Anthropology* 1, no. 1, 74–88.

Lather, Patti. (1991). *Getting Smart: Feminist Research and Pedagogy with/in the Postmodern.* New York: Routledge.

Levitt, Peggy. (2001). *The Transnational Villagers.* Berkeley and Los Angeles: University of California Press.

Lindio-McGovern, Ligaya. (2005). "Transnational Feminism and Globalization: Bringing Third World Women's Voices from the Margin to Center." In *Critical Globalization Studies*, edited by Richard P. Appelbaum and William I. Robinson, 333–48. New York: Routledge.

Maguire, Patricia. (1987). *Doing Participatory Research: A Feminist Approach.* Amherst: Center for International Education, School of Education, University of Massachusetts, Amherst.

———. (2001). "Uneven Ground: Feminisms and Action Research." In *Handbook of Action Research*, edited by Peter Reason and H. Bradbury, 59–69. London: Sage.

Marcus, George E. (1995). "Ethnography in/of the World System: The Emergence of Multi-sited Ethnography." *Annual Review of Anthropology* 24, 95–117.

Mendez, Jennifer Bickham. (2005). *From the Revolution to the Maquiladoras: Gender, Labor and Globalization in Nicaragua.* Durham, NC: Duke University Press.

Mendez, Jennifer Bickham, and Diane L. Wolf. (2007). "Feminizing Global Research/Globalizing Feminist Research: Methods and Practices under Globalization." In *The Handbook of Feminist Research: Theory and Praxis*, edited by Sharlene Nagy Hess-Biber, 651–62. Thousand Oaks, CA: Sage.

Mies, Maria. (2007). "A Global Feminist Perspective on Research." In *Handbook of Feminist Research: Theory and Praxis*, edited by Sharlene Nagy Hesse-Biber, 663–68. Thousand Oaks, CA: Sage.

Mohanty, Chandra Talpade. (1991). "Under Western Eyes: Feminist Scholarship and Colonial Discourses." In *Third World Women and the Politics of Feminism*, edited by Chandra Talpade Mohanty, Ann Russo, and Lourdes Torres, 51–80. Bloomington: Indiana University Press.

Naples, Nancy A. (2004). "The Outsider Phenomenon." In *Feminist Perspectives on Social Research*, edited by Sharlene Nagy Hesse-Biber and Michelle L. Yaiser, 373–81. New York: Oxford University Press.

Observador Económico. (2002). "Zonas Francas Industriales en Nicaragua: ¿Héroes o Villanos?" 119 (December–January). Available at www.elobservadoreconomico.com/archivo/119/zf.html.

Ong, Aiwha. (1995). "Women Out of China: Traveling Tales and Traveling Theories in Postcolonial Feminism." In *Women Writing Culture*, edited by Ruth Behar and Deborah Gordon. Berkeley and Los Angeles: University of California Press.

Parreñas, Rhacel Salazar. (2001). *Servants of Globalization: Women, Migration, and Domestic Work.* Stanford, CA: Stanford University Press.

Patai, Daphne. (1991). "U.S. Academics and Third World Women: Is Ethical Research Possible?" In *Women's Words: The Feminist Practice of Oral History*, edited by Sherna Berger Gluck and Daphne Patai, 137–53. New York: Routledge.

Pesser, Patricia. (2003). "Engineering Migration Studies: The Case of New Immigrants in the United States." In *Gender and U.S. Immigration: Contemporary Trends,* edited by Pierrette Hondagneu-Sotelo, 20–42. Berkeley: University of California Press.

Peterson, V. Spike, and Anne Sisson Runyan. (1999). *Global Gender Issues*. Boulder, CO: Westview Press.

Pyle, Jean L., and Kathryn B. Ward. (2003). "Recasting Our Understanding of Gender and Work during Global Restructuring." *International Sociology* 18, no. 3, 461–89.

Rappaport, Joanne. (2007). "Beyond Writing: The Epistemology of Collaborative Ethnography." Unpublished manuscript.

Renzi, María Rosa. (1996). "Las zonas francas en Nicaragua." *El Observador Económico* 52, 34–44.

Richards, Patricia. (2006). "A Feminist Sociologist's Reflections on Collaborative Research." *LASA Forum* 37, no. 4, 16–18.

Sassen, Saskia. (2001). "Spatialities and Temporalities of the Global: Elements for a Theorization." In *Globalization*, edited by Arjun Appadurai, 260–78. Durham, NC: Duke University Press.

———. (2006). *Territory, Authority, Rights: From Medieval to Global Assemblages*. Princeton, NJ: Princeton University Press.

Smith, Michael Peter, and Luis Eduardo Guarnizo, eds. (1998). *Transnationalism from Below*. New Brunswick, NJ: Transaction.

Stacey, Judith. (1991). "Can There Be a Feminist Ethnography?" In *Women's Words: The Feminist Practice of Oral History*, edited by Sherna Berger Gluck and Daphne Patai, 111–19. New York: Routledge.

Thayer, Millie. (2001). "Joan Scott in the sertão: Rural Brazilian Women and Transnational Feminism." Paper presented at Annual Meetings of Latin American Studies Association, Washington, DC.

———. (2004). *Negotiating the Global: Northeast Brazilian Women's Movements and the Transnational Feminist Public*. PhD diss., University of California, Berkeley.

U.S. Bureau of Census. (2003). *Race and Hispanic Origins*. Washington, DC. Available at www.census.gov/pubinfo/www/multimedia/LULAC.html.

Vanden, Harry E., and Gary Prevost. (1993). *Democracy and Socialism in Sandinista Nicaragua*. Boulder, CO: Lynne Rienner.

Wolf, Diane L. (1996a). "Situating Feminist Dilemmas in Fieldwork" In *Feminist Dilemmas in Fieldwork*, edited by Diane L. Wolf, 1–54. Boulder, CO: Westview Press.

———, ed. (1996b). *Feminist Dilemmas in Fieldwork*. Boulder, CO: Westview Press.

4

Veiling the "Dangers" of Colliding Borders: Tourism and Gender in Zanzibar

Angela Demovic

As a cultural anthropologist, I lived from June to August of 1997 and again from May to December of 2001 in a rural village of coastal Zanzibar, East Africa. I combined participant observation with interviews, some carefully structured and some spontaneous, to try to understand women's lives in rural Zanzibar. This fieldwork became increasingly challenging as I faced fears induced, in part, by veiled and direct threats to me as a foreigner during politically uncertain times and, in part, by my own preconceptions of the region through the lens of a middle-class American woman. A key question from this experience is "How do we understand danger?" We can't always objectively know when we are in danger, but instead we rely on a number of heuristic devices to constantly (and unconsciously) evaluate our risk in any given situation. Particularly from the point of view of an American coming from a society with such a high premium placed on "security," it is difficult to know whether one's evaluation is a valid measure of threat. However, once we are certain of danger, our topic changes abruptly to violence. Ultimately, I can report only my own interpretations of danger, beginning by stating that at times while living in Zanzibar in 2001 I felt that I was in danger. Indeed, this corresponded to the reported feelings of others who were close to me, both African locals and research informants and White Americans.

As far as African locals were concerned, violence was a visible aspect of life in Zanzibar, especially for young Zanzibari males, an observation confirmed by the number of local boys who asked me for bandages and antiseptic once they learned I was generous with them. I bandaged deep and sometimes infected cuts that had resulted from street battles fought with straight razors. The young men were not always able to return to the government hospital for fresh gauze, even when stitches had been sewn there. Moreover, such visits could bring them face-to-face with police, an organization feared by locals—understandably, considering the human rights abuses by police in recent history.

Although there has not been a "politically motivated attack on an American in Zanzibar," as one editorial commenter stated, I felt compelled to spend time calculating whether or not I might be in danger. I met many tourists who had been robbed at machete point of money or passports, particularly common at night when drunk tourists return from bars to guesthouses, whether in town or along desolate beaches. In my own experience, the Tanzanian police in Zanzibar did little to assist such tourists. In fact, on one occasion I witnessed a tourist, trying to file a police report after being robbed on a Friday night, being told by Tanzanian police that he would need to return on Monday morning for anything to be done. For my part, I left Zanzibar at the end of my research, unharmed. Perhaps I was not in danger at all, regardless of some belligerent verbal threats and the intimidating anti–United States graffiti.

THE SETTING

Zanzibar, an island archipelago, is a politically *semi*-autonomous part of the nation of Tanzania. For its part, the United Republic of Tanzania, on Africa's southeastern coast, is sandwiched between Kenya and Mozambique. The Zanzabari island where I performed my research, Unguja, is located twenty-five miles off the coast of mainland Tanzania. Unguja Island, which visiting foreigners commonly refer to as "Zanzibar," is Zanzibar archipelago's largest offshore land mass. Overall, the Zanzibar archipelago has a population of about eight hundred thousand, mostly living on its two main islands. Unguja, the larger, has two important urban concentrations—Stone Town and Ngambo city. Pemba is the smaller, more rural, and more fertile of Zanzibar's two major islands. The majority of the two islands' populations is Muslim.

Unguja Island's most densely populated areas are on its western coast, where approximately one hundred thousand people live in two urban districts. Mji Mkongwe, or Stone Town (also called Zanzibar Town) has long been an important port city for Indian Ocean trade, including slaves, cloves, and now tourism. Stone Town's architecture, built in the nineteenth century by Arab and Indian merchants, includes winding alleys, bazaars, mosques, and ornate Arab houses. One of the most historic and attractive cities in East Africa, Stone Town is a frequent stop for travelers on safari in the Serengeti or climbing Kilimanjaro, who spend a weekend on a Zanzibari, part of the "must-do" African experience. Few of these visitors know of the political unrest in Unguja and Pemba.

Unguja Island's relatively newer Ngambo city district, fringing Stone Town, is viewed as Zanzibar's "African Quarter," a reflection of its inhabitants' slave ancestry and involvement in spice plantations.[1] People in the Ngambo district have roots in mainland Africa, many being later arrivals than the inhabitants of the island's rural east and north coasts. As for the ethnicity of Stone Town inhabitants, Stone Town families often claim "Arab" descent, although scholars have pointed out that this has little to do with any biological characteristics that Westerners often confuse with cultural notions of descent.

Outside of its two cities, the rest of Unguja Island has very low population density; a few populated settlements are attached to fishing communities and near fertile farmlands on the island's westward side. Pointing to the presumed slowness of change associated with rural Zanzibar's relative isolation from globalization, anthropologist Christian De Francisco (2004, 112) claims that the "coastal villages receive modernity solely through the vehicle of tourism." Yet these rural villages are far from isolated from a variety of forms of globalization and the cultural changes associated with life in the modern nation state. In 1997 and 2001, I saw rural people struggling in a variety of ways to survive within the global economy, whose influence included a growing seaweed industry dominated by local female workers and owned by a Filipino company.[2]

On the consumption side, rural Zanzibaris eat sweets imported from the United Arab Emirates—a fairly regular treat. A few villagers own televisions and radios that bring them international news. In other words, Zanzibar remains—as it has always been—an economy that reaches across the Indian Ocean to the rest of the world. Today's tourism is just one component of its "global" profile. Although my research focused on tourism, clearly more research is needed into the many other ways that Zanzibaris and other islanders are entering into more recent forms of global trade for a complete understanding of the region.

Ethnically, while the United Republic of Tanzania is extremely diverse, with approximately 130 named ethnic groups, a minority of its population is Muslim. In contrast, those who identify as having Indian and Arab descent constitute the majority in Zanzibar.[3] Indeed, the most salient aspect of the Zanzibari Swahili identity is Islam, which is practiced by more than 90 percent of the population. In contrast, Tanzania's mainland population is 45 percent Christian and only 35 percent Muslim, with many people still also practicing indigenous African belief systems. Swahili is the Zanzibari populations' primary language, although regional dialects can be found. Known locally as Kiswahili, this language is thought to have had its birth on Zanzibar Island, a belief regularly articulated to me by the Zanzibari educated elite.[4]

TOURISM IN ZANZIBAR

In 1997 and 2001, when I was conducting research in Zanzibar, tourism was mostly of the "backpacker" variety. A few air conditioned hotels and some fine restaurants could be found in Stone Town; those who ventured to the rural beaches were likely to stay in beach bungalows. Living was cheap: For ten to twenty American dollars per person, each night, a tourist could stay on the beach in what a tourist guide would label "an idyllic setting." Such "backpacker" tourism aside, Tanzania has been trying to encourage the development of luxury tourism, which earns higher incomes through fewer visitors. However, the world tourism market is fiercely competitive; during my research most visitors were still students—mostly from Europe, Australia, or the United Kingdom.

Young Zanzibaris in particular have taken an increasingly negative view of tourism. They often frame their discourse through Islamic religious and cultural values, pointing to the negative visitor behaviors that insult and defy Muslim orthopraxy. The strong negative feelings of some Zanzibaris about tourism sprang into the foreground in 1992–1993, when young radicals in Zanzibar Town led demonstrations that included an attack on an Italian-owned jewelry shop. Protestors demanded that Zanzibar join the Organization of Islamic Conferences (OIC) and abolish tourism (Parkin 1995, 200). The demands and associated protests helped to link, in the government's mind, the critiques of tourism with Islam. Indeed, Parkin maintains that youthful Zanzibari men want Zanzibar redefined through affiliation with the Islamic world and a "repudiation of tourism and the sins and degradations associated with Western lifestyles" (200). During my interviews in 1997, rumors circulated around coastal towns that the government was considering a law allowing the caning of tourists whose shorts fell above their knees. Whether this was only rumor or based in fact is not the important point; rather, I would suggest that the exposed body of tourists had become part of a highly charged discourse about morality that links "immorality" to the "polluting West."

Conflicts between Islamic ideals and "polluting" tourist behavior are further reinforced by the negative economic impacts of tourism on Zanzibaris. That Zanzibari tourism represents a strong cultural and economic burden to many Zanzibaris was ultimately supported by my own research. I found that the majority of rural Zanzibari women who reside in tourism villages are experiencing falling standards of living with development of the local hospitality industry (Demovic 2007). Zanzibaris' decreased access to local resources—drinking water and fish, for example—exacerbated by tourism, has impacted negatively upon locals' health, economy, and on their perceptions of tourists. Locals see wealthy foreigners enjoying plenty on their island, while they themselves suffer a parallel decrease in these resources. Those who receive the last share of these resources—poor, aged, and women—feel the decreased access to natural resources that is caused by tourist consumption. Incomes are seasonal, at best, and salaries are sporadically paid. Men control most of the large tourism-related businesses.

Tanzanian tourism, which is under government control and strongly supported by this country's mainland political elites, would not be served by recognizing research findings such as mine. Indeed, any suggestion that Zanzibari tourism be banned (or more strictly controlled) was considered illogical by the Tanzanian elites whom I interviewed. This would contradict the free market ideology currently espoused by Tanzania's ruling party, the CCM, and its neocolonial supporters, the World Bank and International Monetary Fund (IMF). Tanzanian mainlanders have been fervently critical of Zanzibari political demonstrations, designating such activism as dangerously playing up "Islamic identities"[5] and threatening Tanzania's national unity. Parkin (1995) argues that Zanzibaris have been "reluctant to endorse or even speak about" tourism, much less in politico-religious terms (201). This is at least in part due to the Arab notion of *setiri*, or concealment, both in physical person and in unsolicited opinion. In other words, just as family secrets are kept within the walls of the family compound, it is generally the case that the island's political problems should be kept from visiting foreigners.

CONTESTED TOURISM/AMBIENT DANGERS

When I first entered the field in 1997, in addition to my research being potentially controversial for its focus on tourism, it was also potentially dangerous for me to be in Zanzibar due to the atmosphere of local political violence. In the words of Amnesty International in 1997:

> Political tension remained high on the islands of Zanzibar and Pemba where political opponents accused the ruling . . . Party . . . of using intimidation and ballot rigging to win the October 1995 presidential and parliamentary elections. The authorities were responsible, both before and after local elections in March 1996, for further harassment, sometimes violent, of supporters of the main opposition party, the Civic United Front (CUF). . . . Scores of suspected government opponents were tortured and ill-treated by police. . . . On the mainland, criminal suspects were regularly beaten. On Zanzibar, beatings and other ill-treatment and torture were inflicted, including shaving prisoners' heads with broken glass, spraying prisoners with motor oil and forcing them to eat feces. (Amnesty International 1997)

Politically related violence against Zanzibaris was again raging in Tanzania and Zanzibar when I returned to the field in early May of 2001. At the local level, in January and February of that year, political tensions had exploded into riots when mainland police meted out violence against the protesters who were demanding fresh elections for Zanzibar Island's leadership (Ngowi 2001a, 2001b). The confrontations left deaths and injuries in their wake, with even larger demonstrations following as a consequence. Protestors—some demonstrations had more than ten thousand people—demanded democracy in Zanzibar. Although the opposition party's (CUF) leaders were careful to avoid defining themselves as an Islamic party, the Tanzanian mainland government's CCM ruling party continued to disparage the CUF as "Islamic," further fueling the fires of discontent.

In 2001, when I returned to Zanzibar to continue my research, rumors were rampant that the Tanzanian government was engaging in political killings, injuries, rapes, and the torture of political opponents. In the words of News Link Africa in December 2001:

> The recent wave of political violence and the deaths of more than 280 people on Zanzibar and Pemba islands has left a bitter memory in the minds of not only the local people but also the Western tourists who thought they were spending their holidays amidst tranquil islands.

Such violence strongly discouraged the participation of Zanzibari villagers in political debate and public gatherings and it lessened their willingness to take part in my research. Few villagers were willing to risk life or safety to report their economic problems for an obscure academic audience. The ambient threat of violence extended to foreigners, particularly Americans, after the 9/11 attacks in New York City, at the Pentagon, and in the Pennsylvania countryside. The initial reaction of Zanzibaris to 9/11 was sympathy: I was approached the day after the attacks by the local Sheha—a Muslim religious man who is mayor for a section of the village—who wished to officially express his condolences to me concerning the attacks in my country. The elderly man assured me that this was not the work of Muslims; "it is the work of animals," he said.

However, the subsequent U.S. invasions of Afghanistan and Iraq were viewed as anti-Muslim; photos in Tanzanian newspapers depicting the bombings and the resulting "collateral damage" were particularly effective in reducing any feelings of empathy toward Americans. I wondered whether an American woman who was alone conducting research in Zanzibar during a time of international political tensions between Islam and the "corporate West" could carry out research without suffering violence. As an American and a non-Muslim, would I be in danger in Zanzibar? The answers to this question were not always reassuring. Local people repeatedly expressed deep concern for my safety because of rising anti-American anger.

Indeed, increasingly anti-American sentiment was escalating into open threats of violence against foreigners. During one visit to Tanzania's de facto capital, Dar es Salaam, in late August 2001, I was confined to my hotel by a citywide curfew in response to a rumor that there would be a political demonstration after the evening prayers. The front door of my hotel was gated and guarded by two uniformed and armed soldiers. I was afraid to sit in the hotel restaurant; the guards would not let me go down the street to send e-mail. That evening after prayers, the mosque loudspeaker announced to citizens that they "should not be disheartened," as the armed response would "only postpone the protest." My fictive aunt, a civil servant living in Dar es Salaam, had warned me before this trip that the police were finally going to "beat the Muslims." When she told me things like that, her voice would raise an octave—a tone used to indicate anything scandalous, whether she was referring to prostitutes, to thieves, or to the police beating the political opposition.

My fictive aunt's sentiments[6] about the threats to me from Muslims were common: I was repeatedly told in 2001, primarily by Christian urban Tanzanians, that I ought to reconsider my fieldwork on Zanzibar Island if I wanted to avoid being "slaughtered by Muslims." This advice almost led me to change my field site, but I did not, assuming that by studying tourism's impact on women, I would be relatively safe.

I did not fully consider that locals' perceptions and treatment of me might also be shaped by the conflicts surrounding tourism. Knowing that tourism was a polemical subject, I reckoned just the same that the reported human rights violations in Zanzibar, particularly those that had occurred just prior to my entering the field, had been perpetrated largely against members of the Islamic, local opposition party and their families. Not against Christians and other religio-ethnic groups. I assumed that since I was not involved in Tanzanian politics and not associated with any political party, I would be safe.

Yet I continued to be dogged by a range of feelings and emotions about my safety, about maintaining the professional integrity of my study, and about the safety of those I would study. Without raising any unnecessary alarm concerning the hospitality and intentions of Zanzibaris, one objective in this chapter is to examine the behaviors that I viewed during my fieldwork as indicative of danger and discuss the measures that I took to minimize such risks to myself and to my interviewees.

STUDYING ZANZIBAR: RESEARCH HURDLES

My research in Zanzibar involved conducting interviews, surveying households, and carrying out participant observation on women in a rural fishing village on eastern Unguja Island. The aim of my anthropological study was to understand the changes in village life that were occurring with economic globalization, particularly with the development of local tourism. In the process, my own views about the value of tourism for Zanzibar changed. When I first began the field research in 1997, I considered the negative local views about tourism to be curious; Zanzibaris were clearly in dire need of income-producing activities, whether from tourism or otherwise. Might not tourism be one way of achieving "development"? At the same time, I recognized that tourism often generated tensions between local people and tourists, particularly when tourists did not behave or dress in ways considered culturally appropriate by the local Muslim population.

As my field research progressed, any predominantly positive views I'd had about the impact of tourism, particularly as it impacted upon Zanzibari women, shifted. Observing and documenting the negative economic and social consequences of tourism on women and their families led me to place tourism within a new, more negative economic and cultural view. My discoveries had not been openly communicated to me in interviews, but rather suggested in veiled ways during discussions of other topics. Of course, such findings could not be discussed with anyone directly associated with the Tanzanian government, which had elevated tourism to the forefront of Tanzanian development. But where did Zanzibaris stand in relation to tourism?

Pollution Dangers

From the perspective of many Zanzibari Muslims, tourism had serious drawbacks. Zanzibari customs, as applied to tourism, considered such work "polluting" and the people—including myself—who work in or around it "polluted." Could I study Muslim women working in rural tourism, given the politico-religious context that spurned tourism in general, and its involvement of Muslim women in particular? Because gender ideologies in Zanzibar include the belief that women are categorically more susceptible than men to polluting influences, tourism is viewed as a special threat to women's morality.[7] Existing gender role expectations, which seriously limited women's involvement in the island's tourism industry,[8] made those women who worked in the tourist sector socially and personally vulnerable—a status I earned for merely studying them.

In order to carry out my research in the face of the myriad of issues surrounding it, I tried to focus on being professional. This way I could distract myself from fear. I made modifications in my dress and comportment, a challenge to my Western feminist notions about the "modern woman," but such changes helped me to better fit into Muslim Zanzibar. My public attempts at embracing Muslim Swahili feminine gender roles—most visibly through my dress and work—were thankfully interpreted as clear signals of my own positive cultural immersion into Zanzibari morals and of my need for protection. Such perceptions of me helped me to get close to national insiders, both mainland politicians and local leaders, and also helped to allay some of my fears. An additional layer of protection was the "cultural exceptions" offered by Zanzibaris to "currency-spending" foreigners. In order to reduce my own doubts and fears, I did my best to fit into my village and neighborhood as much as possible. In the end, while there was some national and local resistance to my research, and some situations in which I was personally vulnerable, I was fortunately received through multiple lenses and expectations.

Studying Muslim Women

Studying practicing Muslim women had its challenges. There was little academic research on this topic to guide my study, a void certainly addressed in this volume by my own, the Roschanack Eisenlohr, and the Schwandner-Sievers chapters. As our research demonstrates, a woman's status as Muslim cannot be separated from her gender. Zanzibaris have an essentialist view of gender, seeing women and men as very different sorts of people. For example, Zanzibaris believe that men have less pliable characters than women do, a belief they claim is reinforced in the Koran. Thus, because of a man's "more stable, less susceptible" character, Muslim men may marry non-Muslim women, while women—who have more flexible characters and greater moral pliability—are susceptible to having their religious commitment to Islam diluted through a mixed marriage. Whether I liked it or not, such assumptions about women were applied to me as well.

For his part, and according to gendered images of males, my American male traveling companion, who accompanied me during parts of my research, seemed to have been viewed by young men as immutably committed to Western values, a designation that did not always serve him well at a time of anti-American sentiment. Dressed, as my companion generally was, in the clothes of an American, there was often an assumption that he would support American over Zanzibari ideals. As a male and therefore "political," he was perceived as a potential rival. It did not help that my companion reacted to such assumptions, and to other males' challenges of him, by expressing a very mainstream American masculinity. He was ready to physically defend himself and his opinions. Indeed, as I will explain shortly, the only time I ever experienced direct physical threats from Zanzibaris was when I was with this male traveling companion. In the eyes of male Zanzibaris, the role of "protection" had fallen to a person who was a threat to their values. On another occasion, by contrast, when I was alone and lost in Stone Town, a male villager "rescued" me from several "hard-sell" shopkeepers, telling them: "Leave her alone. She is our [the village's] *mzungu* [White person]."

Gender establishes both verbal and nonverbal communication and structural expectations in participant observation. Giovannini (1986, 105) found that, as a foreigner, she was not exempt from the negative impact of indigenous gender-based norms. While I certainly found this to be true, I believe that being gendered female by Zanzibaris actually decreased the danger to me as a Westerner. I believe that I was more protected from danger than an American male researcher might have been. However, unfortunately, my "femaleness" also made any direct assessment of political situation almost impossible. Politics is a male activity among Swahili, therefore, like Giovannini in her research in Sicily, I was limited by the ways that I could seek information about politics. I had to tease information about politics from my informants through indirect means—discussions of travel, work opportunities, and social ties to other areas of the country.

For example, it was because of the large number of Unguja Island southeast coastal village women who reported to me that they had traveled by boat to work on Pemba Island, rather than going to more proximate locations on Unguja Island, that I learned that Pemba Island was seen by these women as politically and culturally "closer" to (e.g., more compatible with) them than those on Unguja Island, because of their extended kin ties to the region. But were the Muslims on Pemba "closer" culturally and politically? I increasingly focused on that question after another serendipitous finding: I was told that it was from Pemba Island that a driver had come who had been involved in attacks on the U.S. Embassy in Dar es Salaam. This led me to ask myself if I had learned something about the political leanings of Pemba Island dwellers that would perhaps be shared by related lineages in this rural village? Of course, answering this would require more research, but I had at least indirectly opened a door to such exploration. Perhaps my decidedly unpolitical questions were uncovering political realities.

Ethnographic (Mis)understandings

Even within the comfort of her own society and a shared language, Tannen (2001) has demonstrated that American men and women can take completely different meanings from the same conversation based upon gendered ways of communicating and perceiving. Tannen likens conversation between American men and women to cross-cultural communication, in which "cross-fires are common and expected." Although we like to imagine ourselves in our own culture as having overcome ascribed differences, including "gendered" communication styles, Tannen (2002) shows that such assumptions are guaranteed neither among family members nor among secondary groups in a shared workplace (2001).

Taking this a step further, an anthropologist working with people of widely different formal and informal learning experiences would find it ethnocentric to assume that the meanings and intentions of our informants can be easily read. Kinesic messages and tones of speech, gestures, and implied meanings are at least as complex and difficult to interpret as a foreign language, increasing the difficulties of cross-cultural communication, in general, and of assessing danger, in particular. Briggs (1970) demonstrated this in her study of the Utku people, which focuses on the contrast between the amazing self-control of these people in their expression of emotions and her own "emotionality" as a mainstream Canadian. For example, Briggs found that her emotional outbursts—her minor expressions of frustration due to a lack of privacy and the constant demands of family members—served to increasingly isolate her from the group on whom her survival depended. Her Utku hosts "read" her expressive nature as indicating a dangerous personality, although this was neither her feeling nor what she desired to communicate. Their feelings that she was uncontrolled emotionally, and therefore dangerous, left her vulnerable to real danger.

During Briggs's extended stay in the Utku camp, being unable to reliably "read" the attitudes of even her own host family toward her, she failed to recognize the real dangers she might face if she continued to transgress the cultural norm of disguising all outward emotional display and was subsequently "abandoned" in an environment where it is almost impossible to survive alone. Such a scenario is not impossible, as the Utku deal with conflict through ostracizing the offender. The true danger was not revealed while Briggs was in the field, it was only after her departure from her host family's dwelling, and her meeting with the town-based Utku missionary's wife, Ikayuqtuq, that Briggs learned the "true feelings" of the informants with whom she had shared close living quarters (Briggs 1970, 261) for more than a year. Indeed, the degree of difference between Briggs's own expression of emotions and that of her Utku hosts was so great that she suggests there may be differences between her own and Utku experiences of those emotional states. It is hard to imagine how to validly assess the feelings of persons from other societies, whether feelings of aggression or otherwise, if indeed our culture creates those emotional experiences in categorically different ways.

An example of another source of ethnographic misunderstanding, the confusion created by intersecting and overlapping discourses (heteroglossia), is illustrated by Boddy (1989, 7). Conducting ethnographic research on the Hofriyati of Northern Sudan, Boddy discovered that in this society where gender asymmetries in power are severe, women and other disempowered individuals have responded by creating counter-hegemonic discourses such as communication through the *zar* possession cult. For the anthropologist in the field, interpreting people's sentiments—through communication that involves eye contact (or not), a shoulder shrug, verbal tonality, a "yes" statement while nodding "no"—is far from straightforward. It is difficult to know exactly what informants are thinking, even when they make every attempt to communicate their sentiments clearly through their own culturally defined symbolic system.

MITIGATING DANGERS

Learning from Research

Not surprisingly, I still do not entirely understand whether I was objectively in danger in Zanzibar. However, through careful attention to signals of acceptance and disapproval from those I was researching, I assume that I was able to at least minimize dangers to myself and those I was studying. Much that I had learned about studying potentially dangerous subjects had come through my previous fieldwork on sex workers in New Orleans. In that research, direct communication about many of the dangers sex workers faced was not possible. For example, the complex network of taboos about sexual negotiations and the illegality associated with sex work constrained what the sex workers could and would discuss with me. Likewise, it was taboo for me to directly ask questions about politics in Zanzibar due to Zanzibari taboos associated with what is thought to be "impolite" conversation, to physical and economic threats to those speaking against the government, and to government policy that forbids researchers' directly investigating politics. These factors made it almost impossible for me to avoid "miscommunications" in assessing the dangers to me during my research.

Being an "Outsider"

My ethnographic understanding was further limited by my being a non-Muslim American conducting research on Muslims in Zanzibar. In order to counter or neutralize the "culturally corrosive" aspects of Western contact, Zanzibari locals operated to preserve their culture by shutting off their "insider circle" to "outsiders."[9] This influenced just how much I was allowed to enter their culture, even though I had visibly adopted such outward behavioral symbols of respect as using proper Muslim dress and comportment for women. But there were still many limits on how far I would be permitted to enter the "inner circle." For example, my interest in gaining knowledge about the Koran was rejected completely when several village elders met to discuss my request to learn to read and study the Koran. The elders decided that, as a non-Muslim, I could not even touch the Koran, much less study it with them. Their insistence was so strong that I did not tell village elders that I owned—and regularly touched and read—an English version of the Koran. Doing so could signal disrespect for their religious values, customs, and authority.

Being unable to assess how my "outsider" status might make me vulnerable to anti-American sentiment and actions, and being unable to obtain information publicly about developing anti-American demonstrations on the island, made me periodically question my ability to remain safe in the field. In response, I turned to a local Koranic scholar for such information. Feeling very comfortable talking with this man, who was my fieldwork informant, I visited his home frequently to try and sort through my fears with him. I asked him about the reported dangers to Westerners on Zanzibar. I wanted to know how many people had attended a recent demonstration in Zanzibar Town. Was there a threat to me in Zanzibar Town? Was there a threat to my safety in our village? Although this trusted informant had previously answered my research questions about economic development in Zanzibar, my queries about safety were initially met with a long silence. This was followed by the scholar's own questions: How had I learned of the demonstrations? Were they known to many other of the *wazungu* (Whites) who were visiting the island? The Islamic scholar then briskly suggested that I not worry about "these political events" and that I "concentrate on my studies of women," a seemingly apolitical and thus acceptable subject.

I later learned—on an evening when the Koranic scholar came under cover of darkness to my house—that I should avoid being in Zanzibar Town. He suggested that I stay inside my house at night and not answer my door, insisting that I use a password to ascertain the identity of friendly potential visitors. A week later, my informant insisted that I cease claiming an American identity, suggesting I tell those who asked that I was French. My informant refused to participate in any discussions about the details of the tensions developing in Zanzibar over local, national, and international politics. I felt too uncomfortable with the ethical implications of his warnings to follow them up. He clearly intended to protect me, but he also needed to protect himself by limiting his own public participation in potentially dangerous conversations.

Losing Networks

I learned later that day that a historian with whom I was acquainted had decided to cut his research project short and leave Zanzibar; likewise, an expatriate friend decided to leave the island to "take an early Christmas." My fears as an American non-Muslim in a Muslim region were exacerbated by the barrage of concerned e-mails that I was receiving from friends and family members, including from some widely traveled anthropologists. The message was consistent: It was time to come home. I learned from an American teacher on the island that anti-American, pro–bin Laden demonstrations had occurred recently in Zanzibar Town and in Dar es Salaam. His information, from the U.S. Consulate in Dar es Salaam, was that that these demonstrations were expected to become regular Friday occurrences, despite threats from the Tanzanian government to mobilize the army to stop them. The consulate advised Americans in Zanzibar to "be diligent" and "to vary their paths and schedules to minimize the risk of violence," and to "remain inside their homes on Fridays after the Muslim noon prayers."

Without a network of knowledgeable locals who were willing to talk about demonstrations with me, and slowly losing fellow researchers with whom I could exchange such information, I knew that I would have a difficult time understanding the reality of my situation and abating some of my fears of danger. I watched local Swahili news broadcasts nightly, but heard nothing about the demonstrations. Since the only broadcast available was the Zanzibari government's ZTV station, I was not surprised by the absence of news about local protests: Anti-Western protest is not good for tourism.[10]

GENDERING PROTECTION

In my participant-observer role, I did my best to fit into my village and neighborhood life. Being professional and behaving in culturally appropriate ways were key to my work. As a graduate student who was both fairly new to field research and to research in Zanzibar, I was uneasy about my place on the island. I had more questions than answers: I wondered how locals perceived me, especially when speaking to young men who held distinctly antitourist political views. If I were considered a tourist, could such a potentially negative designation override my being accepted into my neighborhood? Would being seen as a "professional researcher" nurture my entry into villages? Was it possible for a young woman to ever be seen as a "professional researcher"? What could I do to ensure being placed in the status of a professional?

I knew of the importance to Zanzibaris of self-control in personal expression, particularly as such norms apply to women. Because women's clothing serves as both an ethnic marker and to indicate the purity of a woman's character, I found myself having to focus on the way that I dressed. This had begun in the Tanzanian capital of Dar es Salaam, even before I had reached my Zanzibar Island field site. I found that, although my whiteness was always conspicuous, how people reacted to me as a White female foreigner was very much shaped by my clothes. For instance, although people in both mainland Tanzania's Dar es Salaam and on Zanzibar Island seemed to expect me to wear Western-style clothes, even a Westerner was expected to be "covered up." In addition, throughout Tanzania and Zanzibar people take pride in the "neatness" of their appearance, wearing well-ironed, brightly colored clothes to signal their attention to these values. I did not realize at first that the muted, natural-toned colors often worn by people from the United States were seen as disheveled, old, and not well maintained. Wearing such colors signaled that I was not taking care of my appearance. My informants helped me to dress more "neatly"—using bright and well-ironed clothes.

Modesty garments are also an important part of Zanzibari and Swahili identities. I could see the importance of modesty in dress when even the poorest women, living in the meanest of rural circumstances, covered their heads even though they were "excused" by their age and poor health from Islamic obligations to veil. Just the same, they never left their small compounds without at least a clean *kanga* cloth draped modestly over their head and shoulders. Likewise, village women conformed to rules concerning the use of such modesty garments as the *buibui* (a black outer dress that conceals from ankle to wrist). The women who had the economic means to purchase one would wear a *buibui* and perhaps a fancy *hijab* (head scarf) of colored velvet. A primary school teacher informed me that it would be improper for her to go to the school without her *buibui*, as it would entail moving across land owned and controlled by three families who were not related to her. Within such a cultural context, it would be completely out of place for me to violate proscriptions about modesty in dress. Besides such additional clothing providing a modest layer of protection of a woman's purity, the *kanga* cloth headdress also shielded her from the sun.

Even though the head covering was functional as sun protection, the traditional head covering was not initially an option to me as an "outsider." I knew that respecting the cultural prohibition against my wearing the traditional *kanga* head covering was important. As Giovannini (1986, 111) discovered, research is "reciprocal": The activities of researcher and informant include not only the researcher's interpreting and responding to the informant, but also the researcher's sending out cues about her intentions. Having been discouraged as an outsider from using the *kanga* head covering and needing to reciprocally respect this prohibition, I thus began experimenting with other ways to signal my purity. For example, when I left the village to conduct participant observation on seaweed farms, where, for practical reasons, I needed to cover my head against the sun, I used a scarf or bandana folded to generously cover my head and braid. Using some kind of head covering communicated my intention to respect local ideals about morality and announce that I was not a "sexual threat" to the community. At the same time, my wearing a common scarf—a "Westernization" of the veil—allowed me to expropriate one of the culture's own gendered identity markers while still retaining some of my own Western independence. As time passed, I was urged by local host families to adopt the *kanga* as protection from the sun. I gladly acceded to their pressure out of desire to protect my health, which was much more important to me than challenging those locals who might have seen my using the *kanga* as a norm transgression.

I had learned, especially through examples of violations of dress code expectations, that such norms were taken very seriously. The dress code heavily rewarded covering appropriate body parts and ostracized those who allowed their bodies to remain uncovered. I sometimes learned about such norms through informal conversations: I heard Zanzibari women in my village gossip about the Tanzanian mainland women who had temporarily migrated to Unguja Island for tourism work and who appeared in public scantily dressed. One such woman, who worked as a cocktail waitress in a local hotel, walked past one day wearing a skirt that just touched the tops of her knees. Nothing was said until the woman and the two male hotel workers she was walking with were out of hearing range. Then one of my informants began complaining about having such a "loose woman" in the village. The woman in question, whose name translates as "Praise God," was being criticized for openly walking through town dressed inappropriately and in the company of two male hotel workers. The village women assumed from their reading of her transgressions that "Praise God" was having illicit sexual relations with both men.

Having been a party to this conversation, I came away with a hardened resolve to conform to local gender roles as much as possible; like Giovannini (1986), I needed to be careful to choose an "appropriate" living situation and to use modest forms of dress. Yet as Krieger (1986) found in her research in Cairo, Egypt, I also had to fight against the image of myself as a "Western woman of loose virtue" who is deserving of negative sanctions. This image was reinforced in Zanzibar, as it was in Cairo, by films and television shows imported from the West and by the behavior of visiting tourists. Modifying my behavior to adhere to local norms, through such means as (in addition to accepting modest dress) not being out alone at night, would signal my personal chastity as well as my willingness to respect the cultural norms of my Zanzibari hosts. Being seen as an "appropriate" visitor, I assumed, would allow me to communicate more openly with Zanzibari wives, whom I hoped to interview. I also assumed that by observing culturally appropriate dress, I might be able to create a "safety zone" for myself.

Behavior congruent with local Islamic orthopraxy, I believe, helped me to be a welcome visitor, even during times of political tensions. However, this meant essentially assuming roles considered appropriate by Muslim men for their women—a set of conditions that I, as an American feminist and a young professor of women's studies, could not help but question. I struggled for some time trying to discover the balance between "appropriate" clothing for me—assuming that there were no "cultural exceptions" to modesty if I wanted to be seen as a "good" woman and a serious researcher—while still avoiding encroachment on my own cultural identity. I resolved this dilemma by wearing long-sleeved blouses and a skirt that touched my ankles. It took a while longer to resolve how to cover my head. Experiments wearing the *kanga*, as local women did, or the fancier imported *hijab* headscarves worn by wealthier town women, were met with everyone's curious amusement and only semi-approval. Such modesty garments are markers of Zanzibari identity; I am not Zanzibari. At worst, appropriations of Zanzibari dress could signal that I, a foreigner, was attempting to parody Zanzibari identity. Given the political tensions concerning foreign visitors, such behavior could draw negative attention.

I finally settled on tying a European silk scarf or bandana over my hair, which was neither negatively nor positively commented upon by local women. I was even asked by some elderly women to speak with other foreigners about their "immodesty," because, as these women noted, I "had learned to dress appropriately." I felt even more certain that I had hit upon the correct solution to approved dress when one night I almost left the house without my scarf and a Zanzibari female friend reminded me to put on the scarf, calling me "absentminded" for forgetting it. I knew then that my European scarf had struck just the right cultural tone: "Culturally appropriate" because it was derived from my own culture while addressing Zanzibari cultural expectations. Using a Western cultural marker in a manner that did not usurp the *kanga* or *hijab*, I had become a "Zanzibar-ized Westerner."

FEAR REVISITED: CLASHES BETWEEN THE OBSERVER AND THE OBSERVED

Understanding the intentions of informants within a reciprocal communication system is important to the fieldwork encounter and for assessing and avoiding fieldwork dangers. Swahilis place great value on discreet, reserved communication in which unsolicited opinions are not given. In an illustration of unsolicited information not being given, I was left one day after an interview to wait for the public bus when everyone in the neighborhood knew it would not arrive. I had not asked about the bus route and timetable, and no one had wanted to be "rude enough" to offer an unsolicited opinion.

A communicative system that places a premium on veiling opinions and keeps certain kinds of information secret sometimes resulted in interviewing becoming difficult. My interpreter would sometimes lie to me about what an interviewee had said. For example, in the case of a woman who had provided information that, in the interpreter's opinion, was "too open" about her family's problems, I did not receive her "full story" from the interpreter. One lesson from this could be that a researcher who uses locals to interpret needs to gain the interpreter's trust and understanding of her role before beginning interviews. In this case, even with a clear understanding of my goals, my interpreter was first and foremost committed to the protection of family face.

In an example of how Zanzibari communication norms influenced my knowledge about danger, it was generally taboo to openly discuss politics on the island, making it "politically sensitive" to have discussions about how political conditions might impact upon me. The cultural value placed by Zanzibaris on discreetness, in combination with government's attempts to hide any violence that might impact upon tourism, made it impossible to obtain information about possible dangers to me, a foreigner in Zanzibar after 9/11. As previously mentioned, even my closest informants were hesitant to tell me about anti-American feelings. Yet there was ambient evidence that such feelings existed. In one example mentioned earlier in this chapter, in late September 2001, I rode through Zanzibar town on a bus known locally as *daladala*. This conveyance, a truck converted into public transport by installing benches for seating under a tentlike covering, held about twenty Zanzibaris crammed into the limited space. I entered the *daladala* bus with my American male companion; we were the only Whites on the bus. Knowing that it was not unusual for a few curious tourists to appear on these buses, and recognizing that we were traveling through a particular part of town not usually visited by foreigners, there may have been some reason to have safety concerns. Clearly seeing us as out of place, one older male bus rider suggested politely that he could direct us to (the safety of) Zanzibar City's tourist-friendly Stone Town. We thanked him and remained on the bus, filled with quiet and dignified locals.

Unusual that day was the spontaneous performance of one young male rider. Dressed in tattered pants, flip-flops, a carefully ironed faded shirt, and the Muslim embroidered *kofia* cap, the young man began a "Rap" commentary on international politics. Rhythmically chanting phrases about developing tensions between America and the groups labeled "terrorist" by America, this man brought the otherwise carefully hidden animosities toward Western tourists to our attention. The spontaneous rapper's carefully crafted rhyme proclaimed bin Laden "King of the World" for having "crushed George W. Bush beneath his feet."

The discursive content of the "Rap" and a bus rider singing in public were "matter out of place" in a culture that values expressing opinions in a "reserved" manner, avoiding public discussions of political turmoil, and exercising self-constraint in verbal communication. The man's public performance was judged not only by me, but also by other riders, as an act of aggression. I saw several passengers beginning to look uncomfortable, shifting in their seats or busying their hands with their small packages. One woman began trying to distract her toddler. Other women turned away from the rapper and began covering their head and faces with their loose veils of fabric. This gesture, which was used to socially distance them from their surroundings, was something that I had often observed when immodestly dressed tourists approached local women or when a Muslim Zanzibari woman found herself "uncomfortably" close to a conversation considered "bawdy" or otherwise "inappropriate." It was clear from the women's behavior that a form of "inappropriate" communication was happening.

I was initially uncomfortable with the young man's antagonistic verses and tried to concentrate on information gathering as a means of distracting my fears. I regretted not having my tape recorder thinking this was a good opportunity to understand Zanzibari youth's sentiments about Westerners.

Wanting to at least write down the rapper's words, I began fumbling in my bag for a pen and paper. My response may have also been an unconscious way of distracting myself from the rapper's anti-Western sentiment. In the process of looking for pen and paper, I was unaware that tension was growing between my male traveling companion, the performer, and other young men on the bus. Pen in hand and writing a series of observations, I looked up to find several young men's eyes locked on my defiant companion and his eyes glaring back at them. Bodies poised on the edge of their benches, the young men looked as if they were ready to fight. A religiously observant elderly man—identified by his use of the *kofia* hat and the dresslike *kanzu* that marks the island's pious Muslim men—shot disapproving glances at the rappers, but by then other young male passengers had joined in chanting with the rapper. Fearing that a fight was about to break out, I decided that pretending not to recognize the tension might defuse the situation.

Such hopes were dashed when I looked over to see that my American companion, teeth clenched and fists poised, was itching to fight. Quite irritated with my companion for exposing us to danger and creating a serious ethical dilemma in the process, I knew that I would have to deal with his actions later. On a more proximate level, I became aware that the section of town we were traveling through could explode into violence. I insisted that we exit the *daladala*, feigning interest in a fruit vendor at one corner. There we waited for another bus. Safely back to a more tourist-friendly area, I regretted that I had not been able to record the complex rhyme that should have been a part of this chapter. Indeed, perhaps it could have been taken down, had not my American companion stupidly taken an aggressive stance toward the young men on the bus.

I had learned several important lessons from the experience: The need to carefully "vet," before and on an ongoing basis, those we take into the field with us; that an observer's gender role performances can interface with, challenge, and/or be misinterpreted by the "observed"; that both of these factors can influence the success or failure of cross-cultural communication and observation.

CONCLUSION

During my fieldwork in Zanzibar, danger was a part of everyday life. I was warned by local associates, friends, and by some informants—especially after 9/11—that I should change my field site location. The U.S. Embassy alerted incoming visitors to potential dangers, but demonstrations and violence were unreported in local news. I needed locals to provide such information, but due to cultural proscriptions against giving unsolicited information and the government's prohibitions against creating a climate that would stifle tourism, I faced great limitations on obtaining information about violence and other forms of danger. However, just the same, I was able to allay some fears by getting close to national insiders. These relationships proved critical to improving my field acceptance and integration, and sometimes provided—indirectly and directly—information for making more realistic assessments of danger.

I continued throughout the research to address my safety concerns by being professional—in dress, in comportment, and in research. At the very least, by concentrating on information seeking I distracted myself from tacit threats. To attempt to manage ambient dangers, I modified my gendered behaviors to parallel expectations of the host culture, without totally negating my own identity as a Western feminist. In the end, while there was some national and local resistance to my research, and some situations in which I was personally vulnerable, I was received by Zanzibaris through multiple lenses and expectations. For instance, as a foreigner I was granted some exceptions to violations of Muslim cultural expectations for women: I could do many things that were considered "unfeminine." Such cultural exceptions, I believe, protected me from the negative assessments associated with local women's deviations from Muslim norms and values. In the end, being a Western woman—rather than a Western man—allowed me much fieldwork success and reduced (although did not eliminate) a number of field site dangers. As a woman, I was seen as nonpolitical, which may have allowed me to ask questions that a male researcher might not have been able to ask without being seen as politically and socially threatening. As a woman, I was seen as "spiritually flexible" and "malleable," allowing my adaptation to local customs to be seen as morally "fitting into," rather than culturally mocking, Zanzibari customs.

Finally, my "femaleness" called for male protection, which may have spared me from some forms of male violence. Yet it should be remembered that such protection was not unconditional. When accompanied by an American male ready to demonstrate his hegemonic Western male aggressiveness, local images of a female "needing protection" were neutralized. If my "protector male" did not respect Muslim customs, then my feminine flexible morality would surely be contaminated by his moral failings. This resulted in my being placed in danger. Ultimately, perhaps the biggest challenge to any research is protecting informants. As Giovannini (1986, 114) points out, researchers are social actors who affect the lives of those we study. We are ethically bound to recognize and take responsibility for research consequences. I could have created great danger for my informants if they had honestly and publicly answered some of my research questions. Within a political climate that silences questions about tourism and economic development, a person who even talks openly about these things could be placed in danger. I consistently tried, through concealing the identities of my informants and respecting boundaries of conversation, to protect my informants. In the end, we have much to learn from our dangerous field experiences: their ethical implications and outcomes, how we as outsiders perceive and understand field dangers ("etic" understanding), and whether and how field dangers are defined and understood by members of the "host" society and culture ("emic" understanding). As anthropologists, we may at times expose ourselves to dangers in the course of fieldwork, but we have a duty to do all that we can to refrain from placing our informants in danger.

NOTES

1. For an excellent discussion of the complexity of identity and Swahili culture see Mazrui and Shariff's 1994 *The Swahili: Idiom and Identity of an African People.*

2. Interestingly, this project was originally introduced to men, but by 2001 was totally dominated by female farmers. As one woman reported when asked, "Seaweed is for women; tourism is for men." This division of gender roles also, I believe, separates women somewhat from the disputes occurring over tourism.

3. These two ethno-religious groups make up only 1 percent of the Tanzanian mainland's population.

4. The Zanzibari elite has transformed the claim that its island has the "most pure" form of Swahili language into cultural capital. Zanzibar Town (Stone Town) has a successful international language program that generates substantial incomes for the few.

5. Identity in Zanzibar, which strongly focuses on unity through Islam, has been politically problematized by the Tanzanian government. Parkin (1995) has pointed out that what would have been labeled in 1964 a "bourgeois counter-revolution" is now labeled "Islamic fundamentalism," with the very label contributing to an oversimplified understanding of the island's situation (202). Zanzibar opposition party Secretary-General Seif Sharif Hamad has pointed out (March 2004) that the

Tanzanian government's ruling party has "used the war on ['Islamic fundamental-ist'] terrorism to repress its main political opponent."

6. My fictive aunt in Dar es Salaam tried to convince me to move my field site closer to Kilimanjaro, where I could study in her home village as part of her fam-ily. Because I had assisted her niece in gaining employment as an "au pair" for an American family, she felt responsible to look out for my well-being. Over and over my aunt repeated to me that I would be "slaughtered by Muslims" in Zanzibar. I knew her concern was genuine. I did not know how slanted her view as a mainland civil servant affected the validity of the threat to my safety. I assumed that her views, like my frantically e-mailing mother at home in the United States, were informed mainly by popular media, and mostly reflected an ethnocentric fear of the other and politically biased media.

7. Here, I would argue that Swahili gender ideology is constructed in such a way that the "feminine" is a stronger icon of Swahili culture than the "masculine." This creates an interesting challenge to Ortner's (1974) argument that men are viewed as closer to culture and women to nature in societies with gender asymmetries that favor men.

8. I have argued in my Tulane University Anthropology Department PhD dis-sertation that such beliefs have lead to increased food insecurity for women on the coast.

9. My attempts at adapting to Zanzibari norms were strongly affected by Zan-zibaris' increasing efforts to make their own culture impermeable to outsiders. Swahili people have a strong sense of identity, perhaps highlighted by their close contact with "polluting" foreign outsider "others." Zanzibaris who live in tour-ism areas, as with those who live in other kinds of "borderlands," experience a "cultural collision" with Western notions of decency. Many Zanzibaris respond by "attempting to block the culturally corrosive impact of [two sets of conflicting cul-tural norms] with a counter stance" that emphasizes Muslim Swahili values and norms (Anzaldua 1987). That is, through a "self-ascription" that certain cultural markers are nonnegotiable (Barth 1969), island people on creating overt signs or signals that play up certain cultural traits that help them construct and protect group identity boundaries.

10. During my 2001 field research I had observed a ZTV news team recruit foreigners to help in filming a staged story about how tourism was benefiting the island. At the very least, the Tanzanian government presumably saw no positive value in making public the violent demonstrations.

REFERENCES

Amnesty International. (1997). *Amnesty International Report 1997—Tanzania*. Avail-able at www.unhcr.org/refworld/docid/3ae6aa0568.html.

Abu-Lughod, L. (1986). *Veiled Sentiments: Honor and Poetry in a Bedouin Society*. Berkeley and Los Angeles: University of California Press.

Amory, Deborah. (1994). *The Politics of Identity on Zanzibar*. PhD diss., Stanford University.

Anzaldua, Gloria. (1987). *Borderlands/La Frontera: The New Mestiza.* San Francisco: Spinsters/Aunt Lute.

Barth, Fredrick. (1969). *Ethnic Groups and Boundaries: The Social Organization of Cultural Difference.* Boston: Little, Brown.

Boddy, Janice. (1989). *Wombs and Alien Spirits: Women, Men, and the Zar Cult in Northern Sudan.* Madison: University of Wisconsin Press.

Briggs, Jean. (1970). *Never in Anger: Portrait of an Eskimo Family.* Cambridge, MA: Harvard University Press.

Commonwealth OnLine. (1999). "The United Republic of Tanzania Index Page." Available at www.tcol.co.uk/tanz/tan.htm.

De Francisco, Christian. (2004). *Courting Modernity: Tradition, Globalization, and the Performance of Masculinity among the Papasi of Zanzibar.* PhD diss., Tulane University.

Demovic, Angela. (2007). *Negotiating Purity and Poverty: Tourism, Women's Economic Strategies and Changing Gender Roles in Rural Zanzibar.* PhD diss., Tulane University.

Fair, Laura. (2001). *Pastimes and Politics: Culture, Community, and Identity in Post-Abolition Urban Zanzibar, 1890–1945.* Athens: Ohio University Press.

Giovannini, Maureen J. (1986). "Female Anthropologist and Male Informant: Gender Conflict in a Sicilian Town." In *Self, Sex, and Gender in Cross-Cultural Fieldwork,* edited by T. L. Whitehead and M. E. Conaway, 103–16. Urbana: University of Illinois Press.

Hamad, Seif Sharif. (2004). Speech delivered to the United States State Department.

Hughes, Kirsty. (2003). "Zanzibar: In the Eye of the Storm." *Open Democracy,* September 10.

Krieger, L. (1986). "Negotiating Gender Role Expectations in Cairo." In *Self, Sex, and Gender in Cross-Cultural Fieldwork,* edited by T. L. Whitehead and M. E. Conaway, 117–28. Urbana: University of Illinois Press.

Mazrui, Alamin M., and Ibrahim Noor Shariff. (1994). *The Swahili: Idiom and Identity of an African People.* Trenton, NJ: Africa World Press.

Ngowi, Rodrique. (2001a). "Report: 16 Killed in Zanaibar." Associated Press Online, 27 January.

Ngowi, Rodrique. (2001b). "Heavy Gunfire Continues in Zanzibar." Associated Press Online, 28 January.

News Link Africa. (2001). Available at www.adlinkint-newslinkafri.com/feature.htm.

Ortner, Sherry B. (1974). "Is Female to Male as Nature Is to Culture?" In *Woman Culture and Society,* edited by Michelle Zimbalist Rosaldo and Louise Lamphere, 67–88. Stanford, CA: Stanford University Press.

Parkin, David. (1995). "Blank Banners and Islamic Consciousness in Zanzibar." In *Questions of Consciousness,* edited by Anthony P. Cohen and Nigel Rapport, 198–216. New York: Routledge.

Tannen, Deborah. (2001). *You Just Don't Understand: Women and Men in Conversation.* New York: Quill, Harper Collins.

———. (2002). *I Only Say This Because I Love You.* New York: Ballantine.

II

DANGER AND "SAFE SPACES"

5

Gendered Observations: Activism, Advocacy, and the Academy

Victoria Sanford[1]

> *Quítate el ropaje del pudor para decir con libertad y déjate guiar por el corazón.*

> —Grabe 2000, 12

This chapter is a meditation on the contradictions one confronts when conducting field research on violence and in ambient violence. How do ethics, scholarship, and the rights of communities collide? How do ethical obligations of the researcher shift in war zones and areas of ongoing conflict? How does this impact one's scholarship and one's own worldview? I begin at one of my beginnings with my personal experience working with Central American asylum seekers in the later 1980s during the U.S.–backed wars in Central America. The next beginning is with my master's research on the forced recruitment of Maya youth into the Guatemalan army. Here, I reflect on what it means to work with survivors who are both victims and victimizers. Next, I consider my field research on genocide in Guatemala, the relationship between researcher and survivor, how it feels to investigate crimes against humanity in ongoing ambient violence, and how one struggles to represent this type of research. I conclude this chapter with considerations about the different ways fieldwork on violence has affected me and also how it has carried me on to do new research in Colombia. I close with thoughts about the responsibility of academics conducting field research in violent places. These observations are gendered by my subject position as a woman who, borrowing words from my friend Michael Ondaatje, carries out research in war zones and writes about "a world normally depicted by men."[2]

"A TRUE WAR STORY IS NEVER MORAL"[3]

True war stories are full of contradictions for victims, survivors, perpetrators, bystanders, and, of course, for those of us who come along somewhere in the process to try to document and understand, whether as scholars or human rights activists. In *The Things They Carried*, Tim O'Brien writes, "You can tell a true war story if it embarrasses you. If you don't care for obscenity, you don't care for truth" (O'Brien 1990, 77). Since 1986 I have taken testimonies from survivors of the U.S.–backed wars of the 1980s in Central America. I began taking these testimonies for legal cases to represent Central American refugee claims for political asylum in the United States.[4] When I think back on those first testimonies, I remember feeling embarrassed by the intimacy of the stories. The very personal references that were used by our clients to affirm the "truth" of their testimonies: "I didn't want anyone to see the marks of what they had done. The private places they had shocked me. I couldn't make love with my wife." I was shocked by the violations of dignity that we were forced to carry out by a legal system that refused to believe that Central Americans might flee their country with "reasonable fear for their lives"—the reasonable fear that is internationally recognized and indeed codified into the U.S. legal system as grounds for political asylum. Violations of dignity such as photographing the torture scars on the man who had never even let his wife see them. Three times this man had been detained and tortured by state forces.

We went to court with photographs of his scars and even newspaper articles documenting his disappearance, reappearance, and hospitalization in El Salvador. As the arbiter of truth, the immigration judge found the testimony and evidence of torture to be "credible." We sighed with relief, but too soon. The judge then ruled that our client had no reasonable fear for his life because if the security forces had wanted him dead, they had three opportunities to kill him. Asylum denied, and the war story of our client continued as we searched for safe haven for him. We told his story to different churches and sanctuary houses until we found a church to sponsor him, post a $7,500 bond, and offer him safe (and illegal) haven while we awaited his appeal hearing. "You can tell a true war story if you just keep on telling it. . . . [A] true war story is never about war. . . . It's about love and memory. It's about sorrow . . . and people who never listen" (O'Brien 1990, 91).

THE CONTRADICTIONS OF SURVIVAL

Inspired by my mentor Philippe Bourgois's[5] field research in Central America and Spanish Harlem (Bourgois 1982, 1995), and encouraged by the possibilities of anthropological research presented in Carolyn Nordstrom's

Fieldwork Under Fire (1995), I began collecting testimonies of survival from young Maya men who were living as refugees in California.[6] It turned out that the young men defied the neat categories of victim and victimizer because though they were massacre survivors, they had also been forcibly recruited into the Guatemalan army and had themselves committed abuses during the internal armed conflict that became a genocide taking the lives of more than two hundred thousand Guatemalans.[7] I found it particularly difficult to listen to the stories of abuse, because these young men were my friends. We were friends before I began my master's research project. They were as protective of me as if I were their sister. I loved them as one loves a brother. Mateo was just eighteen years old and finishing high school in San Francisco. I was the co-*madrina* (godmother sponsor) for his prom. He would stare out the window as he recounted his life story to me. We met every Sunday for several months in an apartment belonging to a friend of mine, to avoid the interruptions of my family or his friends. Usually he would talk for two hours. Sometimes, he would talk for three or four hours. He would stand, staring out the window at the San Francisco Bay below as he described finding the mutilated body of his father in the mountains:

After the massacre in Pueblo Nuevo, we lived in the mountain. The army began to burn our homes and our people. They began to burn our animals. I cried because I saw our house burning. They destroyed all our crops. The corn, the beans, everything. They fired bullets. They threw grenades at my father's house. We were left with nothing. We returned to the jungle walking in a stream so we would leave no tracks for them to follow. The army killed my father in an ambush. He had gone to look for medicine because there were many sick people in our community. After the ambush, we all fled in different directions. It was two weeks before we could go back to look for my father.

I was very scared. I was nervous because I didn't know what it would be like to see my father dead. I was afraid from the moment we left. I felt like something bad was going to happen. The people were behind me, but I felt like I was being stalked. But I didn't say anything. I didn't say anything to my stepmother because she was nervous, too. When we arrived, I said, "This is my father's body."

He was in pieces and it made me very scared because I could see bits of his clothing and the things he had with him. Everything was in a path of blood. We didn't see his whole body. He was a puddle of blood. If his body had been more whole, I would have embraced my father. But all I could do was pick up the bones.

We had never seen anything like this. The people were watching to see if the army would come. So, we had to do everything in a hurry. There were frightening spirits there. There were haunted spirits there. Who knows if the spirit was devilish? I don't know. There was such fear there. There were flies and crows. There were hawks. They had been eating him. They had eaten a lot. The flies everywhere. The fear everywhere.

Many people died there. I lost my father. But really it was the children. I believe more little children died than adults. They died because of the cold and they died because they weren't well fed. The mothers didn't have any milk. So, they would give the baby water. Many died. Babies were born dead. Some were born alive, but in two weeks they would be dead. They did not have a great life. Every family lost some children. After my father was killed, I joined the guerrilla. I was a courier. I was eleven years old. (Sanford 2003d, 186–87)

After one year in the guerrilla, Mateo sought refuge in Mexico, where he stayed for two years until he returned to Guatemala. Though only fourteen years old, he was quickly recruited into the army-controlled civil patrols. Before his fifteenth birthday, he was recruited into the army. He described this experience:

Most of the recruits were indigenous, but there were also some ladino[8] students. There were five instructors and they were in charge. They would hit us. Everyday they punished us. The punishment is very harsh. Sometimes they would hang us tied up very tightly to the bed. They would leave us like that for fifteen minutes. Then we would do fifty push-ups. Then, we would go outside and lay on the ground. We had to roll to the other side and back until we vomited. Then they would line us up and go down punching us in the stomach and knocking the air out of us. But by then it didn't hurt so much because we didn't have any food left in our stomachs.

I never said that it hurt because if you said that it hurt they would hit you more. Our training was called the Tiger Course. They explained to us, "You have to complete this course to become a real man." They would say, "You have to know a lot. You can become an important officer. You can order other people. But now you have to suffer three months. If you don't obey the rules, you can die."

There were indigenous recruits who didn't know anything. They didn't know any Spanish; they only spoke their language. The majority of recruits were indigenous. Those who didn't know Spanish had to learn. There were some who only liked to speak their language. They were separated from each other. You could be beaten for not speaking Spanish. Sometimes you got beaten just for looking at someone or something.

There were three recruits who deserted. They were caught on the border because all their hair was shaved off. They were put into an underground jail [a pit]. Each day, water and garbage was thrown on them. They weren't given anything to eat. They were in there for almost a month. They were brought into our classroom all tied up as an example of what happened when you desert. They were kept in that cell for three more months. Then they had to start training all over again.

We were taught to use weapons and practiced with live munitions. Some of the recruits died in training from bullets and others died from bombs. In the third month, they taught us how to beat campesinos and how to capture them. We practiced on each other. They gave us our machine guns. They said,

"It is better than a girlfriend. The machine gun is a jewel." The truth is that it is a pure jewel.

One day, they asked us if we liked our meal. They told us we had eaten dog. I never thought that it was dog. Some people had stomachaches and others vomited. They fed us dog so that we wouldn't be afraid because it would have been impossible for us to withstand everything. I changed a lot after eating dog. I wasn't afraid anymore. I just hated. I hated my compañeros. After three months, I was a very different person. I felt like a soldier.

When I was a soldier, I went to villages. Once I had to interrogate a woman. The woman didn't tell me anything, but she had to respect me because I was a soldier of the government and I had a gun. There was an officer behind me, watching me. I had to do it right because if you don't they beat you and sometimes they kill you. I interrogated the woman. So did some other soldiers. They beat her and I did, too. Sometimes they tell us, "Go get this person and beat him." A man was denounced by his neighbor. We beat him. He said, "I am just a campesino. I dedicate myself to working in the fields and nothing more." The man began to cry in front of us. I had to have such a face. I had to keep a tough face in front of the others because I had my orders and I was obligated to complete them. The man never said anything. The officer sent him to the base and I didn't see what happened to him after that.

The sub-lieutenant would ask the campesinos, "What have you been doing? What have you seen?" The campesinos would respond with their civil patrol titles. The sub-lieutenant would then ask them what they had seen. When they would respond that they had seen nothing, he would contradict them. He would lie and say that he had been told that subversives had been to the village. Then, the poor people would regret their answer and tell the sub-lieutenant, "Yes, we did see that." The army wants the people to give information that is untrue. The only thing that matters is that people will say whatever the army wants them to say. (Sanford 2003d, 187–88)

One day I realized that after particularly rough testimony Mateo would always calmly shift his gaze from the window, look down at me, and ask, "Should I continue?" I discovered that as the testimony moved along, I shifted from sitting on the couch to lying on the floor and would sometimes find myself in a fetal position. On this day, I sat straight up and asked him, "What do you think of this crazy gringa lying on the floor like this when you are sharing your testimony?" Shrugging his shoulders, he responded: "I think you are listening. I know it is difficult. Should I continue?"

While I met with Mateo on Sundays, I met with Gaspar on Tuesday evenings at my house. When Gaspar heard that I was taking testimony from Mateo, he approached me and asked me if I would listen to his story. "My story is different and more complicated," he told me. Indeed, the childhood he recounted to me was so horrible that it made me anxious for him to get to the story of his recruitment because I felt that at least I was prepared for his experiences in the army because I knew what to expect. Still, out of respect and because prerecruitment experiences are extremely important to understanding individual experiences in the army, I listened carefully to his testimony of surviving a childhood of abuse. Gaspar told me:

My mother gave me to a finca owner when I was six. I cut coffee for several months until I could escape. I went back to my mother because when one is little, you always look for the warmth of a mother's love. I never had that. My stepfather would get home drunk and beat my mother, my little sister, and me. He was very strong. He would knock me across the room and tell us that we were garbage because we were Indians, but my mother never wanted to leave him. Instead, she would give us away to another finca.

Once I asked a finca owner for shoes. She told me that my mother told her I didn't like shoes. She threatened me a lot and beat me. They put my food on the floor inside the house where the dogs ate. I wasn't allowed to sit at the table.

I tried to kill myself because I felt that life wasn't good enough, it just wasn't worth it for me. There was a place, a lagoon of water contaminated by the plane that fumigated the cotton. I decided to bathe myself in the lagoon to see if I could die. But I wasn't lucky. Ever since then, I have thought it was bad luck and bad luck follows me. All I got was a rash.

Then, my sister and I went to live with my half-sister in Guatemala City. She told us we were Indians. She was very prejudiced because her last name was Juarez Santos. I have scars on my head from her beating me with burning sticks. She was trying to rid herself of rage. She beat us a lot. Sometimes, she would leave us tied up all day. Sometimes, she wouldn't let us in the house to sleep at night. She left us on the streets. I lived with her for three years and I tried to kill myself. I drank a toxic liquid but didn't get any results. I ran away from her.

I lived in the streets of Guatemala City and ate what I could find. I survived digging through garbage, begging, and stealing. I tried glue and paint thinner, but I didn't like it because it made me vomit. It is because of the way people look at you when you live on the streets. They never know the real feelings we have. Even living on the streets, I still felt I could be someone someday. But the people look at you and say you're lost, worthless, the scum of society. It was out of desperation that my friend Carlos put a rope around his neck. Afterwards, I tried the same thing, but had no luck.

Then, I went back to Mazatenango and got a job collecting garbage. I gave the money I earned to my mother to help her, but she gave it to my stepfather and he beat us. I collected garbage in the day and went to school at night. I wanted to learn and improve myself. But in the class, they laughed at me. They said I came from garbage, that garbage made me. People stopped calling me Gaspar. At school and in my neighborhood, they called me garbage man. Even the teacher called me garbage man.

When I would say my name, they would laugh at me because my surname is indigenous. I even changed my name for a while. But it made no difference, I was Indian because of my features and because that is who I am, whether or not I want to be. This created great conflict in me and I began to see a division between what is ladino and what is indigenous. I was humiliated so much that

I began to hate ladinos. The hatred was so strong that I wanted a weapon. I wanted to kill my half-sister. (Sanford 2003d, 182–83)

We would sit at the kitchen table drinking tea or coffee; sometimes Gaspar asked for a glass of wine. Gaspar always arrived at exactly 7:00 p.m., and when it got close to 10 o'clock we would wrap up the testimony with a conversation about local Maya organizing or his construction work to shift the tenor of our conversation back to daily life. I would feel wasted when he left. I would feel empty, emotionally spent. I would shower and often weep under the flow of warm water. I remember one night when I felt that perhaps I couldn't continue to listen to Gaspar's testimony—that I was too overwhelmed and that I was unprepared to be supportive of him—my husband said, "I don't know what you talk about with Gaspar, but he looks happier every time he leaves here." So I continued to fumble through this intense and intimate testimony. I felt relief when he began to tell me about his recruitment because it represented the end of his miserable childhood:

The army was always recruiting in the park, at the cinema, and anywhere else where young men congregated. I always got away. I was good at slipping away because I had lived on the streets. I saw that the world was made up of abusers and abused and I didn't want to be abused anymore. So, one day when I was sixteen, I let the army catch me. But they didn't really catch me, because I decided I wanted to be a soldier. I didn't want to be abused anymore.

I wanted a chance to get ahead. I saw what the soldiers did. I knew they killed people. But I wanted to see if in reality it could really be an option for me. If there would be an opportunity to get ahead, to learn to read and write. I always thought that it would be very beautiful to learn to read and write. I was always looking for a way to get ahead, to improve myself, but sometimes the doors just close and there is nowhere else to go. The army says we will learn to read and write, but when you go into the army, they teach you very little. They give you a weapon and they teach you to kill. They give you shoes because you don't have any. Many times, you join the army for a pair of shoes. When they grab you to recruit you, they say, "You don't have any shoes."

In the army, I was full of hate. I used the weapons with the hatred I had carried inside of me for a long time. Even though the hatred can be strong, you are still a human being with the spirit of your ancestors, with the spirit of peace and respect. So, inside you have great conflict. It was very difficult for me to find an internal emotional stability.

When I was recruited, there were a lot of indigenas recruited. They were beaten hard and called "stupid Indians" for not knowing how to speak Spanish. The soldiers who beat them were indigenous. The problem in the army is that no one trusts anyone else, even though most of the soldiers are indigenous.

After I was recruited, they told me that I could be a Kaibil[9] because I was tall, fast, and smart. But I wasn't so smart. They took us to the mountains. Each of us had to carry a live dog that was tied up over our shoulders. I was thirsty.

There was no water. Well, we had no water and we were given no water. But our trainer had water. He walked ahead of us on the path spilling water to remind us of our thirst. I was innocent. When we were ordered to pick up the stray dogs on the street, I thought we were going to learn how to train them, that we would have guard dogs. But when we arrived to the camp, we were ordered to kill them with our bare hands. We had to kill some chickens, too. We were ordered to butcher the chickens and dogs and put their meat and blood in a big bowl. Then, we had to eat and drink this dog and chicken meat that was in a bath of blood. Whoever vomited had to vomit into the shared bowl and get back in line to eat and drink more. We had to eat it all, including the vomit, until no one vomited.

The army kills part of your identity. They want to break you and make you a new man. A savage man. They inspired me to kill. There was a ladino recruit who said that Indians were worthless and that we didn't go to school because we didn't want to. I pushed him off a cliff. I would have enjoyed it if he had died. This is how the army creates monsters.

You become very hard in the mountains and sometimes the only thing you feel is fear. You are afraid of any man, or every man. After my first battle with the guerrilla, I decided to escape, because I wanted to improve myself and found no way to do it in the army. (Sanford 2003d, 183–84)

TRUTH AND "POISONOUS KNOWLEDGE"[10]

Gaspar expressed a deep commitment to truth about what had happened. Each time he came to my house, he would begin by saying, "I am going to tell you everything. I am going to tell the truth. It is inhuman, but I will tell you what they made us do." In his sharing of these memories, his stories were always powerful, descriptive. I could see the place where the violence happened. I could hear the pleas of those who were injured or killed. I could feel his disgust and hatred, and also the power he felt at the moment he carried out these atrocities. Sometimes he would shake as he told me of these experiences.

One evening, we had been speaking about violence in the Kaibiles. He had been talking about abuses and atrocities he had committed. We had been talking institutionalized violence and impunity: the systematic violation of rights of Guatemalan men and women, the massacres of villages, and the torture of civilians. But on this particular night, in the midst of a story, he averted his gaze and began to speak in the third person. It was a strange and convoluted story. It was after he fled the Kaibiles but was still in Guatemala. He was on a bus in Guatemala City and ran into another former Kaibil. They began to talk about their experiences as Kaibiles. This other Kaibil told him (on the bus) about working with the death squads in Guatemala City. Gaspar recounted:

They were given the name and address of a young woman—a subversive, or wife or daughter of a subversive. Their job was to stalk her and grab her, take her away to a desolate location where they would torture her and gang-rape her. Sometimes they mutilated the girl and left her for dead. Sometimes they cut off her breasts and mutilated her genitals. They never felt any pity for what they did because these girls were subversives, I don't know what they did.

"I don't know what they did." It is taped on a cassette and transcribed. It is also recorded in my memory. Gaspar didn't know what the girls did? Or what the death squads did? When he said, "I don't know what they did," he also startled himself because he had slipped back in to speaking in the first person. Though I knew as he told this convoluted story that he had not had this conversation on a bus in Guatemala City and that he was recounting something that in his mind was so important that it had to be recounted, if only in the third person, because it was too horrible for him to admit to me that he had done it—or perhaps even admit to himself. I myself was struggling to locate him. "I don't know what they did." "I don't know what they did." He was there when this was done. He helped grab the young women. He saw them raped. It wasn't until he said, "I don't know what they did" that I could also locate him as a perpetrator who felt no pity in the moment of committing a crime against humanity but as he tells the story admits in retrospect that he doesn't know what they did. Visibly shaken by telling me this story, Gaspar looked at me like a child who might just have been caught in a lie. "It comes down to gut instinct," writes Tim O'Brien. "A true war story, if truly told, makes the stomach believe" (1990, 84).

Despite my own revulsion and gut reaction that he was talking about himself and not some other Kaibil who told him a story on a bus, I felt protective of him. I felt pity for him. He was my friend. Each time he came to my house, he would spend a few minutes with my ninety-seven-year-old grandmother. He was a gentle man with aspirations of being an artist. He was also a key activist in the Guatemalan refugee community who would be absolutely ostracized if I shared this particular story with anyone—even as told in the third person—and Gaspar knew this as well. Forced recruitment, understood in the community. Pushing a racist ladino Kaibil off a cliff, understood. Forced participation in army maneuvers, mostly understood. Member of a death squad, absolutely not acceptable under any circumstances. This is the first time I write about this experience in the taking of his testimony that took place more than twelve years ago. And I only write it today because I know that Gaspar is no longer living in California and lives far away from the life he had in San Francisco in the early 1990s. Still, it must also be remembered that Gaspar, like so many others, gave his testimony so that it would be shared with a larger public. It was my decision, not his, to wait more than a decade to share this particular part of his testimony.

I asked Gaspar how his friend had felt about raping, mutilating, and disappearing these young women. He said, "The thing is that you cannot feel anything when you are a Kaibil or they kill you. He didn't feel anything. Well, I imagine that he didn't feel anything." He looked down at the table for a moment, then he looked me in the eyes and said, "I believe he must feel terrible about this now. I imagine that he lives and relives all of this evil. Even if you want to escape it, leave it behind and forget it, it comes to you in your dreams and you wake up sweating. Yes, I imagine he still suffers for what he did because it was wrong and he would know that now." I vomited when he left my house.

The following Sunday, Mateo continued to give his testimony. He was finishing up his time in the army. The next part of his testimony would be about walking from Guatemala to California and his experience as a fifteen-year-old undocumented refugee. In a certain way, this part of the testimony would be the "inspirational" part, because here was a valiant young man who had suffered through so much of the violence in Guatemala and whose life history seemed to embody Guatemala's history of violence and here he was finishing high school in San Francisco, California.

When I take testimonies, I explain at the very beginning that I am trying to understand the violence that happened in the person's life. I told Mateo I wanted to know about *La Violencia* in his life. How was his life before? How did the violence arrive in his community? What happened? I explained that I don't use real names and asked what pseudonym I should use. I explained that I wanted Mateo to tell me his story and that I would not interrupt him. I would write down my questions and wait until the end to ask new questions or clarify points he made.

Mateo had finished his testimony about his time in the army. So I began to follow up with small questions. I went from the small to the specific, then from his individual experience to more generalized patterns of military actions in communities. We began to discuss patterns of army abuse in villages. Though hesitant about becoming an interrogator, I felt I had to ask about the raping of women in attacks on villages. I said, "I have heard that it was a common army practice to gang-rape indigenous women during military actions in villages. Did this happen when you were patrolling villages?" Mateo looked cornered by my question. He took a deep breath, refocused his gaze out the window and responded, "I was very young. I didn't really understand what was going on. I didn't want to participate. I would hold them down while the other soldiers raped them." When I asked him what happened to these women after they were raped, without looking at me, he responded mechanically, "We shot them."

For both Mateo and Gaspar, fear and the desire for truth and justice emanated from the same past, and I never knew whether fear or the desire for truth and justice would weigh in more heavily on any given day. Each had been a victim of *La Violencia*. Each had also been a victimizer. Anthropologist Veena Das (2000) has suggested that "if one's way of being-with-others was brutally injured, then the past enters the present not necessarily as traumatic memory but as poisonous knowledge" (221). It was the unpredictability of this "poisonous knowledge" that shaped each day for Mateo and Gaspar. And after each testimony, I was left to sort out the meaning of this poisonous knowledge not only for my research and human rights in Guatemala, but for myself in my life and my own understanding of the world.

FIELD RESEARCH ON GENOCIDE

As an anthropology graduate student at Stanford University and a research consultant for the Guatemalan Forensic Anthropology Foundation, I took more than four hundred testimonies from Maya survivors of Guatemalan army massacres (see Sanford 2003d). I continued to take testimonies as I completed *Buried Secrets: Truth and Human Rights in Guatemala* (2003d) and *Violencia y Genocidio en Guatemala* (2003c). In the broad stroke, my work clearly shows the calculated and systematic way in which the Guatemalan army carried out three different phases of genocide against the Maya which led to 626 known massacres and more than 200,000 dead or disappeared.[11] One key to this genocide was the systematic incorporation of Maya men into Guatemalan army–controlled civil patrols (also known as PACs). For the majority rural Maya, participation in the PACs was required for personal and familial security and performed under duress. Even a 1990 U.S. State Department memo noted, "Credible reports say that those who refuse to serve in the civil patrols have suffered serious abuse, including death" (Jay 1990, 23). These PACs played a key role in local repression and massacres of neighboring communities.

In its comprehensive investigation, the CEH (Comisión para el Esclarecimiento Histórico—Commission for Historical Clarification [Guatemalan truth commission]) found that 18 percent of human rights violations were committed by civil patrols. Further, it noted that 85 percent of those violations committed by patrollers were carried out under army order.[12] It is not insignificant that the CEH found that one out of every ten human rights violations was carried out by a military commissioner and that, while these commissioners often led patrollers in acts of violence, 87 percent of the violations committed by commissioners were in collusion with the army.[13]

In 1995 there were 2,643 civil patrol units organized and led by the army. In August 1996, when the demobilization of civil patrols was begun, there were some 270,906 mostly Maya peasants registered in civil patrols.[14] This is significantly fewer than the 1 million men who were organized into civil patrols in 1981. Taking into account the population at the time and adjusting for gender and excluding children and elderly, this means that in 1981, one out of every two adult men in Guatemala was militarized into the army-led civil patrols.[15]

One afternoon, I was talking with a group of indigenous men in one of the communities where I had worked for several years. They were talking about their different experiences in the army, PAC, and guerrilla. I remember thinking to myself, *Every one of these men has carried weapons in this war and most likely used them.* The apparently simplistic life of small, rural villages is absolutely ruptured by the complexities of violence. Within communities, people know who did what, who gave up whom, who sacrificed someone else or even used the violence for personal enrichment—these are Holocaust historian Daniel Goldhagen's (1996, 67) "ordinary" citizens[16] who become "willing executioners." I stopped myself from imagining my friends with weapons, receiving orders that could not be refused.

Several days later, I went to a Maya *costumbre* (religious practice) with my translator. Throughout the *costumbre*, there is a sharing of *kuxa*—an extremely high alcohol content, home-brewed beverage. As the cup is passed around from person to person, prior to taking a drink, one offers a little *kuxa* to the heavens and little *kuxa* to the earth. As we entered the celebration site, my translator pointed out a local K'iche man. He said, "Victoria, don't drink out of the cup if he hands it to you. He was a bad man during *La Violencia* and I am certain that one day he will be poisoned at one of these *costumbres*. He has many enemies. That is why no one ever drinks out of the cup after him." And it was true, all the *kuxa* was always offered to the earth after he passed the cup.

THE RHYTHM OF MEMORY

There is a certain rhythm to the giving of testimony. It usually begins with mundane, everyday occurrences. The survivor remembers the security of the daily-ness of life's routine before violence erupted unbidden in his or her life. If the witness (or researcher) is engaged and actively listening when the survivor tells the prelude to violence, the survivor slips into the tale of violence. While sometimes seemingly far away from the witness, the survivor is always checking back in with the witness—making eye contact or directly asking for affirmation of witnessing, "It was crazy, right? Do you see it made no sense? We didn't understand what was happening; who could?" The survivor then continues on the path of memory and recounts the profound pain and immeasurable indignities of survival without losing contact with the scholar witness or activist witness. In *Framer Framed* (1992, 67) Trinh Minh-ha writes, "The witnesses go on living to bear witness to the unbearable." And yet survivors seek out those who will bear witness to their torture, loss, and survival. As Elaine Scarry (1985) notes: "[A]cts that restore the voice become not only a denunciation of the pain but almost a diminution of the pain, a partial reversal of the process of torture itself" (50). The taking of testimony teaches one to listen and to listen carefully. And this careful listening draws survivors to give testimony.

What do I mean by *careful listening draws survivors to give testimony*? I have given more than one hundred talks on my research in different academic and policy venues in the United States, Latin America, Europe, Asia, and South Africa. Whenever I have given a talk that is testimony-driven— heavily weighted by testimony—at the conclusion of the presentation, I have been approached by an audience member who waits until I am alone. "I wonder if you have a minute? I want to tell you something that I think you will understand." Thus, without seeking them out, I have been given testimonies of survival from Rwanda, Sri Lanka, Colombia, South Africa, Pakistan, Sudan, Israel, Palestine, Chile, Ecuador, Argentina, Vietnam, Cambodia, and Nepal, among others. Significantly, the testimonies have often been from individuals one might classify in human rights terms as both victims and victimizers. A Tamil Tiger from Sri Lanka, a former MK commander from South Africa, a former Israeli officer, a retired intelligence officer from Ecuador, a former member of a Guatemalan death squad. What does one do with these stories?

In her work on Argentina's Dirty War, Marguerite Feitlowitz (1998) makes clear that "testimony fulfills the sacred obligation to bear witness, and however discomfiting it may be for us, our pain, though great, is minor compared with that of the victims" (50). Still, sometimes, one no longer wants to hear. When I lived in Guatemala in 1996 and 1997 doing research on massacres, I used to flee from the villages because I felt I could not bear the weight of one more story. "Aren't you overwhelmed?" I asked Julia, my translator, after the fourteenth testimony on a particularly cold, damp day in Nebaj as I looked out at the line of survivors still waiting to give testimony. "Of course, Victoria," she responded. "But they want to talk and who else will listen?" And even when I fled to the city, I never left alone. Because I had a vehicle, I would give rides to people wanting to travel to Guatemala City. And because I lived in a spacious house with a partner who didn't mind if I filled it with my friends from the villages where I worked, I would also offer housing to my friends who ostensibly had some medical, legal, or bureaucratic item to attend to in the capital. But they didn't travel to Guatemala City to take care of such business; they traveled to my house in the capital because they wanted to keep talking, to continue giving testimonies of survival. It was not unusual for people to take buses (more than ten hours from Nebaj to Guatemala City at the time) to visit me in the capital in order to "add to my testimony because I remembered something else important."

I remember sitting at our dining room table in Guatemala City with my friend Magali as she recounted witnessing local officials participate in killing young men in the plaza of Nebaj. I was exhausted, physically and emotionally. We were having dinner. She was animated and speaking with great conviction. She stopped midsentence, "Victoria, where is your recorder? You need to write this down." We were close friends and I felt comfortable enough to say that I was tired. She told me not to worry and went upstairs to my office and brought me my recorder, some paper, and a pen. She set it all up. Then she continued with her story. Every now and again, she would say, "I think you should write this point down," and—obediently—I would.

At the exhumation in Acul in 1997, men and women traveled long distances to join us because they heard we were listening to their stories. I first noticed Doña María as a new face approaching the Acul women with whom I had been working. They pointed in my direction, nodding to her and to me. She came straight over to me, crossed her arms decisively, shyly looked down at her feet, abruptly raised her head, looked me straight in the eye, and said, "I walked here to give my testimony of *La Violencia*.[17] I am not from Acul. I do not have a relative in the grave, but what happened here happened in my village, too. It happened everywhere." I asked her why she came to Acul when many people were still afraid to speak. She told me that she had heard that there was a gringa listening to women. "I was a girl when it happened, but I am a woman now. I want to tell my story. Will you listen?"

RESEARCH IN AMBIENT VIOLENCE

In October 2000 I went to Colombia for the first time. In Bogotá I was invited to give a public talk about human rights in Guatemala at the Colombian Commission of Jurists. Among those attending my talk was a journalist. She approached me at the end and asked if I might be interested in meeting with a group of women who were former M-19 combatants and some of whom had been guerrilla commanders.[18] Fabulous. I told her I would be delighted. I met with the women and the journalist. The women spoke about their current political projects for peace in Colombia. Despite the double stigma of insurgency and the danger their armed participation presented to traditional patriarchal structures, many demobilized M-19 women combatants today dedicate their lives to peacemaking in Colombia. At one point as these former combatants shared their contemporary struggles for peace and human rights, the journalist said, "But this is very dangerous because they are still killing demobilized M-19. They could kill you for doing this and especially knowing who you are." La Negra[19] responded, "Yes, they could kill me. I was willing to die for the revolution and now I am willing to die for peace. The only difference is that now I am not armed."

Out of this group meeting came a packed schedule of individual meetings with these former combatants who wanted to give testimony about their life experiences. Moreover, these women wanted to come back for second and third meetings to continue talking. Dora brought a recorder so that she could also tape her testimony. In 1998 former M-19 commander Maria Eugenia Vasquez Perdomo received the Premio Nacional de Testimonio (National Award for Testimony) for her autobiography *Escrito para no morir—Bitácora de una militancia* that was published by the Ministry of Culture in 2000. Former M-19 commander Vera Grabe published her critically acclaimed memoir *Razones de Vida* (2000) that same year. Grabe's memoir takes the form of a letter to her daughter, born during Grabe's militancy in M-19. Grabe writes: "[T]he heart guides with wisdom and leads to explanations and nuances. And as the poets and *boleros* say: if you know how to listen, you won't be fooled." She explains that she takes the risk of writing this memoir out of "love for the friends who didn't worry about writing their life stories because they risked and lost their lives for us." She writes, "For love of those things that make life worth living."[20] Vasquez Perdomo (2000) writes: "When a person narrates her life and others listen to her or read her life, the protagonist feels like she exists: she feels. If only for this reason, this is enough for me to begin" (13). The critical and popular success of these two memoirs in Colombia indicates that just as survivors and protagonists want to share their testimonies, there is a public anxious to listen and read about these experiences.

FEAR AND SORROW

Fear

People often ask me if I am afraid when I do my field research. The truth is complicated. Was I afraid in Guatemala? No, but I also took Asha—a protection-trained German shepherd—with me for my field research working alongside the Guatemalan Forensic Anthropology Foundation. I first began working with them in Guatemala during the third exhumation in the country in 1994, before the peace accords were signed between the Guatemalan army and guerrillas, before the United Nations Mission in Guatemala (MINUGUA) was started, before the demobilization of the civil patrols, before international NGOs were on the scene. The *forenses*, as locals referred to the forensic anthropologists conducting exhumations of clandestine cemeteries of massacre victims, referred to Asha as my secret weapon because the *campesinos* in rural villages would approach me with curiosity about this apparently docile creature. Forensic team members called her my "secret weapon" because rural Maya peasants were fascinated by her size and apparent docility. They would ask how I trained the coyote. I would explain that she is a German shepherd, not a coyote, and that there are breeds of dogs, just as there are breeds of chickens. Inevitably, it would be collectively agreed in Ixil, Achi, K'iche', or K'ekchi that Asha is a coyote and that I don't know it because I am a gringa.[21] Maybe because I had the dog, I was never afraid. Or maybe I felt a bit safer and that at least with Asha I would have warning if someone approached in the night. Perhaps I was in denial. Or perhaps my fear was simply overwhelmed by other emotions. In Guatemala, more than fear, I felt sorrow. I lived in sorrow taking testimonies from survivors.

The Acul massacre was but one of seventy-nine massacres carried out in the department of El Quiché in 1981. These massacres and others like them were a part of the Guatemalan army's first campaign of genocide against the Maya.[22] Describing the aftermath of the army massacre when fathers were forced to bury their massacred sons, Don Sebastián said, "It fills my heart with sorrow." He recounted, "Then [after the massacre], they asked us, 'What have you observed here? What is it that you have seen?' We did not answer them because we knew that they had killed our sons. We just didn't respond." The soldiers did. They said, "You don't answer us because you don't take good care of your sons. These sons of yours are involved with the guerrilla. That's why you don't answer us. Now, you've seen the dead. You have to return to your homes. You must go tranquil. Go home and eat, relax, and sleep. Don't do anything. You have done good work here. Go home. Go home tranquil."

Sorrow

Don Sebastián was sobbing; he nearly shouted, "But we are not tranquil. We are sad. We went home, but we didn't eat. We are crying. We are not content because we know what they have done. They have killed our sons. I couldn't eat for more than a month." He doubles over, burying his face in his hands between his knees. Still rocking his body, his sobs dwindle to whispers. I turn off my tape recorder. Without a word, Julia and I stand, then crouch, on either side of Don Sebastián. We half embrace him, half caress his back. I can feel each rib, each vertebrae. He is so thin. Powerlessly, I whisper, *"Lo siento"* (I am sorry). Julia says, *"No es justo. Sufrímos mucho. Todos sufrímos"* (It is not just. We suffered a lot. We all suffered). He lifts his head out of his hands. His hard, callused hands pat our arms. He gains composure as he comforts us. "I am still not finished," he says, almost in apology. "There is still more. I want to tell more" (Sanford 2003d, 93–94).

In my writing, I struggled to come to terms with these kinds of experiences. In *Buried Secrets*, I wrote:

> Indeed, in the frenetic escalation of painful memories, there is always more. It seems each time, when I thought we had reached the final ebb, when I felt overwhelmed with their memories of terror, when there just could not possibly be more horror that a human being could suffer and endure, these new friends who accepted me as their confidante would say, "There is more." For the outsider seeking to understand *La Violencia*, the trick is to assume nothing. One must accept the survivor as the guide through the labyrinth of terror. Embrace the path of the memory and allow the survivor to carry it to closure. Even if the path to closure is far beyond the untested limits of one's imagination (2003d, 94).

Laurence Langer (1991) has written extensively about the relationship between the witness and the person giving testimony. His work studying Holocaust survivor testimonies on video revealed a number of interviewer/ witnesses who sought to curtail continued testimony when it became discomfiting for the interviewer or failed to meet the interviewer's expectation of "heroic memory." Dominick LaCapra's (2001, 78) work on witnessing, trauma, and history indicates that a type of transference takes place between the interviewer/witness and the survivor. He concludes that the form this transference takes has much to do with interpretation. LaCapra also suggests that for the study of trauma, it is essential for the researcher to acknowledge this transference because failure to do so has serious, and perhaps unintended, consequences in one's continued research and analysis.[23] In many ways, writing *Buried Secrets* was a meditation upon this transference. And it is a meditation that continues as I take up new projects and expand upon previous projects in Guatemala while pursuing new, comparative projects in Colombia. As writing is always a temporal and provisional project, I sometimes think of new and different ways I would frame my own presence in *Buried Secrets*. If I were to write *Buried Secrets* now, here is how I would begin the book:

> I came back from Guatemala with *susto*. What is *susto*? you ask. The direct translation is scare or fright. But *susto* is really something deeper and far more profound. It is a malady understood in Maya communities and pondered by anthropologists and those who study "folklore." But *susto* is real. People die from susto. For many Maya (and rural ladinos as well) to die from *susto* is to die from a reconfiguration of the individual body and soul, which cannot bear the weight of fear and sorrow in the physical and spiritual realms.

For me, the *susto* was physical and spiritual. Borrowing from Don Sebastian's testimony, my heart was filled with sorrow. In Western terms, you might want to call it secondary trauma or post-traumatic stress disorder. But after having struggled for two years following my field research to work it out of my body and soul, I think *susto* is a better description of the effect my field research had on me. *Buried Secrets* was my therapy, my exit, my act of bearing witness, the fulfillment of my sacred obligation to those who entrusted me with their testimonies. So I have always felt a little perplexed when people have asked me if I was afraid, because I never really felt fear for myself in Guatemala. Those with reason to be afraid have always been the courageous *campesinos* (peasants) in isolated villages that continue to risk their lives for truth and justice.

NEW GEOGRAPHIES OF VIOLENCE

In a random encounter with a local peace activist who lives in a paramilitary-dominated barrio in Colombia, we had a conversation about forced recruitment of youth by the FARC (Fuerzas Armadas Revolucionarios de Colombia/Revolutionary Armed Forces of Colombia) and the paramilitaries. "You are going to write a book about this, right?" he asked. I told him I was writing articles and would write a book in the future. He said, "It would be useful to talk to a paramilitary youth, no?" "Of course," I responded. "But I can't really go around announcing that I want to write a book and would like to interview paramilitary youth about their experiences. That would cause some problems." He then told me that his best friend in the barrio—his best friend since he was nine years old—had just recently joined the paramilitaries. He had been in the paramilitaries for three months and was home on his first leave. His friend was still *de confianza*. Jonathan thought he might be able to ask him to meet with me. Would I be interested? It would all be clandestine. They would come to my hotel room. So that our conversation would not be overheard, we would put the air conditioner on full blast as well as the television while we talked. I trusted this peace activist, so I agreed to interview his friend if the meeting could be arranged.

When they came to the hotel, the woman at the reception desk called with a very serious voice. Instead of the usual courteous announcement that "Señor so and so is here to see you," she said in a very ominous voice, "They have come for you." When I went downstairs to meet the peace activist and the paramilitary, she motioned with her eyes that I shouldn't take them upstairs to my room. But this is a paramilitary-dominated town, so when I smiled at her as we went upstairs, she simply shook her head and returned to her work. The paramilitary, Marlon, was nineteen years old.[24] He had the close-shaven hair and wore the fitted jeans and polo-type shirt that is the out-of-uniform uniform of the paramilitaries. He was tall, slender, muscular, and handsome. He entered my hotel room cautiously. I noticed that he checked the empty bathroom as we walked by it. The room was small, with two twin beds. They sat on one and I sat on the other, across from them. Jonathan explained that this was a confidential meeting and that whatever was said would not be attributed to Marlon's real name and that Marlon would not tell anyone about the meeting either—thus making it clear that it was a dangerous meeting for all present. I asked if I could tape-record the meeting. Marlon agreed, but was then somewhat hesitant to speak. "I haven't really talked about this with anyone. I don't know where to start. Why don't you ask me some questions?" he suggested. I asked him how the paramilitaries recruit in the barrios: "It's not as if they have posters up inviting you to join them," I said. "Yes, they do have posters all over the barrio," responded Marlon. "There is one with a really beautiful girl paramilitary. The paramilitaries can have whatever girls they want." Marlon explained how the paramilitaries recruit and how he joined. Then, he explained his "job" as a paramilitary:

I had no opportunities until one day a friend of mine said, "Come on, let's go join them." As soon as we got there, they gave us camouflage uniforms, rifles, new guns, and other equipment. Those who had no army training went into training. We had been in the army so we went right into operations, which means we went to the mountain to fight the enemy. Who is the enemy? In vulgar terms, the guerrilla. We are enemies, we are in conflict. We are also on the margin of the law. We were taken by helicopter and we began to look for the guerrilla. We started looking in every way among the campesinos (peasants). The campesinos help the guerrilla, so sometimes we have to grab them. Grab them means to kill them. We would ask them if they had seen the guerrilla. First, they say, "no." But then they see that we are going to grab them and torture them, so they say, "yes." And then we have to kill them. They have to respect us because we wear the symbol that says A-U-C: Autodefensas Unidas de Colombia.

When we kill a campesino, it is because there are really few displaced people. What there are [among the displaced] are a lot of guerrilla infiltrators who are very astute and intelligent. When the people know we are coming, they flee; they abandon their communities. We think they do this because they are working with the enemy and they are afraid we will do something to them when we catch them. (Monedto, p. 142)

We have two kinds of helicopters that back up our platoon. They arrive with help and this gives us a lot of support. There is a small helicopter that we call the cricket and large one we call the papaya. Sometimes innocent civilians die because there are some zones that have a lot of guerrilla. Where we work, we are the police because for the people there, it is normal to work with the guerrilla. There may be only 12 police and 1,500 guerrilla in the zone. So, when we arrive, if someone tells us that these people are guerrilla collaborators, then we have to eliminate them. Once, some campesinos told some others when we got to their community. We didn't want the guerrilla to know that we were there, so we had to kill them with machetes, chop them up piece by piece, and bury them. (Sanford 2003a, 3–4)

When the autodefensas (AUC) kill a campesino that lives in a village, it is because we have been given information that this person is guerrilla and that is why we have to eliminate him. But we always say, "nada debe, nada teme" (one who owes nothing, fears nothing). We don't kill anyone without authorization. . . . Sometimes it was painful for me when we got to a town and the civilians would be praying, because I have my family. But they give you an order and you have to carry it out; there is nothing else you can do. I am a patroller and surely, when a commander tells a patroller "kill this civilian," I really cannot ask him why. No, I simply have to do what he tells me to do. And if a higher up patron asks me, "And you, why did you kill this civilian?" Then, I just tell him, "Because my commander ordered me." Then, he can work it out with my commander. So, I just have to follow orders. Because one goes there to kill or one is killed, right?

The AUC has a lot of people because we are everywhere in Colombia. There are people from outside who are not Colombian; I imagine this is because the AUC is just so big. Human rights are a problem because we can't grab 30 people and kill them all at once because that would be a massacre. We are being squeezed by human rights. Now we can't massacre everyone; we have to kill them one by one, one by one. This is a war that Carlos Castaño announced and it is not over. This is a civil war. This is a war without end. If you make a mistake, you pay with your life. I do not wish this work on anyone.[25]

One of the big differences for me listening to Marlon's testimony was that, unlike Mateo and Gaspar's testimonies of abuses, Marlon was talking about atrocities that he had committed just ten days earlier and would continue to do when his leave ended the following week. I couldn't believe he was telling me these stories. Then I realized that he was talking as if I wasn't even there, as if Jonathan wasn't even there. He was verbalizing his experience for the first time. He was processing his own "poisonous knowledge."

FINAL THOUGHTS

As an anthropologist in the field, Marlon's experience is not the lens through which I see Colombia; it is a point of epiphany. It is a naked encounter with humanity's dark side. In fact, it seems to me that the practice of fieldwork is a spiritual experience with nakedness, where the disciplined "normal" becomes out of place and thus challenges the anthropologist (or anyone else in the field) to begin to peel the onion—that is, to begin to make sense of one's own self and the many daily acts and interpretations that customarily guide one through daily life. Fieldwork displaces structures of understanding and disorients trajectories of meaning.

In her film and book *Framer Framed* (1992), Trinh Minh-ha says/writes on and about truth: "Being truthful: being in the in-between of all definitions of truth" (13); "Reality and Truth: neither relative nor absolute" (25); "Interview: an antiquated device of documentary. Truth is selected, renewed, displaced and speech is always tactical" (73); "Of course, the image can neither prove what it says nor why it is worth saying it; the impotence of proofs, the impossibility of a single truth in witnessing, remembering, recording, rereading" (83). Trinh's interrogation of truth touches off much of what I believe is problematic in representation on the intellectual level, but also on the emotional level. For me, this is finding internal balance, rather than shutting down, as I dig and pull bones out of the mass graves before the relatives of victims, witness the sixteenth testimony of survival of the day or listen to a nineteen-year-old paramilitary confess his fears of death without acknowledging the fears of those he kills and tortures.

Trinh's "in-between" space is a place for recognition of my own limitations and contradictions even when I cannot name them; somehow keeping sight of the tactics of my own research and agenda, and not forgetting that others have their own. Sometimes, as in the case of the Marlon's, Mateo's, or Gaspar's experiences, it is easier to fill in the outline of my own agenda than it is to recognize that while I might very well be able to demonstrate the validity of my hypothesis, that this hypothesis may very well have little to do with the daily lives and needs of the communities in which I work—perhaps that is another of the "in-between of all definitions of truth." Of course, it is wholly paternalistic and/or naive to believe that those who provide information do not also have their own agendas. It is not, however, an attempt to somehow measure the sincerity or honesty of those interviewed; nor is it a relativistic position.

The hidden frame for many discussions about truth in fieldwork, particularly with indigenous populations, is the underlying assumption of the "noble savage." This was the case when on one occasion in Guatemala when Padre Luis told me that the Achi Maya do not desire revenge (which they collectively told me they did when I asked the surviving men of the Plan de Sanchez massacre what they wanted from the exhumation of massacre victims). A leader of an international human rights mission in Guatemala once commented, "The problem with these people is that they aren't yet civilized." In Colombia, an international human rights worker told me that Black Colombians lacked sexual morality, while a U.S. academic commented on the "predatory sexuality" she sensed when talking with Black Colombian youth. The hidden frame behind these comments is infused with racism and also assumes the "wily Indian," "unpredictable savage," or "sexual deviant" stereotype when an indigenous Guatemalan or Black Colombian shares an experience that somehow counters the "respected authority." Thus, the indigenous Guatemalan or Black Colombian is "suspect" and must be lying, laying a trap, or has been duped by the "bad guys" and therefore is not authentic because the experts and/or the outside anthropologist better know who truly represents the Guatemalan Maya or Afro-Colombian communities, their hidden desires, and what "these people need."

How can an outsider ever hope to understand, much less convey, a level of terror so great that neighbors massacre neighbors and the exhuming of skeletal remains feels like a celebration of peace, a resurrection of faith, an excavation of the heart, an act of love? In such circumstances, it is easy to romanticize the Maya and Afro-Colombian communities and cultures as "other," as "exotic," as somehow having a different level of tolerance in the face of violence based on cultural difference and hundreds of years of structural marginalization. One of the women interviewed in the video *Surname Vietnam* said, "[T]o glorify us is, in a way, to deny our human limits" (Trinh 1992, 72). It seems that oftentimes, in attempts to encapsulate a culture, anthropologists seek to categorize and compartmentalize, rather than problematize, experience. This is particularly dangerous when one seeks to reveal truths about violence and survival, for it is a slippery slope to reifying survival, difference, and terror, and thereby eliminating all possibilities for understanding (see Sanford and Angel-Ajani 2006). Advocacy and activism, if not the initial impetus for research in war zones, are its inevitable outcome when one achieves an understanding of the lived experience of violence and survival. It is not uncommon within the academy for lived experience to be dismissed as unscientific or not relevant to real, objective scholarship. This is completely backwards because it is the academy that needs to be relevant to the reality of lived experience. Advocacy and activism do not diminish the validity of one's scholarly research. On the contrary, activist scholarship reminds us that all research is inherently political—even, and perhaps especially, that scholarship presented under the guise of "objectivity," which is really no more than a veiled defense of the status quo.

NOTES

1. Victoria Sanford is associate professor of anthropology at Lehman College and the Graduate Center, City University of New York. The author thanks Roberta Culbertson, Asale Angel-Ajani, Lotti Silber, Jose Palafox, Monique Skidmore, Philippe Bourgois, and Shannon Speed for their insightful comments on activism and the academy. Support from the Institute on Violence and Survival at the Virginia Foundation for the Humanities and a U.S. Institute for Peace grant gave me the time to write this chapter. Thanks always to Raul Figueroa Sarti and Valentina for unconditional support. Special thanks to Martha Huggins for including me in this fabulous project. All opinions and any errors are mine alone.

2. Michael Ondaatje, endorsement of *Buried Secrets*, jacket cover, 2003. See also Ondaatje 2000.

3. O'Brien 1990, 76

4. I was the founding director of Oakdale Legal Assistance, a refugee legal program providing free legal services to asylum seekers and refugees from Central America.

5. Philippe Bourgois has been my adviser and mentor since I was a master's student at San Francisco State University. Carolyn Nordstrom (1995, 2004) also became a role model and mentor early in my career. I first called her at Philippe's suggestion. It was the day before she left for Mozambique for one year. She spent more than an hour talking with me about my impending field research in Guatemala and sharing her field experiences. She continues to be an inspiration.

6. All names used here are pseudonyms.

7. See Comisión para el Esclarecimiento Histórico (CEH) 1999.

8. *Ladino* is a term used to connote the non-Maya in Guatemala.

9. Kaibiles are the elite fighting forces of the Guatemalan army.

10. See Veena Das (2000) for this term.

11. See CEH 1999.

12. CEH 1999, vol. 2, 226–27.

13. CEH 1999, vol. 2, 181.

14. CEH 1999, vol. 2, 234.

15. CEH 1999, vol. 2, 226–27.

16. See also Browning 1992.

17. *La Violencia* is the term people use in Guatemala to refer to the time of the genocide.

18. M-19 (Movimiento 19 de abril) was a popular armed insurgent movement that began in the 1970s and disarmed after signing peace accords in March 1990.

19. La Negra is a nickname.

20. Grabe 2000, 12.

21. The word *gringo/a* is used, often contemptuously, to refer to North Americans from the United States. It can also be used as a term of endearment or to connote innocence or inexperience with life in rural communities. Thus, it is used to explain why the gringa doesn't know she has a coyote, can't cross the river or scale the cliff very quickly, makes tortillas like a child, and can't wring water out of her jeans or towels when hand-washing in the river, but can four-wheel drive.

22. For more on genocide in Guatemala, see *Buried Secrets* (2003d) and *Violencia y Genocidio en Guatemala* (2003c).

23. See also LaCapra 1998.

24. Marlon is a pseudonym.

25. On Colombian Peace Comunities, see Sanford 2004b. See also Sanford 2003b, 2.

REFERENCES

Bourgois, Philippe. 1982. "What US Foreign Policy Faces in Rural El Salvador: An Eyewitness Account." *Monthly Review* 34, no. 1, 14–30.

———. (1995). *In Search of Respect: Selling Crack in El Barrio*. New York: Cambridge University Press.

Browning, Christopher. (1992). *Ordinary Men—Reserve Battalion 101 and the Final Solution*. New York: Harper Perennial.

Comisión para el Esclarecimiento Histórico (CEH). (1999). *Guatemala Memoria del Silencio*, vols. 1–12. Guatemala City, Guatemala: CEH.

Das, Veena. (2000). "The Act of Witnessing—Violence, Poisonous Knowledge and Subjectivity." In *Violence and Subjectivity*, edited by Veena Das, Arthur Kleinman, Mamphela Ramphele, and Pamela Reynolds. Berkeley and Los Angeles: University of California Press.

Feitlowitz, Marguerite. (1998). *A Lexicon of Terror: Argentina and the Legacies of Torture*. New York: Oxford University Press.

Goldhagen, Daniel. (1996). *Hitler's Willing Executioners*. New York: Knopf.

Grabe, Vera. (2000). *Razones de Vida*. Bogotá, Colombia: Planeta.

Jay, Alice. (1990). *Persecution by Proxy: The Civil Patrols of Guatemala*. Washington, DC: Robert F. Kennedy Center for Human Rights.

LaCapra, Dominick. (1998). *History and Memory after Auschwitz*. Ithaca, NY: Cornell University Press.

———. (2001). *Writing History, Writing Trauma*. Baltimore: Johns Hopkins University Press.

Langer, Laurence. (1991). *Holocaust Testimonies—The Ruins of Memory*. New Haven, CT: Yale University Press

Nordstrom, Carolyn. (1995). *Fieldwork Under Fire: Contemporary Studies of Violence and Survival*. Berkeley and Los Angeles: University of California Press.

———. (2004). *Shadows of War: Violence, Power and International Profiteering in the 21st Century*. Berkeley and Los Angeles: University of California Press.

O'Brien, Tim. (1990). *The Things They Carried*. Boston: Houghton Mifflin.

Ondaatje, Michael. (2000). *Anil's Ghost*. New York: Vintage Books.

Sanford, Victoria. (2003a). "Learning to Kill by Proxy: Colombian Paramilitaries and the Legacy of Central American Death Squads, Contras and Civil Patrols." *Journal of Social Justice* 30, no. 3.

———. (2003b). "Peacebuilding in the War Zone: The Case of Colombian Peace Communities." *International Journal of Peacekeeping* 1.

———. (2003c). *Violencia y Genocidio en Guatemala*. Guatemala City, Guatemala: F&G Editores.

———. (2003d). *Buried Secrets: Truth and Human Rights in Guatemala*. New York: Palgrave/Macmillan.

———. (2004). "Contesting Displacement in Colombia: Citizenship and State Sovereignty at the Margins." In *Anthropology in the Margins of the State*, edited by Veena Das and Deborah Poole. Santa Fe: School of American Research.

Sanford, Victoria, and Asale Angel-Ajani. (2006). "Excavations of the Heart: Reflections on Truth, Memory and Structures of Understanding." In *Engaged Observer: Anthropology, Advocacy and Activism*, edited by Victoria Sanford and Asale Angel-Ajani. New Brunswick, NJ: Rutgers University Press.

Scarry, Elaine. (1985). *The Body in Pain: The Making and Remaking of the World*. New York: Oxford University Press.

Trinh Minh-Ha. (1992). *Framer Framed*. New York: Routledge.

Vasquez Perdomo, Maria Eugenia. (2000). *Escrito para no morir—Bitácora de una militancia*. Bogotá, Colombia: Ministerio de Cultura.

6

Human Rights in East Timor: Advocacy and Ethics in the Field

Lynn Fredriksson

> We knew from the south zone that the Indonesians had dropped four napalm bombs there. Then they dropped two of these on us. I saw all the flames and heard people shouting and screaming. Some of us set out straight away to help those people. . . . There was nothing but ash and burnt rocks in the whole area, but we had heard those people screaming.[1]

This chapter is grounded in my experience as interviewer, observer, and witness[2] in East Timor, first in 1997 when East Timor was under Indonesian occupation, then in 2000 when it was newly freed from Indonesian occupation, and in 2002 when Timor Leste had become an independent nation. Using intersections of my own biography and East Timor's recent history, I have divided this chapter into five parts and a conclusion. The chapter's first four sections chronicle my work in the field within East Timor's changing international status—"Situating Researcher and Place," "East Timor and Research under Occupation—1997," "East Timor Immediate Postoccupation—2001," and "Timor Leste: Academic as Researcher in Independent Nation—2002." The chapter's fifth section, "Deconstructing Fieldwork Ethics," and its conclusion, "The Choices We Make," revisit the ethical and personal dilemmas and issues identified throughout this chapter—subterfuge, safety, "seduction," taking sides (or not), and managing the emotional "scars" of violence. Dilemmas and dangers assumed different forms at each intersection of my biography and East Timor's recent history. For example, when I was conducting collaborative human rights research in East Timor (1997 and 2000), many dilemmas were associated with guaranteeing my own safety and the safety of my human rights colleagues and informants. Other challenges were associated with secrecy. Still others revolved around not whether or not to take a political position in the situation, since I had entered the field doing so, but rather *when* to do so privately and when publicly. I had not expected to learn that the victims of each "side" could not be easily categorized as "bad" or "good."

In 2002, when I was alone in the field as a doctoral dissertator bound to carry out research as a "scientifically detached observer," I encountered some of the previously identified challenges and a set of new ethical and personal ones, including my own and my academic advisers' inability to cast off completely my professional human rights role. I was told by academic advisers that human rights advocacy clashed with the U.S. academy's ethical and scientific guidelines for research. I was therefore situated within a power dynamic involving myself—a student—and the academic faculty who controlled the definition and course of my field research. My human rights research was seen as "biased" and lacking "academic credibility." I had to negotiate such judgments before and during my field research. In the field, I found it difficult to achieve "scientific detachment" in a country where I had worked as a human rights advocate.

In the post-fieldwork period I struggled with questions about how to explain and narrate for academic readers what I had learned in the field. During the process of analyzing and writing up my findings, I was concerned about advisers' questions about the academic "value" of "data" from professional human rights research and by questions of my own about how to interpret and present informant experiences and voices while preserving informant confidentiality. I wondered whether and how to narrate my emotional responses to the field: Would these important aspects of fieldwork be considered of value in an academic article? Recognizing that such ethical, epistemological, and presentational dilemmas were both field site–specific—in East Timor at three points in the country's political history—and organizationally situated—in my roles as human rights researcher and advocate, later as presumably "detached scientific" researcher—I begin this chapter by introducing East Timor.

SITUATING RESEARCHER AND PLACE

A small Portuguese- and Tetum-speaking nation, East Timor is positioned on the eastern part of an island (which also includes Indonesian West Timor), located in the Indonesian archipelago between Australia and the Indian Ocean. For some 450 years the small half-island nation of East Timor was a Portuguese colony under a form of rule often characterized as "benign neglect." After the Portuguese dictatorship fell in 1974, the new

Portuguese government let go its colonies. The Indonesian government, which had not pursued East Timor since its own liberation from the Dutch, suddenly laid claim, fomenting internal dissent and besieging East Timor. A civil war of three weeks' duration ensued in East Timor, with the Timorese political party that supported national independence emerging as victor. On November 29, 1975, East Timor declared itself an independent nation. Unable to accept this, Indonesia's General Suharto bombarded East Timor by air, land, and sea, killing thousands within days and tens of thousands within several months. Although the United Nations responded with Security Council and General Assembly resolutions condemning Indonesia's invasion and calling for its immediate withdrawal from East Timor, no international action was taken. Indonesia was considered too valuable, East Timor expendable.

Indonesian armed forces brutally occupied East Timor between 1975 and 1999, a twenty-four-year period during which Indonesian authorities systematically used rape, sexual imprisonment, beatings, torture, disappearance, and extrajudicial execution to break the back of East Timor's resistance.[3] This international tragedy went largely unacknowledged until November 12, 1991, when a young man named Sebastião Gomez was memorialized in Dili, East Timor's capital, at a small Catholic chapel facing out to sea. At the subsequent funeral procession to Dili's Santa Cruz Cemetery, more than 270 nonviolent protestors were shot dead by Indonesian forces.[4] This major Timorese demonstration, unlike so many before it, reached the eyes and ears of the international community.

My friend Constâncio Pinto, now posted in Washington, D.C. as Chargé d'Affaires Counselor for Timor Leste (the country's name as an independent state), had been one of the student organizers of what has come to be known as "the Santa Cruz Massacre." It was due to the courageous actions of activists like Constâncio, and my own sense of complicity as a U.S. citizen,[5] that I made my first visit in 1997 to East Timor. I arrived around the time of the sixth anniversary of the Santa Cruz Massacre after having taken the position of Washington representative for the East Timor Action Network (ETAN). I had yet to set foot in the occupied country whose crisis it was my responsibility to bring to U.S. policymakers' attention. With an American woman human rights colleague, I traveled in November 1997 to East Timor, with a stop in Jakarta, Indonesia. My analysis in the next section begins with that trip—which took place while East Timor was under Indonesian occupation.

Fast-forwarding to East Timor's independence from Indonesia, the Timorese people gained formal sovereignty in August 1999 in a United Nations–supervised referendum on national self-determination. Weeks passed, however, before Indonesia fully accepted the results of the August 1999 referendum; Indonesia had to be forced by international pressure from the White House, International Monetary Fund (IMF), and World Bank to withdraw its troops from East Timor. In the meantime the people of East Timor suffered continuous violence as Indonesia was pulling out. In Dili and other towns across East Timor, men in uniform scorched entire neighborhoods, leaving destruction in their wake; tens of thousands of Timorese were kidnapped by Indonesian forces and their militia proxies as Indonesian forces fled across the border to Indonesian-held West Timor. In the wake of this violence I traveled to East Timor in January 2000 with friend and fellow ETAN colleague Gabriela Lopes da Cruz Pinto (Constâncio Pinto's wife) as my guide and translator. As advocates for the East Timor Action Network, Gabriela and I balanced our time between visits with Gabriela's joyful family and interviewing United Nations and Timorese officials, church representatives, human rights advocates, grassroots activists, and people on the streets. East Timor was free, but its people still faced serious limitations on their freedom.

In May 2002 I returned to East Timor as a doctoral student in the University of Wisconsin–Madison's graduate program in political science. I entered the field this time to conduct academic research using interviews about the security agreement associated with the 1999 United Nations referendum[6] on self-determination for East Timor. I learned very quickly that what I had assumed would be a relatively simple period of academic field research—at least, compared to the pervasive dangers associated with my prior professional human rights research—would be marred by challenges that harked back to my human rights advocacy. For example, I was detained at the Bali International Airport, my entry point into Indonesian national territory, before traveling to independent Timor Leste. Indonesian security forces, detaining me for having been deported in 1997 for "illegal journalistic activity" and banned from returning to Indonesian territory, had apparently not received notification from the Indonesian Foreign Ministry that the travel ban against me had been rescinded. I was sent back to the United States, and I only returned again several months later, this time via Australia, to conduct my academic research in Timor Leste.

Entering the field in 2002, I encountered a changed political and research environment: Timor Leste, a politically independent nation, no longer posed elevated risks to my security; new risks were associated with common crime. I was no longer under the political umbrella of the human rights group ETAN and consequently without activist colleagues accompanying me in the field. As an independent academic researcher I was expected to carry out my field research alone, albeit with guidance before, during, and after field research from my academic advisers. Within this framework of relationships—between a student and her academic advisers—and guided by the U.S. academy's organizational mandates—of the Internal Review

Board and academic paradigms for "acceptable" research epistemology and processes—I confronted new sets of fieldwork challenges.

EAST TIMOR AND RESEARCH UNDER OCCUPATION—1997[7]

> But I was different. I was an American. And . . . I [barely] escaped with my life. I've tried to honor my promise in the years that have passed, speaking out in various ways [about the repression]. I've filed lawsuits, I've given interviews, I've testified . . . I've held vigils. But this is the first time [after the brutality against me that] I've dared to write.[8]

From 1975 until 1990 the Indonesian government repressed the East Timorese people using increasingly brutal means. It napalmed jungles to expose small guerrilla bands; displaced entire villages; and "disappeared," beat, raped, tortured, and killed to break the back of near total Timorese resistance to Indonesian occupation. In the process, starvation, disease, and the actions of Indonesian armed forces claimed the lives of more than two hundred thousand people, a third of East Timor's preinvasion population—this was genocide at the level of Cambodia. Yet atrocities in East Timor would remain virtually unnoticed by the international press and the world community until 1991. On November 12, 1991, hundreds of Timorese students gathered at the Motael Catholic Parish in Dili to honor the life of Sebastião Gomez, who had been gunned down ten days earlier by Indonesian forces on the steps of the Motael Church. The subsequent funeral procession to Santa Cruz Cemetery was a nonviolent protest, with students displaying banners proclaiming East Timor's commitment to a United Nations–brokered referendum on self-determination. The student marchers were soon surrounded by Indonesian troops, trapping them within the cemetery's walls. Indonesian forces began shooting, killing more than 270 people that day. British journalist Max Stahl captured the carnage on video, which he hid in an open grave, retrieving it later to show the world.[9] Because of its visibility, this 1991 Santa Cruz Massacre—one among many civilian massacres by Indonesian troops—proved a turning point in East Timor's struggle for self-determination. International solidarity movements sprang up around the world, including the East Timor Action Network, which I joined in 1997 as its Washington representative. Just months before I joined ETAN, the Nobel Committee had awarded its annual Peace Prize jointly to East Timor's Bishop Carlos Ximenes Belo and Timorese resistance leader-in-exile Jose Ramos-Horta.

In East Timor, wholesale violation of human rights continued[10] as I made my first trip there. Wearing a plain white T-shirt over a long flowered skirt, in sandals and bearing a large cross on a chain around my neck, my long hair pulled back neatly in a braid, I was casually posing as a young Catholic nun. Having had extensive experience with nonviolent civil disobedience in the United States, I was not unaccustomed to such subterfuge and clandestine action. But in 1997 I wondered how ethical standards differ for conducting human rights research in the field. Some might say that I was in disguise the day I arrived in Dili. I wondered whether my subterfuge was any different from wearing a ring to feign marriage? Or growing a mustache or dying one's hair as a partial disguise? I believed that I was simply playing a role necessary to guard my safety and gain access to crucial and vulnerable sources. People were suffering and dying in a small country under occupation, should I even worry about a little subterfuge to carry out my human rights mission?

Research Ethics under Occupation

These questions continued to emerge throughout my advocacy work in Indonesian-occupied East Timor, with secrecy and "truth" primary among my concerns: What were my obligations as a human rights monitor in a country whose people's rights are being violated on a daily basis by a powerful occupying country? This question nagged at me as I met with individuals and groups involved in resistance to Indonesian occupation. I entered their world knowing that Indonesian occupiers would consider the information that I was gathering useful in their campaigns against dissidents. At the same time, I knew that when I entered the world of Timorese sympathetic to, or cooperating with, Indonesian authorities, or the spaces of those authorities themselves, I had to narrate their stories to the outside world as well. But how was I to do this? Could I be objective? What constitutes objectivity for a human rights advocate monitoring egregious violations in East Timor? One answer to these questions was clear: As a nonviolent activist, I feigned no semblance of objectivity about violence itself. Whether in the case of Indonesia's violent repression against East Timor or the Timorese opposition's guerrilla violence, I was clear that I could not condone violence. Righteous anger became a way of coping with the cognitive dissonance produced by having to witness the "David-like" East Timorese opposition using violence to fight repression and other brutality of "Goliath" Indonesia. I have since been buoyed by the insight of others like Emerson, Fretz, and Shaw (1995) that "nearly all [researchers] feel torn at times between their research commitments and their desire to engage authentically those people whose worlds they have entered."[11] In my case, as a human rights advocate in a place occupied by a military with the capacity to block most resistance and dissent, "righteous anger" became my main defense.

The need to retain and protect secrecy has implications for human rights research. Who could I trust? Where was it safe to talk? Where could I safely conduct an interview? Sharing a room with a human rights colleague, we were hesitant to discuss events of the day: Could we be overheard? Were our rooms bugged? I had encountered this dilemma several years before in an Arab-owned motel in East Jerusalem: I had taken my privacy for granted and strongly regretted it. In East Timor I was often reminded of that day in East Jerusalem when a deep voice intruded into a private phone conversation, warning me that the nonviolent antiwar demonstration my group was planning was "really not a good idea." As Stephanie Schwandner-Sievers discusses elsewhere in this volume, I also found securing safe places an important and challenging goal.[12] In 1997 my colleague and I took precautions in East Timor to negotiate safe spaces for our meetings. We did this by affiliating with church workers who were scattered in presumably safe locations across the country, or by staying in guesthouses run by Timorese sympathetic to solidarity activists; in addition, I worked closely with my colleague as much as possible. But these precautions were not only partial and insufficient, but in some cases they rendered my human rights work even more exposed. Just being with church people—who often sided with the anti-Indonesian opposition, or were members of the opposition itself, or being affiliated with ETAN as a human rights advocate in a country under occupation, what seemed like safe spaces could quickly become dangerous ones.

It further complicated interviews—while also adding some protection to those being interviewed—that in East Timor in 1997, electricity and other basic services were often inaccessible. Erratic access to electricity and batteries made it difficult to tape interviews and even hindered simple note taking and transcription. I often had to memorize quotations, which I would later record in the near dark of my semiprivate room. In the event that my shared room was under surveillance, I was also reluctant to test my memory against that of my roommate. My inability to record some interviews may have also provided some protection to interviewees: Their voices could not be heard and therefore could not be recognized by Indonesian authorities.

Researching under Occupation

As my colleague and I learned during our weeks together in East Timor, flexibility of planning was crucial. A primary concern was evading notice of authorities, whether police, military, or citizen informants[13] for the Indonesian government. This necessitated our dependence on guides, or, to be more precise, on one particular well-vetted male Catholic Church official. This man, who knowingly put himself at risk to accompany us around

Timor, ended up being both an asset and a liability to my research. Certain interviewees would noticeably alter their responses to our questions, sometimes becoming significantly more reserved, in the presence of our guide. Having a guide also sacrificed certain freedoms—his, ours, and that of our interviewees. Just the same, most Timorese with whom we spoke were still remarkably open and trusting. Of course, we had done our homework, made prior contacts, attained letters of reference, and guarded carefully the secrecy of our guides and interviewees.

Secrecy intersected with interviews through our efforts to maintain anonymity. Interviewees, for their own safety, had to remain anonymous. Their names were omitted from my interview notes. Being Anglos rather than Asians seemed to nurture a kind of "cultural trust": Non-Indonesian Asians were often mistaken for Indonesians and thus seen as potential military collaborators. Gender also engendered a form of "cultural disguise" that allowed anonymity: Being women often led to our being perceived as less threatening, thus increasing interviewees' feelings of safety. Taken together, by respecting interviewees' anonymity, being non-Asian Anglos and women, we seem to have diminished to some degree interviewees' feelings of fear, skepticism, and mistrust. These qualities appear to have made interviewees feel more anonymous to those who would persecute them. I can only assume that if we had been men—or, indeed, Asian men—we would have found less trust among interviewees.

Of course, being trusted guarantees neither the information expected or desired nor the ability to recall valuable information received. In the case of a young priest we interviewed in the village of Baucau, rather than finding that he unquestionably supported the poor that he served, we found this priest was unexpectedly ambiguous. The priest pointed passionately to Timorese youths' lack of discipline, while later predictably noting: "Why should they study? Why should they care?" In contrast, a young priest in Dili was much more consistent in his assertions. This priest, who actively supported the resistance to Indonesian occupation, told us: "I use my own rooms to provide sanctuary to young men [from the resistance] in hiding." In this case, we were left with a different kind of ethical dilemma: Since the church had cautioned this priest "about these activities," we were reluctant to report on his contributions to the resistance, lest we inadvertently betray him.

Woman Fielding Danger

On the morning of November 12, 1997, six years to the day after the Santa Cruz Massacre, I attended early morning mass at the Motael Church. Afterward I walked to the location of what would become a large commemorative demonstration at the University of East Timor. Thousands of student protestors crowded the university sidewalk, others leaned from second-floor windows, many were flowing out of interior courtyards. Scores of Indonesian police in riot gear formed a long line, their automatic rifles directed at the protesters. The students unfurled banners and chanted. At times the atmosphere was so tense it seemed the slightest unexpected move could set off a police attack. I saw no other foreigner in or around the crowd. I had to decide what to do. With the hope that a Western female face might help deter the anxious riot police from a violent response, I decided to stay and make myself obvious. Crossing the street from the crowd of onlookers to the student protesters, I walked along the sidewalk, making eye contact with as many police as possible. Camera hanging from my neck, I slowly covered the length of the sidewalk a couple of times. Drawn by several students into a university courtyard, I was quickly surrounded by other students, happy to see me but furious with the police. I handed my roll of film to a student I knew, hoping to protect it from confiscation. I then returned to the front of the university. Gradually, demonstrators and police withdrew from the demonstration site. I too walked away.

As I withdrew I was approached by a young man who appeared to have been one of the student protesters but who could just as easily have been a police informant. He insisted on writing his name and contact information on a small piece of paper, which I stuffed into my back pocket. Within minutes, fully out of sight of the remaining student protesters, police that I had been watching for hours drove up beside me. First came the motorcycles, then a car to transport me to the local police station. While in the police car I pulled open my camera, exposing what film remained from the demonstration. I can't say that I wasn't scared. But I really began to worry when I realized I was trapped. Over the next twenty-four hours, including twelve hours of interrogation—first by one police official, then by several at a time, in a small room filled with police—I fixated most on the small piece of paper with one student's name which I had stuffed in my back pocket. After the interrogation, I was placed under house arrest, then later deported from East Timor. During the entire ordeal my greatest worry was whether I had placed anyone other than myself at risk. Who might be targeted as a result of my actions? How could I tip them off without jeopardizing their safety? Over and over I ticked off in my mind every item I owned that could be used against anyone I'd spoken with in East Timor.

This had been my central concern when the chief of police and other armed officers were interrogating me: Who was I? My response: I am "a student of Catholicism in East Timor." Interrogators: Who had I met with? My response: No one whose name I could remember. After hours of near-constant interrogation, I was transported by police to the guesthouse where I had stayed. I saw this as an opportunity to get hold of my interview journal and drop it down the hole of an outhouse. But the police had already ransacked my room, packed up my belongings, and confiscated my research journal. My presence there was purely for intimidation purposes—both mine and the owners of the guesthouse.

Next I was taken to a police station further from the center of Dili, to a location where I was less likely to be recognized and arouse public attention. There I was grilled on the contents of my journal and some other papers that had been found in my guesthouse room. Since I had anticipated the possibility of arrest even before the demonstration, I had been careful to alter my already rather illegible handwriting to the point where even my frustrated colleague, and onlooker interlocutors, could not decipher what I was writing. The police interrogators therefore only managed to pull out a few phrases that disturbed them: the quotation from an interview with a Catholic Church official who negatively described what he called "the Javanese mentality." After more hours of questioning at the second police precinct, interspersed with even more disturbing periods left alone to worry about friends and colleagues, I was told I would be "given accommodation" in one of East Timor's "better hotels,"[14] where I would be held under house arrest. Though I was never to see my journal again (no matter how many authorities I subsequently appealed to), the remainder of my belongings were returned. Remarkably, they still included a number of papers and letters. Sure that I hadn't seen the last of the police, and expecting deportation, I waited for several police to leave my hotel room—two would stay behind to guard my door—before rifling through my bags. First I pulled that small slip of paper from my back pocket, tore it to shreds, and flushed it down the crude toilet. Over the course of the next hour I would do the same with almost every scrap of paper left in my possession. When I was finally done, shaking, I sat down and cried.

Later, I demanded of my guards that I be allowed to make a telephone call to a friend in San Francisco who had somehow already heard of my arrest and activated ETAN. This friend and colleague would then contact the U.S. Embassy in Jakarta and inform the Timorese, Indonesian, and international press about my interrogation and imprisonment. Getting the Indonesian authorities to let me make a phone call to the United States turned out to be easy. Harder was sitting through the rest of that very long night—worried, insecure, exhausted, and totally unable to sleep. The night and most of the next morning passed before police arrived at the door to my hotel room. I was surreptitiously escorted to the local airport and flown to the Indonesian island of Bali. A shockingly unsympathetic representative of the U.S. Embassy met me there before I was flown back to New York. Next I remember spending a series of interminably long flights obsessively cataloguing all whom I had met and all whom I had written about in my journal, calculating what actions could now be taken to protect them. I calculated that our church-linked guide and the sister of an East Timor resistance guerrilla leader were at risk.

Blacklisted from Indonesia for "illegal journalistic activity," I knew many who had overcome similar obstacles, so I didn't worry about myself too much. Back in Washington, D.C., I spent the next several days severely jet-lagged, waking in the middle of the night and carrying out rapid e-mail correspondence with friends who could monitor the well-being of those I had met in East Timor. I received almost immediate reassurances about the safety of the guerrilla leader's sister. She joked that she'd taken much greater risks than meeting with me! At the same time, I learned that our church-linked guide had been pulled in by police for questioning. I experienced a powerful visceral response to that news and kicked in a drawer of my desk. Fortunately, our former guide was released in short order, unharmed. Slowly my nightmares and anxiety subsided. I found solace working fourteen to eighteen hours a day to advance the freedom of Timorese people whose experiences I had come to know so much more intimately. My own experience with police repression had given me a deeper, more personal understanding of the sorrow, fear, and anger that Timorese leaders in exile courageously carried on their shoulders every day. Still they were working with impressive dignity to free their people.

EAST TIMOR: IMMEDIATE POSTOCCUPATION—2000[15]

> At one of the rivers we would cross by truck, we tried to determine the depth and current while Gabriela teased naked children playing in the water. She asked in the *Tetum* language, "Where are your pants?" One courageous little boy walked up to her with hands on hips and insisted: "East Timor! Yes, now we have our independence . . . but no clothes!"[16]

Almost the entire population of East Timor had lived in defiant refusal to accept Indonesian occupation. The people would accept no less than a valid act of self-determination. In January 1999 Indonesian president B. J. Habibie, who succeeded General Suharto, conceded to negotiations over self-determination for East Timor. These were carried out between East Timor's former colonizer, Portugal; its occupier, Indonesia; and the United Nations. Indonesia's military stepped up its repressive operations against East Timor by training and arming paramilitary forces to attack rural villages. On May 5, 1999, an agreement to establish a referendum was signed: The UN would administer a plebiscite on self-determination in East Timor (set for August 30, 1999), however, under this agreement Indonesia was allowed to maintain East Timor's "security" through the referendum. This fatal flaw allowed the Indonesian military and its militias to terrorize the people of East Timor for months before, during, and after the plebiscite. While the Indonesian government could not derail the referendum process, within weeks following the plebiscite Indonesian forces and their proxies killed an estimated fifteen hundred people, razed 70 percent of East Timor's infrastructure, and displaced two-thirds of its population. By my second trip to East Timor in 2000, more than one hundred thousand refugees were still being held by military-linked militias. Literally taking their lives in their hands, almost 98 percent of eligible East Timorese voters had turned out for the referendum, with more than 78 percent of these voting for independence. By October 1999 Indonesia relented in its attacks on East Timor, acknowledging the referendum results and withdrawing its troops. An Australian-led force arrived to establish security in East Timor. These were the conditions on the ground when I entered East Timor, five months after the referendum (in January), to begin a second phase of human rights research for ETAN. Ironically, during this phase of my research some of my best findings came when I least expected them. Gathering spontaneous expressions of Timorese public opinion—something that had been dangerous, if not impossible, under occupation—I enriched my understanding of postoccupation conditions in East Timor. Traveling by truck around the eastern half of East Timor with Gabriela Lopes da Cruz Pinto, my guide, translator, and fellow researcher, I still had to cope with many very raw emotions—some painful and others joyful—over people's relief that East Timor was finally free.

Retelling Danger

With truck and driver, Gabriela and I were able to go where few international organizations or nongovernmental organizations had been since Indonesia's exodus from East Timor. Our assignment for ETAN was to assess the amount and effectiveness of assistance from the international community, determine the status of refugees, and gauge international efforts to ease humanitarian crisis and assist development of Timorese civil society.[17] It seemed that nearly everyone we encountered had a vested interest in our work. In Ainaro, a small town high in the mountains of East Timor, I found myself surrounded by families reciting the names of relatives still missing in West Timor. They insisted that I write the names down; it was nearly impossible to actually help them. Sadly, this was not an unusual scenario. Psychological wounds were still very fresh; could we—should we—distance ourselves from them?

On some days it was more difficult than others to achieve "distance" from exposed emotions, recent trauma, and mass killings that had occurred such a short time before. In the village of Suai on East Timor's southern coast, we visited the Nossa Senhora de Fatima Catholic Church, where on September 6, 1999, three hundred villagers had been gunned down, including three priests, with many more villagers killed or maimed when they were thrown from the church steeple. Suai villagers, having taken refuge in the churchyard as sanctuary from the Indonesian military and its militia proxies, paid the ultimate price that day. Evidence of terrible violence was ubiquitous as I walked with my colleague through the church courtyard just four months after the massacre. We passed a forensics tent filled with bones and shards of torn clothing. Piles of hair, clothing, and bones also stood in well-organized piles in the churchyard. We saw an altar memorializing the three murdered priests. We spent a good part of that day recording eyewitness accounts of the carnage. Somewhat later that day, in the village of Liquica on East Timor's northern coast, a UN worker recounted his story of a massacre there, confirming that the Indonesian military had led the assault on the church in Suai. In yet another village, Ainaro, we heard testimony about a burial place called "Jakarta," with vivid descriptions of burned, dismembered, and disemboweled bodies; local leaders provided evidence about "disappeared" children.

What Is 'Truth'?

As a researcher, I am always concerned about the validity of the data I am receiving. Political conditions were sufficiently free by 2000 to allow broad access to potential interviewees, but not so free, or secure, or distant from recent suffering to ensure that they would be fully willing to make an honest presentation of all the facts as they knew them. An additional roadblock to securing and assessing the data that I was receiving was the existence of political, economic, ideological, and experientially situated factionalism. Simply stated, there was clear bias by some groups expressed against others. For example, East Timor's leadership and educated elites in civil society were often in conflict with one another, a circumstance not uncommon in newly independent states. In addition, educated Timorese women appeared to be divided into several politico-ideological and experiential "camps": (1) those working for the new government and international agencies; (2) those working for local Timorese organizations; (3) those from the old guard, of Portuguese heritage, and returning expatriots; and (4) young women who had survived the occupation on the ground. Each group maintained separate loyalties and expressed strong biases against other groups, their common plight as Timorese women with relative political freedom seemed insufficient to unite them in a climate of postoccupation political fragmentation.

These and other biases presented obstacles to our research, a situation perhaps exacerbated by our need, in the interest of time and efficiency, to interview several people simultaneously who might be from conflicting camps. In any case, because my interviewees were already coping with so much, it seemed neither wise nor sensitive to confront their biases head-on, except with very close associates. However, these biases surely colored my findings in ways that I couldn't fully assess. At the same time, such biases helped me learn how to watch how people present themselves. For example, as an additional check on interviewees' narratives I relied heavily on my own and Gabriela's observations, these discussed carefully at the end of each day.

Ethics in the Field

As interviewers we had to respect that East Timor was not yet totally secure against intimidation by the Indonesian military and proxy militias. In addition, we feared the increasingly common politically and economically motivated street crime and random acts of aggression. People were afraid to go out at night for fear of assault, a reality driven home to me one evening when two young men accosted me on a Dili street. More commonly, however, Gabriela and I were at physical risk when we traveled to carry out interviews with hard-to-reach populations. We trekked across steep ravines, down treacherous roads, and along mountain cliffs—along breathtaking vistas in areas where fatal vehicle accidents were a regular occurrence. Almost as treacherous as the unpaved mountain roads was the perilous psychological journey to analyze sharply differing accounts of past and present conditions.

Opinion was divided in newly independent East Timor about returning refugees: How was one to know who among the refugee population had been a former Indonesian military operative or sympathizer? There was deep sentiment in East Timor against refugees who had collaborated with the Indonesian military. Yet at the same time there were those who strongly supported the right of refugees to return. Presuming that the "real perpetrators" among the Timorese—whether in the country or returning as refugees—could be accurately identified, how were they to be handled? Some interviewees—the "average" person we interviewed—favored an international tribunal to prosecute past war crimes and crimes against humanity. Others favored a "truth and reconciliation" process.[18] However, in interview discussions about the "truth and reconciliation" process, multiple perspectives emerged about what constituted "truth" and what "reconciliation" would look like. Sorting through highly emotional interviews and the differing definitions of "truth" and "reconciliation" made interviews and report writing difficult.

Indeed, it wasn't until I sat through the March 2001 federal civil trial of Indonesian general Johny Lumintang that I was able to admit the pain I had been carrying. As a human rights advocate in 2000 I had helped to gather evidence for a case brought against General Lumintang by two U.S. legal groups on behalf of Timorese plaintiffs. I had later identified General Lumintang for a process server at Washington, D.C.'s Dulles International Airport. The server presented Lumintang with a summons for violations of international law in East Timor. Not surprising, the general chose not to return to the United States, but during his trial in absentia, I was present to hear a psychiatrist testify about the long-term trauma among Timorese that had been produced by twenty-four years of brutal Indonesian occupation. Such trauma, the psychiatrist reported, was very likely also felt by those who had documented (and, like myself, directly experienced) Indonesian government repression. As the psychiatrist spoke about post-traumatic stress and secondary trauma, I began to think about myself.

In East Timor in 2000, it further complicated matters that we, as interviewers, were finding it difficult to differentiate Timorese victims from perpetrators—the indicators and indications of each had been conflated in post-independence. It had become easier to see former perpetrators as victims. We learned of their forced recruitment, of threats they received from both sides of the conflict to ensure loyalty. Their accounts blurred the categories of "perpetrator" and "victim." Back home in Washington, D.C., sorting through our findings, preparing them for presentation to the American public, to human rights and humanitarian groups, and to the press and elected officials, I was caught in a spider web of perspectives. Returning to my role as a human rights advocate, I was able to cut through a wealth of data and questions and related emotions to highlight what was most critical in order to present a picture of recent political and economic developments in East Timor. By this I mean that being a human rights advocate for ETAN, the goal of which was to obtain the information necessary to inform the American public of human rights abuses in East Timor, I knew whose "side I was on." In a conflict where those who resisted Indonesian occupation were brutally repressed, I was under a personal and moral obligation to report the brutal violations of fundamental human rights suffered by that "side."

However, the road to placing our narratives and other data in a communicable form would still be littered with my own and my interviewees' emotional baggage. As a scholar carrying out data analysis and as a human rights advocate interpreting what I had found, my personal defense mechanisms frequently kicked in. I found that I no longer experienced the elation or the suffering I had felt in East Timor. I was still not conscious of how, and to what extent, my work in East Timor may have affected me. I simply wrote the surface of my experience, and that was enough to satisfy the requirements of my human rights advocacy with ETAN.

TIMOR LESTE: ACADEMIC RESEARCHER IN AN INDEPENDENT NATION—2002

> Culture defines who is an insider and who is an outsider. It sets up boundaries between those who should and those who should not be taught the rules. To learn about culture, an interviewer doesn't necessarily need to become an insider but must be allowed to cross the boundary and become accepted as one who can be taught.[19]

Today East Timor is free, the first newly independent nation state of the new millennium—the Democratic Republic of Timor. When I returned to Timor Leste in 2002 as an academic student researcher in a doctoral program, I had changed. I was visiting East Timor with the primary purpose of answering academic questions for my academic research about the May 5, 1999, agreement, and about the September 1999 exodus from East Timor of internationals who were there as vote monitors.[20] The agreement had allowed Indonesia to maintain control over security during and immediately after the referendum process. The exodus had allowed the Indonesian armed forces to wreak havoc on East Timor with no one to stop them. I suddenly decided that what I was doing academically was fairly superfluous. The hard work of nation building was going on all around me. Everyone had moved on from 1999, and there I was researching the past. Was my work on East Timor still valid and useful to the country's development? Would my academic research eventually position me in a place to assist in the nation-building process? I was entering a new country with a new way of conducting research. I had supposedly become a "scientifically detached" doctoral student researcher. I was no longer carrying out collaborative human rights research; I was alone in the field, an independent researcher in a changed terrain.

Independent Researcher

The urgency I had felt in 1997 as a human rights advocate, and the energy that had motivated my work in 2000, had been eclipsed by frustration and disappointment. On this field mission I was the safest I had been during five years of human rights work, yet I felt frustrated, vulnerable, and overwhelmed. It was actually harder to get around to accomplishing my research goals in 2002 than it had been when I was conducting human rights research under more difficult circumstances. One factor that complicated matters was the near total absence of street addresses, while practically everyone I knew had moved. In addition, phones didn't work. In Dili, power would frequently go out, and we never knew when to expect it. And the wind in Dili could still kick up one hell of a dust storm, which left me walking around with tears in my eyes.

I found the environment surprisingly sorrowful in 2002, which drained my energy. I had nightmares: A huge snake was about to bite an old grandmother and—like almost everyone else in my dream—I stood back and watched from a distance, yelling to the grandmother to leave the snake alone. One man among the bystanders walked into the danger, picked up the grandmother, and carried her to safety. The huge snake then ate a poisonous plant and died. My dream raised questions for me about being an independent academic researcher in Timor Leste: Was I little more than an onlooker in my new role as researcher? Had I fully abdicated my previous role as human rights advocate—as someone who walks into danger rather than studying it from afar? Was the snake's death a metaphor for my own as a person who had chosen academic dispassion over human rights advocacy and intervention? Whatever the answers to these questions, I often awakened from such dreams thinking about the pain that lay immediately beneath the surface of East Timor's new freedom.

In 2002 I spent most of my time in meetings and conducting interviews. I met with officials from the United Nations, World Bank, and the Timorese government, as well as nongovernmental organizations and church workers. It was amazing to sit for hours listening to these actors' stories, but unnerving to comprehend the degree to which so many had compartmentalized their politics to contain their own small pieces of the big nation-building puzzles. I noted with discouraged curiosity the criticisms of women by women, of Timorese by Timorese. I heard about political scandals, experienced mistrust, and heard damaging gossip. All of these were more pervasive in 2002 than they had been in the prior periods when a "common enemy" had brought dissidents together to end the occupation. I was disheartened when I interviewed an official from a prominent Timorese family who had taken an active role in the struggle against Indonesian occupation, but had become so disillusioned that he had already resigned from the new Timorese government. It was strange to hear Timorese express nostalgia for the relative economic stability of the occupation period. I attempted to stay neutral, as was expected of an independent academic researcher.

I discovered that I could not always remain neutral. I felt angry when a Timorese public official expressed disgust at "the disrespectful, uncosmopolitan, and xenophobic attitudes of Dili youth." I was disappointed when a young Catholic woman doing aid work focused her anger at "what colonization and occupation have done to the mentality of the young people," whom she called "lazy" and "dependent." Indeed, more sensitively expressed, I heard Timor Leste's then-president Xanana Gusmão argue that his country needed more than anything, a "change in attitude." In 2002 I found it difficult to get past my progressive politics and idealistic thinking and admit the validity of such nuanced perspectives. I was still struggling with the tensions between my prior roles as human rights advocate and researcher and my new role as empirical academic researcher.

A New Role: Dispassionate Academic

I found it difficult in 2002 to balance my identity as a human rights advocate with my new role as an academic researcher. I was living the paradox of power and vulnerability that Donna Goldstein discusses elsewhere in this volume.[21] In one sense I had everything, and in another I had nothing. It was hard to maintain my balance. Assessing East Timor's political situation, conducting interviews, and carrying out participant observation, I was asking myself many new as well as some of the same old questions. How can one bridge academic research and human rights advocacy? Are the requirements of academic research and human rights advocacy largely contradictory? Are they especially at odds in situations of violent conflict? Can advocacy and academic neutrality ever be congruent? Can safety and calculated risk be satisfactorily conjoined? How do we cope with armed combatants—are lies and subterfuge sometimes necessary? Under what circumstances should we intervene in situations of violence or threatened violence? How are we to record and understand the prejudices and political agendas of our informants? How do we convey subaltern or conflicting voices? How do we situate ourselves within the process of interpretation? How do we work with our own emotional responses—of fear, anger, sorrow, attachment, exhaustion? Is there even a place for such "emotionality" in academic research? I had many more questions than answers.

As a new academic, I felt unprepared to walk the dangerous terrain between academic scholar and human rights researcher. During my first two missions to East Timor (1997 and 2000), my task had been to record testimony so that Timorese voices could be heard inside the United States and beyond—albeit through me. In 2001, when I had visited the ruins of what had been a grand cathedral in Suai, I recorded survivors' stories. The massacre they had survived had claimed the lives of priests and parishioners, all gunned down in cold blood. Back in the United States, I testified in Congress, gave press interviews, and spoke at rallies—fulfilling a responsibility to make firsthand information as accessible as possible to the wider international public.

Somewhat later, as a doctoral student, I would learn that such a responsibility is an often-controversial choice for academic researchers. Student researchers are expected to use "objective" research practices to produce a dissertation, articles, and ultimately books, and are seldom encouraged to transmit their data analysis in a timely fashion to policymakers and the American public. In another difference between human rights research and academic research, on my early trips to East Timor, I couldn't possibly have feigned objectivity; I wouldn't have wanted to even try. As an independent doctoral student researcher, I was encountering very different views about a researcher's obligations to "objectivity," at least inside my little corner of the academy. I discovered that there were academic biases against my firsthand advocacy experience. The assumption was that such experience was one-sided, "atheoretical," and therefore irrelevant to academic research. Applied social science seemed to be considered anti-intellectual and "impure," especially when its findings had come from qualitative data or when these findings cast doubt upon academically accepted ideas. While the claim is often that human rights research that informs advocacy is politically biased, in fact, I have found academic research to be highly politicized—its claims to relative objectivity notwithstanding. Research topics are chosen according to what will "sell" to foundations, what will prove most popular for publishing, and what locations are safest to research. Questions are fashioned according to the (often political and ideologically motivated) outcomes desired. Informants are selected according to often highly restricted criteria, and statistics are highly subject to interpretation. These are only some of the many ways in which supposedly neutral research becomes biased and politicized.

I was especially surprised by attitudes within academia about students conducting research in areas experiencing conflict. My academic advisers were clearly more concerned about my safety, something that had not deeply concerned me as a human rights advocate in Indonesian-occupied East Timor. Indeed, I experienced very little fear going into East Timor in 1997 and 2001. As a nonviolent activist, I was accustomed to U.S. protests, sometimes violently halted by police; familiar with the insides of jails and prisons; acquainted with political repression. I believed that as a well-educated American in a privileged position and an advocate for the East Timor Action Network, I was obligated to take calculated risks for a people suffering unknowable horrors under an occupation supported by my own government. I believed that the more isolated and dangerous the field situation, the greater the need for research. In the end, whether or not I went to Indonesian-occupied East Timor was a decision that I would make for myself. This all changed when I became a doctoral student: There were people and organizational policies (the Internal Review Board, for example) that could block or require that I modify my research, or forbid my entering the field (for example, due to the liability that my research might place on the university), or, in the case of my academic advisers, simply worry about my safety. I failed to see how liability issues could be involved in conducting research in a newly independent nation. Furthermore, I still believed there was an ethical imperative to provide help where help is most needed. I found myself experiencing a profoundly disturbing form of cognitive dissonance: When so many must live in potentially deadly circumstances, why should graduate students be required to avoid researching such areas altogether? What does this do to our collective understanding of violent conflict and oppression? Will the academy ever fully understand such circumstances if someone does not study them? Many of my arguments fell on deaf ears, but with sufficient revisions in my project I was finally permitted to enter the field.

DECONSTRUCTING FIELDWORK ETHICS

It's not easy to discern the often-contradictory ethics of research in general, and even less so to sort out particular fieldwork ethics in potentially dangerous field situations. One glaring contradiction for interviewers is that we are advised to win the trust of informants while being cautioned about "going native"—that is, getting so close to our informants that we cease to be able to be "objective." As a graduate student I came to see that human rights research is often seen within academia as having "gone native" even before the advocate enters the field. The assumption seems to be that because a researcher is working for an organization that advocates for one side in a conflict over another, this researcher cannot conduct "legitimate" social science research—she is "too close" to some informants to see their negative "objective realities" and is unwilling to examine the narrative and lived "realities" of their opponents. Quite to the contrary, as I have demonstrated in this chapter, one of the ethical dilemmas I grappled with in my human rights research in East Timor was coming to see those actors whom we in ETAN had defined as "perpetrators" as "victims" themselves.

As I lived out ethical dilemmas as a nonviolent human rights advocate in volatile field sites, I quickly learned that no side in armed conflict is ever completely "right" or totally blameless. For example, I had a close woman friend who took sides in the 1980s in the Farabundo Martí National Liberation Front's (FMLN) guerrilla war against the U.S.-supported military government of El Salvador (see Viterna in this volume). My friend had worked with the FMLN because she believed them to be saviors of the poor. However, the FMLN ideology of respect did not uniformly apply to women in their movement. My friend was degraded and sexually assaulted in an FMLN camp by her guerilla comrades. She fled to the United States suffering from trauma-induced schizophrenia. Sometimes the sides we take can end up victimizing us, a fact not easy to live with and seldom included in our advisers' caution that an objective researcher must not take sides.

Likewise, our fieldwork preparation seldom discloses that field research involves challenges to "take sides" every day, with no easy script for how to decide which side to sympathize with and how to negotiate and work with those who repel us. The complicated nature of sympathies is illustrated in this volume, especially by Sehgal, Gleebeek (in Huggins and Glebbeek), and Viterna. However, as I see it, the problem of whether or not to "take sides" becomes less of an operational dichotomy—at least for me—in violent field sites: Seeing on a daily basis the human consequences of violence, if nothing else, convinces one about the value of nonviolence and the importance of nonviolent means to achieve political and social ends.

Being a human rights advocate neither insulated nor protected me from the grinding realities of pervasive ambient violence. Sometimes my nonviolence was challenged to the limit: In 1997 I was asked to deliver messages and other kinds of support to those backing the anti-Indonesian guerrillas. As a nonviolent activist, I tossed and turned many nights before I could conjure up the will to deliver the requested assistance to those carrying out armed conflict. As I delivered the outsider support to the Timorese guerrilla supporters, all I could do was request that the support be used for humanitarian purposes only. Was it so used? I can only hope that my stand for humanitarian assistance was honored.

Related in another way to the subject—and an area not taken up by most graduate school field research programs—how does a researcher cope with violence? One kind of violence is the direct physical violence she may see; related are the ubiquitous signs of past violence—bullet scars, bandaged limbs, testimonies about rape, emotional wounds. In January 1991, when I was touring with the Middle East Children's Alliance in Israel and Palestine, people on both sides of the conflict would raise their shirts to show me their battle scars. In 1997 I had the same experience in East Timor, when a guerrilla leader's sister exposed her conflict scars to me. What do we say; how do we respond to these manifestations of violence? What does the researcher—human rights advocate or academic—do to keep going? In 1991 in Israel and Palestine, I remember attempting to neutralize my reactions to the pervasive human acts of cruelty by what amounted to a psychology of "comparing atrocities": Are the things I am seeing really any worse than what I have seen and lived through in other situations? I had already worked for years on both east and west coasts of the United States with homeless people in shelters and soup kitchens. I told myself, "They have scars too—both emotional and physical." I told myself that the scars of conflict I was seeing were "no worse" than theirs.

Taking this reasoning a step further, I would repeat to myself what became my fieldwork mantra: "You aren't allowed to cry." Sometimes this painful demand worked and sometimes it didn't. In 1997 I broke down when a brave woman showed me the cigarette burns on her back, a sign that she had been tortured; she confided that she had also been raped. In East Timor in 2000, I cried when a woman showed me photos of her brother, whose skin had been ripped from his body. Again I broke down when I learned that my friend Jafar Siddiq Hamzah, a human rights lawyer from Aceh, had been kidnapped and tortured to death in Medan, Indonesia. And I broke down and cried after twenty-four hours of interrogation, once my interrogators had left my room after placing me under house arrest in Dili.

However, I had to continue seeking ways to cope with and record raw brutality, usually falling back on "comparing atrocities," willing myself not to cry, and recognizing that at times I would still break my own "coping" rules, usually waiting until I was alone. Within such a framework of recognized vulnerability I came increasingly to see the utility of compartmentalizing my responses to human tragedy into front- and back-stage spaces. When in public, in front-stage spaces I willed myself to conceal my feelings—of fear, sorrow, anger, despair, exhaustion, of gratitude, attachment, or transference. When safely ensconced in private back-stage spaces, I would sometimes allow my emotions free rein, but more and more frequently I squelched them even in private.

As for the problem of the "truthfulness" of informants in 1997 in Indonesian-occupied East Timor, I was certainly lied to, sometimes suspected of being a liar (or something worse), and sometimes tricked into accepting a respondent's political or personal agenda. Looking back to my human rights research in East Timor, I would say that outright lies and other subtle forms of subterfuge were relatively rare. How can I be certain? I suppose I can't—not entirely, that is. But in the field, when one knows a country, its people, and their customs, it is possible to develop a fairly accurate sense about truth telling and lying. Such educated intuition can be further verified by triangulating findings.

My fears about gender-related victimization inspired me to play into patriarchal behavior as a means of self-preservation. Rather than trying to eliminate sexist stereotypes about myself, I sometimes allowed or even encouraged them. Often unintentionally, sometimes not, I found myself using my national status and appearance—that of a young Western woman—to obtain information, to receive protection, and to secure trust. For example, I found that when I was interviewing women, being a woman was more of an asset than a problem. The fact that we shared the experience and mutual vulnerability of living among violent men seemed to produce a bond between us that invited conversation and openness. With men, I used my gender in a calculated manner to elicit a protective response and to secure their trust.

CONCLUSION: THE CHOICES WE MAKE

Interpretive methods are based on the presupposition that we live in a social world characterized by the possibilities of multiple interpretations. Dispassionate, rigorous science is possible—but not the neutral, objective science stipulated by traditional analytic methods.[22]

How do we construct the conditions of our field research and how much do those conditions construct and constitute our research? One lesson learned in my partial transformation from human rights advocate to academic researcher is that firsthand accounts under dangerous conditions may not yield totally accurate answers to our questions. A corollary to this is that determining the authenticity of our own and others' accounts requires interpretation and a constructivist approach. Another lesson relates to the intersection between biography and politico-geography. In 1999 I made choices in occupied East Timor that reflected my primary self-identification as a human rights advocate. My ethics took into account only one side of a brutally violent conflict: the Timorese who were fighting for their country's freedom. In the position of human rights advocate, I was in imminent danger twenty-four hours a day. I took conscious steps to conceal my identity. I moved into violent settings when necessary, witnessing a demonstration that I knew would put me in harm's way. I believed that the ethics of personal concealment and the risks were secondary to providing witness to the international community about conditions in Indonesian-occupied East Timor, a window into the country's struggle for self-determination, and a voice for the pressing need to save lives.

By 2000 the worst of the political violence in East Timor had dissipated, with danger confined to its borders and street crime. But while physical dangers were greatly lessened, ethical dilemmas had become much more complex. By 2002, when I returned to carry out academic research, the field itself was no longer dangerous. However, from a personal and ethical standpoint I was coping with the effects of my own and my informants' unhealed physical and psychological wounds.

As researchers, we face difficult choices not just in the field but back home at our desks. How do we present findings from violent, threatening, and complex political and social environments? How fairly and accurately can we record and write subaltern voices and experiences? How fairly and accurately can we record and present our own voice? On the one hand (typically that of the human rights advocate), it is simply too easy to romanticize the voices and reify the perspectives of our informants. On the other hand (that of the academic researcher), there is a tendency to problematize our informants' comments and experiences. But there is another alternative, one often chosen by women academics like those in this volume: to present our conclusions alongside our informants' and to explore the inherent complexity and contradictions of both. My first and primary task in unraveling my experiences in East Timor was to admit and expose my own agendas at each of the three periods of my research. But this task became progressively difficult the further I moved from *pure* human rights advocacy (the first two periods of my work in East Timor) toward *pure* academic research (the last of the three research periods). As Victoria Sanford has noted elsewhere in this volume, "Fieldwork displaces structures of understanding and disorients trajectories of meaning."[23]

I believe we can draw inspiration as women and as researchers from the social justice approach of political scientists Margaret Keck and Kathryn Sikkink,[24] who readily admit to and incorporate their progressive political and social agendas into their research. We can also draw wisdom from sociologist Jennifer Bickham Mendez,[25] who incorporates the progressive agendas of the programs that she studies into her academic-advocacy research, recognizing that she and they are shaped by and in turn shape global contexts and processes. Academics and their informants live in a complicated universe of power and control shaped by local, national, and global dynamics. Applying this to my own case as an academic researcher, I had to learn that in the process of constructing a research proposal, defending it to an academic department, carrying out the research, and analyzing it in the relative comfort of the academy, my work and its academic value is inserted into—using a version of Bickham Mendez's argument—"power differentials [that are not] detached from a global context."

I have no easy answers to the many ethical questions inherent in conducting research in dangerous field situations. Perhaps the greatest value of this chapter lies not in any ultimate answers but in the fact that it encourages field researchers to continue to raise the questions, to be disturbed by them, and to allow the reporting of findings and be influenced by them. Such realizations give depth to the data we present and the stories that we convey. As women, I believe we are often at great risk in danger zones, however, I maintain that it is at the intersection of gender and risk from which some of our most brilliant social science research and theory derive. What should worry us most is not the questions with which we grapple, but that so many questions seem already answered are therefore left unasked.

NOTES

1. Michele Turner (1992), *Telling East Timor: Personal Testimonies 1942–1992* (Sydney: University of New South Wales Press), 114. From an interview with an eyewitness to the carnage in East Timor in 1975.

2. As a human rights advocate, the term "witness" refers to my physical presence in solidarity with local people who have survived human rights violations.

3. John Taylor (1999), *East Timor: The Price of Freedom* (London: Zed Books), 100.

4. Constâncio Pinto and Matthew Jardine (1997), *East Timor's Unfinished Struggle: Inside the Timorese Resistance* (Boston: South End Press), 191.

5. In the wake of the United States' devastating defeat in Vietnam, then-president Gerald Ford and Secretary of State Henry Kissinger were in Jakarta meeting with Suharto only hours before the initial invasion of East Timor. What was to become almost a quarter century of brutal occupation began with a U.S. green light. It continued with increasing commitments to support, fund, and arm Indonesia's security forces—providing 90 percent of the weapons used in the first days, mounting during search and destroy missions of the 1980s, and topping $1.1 billion by 1999.

6. Ian Martin (2001), *Self-Determination in East Timor: The United Nations, the Ballot, and International Intervention* (Boulder, CO: Lynne Rienner).

7. Reprinted with permission from the Interhemispheric Resource Center and the Institute for Policy Studies.

8. Sr. Dianna Ortiz, with Patricia Davis (2002), *The Blindfold's Eyes: My Journey from Torture to Truth* (Maryknoll, NY: Orbis Press), 9.

9. American journalists Allan Nairn and Amy Goodman would also bring their personal accounts to American radio.

10. Arnold Kohen (1999), *From the Place of the Dead: The Epic Struggles of Bishop Belo of East Timor* (New York: St. Martin's Press), 220.

11. Robert Emerson, Rachel Fretz, and Linda Shaw (1995), *Writing Ethnographic Fieldnotes* (Chicago: University of Chicago Press), 20.

12. Stephanie Schwandner-Sievers, "Securing 'Safe Spaces': Field Diplomacy in Albania and Kosovo," chap. 7 in this volume.

13. "Informants" in this case are those who collaborated with the military occupation, in contrast with use of the word "informants" to indicate interviewees.

14. This confirmed earlier warnings that official hotels were collaborating with the Indonesian authorities.

15. Reprinted with permission from the Interhemispheric Resource Center and the Institute for Policy Studies.

16. Lynn Fredriksson and Gabriela Lopes da Cruz Pinto (2000), *East Timor in Transition: Observations and Analysis for Political Advocacy* (unpublished report).

17. Jarat Chopra (2000), "The UN's Kingdom of East Timor," *Survival* 42.

18. "Truth and reconciliation" commissions have taken many forms, with most having the objective of discovering and revealing past wrongdoing by a government or its militia associates, with the hope of resolving conflicts and abuses of the past. Some "truth and reconciliation" commissions include, besides the objective of clarifying and recording abuses, also determining whether to award amnesties for perpetrators and reparations for victims.

19. Herbert Rubin and Irene Rubin (1995), *Qualitative Interviewing: The Art of Hearing Data* (Thousand Oaks, CA: Sage), 171.

20. John Martinkus (2001), *A Dirty Little War* (North Sydney: Random House Australia), 300.

21. Donna Goldstein, "Perils of Witnessing and Ambivalence of Writing: Whiteness, Sexuality, and Violence in Rio de Janeiro," chap. 9 in this volume.

22. Dovra Yanow (2000), *Conducting Interpretive Policy Analysis*, Qualitative Research Methods Series 47 (Thousand Oaks, CA: Sage), 5.

23. Victoria Sanford, "Gendered Observations: Activism, Advocacy, and the Academy," chap. 5 in this volume.

24. Margaret Keck and Kathryn Sikkink (1998), "Transnational Advocacy Networks in International Politics: Introduction," in *Activists Beyond Borders* (Ithaca, NY: Cornell University Press).

25. Jennifer Bickham Mendez, "Globalizing Feminist Research," chap. 3 in this volume.

REFERENCES

Chopra, Jarat. (2000). "The UN's Kingdom of East Timor." *Survival* 42.

Emerson, Robert, Rachel Fretz, and Linda Shaw. 1995. *Writing Ethnographic Fieldnotes.* Chicago: University of Chicago Press.

Fredriksson, Lynn. (2000). "East Timor." *Foreign Policy in Focus* 5: 43.

———. (1997). *Jakarta and East Timor.* Unpublished report. Washington D.C.

Fredriksson, Lynn, and Gabriela Lopes da Cruz Pinto. (2000). *East Timor in Transition: Observations and Analysis for Political Advocacy.* Unpublished report. Washington D.C.

Keck, Margaret, and Kathryn Sikkink. (1998). "Transnational Advocacy Networks in International Politics: Introduction." In *Activists Beyond Borders.* Ithaca: Cornell University Press.

Kohen, Arnold. (1999). *From the Place of the Dead: The Epic Struggles of Bishop Belo of East Timor.* New York: St. Martin's Press.

Martin, Ian. (2001). *Self-Determination in East Timor: The United Nations, the Ballot, and International Intervention.* Boulder, CO: Lynne Rienner.

Martinkus, John. (2001). *A Dirty Little War.* North Sydney: Random House Australia.

Ortiz, Sr. Dianna, with Patricia Davis. (2002). *The Blindfold's Eyes: My Journey from Torture to Truth.* Maryknoll, NY: Orbis Press.

Pinto, Constâncio, and Matthew Jardine. (1997). *East Timor's Unfinished Struggle: Inside the Timorese Resistance.* Boston: South End Press.

Ramos-Horta, José. (1996). *Funu: The Unfinished Saga of East Timor.* Lawrenceville, NJ: Red Sea Press.

Rubin, Herbert, and Irene Rubin. (1995). *Qualitative Interviewing: The Art of Hearing Data.* Thousand Oaks, CA: Sage.

Taylor, John. (1999). *East Timor: The Price of Freedom.* London: Zed Books.

Turner, Michele. (1992). *Telling East Timor: Personal Testimonies 1942–1992.* Sydney: University of New South Wales Press.

Yanow, Dovra. (2000). *Conducting Interpretive Policy Analysis.* Qualitative Research Methods Series 47. Thousand Oaks, CA: Sage.

7

Securing "Safe Spaces": Field Diplomacy in Albania and Kosovo[1]

Stephanie Schwandner-Sievers

Albanian local identity politics have been at the core of the plot that have I followed over the last fifteen years through multisited comparative ethnographies. In both postcommunist Albania and neighboring postwar Kosovo I have conducted ethnographic research on local actors re-evoking local, precommunist pasts during periods of political transition, state collapse, and other such crises (Schwandner-Sievers 1999a, 1999b, 2001, 2004a). I have discovered that "retraditionalization" can be a very modern political process, even if this concerns the reinvention of precommunist customary law for mediating local conflict, such as happened during the early 1990s in the northern Albanian mountain villages.[2]

From the beginning of my long and short fieldwork residencies in the conflict-riven western Balkans since the early 1990s, I have seen that my friends and family were much more concerned about my personal security than I was. Loved ones worried that conducting research in regions experiencing great political and social turmoil, and focusing on people taking justice into their own hands, could surely result in violence against me—even my death. However, as this chapter will demonstrate, I increasingly discovered as a woman working on my own that the greatest threat was not the risk of violence toward me, but rather not being taken seriously as a researcher by my interlocutors. As a consequence, I had to discover, and then negotiate my way into, the various local cultural standards and practices that would protect me. I did this through a process that I label "field diplomacy."[3]

As this chapter shortly illustrates, an essential first step in conducting effective "field diplomacy" was being culturally knowledgeable about those I was studying. One step in this direction was understanding the role of traditionalism in social change after the fall of the communist state. I will show that what may appear paradoxical—appealing to forms of traditionalism often stereotypically associated with Albanian violence—turned out to offer me the greatest protection in some research settings. However, it was not just in those regions where precommunist customary law was deliberately, ritually, and ideologically reinvigorated that I symbolically and physically aligned myself with cultural notions of social honor, family, and gender. In conducting culturally sensitive "field diplomacy," I hoped I would be safe from ambient dangers, be taken seriously as a researcher, and carve out safe and productive research spaces for myself.

SITUATING MYSELF WITHIN "THE FIELDS"

In the 1990s each of my research sites, whether in Albania or Kosovo, was experiencing great economic, political, and social turmoil. Conducting anthropological research on conflict and indigenous traditions of reconciliation, I spent a good deal of field time in Albania—a country just a little larger than Massachusetts and slightly smaller than Maryland. Mostly mountainous, Albania's domestic economy was dominated by subsistence agriculture. Still today, a quarter of the population (of approximately 3.5 million) is estimated to live below the poverty line. Greece to Albania's south and Italy across the Ionian Sea to the West—with their relatively proximate locations, more developed economies, and European Union status—have been a magnet for Albanian migrants. During my research nearly every Albanian family relied on remittances sent by a migrant relative for survival, and the country's gray economy was thriving.

During Albania's communist period (1945–1991) in general, and particularly during and after the 1960s, when Albania was the only European ally of Maoist China, Albania had been completely isolated from the outside world. Its impermeable geographic and ideological boundaries extended even to its fellow socialist neighbors. When the Iron Curtain fell, Albania was regionally the last country to open to the West. In 1967 communist Albania was declared an atheist country in order to overcome its internal religious divisions (approximately 70 percent of the population was Muslims of majority Sunni and minority Shiite orientations, 20 percent were Christian Orthodox, and 10 percent were Catholic). Any religious or political affiliations that diverged from Communist Party of Labor doctrines under dictator Enver Hoxha were brutally suppressed.

Today, apart from newly independent Kosovo (more than 80 percent; Bosnia-Herzegovina with 40 percent), postcommunist Albania is the only European country holding a Muslim majority (70 percent). However, Albanian Islam is dominantly secular and pragmatic. Religion per se was not a preeminent source of contestation, friction, or risk during my fieldwork in Albania. Neither were national, regional, kin, and ethnic affiliations that provided more important identities. But during the turbulent years of postcommunist transition in Albania, the recent communist history of persecution accounted for unrelenting animosity and political friction between those Albanians who had profited from the former totalitarian regime and those previously persecuted as "enemies of the people" (Saltmarshe 2001).

During the 1990s Albania experienced a particularly rocky transition from communism to a multiparty "free-market" system. This period was dubbed Albania's "years of anarchy" (Vickers and Pettifer, 1997) for its repeated political, economic, and social crises. I first experienced this crisis climate in 1992, soon after political violence and social disorder had surged when nearly five decades of communist rule crumbled. At that time my research focused on how people in the northern Albanian mountain regions, accustomed to a paternalistic and overbearing government making all decisions affecting their lives (Backer 1992), had to find in the sudden absence of state power new ways of dealing with the freshly arising family and community disputes over land ownership and boundaries. It was then that they rediscovered precommunist ritual prescriptions regarding blood feuds, mediation, and reconciliation, which in this region are known as *kanun*.[4]

The next major crisis during my field research in Albania was triggered by the fraudulent 1996 elections, followed in 1997 by the collapse of government-sanctioned "get-rich" pyramid schemes. An estimated two-thirds of Albania's population had invested in these schemes, suffering great economic losses as the schemes fell apart. Overnight the repatriated earnings from arduous years of migrant labor abroad evaporated—adding an additional misery to the long years of family separation. Many Albanian families had used their homes or livestock as collateral to invest in pyramid schemes, resulting in their losing their last family asset (Jarvis 2000).[5]

With a complete loss of faith in the Albanian government, vigilantism and protracted gun crime prospered. The Albanian state suffered a virtual meltdown (Shala and Chavez 2002). There were riots, and the population ransacked the old communist weapons depots to arm itself. Even though international troops temporarily intervened in Albania, in the backwaters of this situation serious crime began to flourish—including trafficking in heroin, in refugees, and in young women and children kidnapped or lured into forced labor—including prostitution—in western Europe.

Kosovo—just northeast of Albania and landlocked between Montenegro to the west, Serbia to the north and east, and the Republic of Macedonia to the southeast—is just slightly larger than Delaware. It was once an autonomous province inside the former Yugoslavia. Serb leader Slobodan Milosevic,[6] later tried at The Hague for his war crimes, revoked Kosovo's autonomy in 1989 and thereby initiated virtual apartheid: During the 1990s the minority local Serb (Christian Orthodox) population held all government positions while the majority Albanian (majority Muslim)[7] population withdrew into a parallel, self-organized world of education, social services, and health care outside the official Serb-dominated state system. By 1999, Serb human rights violations and massacres against the Albanians in Kosovo caused the North Atlantic Treaty Organization (NATO) to intervene militarily. Almost 1 million (out of a population of 2 million) Albanians fled Kosovo before it became a United Nations protectorate in June 1999. Not after long, local Serbs and affiliated minority groups, such as the Roma, were retaliated against—a process labeled "reverse ethnic cleansing," with more than one hundred thousand non-Albanians fleeing Kosovo. Today, Kosovo has a population of more than 2 million and is 92 percent Albanian, who are mostly Muslim, with a few Roman Catholics. The predominantly Orthodox Christian Serbs today account for only 5 percent of the overall population (due to both diverging birthrates between the ethnicities and flight), down from more than 18 percent in 1971.[8]

There was a major postwar crisis in Kosovo under UN and NATO protection in March 2004, when Serb houses and major Christian Orthodox symbols and monuments were attacked across the country and a number of people killed. These events shed severe doubts on the ability of international peacekeeping to secure multiethnicity and safety and suggested the continuity of potentially strong, informal power structures of the formally disbanded Kosovo Liberation Army (KLA).[9] Some sources held the (officially registered) KLA veterans' organizations[10] responsible for having orchestrated these nationwide riots in 2004 (Human Rights Watch 2004, 17–18). During that period, I was studying the KLA veterans' martyr cult commemorations of the KLA members who had died during the 1998–1999 fighting. These martyr cults more generally celebrated Albanian militancy and resistance (Di Lellio and Schwandner-Sievers 2006a, 2006b).

Interacting with former Albanian KLA guerrilla fighters who were growing increasingly impatient with international (UN protectorate) rule in Kosovo, my goal was to understand from the inside. The KLA guerrilla fighters were labeled "liberation fighters" and "heroes" by the Albanian side but "terrorists" and "criminals" by the Serbs. The international community felt deeply uncomfortable with anything that suggested the power and popularity of KLA ideology among the majority Albanians. Tensions were exacerbated by regional propaganda labeling the KLA and its successor organizations an "Islamic threat" following 9/11 and by the prosecutions of prominent KLA leaders at The Hague, for which I was producing an independent background report at the time.[11]

Ironically, I was learning that the greatest threat to my fieldwork was neither Islamic spillover from 9/11, nor the culturally endorsed militancy, nor my own association with the perceived adverse geopolitical powers (the International Criminal Tribunal at The Hague). My response to ambient tensions in Kosovo and Albania was to seek cultural mechanisms for keeping myself out of harm's way. The way to do this, I learned, was to utilize the local concept of social honor, or *besa*,[12] which I had first set out to study in the early 1990s in northern Albania. The KLA had explicitly rediscovered and cherished *besa* as a marker of distinct Albanian identity, solidarity, and military honor (Schwandner-Sievers et al. 2005). Although *besa* is a traditional concept of hospitality, truthfulness, personal loyalty, and protection that is associated with *kanun* customary law, in my research settings it had acquired a new and modern significance. Both in postcommunist Albania—described as the "periphery of the periphery" by Albanian sociologists (Fuga 2004)—and in postwar Kosovo, where ex-KLA members struggled to avoid marginalization from the mainstream processes of development, this concept served to generate interpersonal trust, reliance, and security in the face of state powers experienced as absent, abusive, unreliable, or simply alien.

FIELDWORK CHALLENGES: GAUGING CULTURE

My family and other loved ones were worried about my living alone in mountain villages or working with people known for taking the law into their own hands. For my part, I knew that violence and risk were urgent realities for Albanians, whether in Albania or Kosovo, and by extension for anyone interacting with them during the time of my research. But I was not clear about whether the intra- and interethnic violence would become a risk for me—a nonlocal outsider? As a young, independent, "modern" Protestant (actually a "religious agnostic") woman from the "prosperous West" (Germany), would I be seen as a *non*-threatening outsider to those I was studying? Would these facts of my biography perhaps provoke material or other aspirations that I could not meet? How could I even enter the community without knowing anyone? I reckoned that in countries where violence had been used against ethnicities different from my own, my foreign identity would serve me well.

I did not fit into any of the social, ethnic, or political categories most susceptible to violence. However, being safe was only one layer of my concerns. I also needed to be accepted by those I was studying. Could I assume, as Georg Simmel has written, that "the stranger" in a local community who stays for a long time and can leave any time would be rewarded by receiving "the most surprising openness"? Would I hear interlocutors' confidences—delivered to me "like a confessional [and] carefully withheld from a more closely related person" (Simmel 1950, 404)? I would come to see in the weeks, months, years ahead that gaining an interlocutor's acceptance would be somewhat more complicated than envisioned by Simmel and that negotiating my personal safety would be easier than garnering respect as a woman conducting research. Negotiating indigenous mechanisms for dealing with strangers as "guests," through social honor—as embraced within the concepts of *besa* and silence—of giving one's word and not talking about certain things but being truthful and upfront about others, all seemed to be a possible avenue for engendering trust and security—but this would also incur social obligations on my part.

As a woman, in order to be safe and professionally efficient, I would need to perform according to local cultural expectations for a "good woman" who deserved respect. This would mean balancing being a foreigner and being a "good" woman (in local terms), while engaging in activities necessitated by research that local culture reserved exclusively for men. "Good" local women could not and would not do what I was doing: I intended to make independent decisions about those with whom I would talk and where and when I would travel—both sets of activities traditionally reserved for men in my chosen research settings. As an economically independent foreign woman, I could make independent decisions and plans, even though as an "honored guest" under *besa* protection I had to be accompanied from one host household to the next by a representative of a local village household. Perhaps, in the latter respect, I would be like local women: the young married women in my field locations, fully dependent on the men of their family and on the larger family itself, could not be in public without someone from their in-laws' family. Would this model be applied to me, and how would I negotiate if I could not adhere to it? What would the cultural consequences be, and the impact on my research, of ignoring such cultural expectations? Wouldn't my insistence on research independence and mobility lead to a loss of connectedness to local cultural and power networks, the latter providing a cultural shield against ambient violence?

NO NEUTRALS ALLOWED

In the 1990s in Albania and Kosovo, "the field was both dichotomized and highly polarized" (Dudwick 2000, 14; cf. Buroway and Verdery 1999), although not primarily along religious lines. My interlocutors, facing uncertainty and loss of security in postcommunist Albania and postwar Kosovo, were focusing on carving out and consolidating new identities to replace those lost with their previous social order. Social prestige and structures of power were being reshuffled and aligned in my research sites. Particularly in northern Albania, patriarchy was being reestablished and with it a range of associated informal social values, expectations, and regulations. Here, the conflicts over power, identity, and property resulted in murderous "blood feuds" among kin and neighbors (De Waal 2005, 225). Such violence affected my interlocutors, not myself: Interlocutors knew that I had no stake in the outcomes of their conflicts; likewise, my place outside the societal power structure kept me from being seen as a threat (cf. Simmel 1950).

Yet, just the same, ambient societal friction still influenced how I positioned myself personally and as a researcher in relation to those I studied: Where conflicts over political, regional, tribal, or personal allegiances are visible, contested, and palpable, the lines between who is "in" and who is "out" are likely to affect interpersonal relations and by extension research processes and outcomes. I had to confront at each stage of my fieldwork the assumption among prospective interlocutors that "those who are not with us are against us" (Dudwick 2000, 14). For example, among my ex-KLA interlocutors in Kosovo I felt at risk of being regarded as a "spy" and as untrustworthy for my collaboration with The Hague. At the same time, in Albania and Kosovo during the period of my research, the lines between national insiders and outsiders were not always clear. For example, Catholic north Albanian men discussing Muslim southerners saw the latter as lacking *besa*—in their view, not trustworthy because they had been "corrupted" by the Ottomans when they converted to Islam (Schwandner-Sievers 2001). Such "betrayal" of one's presumed original collective identity was regarded as dishonorable and effeminate and therefore not to be trusted.

In contrast, in northern Albania or in Kosovo, when traditionalist interlocutors praised masculine valor—their own, that is—they spoke of honor and trustworthiness, framing their arguments along the lines of how such attributes imparted *besa* (Schwandner-Sievers et al., 2005; Di Lellio and Schwandner-Sievers, 2006b). To "have *besa*," therefore, is to be seen as being trustworthy, faithful, and loyal, a quality ascribed to local collectivities. For example, northern (Catholic and Muslim) Albanians regarded the Albanian government between 1997 and 2005—dominated at the time by southern Albanians—as "not having *besa*." This was due to their suspected past "collaboration" with the Greek government that had allied itself with Serb interests against the Albanian cause in Kosovo (Serbs and Greeks are Christian Orthodox, as are many southern Albanians). How could I expect to be rewarded with any research-relevant information by my interlocutors if they associated me with the "wrong" political side—for example, for collaborating with The Hague or for having private and professional links to Greece?

Besides such politico-cultural divisions within my field sites, another factor complicating field research, where "no neutrals are allowed," was my gender and nationality. I could not disregard that, at the very least, as a female foreigner I was likely to be seen by my interlocutors as having either questionably ambiguous identity characteristics or identity markers incompatible with their own. Could this feature of my perceived identity make me seem threatening, or, alternatively, put me at special risk? Might the striking differences between myself and my interlocutors decrease my effectiveness within an already culturally and politically polarized field setting? As I focused on these questions, I came to see that at a time when my own family and friends were fretting about my physical safety—indeed a consideration for me as well—I was focusing most upon whether the cultural and political differences between myself and potential interlocutors—factors that I had initially assumed would work in my favor—might actually block my conducting research at all.

Knowing about and studying the importance of *besa* for interlocutors, I wondered if there might be a place for me—an outsider woman—in relation to *besa* that would engender trust between them and myself? Were there alternative ways to engender trust in research contexts where *besa* did not matter to interlocutors?

FIELDS OF RITUAL POSSIBILITIES

Besa, a polysemous term that cannot be translated into one word, was at the core of my earliest ethnographic research investigations. Understood as a quality that a person "has" or "does not have," *besa* is thought to be manifested in a person's conduct and actions. Translations of *besa* cover a range of definitions, all pointing to the combined personal characteristics of honor: the given word, trust, faithfulness, magnanimity in reconciliation and hospitality procedures, and loyalty. These qualities, assumed to be held by a person "with *besa*," are situated within a patriarchal system that provides protection for and retaliation against those who violate *besa*. Such violations are seen as constituting an affront to a person's or a household's honor. *Besa* has sometimes been compared to the Italian Mafia's *omertá*, the doctrine of silence resulting from obligations of group allegiance (Xhudo 1996). However, *besa* is much more than this: In traditionalist northern Albanian and rural Kosovar contexts, "having *besa*" makes a man a man; being "with *besa*" transforms a man into a potential friend; and a man "without *besa*" is seen as a potential "traitor." Those who "break *besa*" are considered socially dead, and such traitors indeed are seen to deserve physical death (Schwandner-Sievers 1999a).

Within the patriarchal system underpinning the concept of *besa*, where does a woman fit? In historical terms of *kanun* law, the larger traditionalist framework that embraces *besa*, female honor is bound up with male obligations: The men of a family are duty-bound to protect and control their sisters, daughters, and wives; the man represents his family to the outside world. A woman's proper conduct, in compliance with norms of chastity both before and after marriage, requires her demonstrating faithfulness, industriousness, and deference to men (cf. Reineck 1993).[13] Women are also traditionally depicted as the root of trouble because they talk too much and thus stir up unnecessary misfortune. Theoretically, therefore, a woman can also "have *besa*" if she is faithful, brave, trustworthy, and, by implication, careful about her words—"just like a man." However, within traditional village contexts the "proper" woman is still defined largely by her reproductive sexuality and purity, which, in turn, is seen as posing a potential challenge to the *besa* of the men who protect a woman's and family's honor (cf. Amnesty International 2006).

In traditionalist contexts, I also found that women regarded as brave and trustworthy could also be seen as "having *besa*." Such women, assessed in terms of ideal male qualities, had bravely risked their own well-being to support the KLA during the 1998–1999 war in Kosovo. Sometimes described as *burrneshë*—"of male quality" (derived from *burrë*, the term for man)[14]—such a woman was accorded a special status within a patriarchal culture that would normally not primarily value her in terms of "having *besa*." However, because she had performed according to highest male role expectations, she had moved in a positive way beyond traditional role expectations for women.

Obviously, the importance given within the northern Albanian and rural Kosovar research contexts to *besa* as the criterion for trusting *a man*, and the fact that I am a woman, seemed at first to preclude my establishing a trust relationship with male interlocutors. I could not help but wonder: As a foreign "alien" woman, could ever I be seen as "having *besa*" and thus be appropriately respected? This question gave rise to other much more troubling ones: If I were respected, would I be required to ally with the political causes of those interlocutors who had accorded me *besa*? In field sites where "neutrals" are suspect, could I remain politically neutral and still receive interlocutors' trust and, by extension, their *besa* designation? Turning to questions about my safety, I wondered: Would being seen as not "having *besa*" jeopardize my personal security? If so, were there ways that I could at least profit from the *besa* of others—particularly, from the *besa* obligations of my hosts? Lastly, how could I sensitively insert myself into research settings where *besa* was not adhered to, or not anymore? Was there any alternative culturally aware method of carving out safe and satisfying research spaces?

The following sections of this chapter demonstrate how these questions were addressed through field site negotiations aimed at discovering a workable research identity, carving out "safe spaces" for myself and for the research, and for completing the research itself.

NEGOTIATING STATUS

Rather than my ever being completely successful within any one interview at resolving the interactive contradictions between my own identity features, my presentations of these, my interlocutors' perceptions of me and of my identity "performances," in fact, this dynamic was on-going and changing in response to situational, cultural, locational, and gendered conditions. By dynamically re-staging my research persona during each interview setting, I was able to address on the spot a range of multifarious research challenges. The dynamics of this "re-staging" is difficult to communicate; certainly, I have no static formula for doing so. However, my research experiences do offer a number of fieldwork guidelines, beginning with the necessity to develop a "field persona"—a presentation of self that represents an amalgamation of who, by local cultural norms, I *should be* and who I *am*, according to my own and my discipline's expectations. Expectations for myself, as I saw them, had to include the realities of my ethno-social and international position, as well as who I thought I *needed to be* in order to conduct research safely and effectively. In the process, such a persona helped me to carve out a safe space for myself by inserting myself into the cultural framework of local actors and their norms, ideals, and practices—all, of course, negotiated within their standards and expectations for me.

Cultural Competence

The first step in developing a successful research persona, as I have said, is "cultural competence" about one's research field (Lee 1995, 74). Having knowledge about the people and culture that one is studying in advance of entering the field, cannot be reduced to "having respect" for interlocutors and their culture. Cultural competence translates into an ability to appropriately and convincingly carry off the *performative* aspects of a group's cultural expectations. Of course, speaking the local language, even if not perfectly, was indispensable to my negotiating a culturally competent fieldwork identity. But the next step was successfully translating my knowledge of culture, history, and language into culturally competent research performances.

Research Performances

Negotiating a culturally competent research identity proceeded within a dynamic of real and imputed "facts" about me: A Western female foreigner, I first entered the field as a young "married" woman in Albania, although my family—a daughter and "husband" (actually, a boyfriend)—were conspicuously absent from the field itself. By background and status, I was easily identifiable a national and cultural outsider to the group I was studying; however, I could enhance my position as a culturally educated "insider" by demonstrating a serious interest in the region's cultural customs. Yet my background and cultural preparation seemed to still present a number of personal and research challenges. Among these was *effectively* carrying off convincing cultural performances.

This required seeing myself as one actor among a range of other cultural actors, with all "performers" switching between back- and front-stage positions during a research interaction. After Goffman (1959), some methodologists have pointed to the essence of such performances as "impression management" (Hammersley and Atkinson 1995, 83), arguing that the personality of the researcher is usually regarded as more important by interlocutors than the research project itself. In consequence of such interlocutors' prioritization of interest in my person, I frequently had to consciously perform front-stage impression management. For example, as a woman alone in places where women hardly travel without male protection, I would wear a wedding ring—I called it my "Balkan ring." The ring was a standard feature ("prop") of my research portfolio long before I actually married my then-boyfriend. The ring stated symbolically that as a woman already under a husband's protection, I was not looking for marriage proposals. To reinforce this impression I carried photographs of my boyfriend and daughter, which I could show when asked—and this always happened. Such performative aspects of my research, indeed, often (at least, momentarily) back-staged research objectives.

Understanding Silences

After having been married briefly to the German boyfriend, I returned to the field, this time divorced and remarried to a British man. Knowing that such information about me would be quite incompatible with local norms in conservative Albanian villages, I knew that I had to take care in how I communicated it to locals. When asked about my family by those who had known me previously, I did not want to lie, so I explained generally about my new marital situation, noticing that most people did not request that I explain further. These silently curious people seemed to be helping to keep unsaid those facts that would be culturally damaging to both sides of our interaction. However, I also noticed that the "embarrassing information" that I was disclosing sometimes provoked a "community of the shamed," with my "shame" opening the door to similar accounts from my interlocutors. For example, when a local farmer of already low reputation in the community suddenly realized that I had "changed husbands" since last visiting him, he admitted—with a wink—his own private "disaster": His wife had left him because he beat her too much! Such intimate and shameful information would otherwise hardly ever have been shared with community outsiders.

I have come to see that in all my rural research sites, cultural strategies of silence served the function of deliberately allowing something shameful that had happened to be *performed* as if socially untrue or irrelevant. This allows something that should not be talked about to be ignored. It follows that something not made "real" through discussions of it does not require action to rectify or punish it. For example, in 1994, the "shame" of a man in a northern mountain village who was overdue to "take blood"—that is, retaliate—in a feuding cycle motivated by the death of his grandfather, was deliberately not spoken about. This temporarily prevented this man from having to kill the person who had taken his grandfather's life (the killing nevertheless happened two years later, in 1996). In another example of strategically employed silences, a man never talked about his first daughter, who had been abducted in the village and forced into prostitution abroad. By regarding his daughter as "socially dead"—indeed, as a person who had never even existed—the "shamed father" was able to remain a respected member in the community. Although everyone in the village knew about the man's daughter's kidnapping and about the family's subsequent erasing of their daughter's existence, villagers did not speak openly about this. There was an implicit consensus that the daughter would only be spoken about "in confidence," an act that respected the family's pretence that the daughter had never existed. The father's *besa* was unspoiled: He had no responsibility to protect a daughter who had never existed. Knowing the culture of silences in the villages I was studying helped me to effectively insert my own questions about my safety into the logic of these silences.

Talking and Disclosure

Just as "silences" had to be culturally understood and effectively negotiated, sensitive decisions had to be made about what could be said openly. For example, I decided not to make any secret of my work for The Hague to ex-KLA interlocutors in Kosovo. After all, there was little else I could do in order to defuse suspicions that I was a spy than offering transparency. To my astonishment such truthfulness proved even status enhancing; for example, an unintended consequence was that some respondents believed me to be a "sympathetic spy" (who sometimes was then furnished with even more delicate information than required!).

Staging Performances

I also discovered the immense value of symbolically communicative "props" for staging my research persona and performances. The function of these "props" was to explain who I wanted to be—a professional researcher—within a setting where such a status was largely limited to men. "Props" also had the function of explaining my researcher status so that even the annoyances I caused would be culturally understood. To put this another way, "props" assisted in garnering acceptance for my positive social and professional standing, while making my "cultural faults" seem negligible. For example, it was essential to my professional enterprise that I stick my nose into interlocutors' private affairs. But how could I do so without being seen as a socially annoying "busybody"? How could I maintain the professional standards of my research—to protect interlocutors' safety and confidences—while engaging in interpersonal interactions of a private nature?

It was by balancing all of my imputed and real identities, along with the positive and negative consequences associated with each, that I negotiated not only my own research status, and the "degrees of action" freedom within that status, but also carved out "safe spaces" for myself and interlocutors. Balancing my own and the culturally imputed versions of these identities determined whether and how I could stay true to myself, to interlocutors, to my research, and to the ethical standards of my discipline.

"PROPPING UP" IDENTITY

I discovered that certain physical and personal "props" enhanced my professional status and smoothed over some status inconsistencies. *Increasing age* seemed to enhance my status as a researcher: I had begun my research career as a young woman and grew "acceptably" older as time passed. Age itself thus became a "prop" for others seeing me as a "professional" researcher. *Evidencing familial connections*, by wearing my "Balkan ring" and showing family pictures to interlocutors, demonstrated culturally important aspects of my identity, even though people kept wondering why my husband would let me travel on my own. I still had to seek local "proxy protectors," which was facilitated by *paying respect* to the local status order. Honoring those of importance was a visible way to enhance my professional persona and gain such people's *besa* protection. This could be accomplished by declaring an interview with an important person "of utmost importance to my research," even if it was not. It could be achieved by staying with the proper family—a choice not always up to me; nevertheless, as a guest, I benefited from the respective host family's protection. I strove to use the culturally correct formal words and gestures of gratitude. In such ways I manifested respect for the *besa* of a respected local household or person. While all such actions are universals of professional politeness, they had the additional outcome in my research of paving the way for powerful community gatekeepers to watch over my security and further my research.

All such performance-enhancing "props" were of course combined with other *observable evidence* that I too saw myself as a researcher: Being "dressed up" at the right occasions—rather than casual; carrying a tape recorder and other research paraphernalia—a photo or film camera, papers and pens. It also helped to carry letters of recommendation into the field (serving as the extended *besa* of an important person in the city); to work in company of local or international colleagues; to make an interlocutor a gift of one of my publications; to demonstrate connections to local academics—mentioning their name, for example, in an interview. An added incentive for performing professionalism was that as a "professional researcher" I could keep a controlled distance from interlocutors and create a personal space that made me relatively safe from unwanted sexual advances. (I soon learned to avoid eye contact with men to whom I had not been properly introduced). Performing professionalism through my conduct and through gadgets and by how I was dressed helped to reduce the partisan political pressures on me to "take sides" inside a field situation where no neutrals were allowed. Along the way, such personal and professional distance also helped develop the necessary research freedom for healthy intellectual skepticism.

Some other strategies for "propping up" my professional identity included the *social capital* of driving my own car—highly unusual for a young woman in Albania at the time. I found that arriving at a village in my own vehicle gave—besides a designation as "exotically different"—a sign to others that I possessed an important resource. This translated into enhanced professional prestige by announcing my material capabilities—but, even better, I could use my vehicle to exchange favors with interlocutors by offering rides for visits and transport. Lastly, by having my own car, I could withdraw at will from a research community—a valuable resource in a situation of potential or real risk.

WHO WAS I BECOMING?

As my time in the field progressed and I mulled over my emerging research persona, I realized that it was unquestionably being shaped by patriarchy—a fact that was nonetheless greatly facilitating my research in the northern Albanian and Kosovar villages, but not just there. Patriarchy had also shaped my research possibilities within a two-man, one-woman Western research team. Surprisingly, however, in the case of the latter, counterintuitively, I found myself more exposed to risk as the only female on that team, than when I negotiated safe spaces for myself through patriarchy within traditional Balkan villages and by becoming "like a man." As a researcher alone—whether as guest under a local family's *besa* or as a person accompanied and/or recommended by a local—I gained respect as a female researcher doing a "man's job."

Woman-as-Man

When an Albanian interlocutor from Kosovo, somewhat self-aware about his use of such a traditionalist label, called me *burrneshë*—"a woman like a man"—I knew that my overall status had been elevated and that I had carved out a space of respect for myself. As a woman who is "like a man," I could be a professional foreign female researcher. Being designated as "like a man" meant that I could encourage and engage in discussions of political and controversial themes. Likewise, categorized "like a man," even in a highly traditionalist context, my presence was allowed within some male-only household spaces—the men's *oda* room,[15] the ritual space for receiving guests and exclusively male company, where discussions take place and from where traditional households exclude women.

I had found some years earlier, as a female "associate" of a Western male research team in remote villages, that the male-only *oda* room had been off-limits to me. Lacking access to this public front-stage of a household had implications for what I could learn about certain aspects of village life and customs. I found myself literally assigned to the private back-stage of the house, the spaces designated exclusively to the women and children. This was a space off-limits to my male colleagues, which— although I felt excluded and even humiliated at the time—provided an entirely different and important set of perspectives on life in Albanian households and villages and about attitudes toward feuding practices. In contrast, as a researcher on my own I found myself having better access to both worlds: As a guest I was invited, "like a man," to the household's public front-stage—the *oda* room—and, as a woman, I had special access to the female social worlds that within traditional contexts could be a back-stage inaccessible to male researchers.

Under *Besa*

As part of the Western research group, our teamwork had provided proxy *besa* for me inside a remote northern Albanian village. But when the two male colleagues left me on my own for a short period to conduct my own research in the village, I found "safe spaces" had vanished: Without male protectors I became the focus of young local men's sexual advances. At first I wondered if I would ever be able to conduct research while fending off local males' sexual jokes, advances, and unwanted intrusions into my private spaces. I felt objectified by those I aimed to study. I was losing command over my research autonomy. My response to the persistent sexualized threats from local males was to withdraw more fully into the cultural and literal shelter of my host household, a response that of course placed restrictions on my personal and cultural independence. In fact, I initially questioned whether I had actively shut down my research.

Instead, I learned that through inserting myself into the hospitality protections of the aged widow in whose house I was living, I had enhanced my safety and facilitated my research through her *besa*, the set of customs that placed me, as her "honored guest," under the protection of her household's "honor." Initially I remained near her dwelling and conducted research on this woman alone. Before too long, as I came to be seen as the old lady's fictive daughter, this status further enhanced my *besa* protections and provided me a wider safe space for carrying out quasi-independent research.

Acting as my protective shield, the distinguished older woman opened doors to interviews with others—first by inviting villagers to her house, where I interviewed them under her close "guardianship."[16] Later, when I ventured out to other interlocutors' houses, she accompanied me to each new dwelling. There, I was "protected" by the interlocutor's household *besa*. After each of these interviews, a family member from the household would then accompany me to my residence, where I would once again come under the protection of the respected old lady's *besa*. (I avoided interviewing young, unmarried men during that period).

Overall, by crafting safe research spaces for myself through *besa*, I was able to avoid a dilemma frequently faced by female researchers: Allowing men to treat them in a demeaning sexually available manner—in order to get desired research information—or spurning male informants' sexually aggressive behaviors and risking closing the door to any but the most superficial research (Lee 1995, 58). I worked around this, as I have said, by using my "foreign guest" status to gain entree into a household's *besa*.

Becoming Family

Whether in developing relations with women or in being allowed to enter the spaces of men, there were benefits and pitfalls to having a persona based upon the patriarchal customs so evident in northern Albania's mountain villages. Yet similar research requirements became evident during long-term fieldwork in the south of Albania, as well, where there was no locally recognized tradition of *kanun* customs and law including the rituals and rhetoric of *besa* (Schwandner-Sievers 1999b, 2001). In these regions, I negotiated a persona for myself and gained access to private household spaces by entering into a household's "fictive kin" networks, similarly as the previous example illustrated but without any reference to *besa*. This involved emphasizing my "shared sisterhood" with local women, often initially through our mutual connections to "motherhood" and then through my position as the household's fictive "daughter," "sister," or "cousin." Such statuses, generally available for women to privately bond with families and households in traditionally patriarchal Balkan contexts, facilitated my "incorporation into a role perceived as fit for the host society" (Birkett 2000, 212, 214). Especially in my longer-lasting fieldwork, fictive kinship offered a secure option for becoming "sufficiently native" to ethnographically explore a bottom-up perspective on social life and sufficiently safe to do so over an extended period of time.

Becoming a household's "fictive cousin," and developing the interpersonal and community dynamics required to support this identity, was complicated. Everyone knew that I was not a "real cousin," yet they were still perfectly willing to enter into this social role relationship with me while fully recognizing that I was "really" an outsider. Initially I was introduced to others by my hosts as their "cousin" in a joking, sometimes even ironic manner. Yet I still benefited from the cultural practice, discussed earlier, of insider cultural actors' *not speaking* publicly about incongruent or culturally embarrassing information. In effect, I found myself socially related to as if I were really this family's cousin. Hence this became a shared social "truth" in practice, even though, if pressured, everyone would have known that our shared "truth" had been jointly constructed. This system of "strategic cultural silences" helped me to craft and sustain an effective safe space for conducting research within cultural spaces shot through with risks outside the shelter of family protections.

However, for my part, being in a fictive kin relationship still involved a complicated balancing act. On the positive side, being inserted into fictive kinship statuses and networks protected me from being sexualized within a cultural context in which Western female foreigners cannot easily acquire the cultural protections designated for local women. On the other side, cultural incorporation through fictive kinship has the capacity to severely restrict a female researcher's freedoms. Most women anthropologists of Balkan villages—including Ernestine Friedl in 1930s Greece (1986), Diane Freedman in 1980s Romania (1986), and Barbara Kerewsky-Halpern, in 1950s Serbia (2000)—who entered into fictive kinship relations with local households found that, as Birkett (2000) has observed,

> as a woman traveler [or ethnographer] was drawn closer into village life as a [family's] child, [sister, cousin], wife or mother, she would also be expected to conform more and more to the behavior expected of a woman in that world. Transgressions of acceptable behavior would not be [as] tolerated as they were when she had been a stranger and honored guest (213).

In short, the "privileges of an outsider had been lost" (Birkett 2000, 214) once the outsider had entered into the social roles expected of local women. In addition, by becoming culturally close to her research subjects, via quasi kinship incorporation, the female researcher might lose the distance required for research independence and mobility—a troubling "paradox of intimacy" in the ongoing negotiation of appropriate proximity and distance to the interlocutors.

Invited into Patriarchy

For foreign female field researchers the relative advantages of remaining a "foreign" outsider with greater social and cultural freedoms, versus becoming a "protected" (and socially constrained) female cultural insider, may mean balancing, as Mitchell points out, the "high degree of trust achieved early in an investigation" (through being part of a local household), with being independent and seeing one's "freedom to look and ask" curtailed (Mitchell 1991, 103, cited in Lee 1995, 25).[17] At the same time, as Dudwick (2000) has highlighted, developing proximity and trust and establishing an "acceptable" position within one's research community is particularly important in societies ridden with war, by identity conflicts, or by repeated state disintegration. In such cases, safety may override a researcher's considerations about the loss of freedom from being enmeshed into patriarchy, as I discovered in the 1990s in selected parts of Albania and later in rural Kosovo.

Being a researcher on my own in the Balkans and being seen as *burrneshë*, "like a man," particularly in the most traditional contexts, was somewhat compatible with certain identity choices that I had made for myself. Knowing that the best course for a female researcher in traditional settings in Albania and Kosovo was to "arrange with" patriarchy, I elected to straddle insider-outsider definitions and pressures. It was in the performative dynamic of static status combinations—being a woman, foreign, an honored guest under *besa*, and a "woman-as-man"—that I negotiated being accepted as a professional researcher and maintained a sufficient degree of research independence. However, as the next section illustrates, discovering the optimal role performance for each research setting was far from simple.

DISCOVERING THE "IDEAL" PRESENTATION

"Vulnerable Woman," "Honored Foreign Guest"

Whether in Albania or Kosovo, I realized that each research setting required somewhat different research personas, depending upon local and cultural conditions. My acceptance into, and the extent of my eventual socialization within, varying Albanian and Kosovo field sites usually turned on aspects of "essentialist objectification." I could be treated as a "vulnerable woman," "fictive kin," or as an "honored foreign guest" with positive male qualities. In the first case, I was exclusively defined by female gender images and norms, as these are understood by the Albanian rural-traditional cultures of the region. This resulted in my being seen as vulnerable and thus unreliable and therefore "needing protection" under a host household's *besa*. The second designation, that of "fictive kin," provided sufficient protection, yet also included the obligations and (gendered) limits associated with ritual kinship affiliation. The third alternative identity—being an "honored foreign guest" with positive male qualities—defined me almost exclusively in terms of my foreigner professional status. Such a designation allowed me to be seen as "honorable and respected"—as a woman who potentially "possessed *besa*" herself because of her likeness to men. Nevertheless, even in this case I was still primarily a "female foreigner." The latter designation gave me more research freedom than either of the former two taken alone. However, such a globalized designation of my status had implications for how I could carry out research, as I explained previously.

Likewise, as a "vulnerable woman" my research subject was constrained: As a woman in need of patriarchal protection I found myself potentially excluded from certain front-stage household locations and certain kinds of ritualized processes. As a designated "family member" I could only interview those people regarded as friends and allies of "my" host family. As an "honored foreign guest," which also involved a certain degree of ritual infantilization and social constraints, I gained the respect allocated to a short-term "guest," which gave me somewhat more command over fulfilling my research plans, unless or until my locally defined *female* status trumped my "foreign honored guest" designation. In such cases, I was restricted from entering some household and community areas. My ultimate response to the various costs and benefits associated with each static designation of "*who* I was seen as" was to seek new ways of crafting out and elevating the "honored guest" status to a level above that of the more professionally constraining social definitions of me.

By negotiating a research persona that emphasized my "foreignness" over my "femaleness," I was usually able to negotiate research-friendly degrees of independence, of intimacy, and of control. Of course, as the word "negotiation" suggests, the process of establishing a research-friendly identity was ongoing and dependent upon being able to insert myself into, and negotiate in terms of, local cultural customs and norms that militated against seeing me as a professional researcher. The key to a successful identity negotiation was learning to balance identities—those that I preferred, those being designated to me, and those I was negotiating. I discovered that each research focus—for example, studying women's or men's attitude toward conflict—called for my being in different research spaces—be this taking the front-stage in the men's *oda* room or entering the back-stage of a household's private room or kitchen. Each research space, of course, called forth different aspects of a research persona.

ONE RESEARCH PERSONA, MANY VARIATIONS

Of course, contemporary anthropologists are not the first to rely on cultural norms for carrying out "field diplomacy." Many early female travelers and ethnographers used their foreign status to secure a "culturally known" location within the host society and become "honorary men."[18] For the Balkans, and particularly for northern Albanian regions, Edith Durham, Rose Wilder Lane, and Margaret Hasluck, who traveled alone in the early twentieth century, "were allowed into the society of men and rich men at that, giving them more social power than they could dream of in Britain" (Clark 2000, 136; cf. Young 2000b; see also Durham 1985; Lane 1923). As one writer put it, being "foreign and acting outside the parameters deemed fit for feminine behavior (both in her home and the host society) meant she could be considered *as if male* [emphasis added], a privilege not enjoyed by women journeying with a husband" (Birkett 2000, 210). This apparently compensated these Victorian English women for traveling alone to regions where the everyday performance of masculinity resulted in strongly "masculinized" honor codes, warrior cults (including blood feuding), and strictly patriarchal and patrilineal kinship organization.

But how did these early female travelers negotiate into their "culturally known" location within the host society? One answer lies in the "benefits" to be derived from patriarchy itself. As "honored guests" the early-twentieth-century foreign female travelers to the Balkans were eligible to be seen as "like a man," a respectful status that was (and is) culturally available for understanding some outsider women. Being seen as an independent woman who is "like a man," but not a man, offered a workable alternative to other readily available status alternatives—solely "an honored guest" under protection of a local patriarch's household; "sexually loose" and therefore sexually available; a "good" foreign woman seeking marriage among locals; a powerful outside competitor to male power. I found that being integrated into local cultures through a combination of household "honored guest," "fictive kin," and foreign woman and "like a man," best served the positionality amalgam of "who I am" and who interlocutors wanted me "to be."

CONCLUSION

Establishing safe research spaces within my field sites, or "safety zones" (Lee 1995, 44–46), was contingent upon discovering and using culturally resonant identity presentations. One element in this process, *identity negotiation*, involved, as I have explained, adopting some "culturally ready" definitions of myself and employing actions normatively associated with these. Being seen as "from the powerful West" and "a woman"—whether such designations were taken alone or in combination—had consequences for me and for my research. Without doubt, gender and nationality set the terms for how I was treated, what I would be told, and which of my behaviors would and would not be tolerated. It was within the process of negotiating with interlocutors over the meaning and preeminence for each of us of my "real" and "perceived" identities that interlocutors' attitudes about—and expectations for—me were shaped. Central to this negotiation was patriarchy; it became—rather than an absolute inhibitor—a strategy for research and for working out safe spaces for myself and my research.

It has often been noted that "the risks female social scientists face in doing research remain under-documented" (Lee 1995, 56; Warren 1988). This is, in part, the case because the safety issues specific to female researchers have previously provided arguments for their exclusion from carrying out certain kinds of research assignments (Lee 1995, 57; Golde 1986; Lutkehaus 1986). Such exclusion has also likely resulted because some female researchers have not wanted to recall—out of "shame" or professional embarrassment—the personal research experiences involving their "objectification," making such experiences underthematized by scholars. I especially experienced patriarchal forms of objectification at the beginning of my research career; later on, I learned to negotiate patriarchy to my advantage. This transformed what some might call "victim-objectification" into agency for negotiating patriarchy to serve my research.

I argue that cultural awareness is necessary for negotiating safe and gratifying research spaces. Researchers must look to the *performative* character of culture, which requires cultural competence about local rituals and values. I negotiated these rituals by learning to recognize the difference between front- and back-stage of cultural performances, particularly with respect to the ambiguities and rigidities associated with my being a "foreigner," a "female," a cultural "stranger," and a researcher—the latter seen as "man's work." These "double-binding," often ambiguous, frequently contradictory statuses and status combinations necessitated my shifting between statuses and roles and front- and back-stage performances. In the process, ambient violence took a back-stage to my working out a culturally resonant and productive research interaction under protection of local hosts and families. I learned in the process that a culturally resonant research interaction was the best insurance against being victimized by ambient violence while maintaining a sufficient degree of research autonomy.

NOTES

1. With great thanks to Martha Huggins for her critical, constructive, and thorough engagement with the preceding versions of this chapter.

2. The Ottoman Empire (late thirteenth century to 1922)—which included present-day Albania and Kosovo—had ruled its provinces "indirectly" by fostering local self-regulation through the system of rural community law called *kanun*, from old Greek word, *canon*—i.e., rule of the measuring stick. Such local customary law was orally transmitted over centuries in sayings and proverbs that were

proscriptive but not necessarily descriptive of social realities, and negotiated in tribal assemblies. In the international literature historic, northern Albanian customary law is still commonly been subsumed under the Ottoman term *kanun*. However, today this term is also more often than not used in stereotypical ways to explain (or, by local criminals themselves, to seek culturalist defense for) practices of blood feuding and revenge killing in Albania that are modern in origin, aims, and practices (Schwandner-Sievers 2004b). True sociocultural continuities originating in *kanun* customs of the nineteenth century can still be found in selected and remote northern Albanian and rural Kosovar settings, but these are not always referred to as *kanun* anymore by the involved locals themselves.

3. A term suggested to me by Martha Huggins and inspired by the notion that "private diplomacy" is necessary for negotiating safe research space during face-to-face research interactions (Lee 1995, 58).

4. See note 2.

5. According to Christopher Jarvis (2000), "The pyramid scheme phenomenon in Albania is important because its scale relative to the size of the economy was unprecedented, and because the political and social consequences of the collapse of the pyramid schemes were profound. At their peak, the nominal value of the pyramid schemes' liabilities amounted to almost half of the country's GDP. Many Albanians—about two-thirds of the population—invested in them. When the schemes collapsed, there was uncontained rioting, the government fell, and the country descended into anarchy and a near civil war in which some 2,000 people were killed. Albania's experience has significant implications for other countries in which conditions are similar to those that led to the schemes' rise in Albania, and others can learn from the way the Albanian authorities handled—and mishandled—the crisis" (Jarvis 2000, 46).

6. See Traynor 2006.

7. Religious difference serves as a marker of ethno-national opposition to the Serbs. Yet during my research amongst mostly Muslim Albanians of Kosovo, the only "religion" that mattered was Albanian ethno-nationalism—a legacy of both nationalist and secular Albanian self-understanding, according to which "the religion of the Albanians is Albanianism" (Duijzings 2000).

8. The Albanians are said to have one of the highest birthrates in Europe. The remaining three percent of the overall population is Roma—who are Muslim or Orthodox Christians—as well as Turks, Bosniaks, and Gorani—who are Muslim—with the latter two groups linguistically distinguished as Slav speakers (Statistical Office of Kosovo 2008, 7). Those of "ambiguous" ethnic identity, such as the Bosniaks or Gorani—who share Muslim religion with the Albanians and their language with the Serbs—have often suffered pressures for allegiance to one ethno-religious group or another and have faced persecution from both the Albanian and Serb sides. Also, these two ethno-religious groups have fled Kosovo in large numbers in the postwar years.

9. The Kosovo Liberation Army developed in the early 1990s out of a handful of clandestine, radical Albanian splinter groups created in the diaspora and rooted in the remote villages of Kosovo that were worst affected by Serb police violence. Some of these early KLA activists engaged in killing Serb policemen while others in gun running. In 1998 the KLA transformed into a mass guerrilla movement in response to Serb massacres of entire Albanian families in some of the home vil-

lages of these early KLA fighters. (Judah 2000; Di Lellio and Schwandner-Sievers 2006a, 2006b).

10. Formal KLA postwar successor groups included the KLA veterans' associations, two successful national political parties, which have since provided two prime ministers, and the police and civil protection forces which had officially absorbed large numbers of the disbanded KLA.

11. In 2003 and in 2005 the International Criminal Tribunal for the former Yugoslavia at The Hague charged prominent former KLA leaders with war crimes, allegedly committed by the KLA during the 1998–1999 combat period against Serbs and their Albanian collaborators. Nearly all KLA were later acquitted (respectively in 2005 and 2008) and have since resumed leading political roles in Kosovo. See also www.un.org/icty/limaj/trialc/judgement/index.htm.

12. Definitions of *besa* include "the honor of the house," "faithfulness to a man's given word," "a protection guarantee," "a man's quality of trustworthiness, reliability or loyalty," and the social obligation of reconciliation—resulting in an oath-bound ritual after a blood feud (Schwandner-Sievers 1999a).

13. By the same token, women from traditional, rural background who were abducted and forced into prostitution (northern Albania) or suffered war rape (in Kosovo) were typically rejected by the family and had to take the social blame. (cf. Amnesty International 2006; Schwandner-Sievers 2006).

14. This concept should not be confused with the better-known northern Albanian traditional concept of the "sworn virgins" (see Young 2000a; Gremaux 1994), which historically applies to women who have ritually sworn eternal virginity, usually in order to evade an unwanted marriage or lead a parental household without male heir; these women have thus never married and have no children of their own, and thus always remained living with their patrilineal kin group. *Burrneshë* can apply to any woman, married or unmarried, including married mothers who conduct themselves according to values culturally understood as typically male; and I found this a concept still commonly used in everyday speech among my traditionalist interlocutors, contrary to the highly culturally and historically specific concept of a "sworn virgin."

15. In traditional Albanian houses—which often hold large extended families—learning about male cultures requires being able to access the *oda* room. This area is traditionally both a formal reception room and the place where the men sleep, eat, lounge, sing, and tell stories—a place exclusively reserved for men. In many houses that I visited in northern Albania or rural Kosovar mountain villages, the *oda* was still furnished in a manner reminiscent of the old Ottoman style: low benches along the wall are covered with woven throws, yet the traditional fireplace has sometimes been replaced by an electric heater. Indeed, in highly traditionalist houses an overnight guest might never see the women of the house. Although the women prepare the household's food, they do not serve it to *oda* room guests: Just outside the room the food is handed to, and then served inside by, the household's younger, less prestigious men. In the somewhat less traditional households, when a guest's stay extends beyond a few days, the women will serve the food but will not always sit with the guests.

16. She quite enjoyed the "entertainment" value of my interview work and, with the exception of preparing coffee for the guests, always actively participated in conversations and thus contributed and shaped research outcomes.

17. An interesting question is how a man would experience familial incorporation—would being a man, even a foreign one, constrain the researcher in the same ways that it constrained a foreign female researcher? Likewise, would being a fictive family member constrain the male researcher's "freedom to look and ask"?

18. Among these were Africanist female anthropologists Audrey Richards, Phyllis Kaberry, and Lucy Mair, who experienced, in the late African colonial periods, being perceived as an "honorary man" in the tribal societies they studied. I wish to thank Richard Fardon for pointing me to this similarity.

REFERENCES

Amnesty International (AI). (2006). "Albania: Violence against Women in the Family: 'It's Not Her Shame.'" *Amnesty International Report*, Index EUR aa/002/2006, March 30. Available at http://web.amnesty.org/library/index/engeur110022006.

Backer, B. (1992). "The Albanians of Rrogam." BBC/Granada Films documentary series *Disappearing World*.

Birkett, D. (2000). "Bucks, Brides, and Useless Baggage: Women's Quest for a Role in Their Balkan Travels." In *Black Lambs & Grey Falcons: Women Travellers in the Balkans*, edited by John B. Allcock and Antonia Young, 208–16. New York/Oxford: Berghahn.

Buroway, M., and K. Verdery, eds. (1999). *Uncertain Transition: Ethnographies of Change in the Postsocialist World*. Oxford: Rowland and Littlefield.

Clark, M. (2000). "Margaret Masson Hasluck." In *Black Lambs & Grey Falcons: Women Travellers in the Balkans*, edited by John B. Allcock and Antonia Young, 128–54. New York/Oxford: Berghahn.

De Waal, C. (2005). *Albania Today: a Portrait of Post-Communist Turbulence*. London: I. B. Tauris.

Di Lellio, A., and S. Schwandner-Sievers. (2006a). "The Legendary Commander: The Construction of an Albanian Master-Narrative in Post-War Kosovo." *Nations and Nationalism* 12, no. 3, 513–29.

———. (2006b). "Sacred Journey to a Nation: Site Sacralisation and 'Political Reproduction' of a New Shrine to the Kosovo Nation." *Journeys: The International Journal of Travel and Travel Writing* 7, no. 1, 27–29.

Dudwick, N. (2000). "Postsocialism and the Fieldwork of War." In *Fieldwork Dilemmas: Anthropologists in Postsocialist States*, edited by Hermione G. De Soto and Nora Dudwick, 13–30. Madison: University of Wisconsin Press.

Duijzings, G. (2000). *Religion and the Politics of Identity in Kosovo*. London: Hurst.

Durham, M. E. (1985). *High Albania*. Boston: Beacon.

Freedman, D. (1986). "Wife, Widow, Woman: Roles of an Anthropologist in a Transylvanian Village." In *Women in the Field: Anthropological Experiences*, edited by Peggy Golde. Berkeley and Los Angeles: University of California Press.

Friedl, E. (1986). "Fieldwork in a Greek Village." In *Women in the Field: Anthropological Experiences*, edited by Peggy Golde. Berkeley and Los Angeles: University of California Press.

Fuga, A. (2004). *Shoqëria periferike*. Tirana: Ora botime.

Goffman, E. (1959). *The Presentation of Self in Everyday Life*. Harmondsworth, UK: Penguin.

Golde, P. (1986). *Women in the Field: Anthropological Experiences*. Berkeley and Los Angeles: University of California Press.

Gremaux, R. (1994). "Woman Becomes Man in the Balkans." In *Third Sex, Third Gender: Beyond Sexual Dimorphism in Culture and History*, edited by Gilbert Herdt, 241–81. New York: Zone Books.

Hammersley, M., and P. Atkinson. (1995). *Ethnography: Principles in Practice*. London/New York: Routledge.

Human Rights Watch (HRW). (2004). "Failure to Protect: Anti-Minority Violence in Kosovo, 2004." *Human Rights Watch Report* 16, no. 6 (D), July 2004. Available at www.hrw.org.

Jarvis, C. (2000). "The Rise and Fall of Albania's Pyramid Schemes." *Finance and Development* 37, no. 1, 46–49. Available at www.imf.org/external/pubs/ft/fandd/2000/03/jarvis.htm.

Judah, T. (2000). *Kosovo: War and Revenge*. New Haven, CT/London: Yale University Press.

Kerewsky-Halpern, B. (2000). "An Anthropologist in the Village." In *Black Lambs & Grey Falcons: Women Travellers in the Balkans*, edited by John B. Allcock and Antonia Young, 187–207. New York/Oxford: Berghahn.

Lane, R. W. (1923). *Peaks of Shala*. New York: Harper and Brothers.

Lee, R. M. (1995). *Dangerous Fieldwork*. Qualitative Research Methods Series 34. London/New Delhi: Sage.

Lutkehaus, N. (1986). "She Was Very Cambridge: Camilla Wedgwood and the History of Women in British Social Anthropology." *American Ethnologist* 13, 776–98.

Mitchell, R. G., Jr. (1991). "Secrecy and Disclosure in Fieldwork." In *Experiencing Fieldwork: An Inside View of Qualitative Research*, edited by W. B. Shaffir and R. A. Stebbins. Newbury Park, CA: Sage.

Reineck, J. (1993). "Seizing the Past, Forging the Present: Changing Visions of Self and Nation among the Kosova Albanians." *Anthropology of East Europe Review*, Special Issue: War among the Yugoslavs, 11, no. 1–2, 85–92.

Saltmarshe, D. (2001). *Identity in a Post-Communist Balkan State: An Albanian village study*. Aldershot, UK: Ashgate.

Schwandner-Sievers, S. (1999a). "Humiliation and Reconciliation in Northern Albania: The Logics of Feuding in Symbolic and Diachronic Perspectives." In *Dynamics of Violence: Processes of Escalation and De-escalation of Violent Group Conflicts*, edited by Georg Elwert et al., 133–52. Berlin: Duncker & Humblot.

———. (1999b). *The Albanian Aromanians' Awakening: Identity Politics and Conflicts in Post-Communist Albania*. Working Papers #3. Flensburg, Germany: European Centre for Minority Issues.

———. (2001). "The Enactment of 'Tradition': Albanian Constructions of Identity, Violence and Power in Times of Crisis." In *Anthropology of Violence and Conflict*, edited by Bettina E. Schmidt and Ingo W. Schroeder, 97–120. London: Routledge.

———. (2004a). "Times Past: References for the Construction of Local Order in Present-Day Albania." In *Balkan Identities: Nation and Memory*, edited by Maria Todorova, 103–28. London: Hurst.

————. (2004b). "Albanians, 'Albanianism' and the Strategic Subversion of Stereotypes." In *The Balkans and the West: Constructing the European Other, 1945–2003*, edited by Andrew Hammond. Aldershot, UK: Ashgate.

————. (2006). "'Culture' in Court: Albanian Migrants and the Anthropologist as Expert Witness." In *Applications of Anthropology: Professional Anthropology in the Twenty-first Century*, edited by S. Pink, 209–28. Oxford/New York: Berghahn.

Schwandner-Sievers, S., with S. Cattaneo et al. (2005). "Gun Culture" in Kosovo: Questioning the Origins of Conflict." *Small Arms Survey 2005: Weapons at War*, 205–27. Geneva: Graduate Institute of International Studies; Oxford/New York: Oxford University Press.

Shala, A., and D. Chavez. (2002). "Albania: From Anarchy to Kanun Politics and Society." In *Searching for Peace in Europe and Eurasia: An Overview of Conflict Prevention and Peacebuilding Activities*, edited by P. van Tongeren, H. van de Veen, and J. Verhoeven. Boulder, CO: Lynne Rienner.

Simmel, G. (1950). "The Stranger." *The Sociology of Georg Simmel*, translated by Kurt Wolff, 402–408. New York: Free Press.

Statistical Office of Kosovo (SOK). (2008). *Demographic Changes of the Kosovo Population 1948–2006*. Pristina: Statistical Office of Kosovo/Ministry of Public Services. Available at www.ks-gov.net/ESK/.

Traynor, I. (2006). "Obituary: Slobodan Milosevic." *Guardian*, March 13. Available at www.guardian.co.uk/news/2006/mar/13/guardianobituaries.warcrimes.

Vickers, M., and J. Pettifer. (1997). *Albania: From Anarchy to a Balkan Identity*. London: Hurst.

Warren, C. A. B. (1988). *Gender Issues in Field Research*. Newbury Park, CA: Sage.

Xhudo, G. (1996). "Men of Purpose: The Growth of Albanian Criminal Activity." *Transnational Organized Crime* 2, no. 1, 1–20.

Young, A. (2000a). *Women Who Become Men: Albanian Sworn Virgins*. Oxford/New York: Berg.

Young, A. (2000b). "Rose Wilder Lane: 1886–1968." In *Black Lambs & Grey Falcons: Women Travellers in the Balkans*, edited by John B. Allcock and Antonia Young, 99–112. New York/Oxford: Berghahn.

III

NEGOTIATING RESEARCH IDENTITIES

8

Negotiating the Field in Rural India: Location, Organization, and Identity Salience

Mangala Subramaniam

Research in gender studies has emphasized bringing *women* to the center of inquiry (Acker 1989; Stacey and Thorne 1985), arguing that this fosters an understanding of women's lived experiences. However, much gender studies research has pointed out that women's experiences vary by location—social and geographical—as well as within different organizational contexts; women and their experiences must be explored in terms of these varied dimensions as well (Lal 1996, Mohanty 1991, Wolf 1996). And, of course, in addition, women's experiences vary according to how power relations are organized, making understanding "women's experiences" complex, particularly in multisite and multilocation field-based research (Mohanty 1987; Purkayastha et al. 2003). Indeed, I would argue that the central dilemma for contemporary feminists conducting fieldwork on women is how power, unequal authority, status hierarchies, and social control manifest themselves within and between different social and geographic locations and organizational and social contexts.

With respect to the focus of this book, I would argue that the ubiquitous danger to gender studies field research is the failure to assess the myriad conditions that affect women's lives, particularly within field settings where such conditions cannot be "held constant" either for the researcher or for those being researched. Thus, this chapter—rather than recounting the dramatic and immediate physical or psychological dangers that I experienced as a researcher—points to the banality and social regularity of the myriad dangers associated with gender research. I explore these, on the one hand, in terms of carrying out field research in developing countries, and on the other, with respect to the challenges of multilevel gender-focused field research in rural India.

The focus of my larger field research project, based on four months of field research in rural India, is the village-based poor women's groups of the Mahila Samakhya Karnataka (MSK) Program. With respect to the MSK Program's name, *Mahila* means "women" and *Samakhya* is a compound of two Sanskrit words—*sama*, meaning "equal," and *akhya*, meaning "to be valued or weighed." My research explored the Indian government initiative to promote literacy among poor, low-caste women through MSK. The village collectives that were the foundation of the MSK Program had the broader objective of empowering poor rural women to resist and challenge gender and caste power structures, hence living up to its name of giving Indian women equal value to men. By focusing my research on larger contextual relations of power and authority, and then on how such inequalities between myself—the observer—and those I was observing—poor, lower-caste, rural women—played out within different research settings, I use this chapter to illustrate how I, a graduate student researcher, came to "know," interact with, and negotiate identities within different MSK organizational contexts.

Divided into five themes, this chapter begins with a discussion of "researcher and researched," focusing on academic methodological debates about the roles of "insiders" and "outsiders" in research. I recommend employing a "reflexive" research process—a dynamic interaction of roles—rather than seeing research relationships as existing between static "insiders" and "outsiders." The chapter's second theme, "research context/focus," situates my research within southern India and locates me and those I studied, socially and professionally. In section three, dealing with "infrastructural dangers to research in Indian villages," I identify the challenges of third world infrastructure in its own right, as well as how such challenges intersected in my research with class, caste, and gender. In the chapter's fourth section, "negotiating roles," I elaborate upon research roles and their negotiation within different research contexts. This chapter's fifth section, discussing "organizational structures, hierarchies, research outcomes," explores role negotiation within three socio-organizational contexts—an urban, formal bureaucratic setting close to national power; a middle-level district regional, "family-like," organizational context; and the micro-level contexts of poor women's *sangha* collectives. The chapter's conclusion identifies the contributions of my scholarship to field research on women.

RESEARCHER AND RESEARCHED

Recent methodological analysis that adopts a "reflexivity" perspective suggests that "the self" should be fully articulated in research and writing rather than minimized or neglected (Krieger 1991; Stanley 1990). As Wainwright (1997) explains, reflexivity "refers to the researcher's conscious self-understanding of the research process, or more specifically, to [being able to adopt] a skeptical approach to the testimony of respondents." Wainwright adds that "the purpose of reflexivity is not to produce an objective or value-free account of . . . phenomen[a]," but rather, as Ward-Schofield (1993) argues, to produce "a coherent and illuminating description of and perspective on a situation that is based on and consistent with detailed study of the situation" (202).

While reflexivity has been commonplace in much field research (Ghose 1998; Rayaprol 1997; Stacey 1991; Stanley 1990), it is seen by many positivist-oriented survey researchers as "unscientific." In response to such critiques, the researchers who pursue reflexivity often argue that its absence can also be "unscientific." By placing "the self" in the front stage of research and writing, the researcher can see and be present in aspects of subjects' lives that positivistic detachment would not permit. Moreover, by explicitly specifying the parameters of one's emerging reflexive relationship to those being studied, the researcher manifests greater openness about her research than by portraying "objectivity" within research situations that are inherently "personal." By feigning "detachment" and claiming "objectivity," the positivist can misrepresent the research process and fail to acknowledge key behavioral outcomes.

After adopting reflexivity as a valid research process, the researcher must make decisions about *her status* vis-à-vis those being researched and become conscious about *their status* in relation to her, the researcher. This has led to scholarly debates about the constituent parts of a reflexive role relationship and how these fit or not into an interaction as a whole, and the actors best suited to operate effectively and ethically within such a reflexive relationship. Seeing the reflexive research relationship in terms of a dynamic whole that is more than the sum of its parts, some methodological scholarship has presented reflexivity as if role relationships are relatively fixed, strictly dichotomous, and fairly static. Within such a methodological approach to reflexivity, the two elements of a reflexive relationship—researcher and researched—have often been seen as in a static "role-set" relationship consisting of "insiders" and "outsiders," or "natives" and "others," or "self" and "other."

Such an approach has led to debates about who is eligible to study whom. A researcher who shares the same gender, racial, ethnic, and social-class background as her subjects is considered to be an "insider" with them, while one whose status characteristics differ from those of her subjects is considered an "outsider" (Baca Zinn 1979; Merton 1972). During the 1960s and 1970s, the distinction between "insiders" and "outsiders" generated a debate about who could *acceptably* conduct research on minority communities (Bridges 1973), with some Black scholars claiming that poor and minority communities—because they have been exploited by the research practices of White researchers—should not be studied by non-Blacks.

Scholars who critique the dichotomous notions of "insider" and "outsider" argue that ethnic "outsiders" are very capable of studying those of classes and ethnicities/races different from their own. They justify this with the positivist argument that an "objective" social scientist can be "neutral" (e.g., "professional") in research and analysis (e.g., Horowitz 1983; Sanchez-Jankowski 1991). Some positivists might even argue that *only* an "outsider" can be sufficiently detached to research and write scientifically about what they see, study, and describe. Whether this is true or not, in fact, in sociology some white men and women have produced insightful studies of groups whose class and/or ethnicity/race are not the same as their own (e.g., Bourgois 1988; Miller 1986; Moore, 1991; Stack, 1983; White, 1993).

Returning to the argument that "outsiders" are the only ones who *can* and *should* study other "outsiders," some critics have pointed out that *even* researchers who share *the same* identity markers as those they study can come away from the field without a "full" picture of what is going on there, as Meera Sehgal has pointed out in her chapter for this volume. In dissecting what being a minority scholar entails, Baca Zinn (1979) has argued that "field research conducted by minority scholars may provide a corrective to past empirical distortions" in that they are "better able to get at some truths" (218). At the same time, she notes that the minority scholar's identity and commitment to be accountable to the people they study can also pose unique problems, such how to interact within their community and how to effectively leave the field. However, it should be noted that such problems were also experienced by Viterna, a U.S. outsider to El Salvador, as her chapter in this volume illustrates. Indeed, in the case of third world women of color, South Asian women have reported a troubling sense of "difference" even in their interactions with other national "insiders," recognizing that class, caste, and status differences can create disparities between themselves and their "insider" sisters (Mani 1990). Looking at "insiders" and "outsiders" through a similar lens, Pierce (1995) and Hill-Collins (1986) have pointed out that there is no *true* "insider" or "outsider"; even an ethnic equal can be a religious, caste, or class "outsider" to those in her ethnic group, as I in fact found during my research in southern India.

Yet many proponents of research reflexivity would still argue that being an "insider" can greatly facilitate initial access to "insider" communities or groups (Hill-Collins 1986). While on some level this is certainly true, it is not always the case, as I discovered. Insider community access may depend upon more than being ethnically similar to those being studied, since "insider" ethnicity can be complicated by a researcher's incongruent *"outsider"* social location—gender, status, caste, or class position—vis-à-vis those being studied. For instance, the *sangha* women who were the focus of my research belong to the lowest caste; among the poorest, these women had seen little beyond their immediate community. While this was not necessarily the case with the state-level MSK Program staff, there were still differences in status between myself and these women with regard to education and access to institutional power (such as the government bureaucracy). Moreover, academic training can make researchers and subjects look at the world in different ways. For example, what might be a positively valued, "honored practice" to a group of cultural "insiders" could, to an educated field researcher (even of the same ethnicity), represent an act of "cultural violence." Note also that academic field researchers have not always held the same "educated" assessments over time: Once accepted as a necessary system of occupational stratification, caste has now been described by many research scholars as systematic structural violence, especially against those engaged in menial forms of occupation. For a variety of reasons, researchers and those being researched can be "outsiders" to one another even when they share similar "insider" national origins, class/castes, and genders. As I discovered in research on India's MSK Program, organizational setting and its functionaries' need to protect information kept some ethnic, class, caste, and gender equals from treating me as an "insider."

I would argue that one way to breach the "insider"-"outsider" logjam is to see field research identities as *dynamic* and *multiple*, rather than—as often presented in methodological texts and in some academic discussions—as role-set *static opposites*. Certainly, one of my biggest field challenges was *negotiating* my research identity within different and changing field settings, something I had not been academically trained to do, although from past experience traveling in rural India I was vaguely aware of the need to do so. Indeed, my exposure to academic literature that represented researcher and researched as *either* "insiders" or "outsiders" to one another provided little or no help to enter a field setting infused with identity dynamics. Moreover, such role designations as "researcher" and "researched" were usually discussed in the academic literature as if "classless," "ethnicless," "statusless," and "genderless" in their content and dynamic. In sharp contrast, I found myself in the field in southern India trying to *negotiate* research roles and identities in situ (Pierce 1995) and recognizing field research identities as changing, flexible, and often multiple—as dynamic "multiple mediations," as Mani (1990) describes the research process.

In addition to these problems directly associated with my preparedness to carry out field research, I was also challenged by the glaring misfit between my *academic Western* methodological training and the actual field conditions that I encountered in a "third world" country. I would argue, on the one hand, that U.S. academic training—in its promotion of Western-based methods for field research—does not prepare researchers to work in third world contexts. In the field in India, I was challenged to consider the practicality and utility of such methods for research outside Western fieldwork contexts.[1] Unlike in most developed-country research, fieldwork in developing ones, especially when carried out in rural areas, can be physically demanding and logistically challenging. I encountered poor-quality transportation facilities, a lack of regular transportation to many rural villages, and difficulties with lodging once there. In each district where my research took place, only a few major towns were connected to one another by buses and/or trains. The smaller villages had to be reached by a precarious tramlike pedicab and/or a hired private car. Either of the latter options, as well as lodging, had to be negotiated in terms of my status as a woman in general, and as an Indian woman of a privileged class and caste position in particular.

RESEARCH CONTEXT/FOCUS

Before working on an advanced degree at a United States university, I had grown up in urban and suburban India. Learning to speak English while young and later graduating from a prominent New Delhi college, I defined myself as an educated, upper-caste *Indian* woman. Like many socially privileged Indian women, I took for granted the class and caste privileges associated with my Indian background, beginning with an assumption that my exposure to various regions of India could facilitate entering the field in India. Not particularly trained for field research, I returned "home" to India to begin my fieldwork in a geographical area outside urban and suburban India, the places I had known. My research site was in rural Karnataka state (formerly known as Mysore), a southern Indian state bordered on the west by the Arabian Sea, to the northwest by Goa and Maharashtra states, and to the south by Kerala state.

The primary focus of my larger research project—poor, rural women in village-based women's groups organized by the MSK Program—involved my studying women who were very different from me in class, caste, and education.[2] As an educated Indian woman and a future educator, I empathized with the MSK Program's explicit goal of promoting literacy for poor Indian women, itself a route toward the MSK organization's wider objective of reducing gender, caste, and power differences within my country—a goal I also accepted. The MSK organization's central mechanism for promoting such changes was to encourage the formation of village-based *sanghas*. These were to foster social change by raising poor women's consciousness about—and then empowering them to challenge—gender and caste power structures. These are important objectives for the northern rural districts of Karnataka state,[3] where overall economic development is poor (Government of Karnataka 1998), compared to the achievements of the state's capital, Bangalore, dubbed India's "Silicon City" for its important position within India's growing software industry. In a state where modern urban wealth and urban and rural poverty square off every day, the MSK Program could be a class, caste, and gender equalizer, at least for the state's poorest of poor women.

However, in 1998, when my doctoral research was being carried out, the MSK Program was only functioning in four of the state's twenty-seven administrative districts—Bidar, Bijapur, Gulbarga, and Raichur,[4] areas where my research was conducted. A great challenge to the longevity of collectives is that the *sanghas* are expected to evolve gradually, over a year or more, into a unique women's space and forum that is "owned" by its members, rather than being artificially propped up and maintained by outsiders whose withdrawal might leave the *sangha* vulnerable to collapse.[5] Such a philosophy is certainly partially responsible for the slow implantation of *sangha* collectives. But other factors are surely involved as well.

Most of the women in MSK *sangha* collectives are *dalits*—from India's lowest caste—a caste that constitutes more than one-sixth of India's population.[6] With about 160 million Indians enumerated as *dalits* (Government of India 1999), these "downtrodden people"—as the name is translated— live in extreme poverty, without land or other opportunities for bettering their education or income (Human Rights Watch 1999; Mendelsohn 1998; Mendelsohn and Vicziany 1994). Only a minority of *dalits* have benefited from India's existing policy of educational and government job quotas; the majority still perform the most menial tasks, with some even sold into bondage to pay off their debts—even the very youngest *dalits* (Human Rights Watch 1999). Increasingly frustrated with the pace of Indian Government "reforms," *dalits* have begun to resist subjugation and discrimination, mobilizing *dalit* organizations—particularly since the early 1990s—to protest peacefully the human rights violations against their community. In turn, such resistance has created an atmosphere of increasing intolerance toward *dalits*, leading to violence against them in general, and toward *dalit* women in particular. Such violence has steadily climbed since 1994 (Human Rights Watch 1999).

The MSK program believes that *dalit* women's participation in its *sangha* collectives will provide a means for them to challenge the power structures that promote various forms of violence against them and their families, a claim that was examined in my larger research. To explore this proposition and a range of others about MSK initiatives, I gathered data for an almost five-month period in 1998–1999, systematically selecting thirty-one *sanghas* across the four districts mentioned above (Subramaniam 2001). Using a sample consisting of 502 women from the thirty-one *sanghas* and 103 women not in such collectives, my final sample contained 605 women. All participants were administered a structured survey[7] that covered demographic characteristics about the individual and information regarding decision making within the family and community, as well as involvement in local village-level institutions. Members of *sanghas* were asked additional details about participation in a *sangha* collective. I also administered a structured survey to the thirty-one *sangha* facilitators for information pertaining to the *sanghas*. In addition, I attended *sangha* meetings where, as an observer, I audiotaped the deliberations. During my fieldwork, I also observed program activities, conducted informal interviews with employees, including the *sahayoginis* (facilitators who are employees of MSK and mobilize women in villages to form a *sangha*) of the MSK Program, and I visited several *sanghas* in the four study districts.

INFRASTRUCTURAL DANGERS TO
RESEARCH IN INDIAN VILLAGES

Unlike in developed countries, fieldwork conditions in developing ones, especially when carried out in rural areas, can be physically demanding. One ever-present problem is the poor quality, infrequency, and general unavailability of public transportation. In each district where my research took place, a few major towns were connected to one another by public transportation—bus and/or train. For the most part, villages closer to the main towns in the district—for example, Udhunur village in Gulbarga district; Babaleshwar village in Bijapur district—were more frequently served by buses. However, the frequency of most intervillage bus service is commonly very low.[8] Especially infrequent is regular bus transportation between the smaller villages of Karnataka state's interior, making me rely upon either the privately owned three-wheel vehicles ("tempos") or private car or jeep. Needless to say, transportation was a constant challenge to conducting research; even where there was some form of public transportation, there was often no way of obtaining a transportation timetable. I usually had to plan my travel by seeking departure and return timetables from the local people.

Another research challenge was seasonal climate problems—rain and mudslides—which, when combined with the fragility of transportation infrastructure, made travel almost impossible. With heavy rains, travel became extremely unreliable, with roads washed away and power lines downed. It complicated matters that I usually had to be totally reliant upon some form of public transportation for getting from one village to another. Although travel by hired jeep would have saved me time, several considerations made this prohibitive. Hiring a private jeep and a driver was expensive—a matter for concern considering my limited resources. However, of even greater concern was that a single woman traveling alone with two men—a hired jeep would include a driver and his helper—would have been unsafe and, more importantly, construed as violating cultural norms. Such impressions could cast a negative shadow on my research.

Thus, even though numerous physical dangers could be associated with my using public transportation—for example, the catastrophic accidents associated with buses passing on curves, driving too fast, traveling on bad tires, or drivers falling asleep at the wheel—I felt that the best means of transportation for me was public transportation. Of course, I had to be constantly prepared for untoward events that would upset my research schedule, particularly remembering the time that I was stranded overnight on a broken-down bus. As the only woman among the passengers in pouring rain, I was traveling from Raichur to Bijapur when the bus broke down after encountering a mudslide. It was impossible for the driver and conductor to check what was wrong with the bus, so the driver decided to simply wait in a lonely, dark place until the rain stopped. I had no food or water with me, having expected to reach my destination late in the evening. I feared the men might take advantage of me. Although tired, keeping awake appeared to be the best option. It was a challenge to stay vigilant and at the same time present an image that traveling alone was "normal" for me. While nothing untoward occurred, the possibility of physical danger loomed large in my mind.

Another challenge to my research was the caste proscriptions. An Indian woman from an upper-middle-class and upper-caste Indian family, I was studying poor *dalit* women in small rural villages. Such differences between myself, the researcher, and those I was studying, my research subjects, *might have* been easier to negotiate in a more urban research setting. However, where the researcher is in a small traditional village, focusing on the lives of lower-caste women—where caste differences very strongly proscribed where I could stay, with whom I could associate, and what and with whom I could eat—the mere act of *navigating* caste was complicated. For example, caste influenced where I could sit or eat or with whom I could stay overnight. While I could not fully ignore such norms and rules, I made conscious attempts to convey that I did not believe in and did not want to adhere to them. While the *sangha* women and *sahayoginis* from among the lower caste appeared to appreciate this, other MSK staff as well as the government officials I interacted with did not always consider my caste "freedoms" positive. For example, a senior government official, known to my family, frequently reminded me to make lodging arrangements in the town nearest to the villages I was covering for this research, rather than stay in the villages. I was often caught between ignoring caste proscriptions and being pressured to adhere to them.

Spatial distribution designates and defines caste and purity. My field research had to take into account the extent of space "available" to (e.g., legitimate to be used by) a particular caste group. Households were located in relation to assumed caste purity, with the lowest castes and the Muslim households (if the latter were in a village) located farthest away from the main village area. This of course meant that after I had arrived in a village, I had to trek back into its periphery to conduct interviews and observations with those of the lowest caste, a spatial location considered polluting to members of my caste. Similarly, Muslims and the village's lowest castes are restricted from entering the village's central location, which contains the village's main temple, the community hall (if a village has one), the school, and the *panchayat*—the elected village council's office.[9] The various gradations of purity and pollution associated with caste, with the "untouchable" caste at the very bottom, were reflected, as I have explained, in household groupings. The village area that contained the huts of the lowest, "untouchable" castes is labeled *harijankere*—the village area of the *harijans* ("children of God")—the latter designation given by Mahatma Gandhi to India's "untouchables." The restrictions upon entry into the village's main area are well understood by the *harijans*, who may attend a meeting of the *panchayat* village council, but cannot venture along the way or afterward near the households of upper-caste groups. These were the caste rules I had to be aware of in order to interview the *dalit* women. Combined with these proscriptions were issues of hygiene; I had to take care in eating food and drinking water or coffee that I did not consume something that would make me ill. I did not decline food or water when offered by women from *dalit* households, to ensure that I was not perceived as an upper-caste woman conscious of being "polluted" by her respondents. Being cognizant of these issues was strange: They would be inconsequential associating with people from my own caste and class.

As a researcher I had to be cognizant of such caste customs while conducting my research. For example, as someone from a high caste, there were implications for my associating with those of the lowest caste—or, as some friends put it, "risking" staying overnight in the *harijankere*. This influenced the decision I made to not stay overnight in any of the villages covered in the study. I spent long hours, even late into the evening, but always returned to a nearby town to stay at a government-owned residential place (often reserved for government officials visiting these areas) or a hotel. My interaction with *dalits*, as part of my research, was to some degree acceptable to upper-caste people, such as government officials known to my family or me, because I live and study in the United States. My U.S.–based graduate student and scholar identity facilitated overlooking to some degree the concerns of being polluted.

NEGOTIATING ROLES

While in the field, my gender, class, caste, and status—for example, as an upper-caste and privileged class Indian woman and a graduate student researcher—never actually changed, although each of these positions had more or less salience depending upon my geographical location and the formality of the interaction situation within a particular organizational size and makeup. Whether such characteristics were "real" or merely assumed by other actors was less important than the rich dynamic over them within each research interaction. In this section I identify the ways in which I negotiated my research identity. But before identifying the dynamics of an interview, there were certain more static identity-negotiating constraints. For instance, interactions set near or in a city and close to governmental institutional power were more formal, bureaucratic, and secretive. Interactions set in districts and villages more distant from state government could be either formal or informal. At the district level, my interactions with government employees were somewhat formal but relatively more open than those at the state level. Yet unlike the latter interactions, the district-level ones often took a familial turn and were less secretive. The village-level *sangha* women were most personalistic, completely open, and seemed to have no bureaucratic rules whatsoever.

Certain other patterns were also revealed in research interactions. Sometimes research subjects responded to me as "a researcher with connections to Indian government bureaucrats," a designation that seemed to make especially the state- and district-level MSK staff perceive me as having status and power. In contrast, when I was seen as "a woman and a researcher," this rendered me more subordinate and thus less prestigious and powerful. The potential for one or another designation to have salience varied by the formality of organizational setting: In the least formal of the organizational settings that I studied—the collectives of poor, rural women—it was often difficult to even make my "real" status, as a "graduate student conducting research," understood. My acceptance within such a setting was based upon my being a young woman, like the women's daughters or sisters, interested in knowing about the women's lives. I learned from my field research experiences that a researcher takes into the field a variety of roles that make possible multiple field-level identities; research subjects may accept or reject one or more of these, taking those aspects of a researcher's "real" and "presented" identities that have salience within the research subjects' social, cultural, and organizational milieu.

Related to this insight, I discovered that the multiple cultural and social meanings associated with a researcher's various roles have consequences for what subjects convey during the research process. With this in mind, I negotiated *situationally salient* field-level identities, often multiple ones within a particular research setting, by presenting the "noticeable" or "prominent" aspects of a situationally viable identity, rather than employing one single identity in each and every research interaction. Unavoidably, the many locations in which I found myself, and that shaped my identity and notions of self, clearly influenced my choice of a "working" identity. Without doubt, however, the most defining feature in my identity negotiations was being an *Indian* woman. While one might assume that being an Indian woman in and from India might facilitate conducting field research there, in fact my privileged and secular Indian upper-class and upper-caste background situated me within the category of "an Indian woman different from" those belonging to other classes and castes. It was by constantly *balancing* the "similarities" between myself and my research subjects—being Indian, being a woman, and having rural work experience—with our "differences"—my being upper class and caste and they being poor and of the lowest caste—that I sought to locate myself within identity negotiations. From such positions, I became aware of the problems associated with assuming that only a "native insider" could research other "native insiders." Among other things, such a designation reduces the "native" to a static, unidimensional entity.[10] At the same time, it is important to note that an "outsider" (someone who is not from India or has had no experience with India's rural areas) is unlikely to recognize these complexities or understand them.

NEGOTIATING ROLES: ORGANIZATIONAL STRUCTURES, HIERARCHIES, RESEARCH OUTCOMES

MSK State-Level Offices

At the MSK Program office in Bangalore—the Karnataka state capital—location, size, and level of formality indicated importance. The program directorate was in a private residence in an important upscale residential area of the city. Within the directorate offices, the MSK Program director's office situated at the far end of the directorate offices, the director's office suite located such that one could freely enter. Meeting the director required a prior appointment; visitors were ushered into her office by an office *peon* (a low-paid officer worker) only after permission had been granted by the director. Within the directorate offices, the more important administrative staff occupied one large room, while lower-level staff had a smaller room. Computers were housed in yet another room.

Visitors to the MSK offices often waited in a hallway that contained framed pictures of MSK activities on the wall. Some visitors could be seated in chairs along the hallway; others were placed in a visitors' waiting room occupied by a part-time staff member. While waiting to see an MSK official or staffer, I often sat in this room. My first visit to the MSK directorate came about six months after I had obtained written consent from the director to begin the study. However, needing a face-to-face visit to work out the details of my field research, I scheduled a meeting with the director. On the day of the scheduled appointment I waited for more than an hour to meet with the director, at the end of which I was informed that the director could not see me. Other MSK staff refrained from providing me with assistance; they needed instructions from the director to assist me in any way. Throughout the following week, I made several calls for an appointment, but was unsuccessful. Concerned that I was losing research time, I approached a senior government bureaucrat known to my family, who, in turn, helped me secure an appointment with the MSK program chairman, also a government official. My meeting with the chairman was very useful; he appeared receptive and expressed tremendous interest in my dissertation research, adding that systematic research would enable the government and MSK to consider avenues to strengthen the program. He suggested that I call the MSK directorate and request a meeting with the same director whom I had been trying to see. Being familiar with what makes Indian bureaucracy work, I understood what the chairman did not explicitly state: He would intervene and make sure that I got an appointment.

As a female graduate student, I was clearly an outsider to the MSK Program, a fact continually reinforced by MSK Program functionaries. Shulamit Reinharz (1992) has cautioned that inexperienced fieldworkers may have problems maintaining their identity as sociologists because their professional identity is not fully developed. Not only was my own professional training incomplete when I undertook this research, but my research experience and academic course work—which had encouraged critical thinking—had led me to believe that this too would facilitate my field research. The latter strongly shaped my views and behaviors in the field, especially when I first entered it, and nurtured my problematizing and questioning what I saw. This did not sit well with MSK state functionaries, who tended to neutralize my critical stance by reducing my status, as a later discussion will illustrate.

Once I had gotten to see the MSK director, she assured me that she too recognized the importance of the research. She appeared forthcoming, while attempting to determine my connection with the MSK chairman, her superior. The director offered to help my research process in any way and designated a part-time employee as my state office research contact.[11] Just the same, my knowledge of how things work in India led me to treat the director's promises as tentative. Program officials and their staffs exert power and authority by giving (or not) information and resources. By offering to assist me—or, more accurately, by offering me "a contact" from her office—the director was asserting her power over my research and ultimately bolstering her power over her office and her functionaries.

While the MSK director assured me that my proposed research was designed with rigor, she feared that the research might reveal weaknesses or negative impacts of the MSK Program. To ensure that this would not happen, prior research—usually conducted by the MSK itself or contracted out by the MSK—had typically involved visits to selective regions and villages (not systematically sampled but chosen by MSK) and interviews of carefully chosen *sangha* women. My proposed research was certainly a departure from these earlier studies: It had a clear, methodological plan that would involve a rigorous selection of *sanghas* and of the women to be interviewed. Although I felt pressure to make sure that my findings were favorable to the MSK programs, my training in research, background in research ethics, and interest in the poor, illiterate women I was studying made it impossible for me to provide the MSK director with any such guarantee.

Needless to say, my interactions with the state-level MSK Program office functionaries were far from smooth. I got little assistance from the staff, who claimed to be unable to even provide me with a list of the functioning *sanghas* in each of the four districts my study would cover. I repeatedly emphasized that such a list was essential to constructing a sampling frame, but I still did not get the requested information. When I finally insisted that I needed such information, I learned that the requested list had to be prepared—it apparently did not already exist because documentation was not a priority of the program, nor did staff have the time to attend to such work. Eventually, I obtained a tentative list. List in hand, I followed up with visits to each of the four district offices to confirm that I had a somewhat complete list of *sanghas*. While in this case the information that I had requested apparently did not exist, a related and culturally rooted reason for keeping me away from MSK organization information had to do with Indian notions of authority. Entering "too far" into the workings of the MSK organization would represent a violation of Indian and organizational norms about proper deference to authority.

The authority structure of the formal state-level MSK organizational offices was reinforced at each meeting by MSK functionaries, who dealt with me as if I were a "naive" scholar without knowledge of the "practical realities" of their programs. Officials demonstrated this by interacting with me as if I were unfamiliar with their work; with the local language, Kannada, which I could speak fluently and read and write as well; and even with the subtle nuances of social science research. For example, in preparation for distributing my structured survey to the sampled women and the MSK *sahayoginis*, I (with help from friends) had translated the questionnaire from English into Kannada. While waiting for a local printer to pick up the typed survey from me, two MSK staff members began to look at the English and Kannada versions of the questionnaire. They were critical of several words of translation, implying that I was not competent in Kannada language. I did not respond to the subtle critiques because I recognized that I had control over what would be printed. My silence reaffirmed their notions of my naïveté and "outsider" status. One of the ways that my "outsider" organizational location and status was reinforced by these MSK functionaries was interacting with me as "an educated woman from the United States"—a designation seemingly demonstrated by my alleged inability to translate English into Kannada. This positioned me as a naive—yet potentially dangerous—organizational "outsider."

Sometimes I was explicitly reminded of my "outsider" status when staff members related to me as "a person who knows little about the MSK program." For example, my pressure to obtain a list of functioning *sanghas* from MSK was viewed as demonstrating a lack of knowledge about MSK priorities. The organization had better things to do than draw up lists for an "outsider." As a consequence of the ways that I was viewed and treated by the state-level functionaries, it was difficult to build relationships at the MSK state office level. In my attempts to develop rapport, I found myself drawing on different components of my identity, depending on the situation and the issue involved in an interaction. I sometimes drew on my status as "an educated and well-trained graduate student"; at other times I was assumed to be "a U.S.–based graduate student who knows little about local practices or language"; at still other times I was seen as "a middle-class and upper-caste woman with access to government officials." At no point when a status designation was in play did I directly challenge MSK staff or question their assessment of me. However, I mediated my identity performances to prevent conflict in any form. In the end, most of my data collection was based at the district and village levels; thus, I did not spend a lot of time mediating these often very different definitions of me by the MSK state-level officials.

MSK's District-Level Offices

The MSK's district-level offices are located in the main town of each of the four districts: Bidar, Bijapur, Gulbarga, and Raichur. The MSK's district-level subunit is called the District Implementation Unit (DIU), headed by a district program coordinator (DPC). The program coordinator is assisted by "resource persons"—with a maximum of four such staffers in any district—as well as accounting and other administrative staff. The *sahayoginis*, between ten and fifteen in each district, oversee a cluster of (usually ten) *sangha* collectives; the *sahayoginis* are supervised by the DPC. All of the district MSK positions are held by women; the office accounting position is held by a man.

The district offices are located in rented houses, albeit much smaller ones than where the state-level office is located. The DPC generally occupies one room, the accounting staff has another room, leaving two small rooms for the program coordinator and facilitator *sahayoginis*. Since the *sahayoginis* and the resource persons are expected to spend most of their time in the field visiting the district's *sangha* collectives, their office is less used than the other ones. The offices have minimal furniture, with only the office basics. Each district office has at least two jeeps with drivers for traveling to the *sanghas*; the jeeps are never used by *sahayoginis*, as they are designated for the program coordinator and resource persons. However, this hierarchical system is embraced within an otherwise relatively flexible working structure. For example, the district offices, while also essentially bureaucratic in their organizational arrangements, are characterized by an informal interpersonal dynamic. The program coordinator does not use her office as a bulwark against the outside world, as the state MSK director does; rather, she often travels to *sangha* collectives with the resource persons and *sahayoginis* and is active in discussing issues related to the *sanghas* or in organizing new *sangha* collectives.

At the district level my knowledge of the local language and my familiarity with the geographical area, no doubt, facilitated my acceptance by district officials and staff. However, the district-level staff also appeared to focus on another aspect of my identity, considering me a "native insider," while recognizing my "upper caste and class" background as different from their own. For example, the majority of the *sahayoginis* in all four of the MSK district programs that I observed belonged to the lowest caste, and the program coordinators and other staff were from the lower to middle castes. At the district level, I downplayed my caste and class status and most frequently drew on my identity as a researcher—someone who wanted to know about the work of the district offices and the lives of *sangha* women. However, this did not stop district staff and the *sangha* collective women from wanting to probe more deeply into my biography. For instance, in matters pertaining to my travel, lodging arrangements, or meals, the *sahayoginis* and district staff were initially cautious about my upper-caste status, presumably in part because caste proscriptions would shape travel, lodging, and meals, but also because my caste would influence how they could interact with me. However, as I continued to interact with these MSK personnel, they became more interpersonally informal and included me in their lunch get-togethers or, in the case of the *sahayoginis*, invited me to stay overnight with them when we returned late from a *sangha* visit. Indeed, such inclusion is typically engaged in by Indian families: A person who participates in family-related activities with family members is often treated as a special category of family "insider." However, the view of the district office as a large Indian extended family was probably also projected because the majority of the staff are women.

For instance, I recall the evening we heard about protests by *sangha* women in Kallur village for the refusal of a shop owner to help *dalit* women try on bracelets.[12] Word of the protest in Kallur came through a *sahayogini* who had returned from visiting a village near Kallur. Although the program director and her staff had few details about the protest, they immediately contacted me, asking if I would like to go with them to Kallur village. They mentioned that such protests could turn violent and often involved local police. There was no secrecy about the incident; I was permitted to be present when the program director spoke openly with her resource personnel. I recognized the program director's approach as a significant departure from how state-level officials would very likely have responded to such information. Such officials had made certain that I knew that I was an "outsider" to the daily work of the MSK organization by including me in such information only after MSK state-level staff was certain that the information I received would not damage the MSK organization's (or the officials') reputation. In contrast, the district-level MSK staff involved me in discussions as if I were one among them.

Consequently, at the MSK district-level offices, I experienced a congenial working atmosphere—treated as a member of the district "family." Perhaps, as a result, much potentially negative information about the MSK organization was not withheld from me as an "organizational secret." For instance, I explored delicately the reasons for the alleged lack of data at the district level about the *sangha* collectives, in light of the seeming absence of such data at the state level. The district program director as well as other staff members were forthright with me: Their extremely tough and tight working schedules, the long hours that they worked, the programmatic uncertainties, and the lack of adequate staff all kept them from carrying out such bureaucratic necessities as collecting and maintaining statistics on the district's MSK programs. They showed me their past (failed) initiatives at record keeping, which were abandoned for lack of time and staff support. The district coordinator shared with me her frustration that the state program director and most of her staff do not speak the Kannada language. From the continuing openness of such communication, I concluded that the district-level coordinator and her staff saw me as a researcher in whom they could confide. In doing so, they probably expected me to empathize and acknowledge the hard work they do—which I did in my dissertation and the book that followed (Subramaniam 2001, 2006).

While I consciously played down my upper-caste status and heightened my graduate student researcher role, my caste and class and access to government officials were noted by MSK district staff. My interactions with government officials, particularly in the Gulbarga and Raichur districts, were seen by MSK district staff as a sign of power and privilege. One district program director even asked that I share some of her district's concerns—particularly the weak connections with the MSK state office, with government officials. I drew on my researcher identity to explain that I am not an employee of the government or of the MSK, so it might be inappropriate for me to comment on these connections. At the same time, I assured the program coordinator that my research would bear testimony to the work of her district staff in organizing *sanghas* and promoting social change. This explanation did not negatively influence my relationship with these district officials; in fact, it strengthened it.

Even in the face of an unexpected, visible failure of one of its district *sangha* collectives, I was included in this district's insider information. For example, being keen to facilitate my being able to talk with *sangha* women, an MSK district coordinator offered to take me to a village *sangha* that the staff described as "very active, with a group of vibrant women" ready to build their collective. Just the opposite was visible when, late one November evening, we visited this *sangha* collective. The *sangha* members had not even met for several months; the women that we met did not respond to the many questions raised by the district coordinator and her staff. As we left the village after a one-hour visit at the *sangha*, an MSK staff member expressed her disappointment to me about what had happened (or not happened) at the collective. On our ride back to town we continued to discuss the collective, trying to understand why the *sangha* women had seemed so unconcerned about their collective's survival. As each of us—the district coordinator, her staff, and myself—expressed our views about the visit, I realized how open these officials were to voicing their concerns about a collective that they had previously described to me as "one of the district's great successes." Rather than trying to backpedal and cover up their lack of knowledge about the collective or refrain from discussing it at all, the district-level administrator and her staff included me in openly evaluating the collective. The program coordinator solicited my input with the explanation that since the program staff work very closely with the *sangha* women, the staff might not see things that someone like myself might observe and be able to evaluate.[13] Thus, as a positively esteemed, special type of "outsider," I was seen as someone who could be a trusted "insider." The many layers of my fieldwork identity—from family insider to a woman like others in the district to an educated graduate student researcher—seemed to come together at the moment of one *sangha* collective's crisis to reinforce my relationship with the district coordinator and her staff and to facilitate an exchange of information for my study.

Village-Level *Sanghas*

In large part, women in the *sanghas* were very interested in sharing their experiences and in presenting the details of their collective's activities, relating past events and encounters and inviting me to participate in activities arranged by the district or by the collective itself. It nurtured the easy exchange of information between myself and *sangha* women that village-level *sanghas*, which are made up of poor village women, are not directly subordinate to the larger MSK structure. They do not even function "officially" at the MSK level, a fact central to MSK state-level operational directives. Thus, although resources (funds and staff) are regulated through district and state MSK policy, these administrative entities have little say about what a local *sangha* collective does or chooses not to do. By its own organizational rules, the MSK program's goal is "to establish a decentralized participative mode of management, with the decision making powers devolved to the district level and to the *mahila sangha* which in turn will provide the necessary conditions for effective participation" (Government of India n.d., 2).

The link between a *sangha* collective and the MSK district and/or state office is flexible (Subramaniam 2006). On the one hand, *sangha* members pay little attention to formality and procedure in the operation of their collective. For example, most *sanghas* meet once a week or somewhat more, depending upon their members' need to work long hours for wage labor or when monsoons make wage labor unavailable and free the women up for *sangha* collective activities. *Sangha* meeting locations are flexible as well. Women meet in the village community hall, under a tree, in front of a temple, or in a *sangha* hut (*mane*). (Some of the older *sangha* collectives had constructed a community hall by raising resources from various sources—in some instances even from contributions from *sangha* members' savings). Most commonly, *sanghas* had no specific space for meetings, sitting on a bare floor or on a carpet to do their cooperative's business.[14] Just as *sangha* organization is informal, so also were my conversations with *sangha* women. My conversations with *sangha* women became free-flowing, although in some cases sooner than others. Some *sangha* women responded to me with caution, presumably focusing on my high caste status, a woman of privilege who had access to government (or some other form of distant institutional) power. Other *sangha* woman made me feel included in their community, as a woman who spoke their language and was interested in their lives. Perceiving my identity as primarily that of "an Indian woman and a researcher," these women were comfortable in narrating their experiences to me. Considering that one source of data for my study was the firsthand narratives of *sangha* women, I promoted the identity that best promoted this intersection of mine and the *sangha* images of my and their identities. Demonstrating their acceptance of me as an "insider," *sangha* women shared tea with me and/or invited me to join with them in ritual singing.

One very likely sign of my acceptance by *sangha* women was their desire for me to return to their village. For instance, *sangha* women in Babaleshwar village were insistent on knowing when I would be returning to their village. Although I did not have my schedule of visits on me, they would not relent until I committed a date for my next visit. I returned to Babaleshwar a week later, where I had planned to spend a couple of hours and then go to other *sanghas*. I spent almost the entire day: The women sang a song they had composed about my previous visit, when they had come to know me and included me in their community of women. This was an emotional moment, I reckoned, because, in part, it made my identity as an Indian woman salient. At the same time, our coming together had provided me an added opportunity to ask a variety of questions about the *sangha* and its members' lives. Building upon such relationships facilitated gaining insight into these women's lives; lives that were structured within the family and community by gender, caste, and class norms.

A critical issue for my research at the village level was being aware of the significance of such cultural, caste, and class signifiers as dress, language, and behavior. This knowledge, and how I used it, would influence how and whether village women would interact with me. As caste affiliations are identifiable from names and appearances, the power and identities attached to caste were important elements in field interactions. While in the field, especially at the district and village levels, I dressed in traditional Indian style. My intention was to emphasize my similarities with local women and downplay our differences. I wanted to be perceived first and foremost as an Indian woman, albeit one pursuing a higher education degree. By using traditional Indian dress, I was able to facilitate my initial acceptance into traditional villages—the "Indian woman" side of my identity—and avoid being perceived as a "modern woman who had adopted Western values"[15]—the "modern graduate student" side of my identity.

However, dress did not sufficiently back-stage for rural women my upper-caste/class status. Belonging to the lowest caste, *sangha* women were sometimes deferential toward me, which certainly had implications for how much and what they narrated to me. Caste and class also impacted upon the field identities available to me. For instance, I attended a *sangha* meeting in Chambola village, where *sangha* women had constructed a meeting hall. As the *sahayogini* facilitator and I entered the hall, the women picked up the carpet that was used for seating and laid it out for us to sit on. While seemingly a mere act of courtesy, this act had much more important significance. As we sat on the carpet, we saw that the *sangha* women sat away from the carpet, even though I was encouraging them to sit on it with us. The carpet symbolized both my "inclusion" into their world—because I was offered a seat on it—and "outsider" deference—the lower-caste women sat on the floor at a distance from a higher-caste women and the *sahayogini* facilitator. An event that mixed deference and respect, based on caste and class proscriptions, certainly had implications for obtaining women's narratives.

During my field research, I also had to attend to gender in rural Indian social life. Drawing from my fieldwork experiences,[16] it was clear that *sangha* participants did not understand what it meant that I was in "a doctoral program" and was "collecting data" as part of that program. When told that I was "a student," their most frequent question was: "Which class are you in?" meaning "How much schooling do you have?" In some instances, my response evoked questions from the women about my marital status. Such questions provided an interesting springboard for learning more about the women themselves, about their literacy levels and expectations, and about their sense of empowerment. But such questions not only brought my gender identity into sharp focus, but also highlighted differences between myself and the poor women in *sangha* collectives. Young women in rural India do not have the opportunity to complete high school and are often married very early. I was attending a university and not married. To help smooth over our differences, I occasionally explained that my immediate goal was to complete my study and then consider marriage and family. Most *sangha* women seemed more accepting of my personal narrative when I mentioned that my parents agreed with my course of action, a resolution of differences that returned us to gender and its expectations and constraints. In India, young women do not make decisions independently, but rather in consultation with elders.

CONCLUSIONS

My fieldwork experiences suggest several important insights. First, that formal organizational setting, location, and informal organizational dynamics are fluid in field research, with a researcher's salient identity changing in terms of organizational setting and dynamics. Second, the positions of "subject" and "researcher," in reference to role-sets, can vary in relation to and/or in opposition to one another within the very same field setting. This can lead to the production of multiple identities in interactions between the researcher and the researched. Third, dichotomous categories such as "insider and outsider" or "native and outsider," are inadequate to explain identity *negotiations* in field research. Such static designations are especially unhelpful when a "native" returns "home" for research, as several articles in this volume have illustrated. As has been illustrated, an ethnic "native" can expect to be an "outsider" even within her own country and even among those—as in my case—of similar class and caste statuses, who have different occupational interests and/or gender identifications, or both.

Fourth, in fact, multiple identities are constructed as researchers negotiate complicated organizational and occupational, as well as the intersecting class, caste, and gender realities in the field. As sociologists of identity have argued, often quite emphatically: "[I]dentity is not simply imposed. It is also chosen and actively used" (Pettman 1991, 191). Geographic location and organizational structure and dynamic, among other things, can nurture identities; there is no easy and formulaic way to communicate how identities will work out in an actual field setting. However, as this chapter has suggested, the researcher who transcends several kinds of field locations and organizational settings should be prepared for her identities to shift and change—with different identity combinations and possibilities becoming salient within different organizational realities.

The biggest danger to successful and ethical research is to assume that one must be able to enter the field fully prepared to predict how various identities will play out in situ. Instead, researchers must understand that identities can take shape in different ways according to location; organizational mandates and structures; and class, caste, and gender, as I have argued. I would suggest that a distinct danger to research is when a researcher is unaware that the position of a researcher, vis-à-vis those being studied, involves constant negotiations of power. For example, the MSK higher functionaries and staff at upper levels of organizational hierarchy, on the one side, and the *sangha* women at the lowest organizational level, on the other side, each represent people who are differentially situated within their own power hierarchies, as well as vis-à-vis my status as an upper-caste female graduate student from the United States. I had to be prepared to negotiate in terms of such groups' designations of my status and identity, using different permutations of these designations as they were understood by myself and by those with whom I interacted and was attempting to study. I have concluded that *the real* danger to research is being unable to navigate such changes and the expectations associated with them in an ethical manner.

NOTES

1. In spite of the highly visible trends in globalization, sociology, compared to most other social sciences, has yet to "internationalize" its curriculum. While international issues may be dealt with in a specific course, often involving cross-country comparisons, it fails to be systematically integrated into a course.

2. An intervention of India's federal government, the MSK Program was born out of India's 1986 New Education Policy, with the intent of creating conditions for fostering women's equality (Mahila Samakhya Karnataka 1996). *Sahayoginis* (or facilitators), who are MSK Program employees, are responsible for organizing the village-level collective referred to as the *sangha* (one in each village). Each *sahayogini* oversees *sangha* collectives in up to ten villages/hamlets; such hamlets are part of an administrative subdistrict called a *taluka*.

3. Divided administratively into twenty-seven districts, Karnataka State contains 175 subdistrict *talukas*.

4. Activities in one other district, Mysore, were temporarily suspended in 1998.

5. The *sanghas* are supported by a District Implementation Unit headed by a program coordinator and backed up by a State Program Office with a state program director (Mahila Samakhya Karnataka 1996).

6. Perceived as a particularly rigid and oppressive form of inequality, the origin of the caste system is a subject of debate. See Joshi (1986) for details of the debate. "Untouchability," along with rituals and ritual prohibitions, are an essential feature of the caste system. The practice of untouchability isolates those from among the lowest caste, especially the Scheduled Caste (also referred to as the Harijans or *dalits*), from those belonging to the higher castes. However, it is unquestionable that *dalit* women struggle against great inequalities at the intersections of class, caste, and gender that shape their experiences.

7. The structured survey form or interview questionnaire originally prepared in English was translated into the local language, Kannada, and printed for use. All members from each of the sampled groups and the sampled nonmembers were targeted for the structured survey. The questionnaire was administered to individual respondents in the local language by trained field investigators because the *sangha* women are illiterate. Responses to the questions were checked/written in by the trained field investigators. For additional details, and particularly the process of training of field investigators, please refer to Subramaniam (2006).

8. District-level government offices are based in the town, designated as the district headquarters, and it is therefore a major town.

9. The *panchayat* is a village governance institution comprising elected representatives that makes decisions on issues key to the village's social, cultural, and economic life. See http://encyclopedia.thefreedictionary.com/panchayet.

10. These dynamics also concern the variations among "native" women as well. Mohanty (1991) challenges feminist scholars with important questions about power and location: "Who produces knowledge about colonized peoples and from what space/location? What are the politics of the production of this particular knowledge?" (3). Mohanty unsettles not only the category of the "Third World Woman" but also the assumptions of unity underlying "women" as a central category of analysis. These aspects raise additional concerns about what happens when the traditional boundaries between the knower and the known begin to break down, are reversed, or are crosscut with mixed and hybrid identities.

11. The employee, with formal training in social sciences from a reputed institution, had negotiated for this part-time job because of family commitments. However, she quit her job with MSK at the time I was completing the fieldwork. The qualifications and ability of the staff at the state-level office did not match her knowledge and capabilities, and as a part-time employee she commanded little authority. Her lack of knowledge of the local language and personal contact with the district staff further complicated her position. On several occasions I found that the information and guidance she gave me differed from the opinions of the other officials and staff.

12. The *sangha* women were protesting a caste-related tradition. As a time-bound tradition, a local store owner refused to help *dalit* women try on bracelets he sold for a local festival. He did not want to touch them because they are *dalits* and so considered impure. The local women organized a protest by sitting outside the store

and refusing to move and buy bracelets. Men from the lower caste and women from other villages joined the sit-in. The store owner gave in. These forms of resistances question the embedded system of caste relations.

13. The district-level program staff sought critical feedback and I provided it. In so doing, I assumed a more egalitarian relationship and responded as a peer. Although this may have violated an unstated norm that is to refrain from commenting on the program, I believe it facilitated establishing a professional and, at the same time, a friendly relationship with the MSK district coordinators and their staff. It was almost impossible for me to refrain from expressing my opinion and participating in the discussion. Not participating in the discussion could be construed as disinterest or a lack of enthusiasm on my part to understand the activities of the program.

14. Such a carpet is often referred to as a *durree* in India.

15. Stereotypical notions of Western values included lack of integrity, honesty, and sexual promiscuity.

16. The rich experience of the fieldwork for a little over four months cannot, by any means, be covered in a single chapter. I narrate experiences selectively as relevant to the arguments being made here.

REFERENCES

Acker, J. (1989). "The Problem with Patriarchy." *Sociology* 23, no. 2, 235–40.

Baca Zinn, Maxine. (1979). "Field Research in Minority Communities: Ethical, Methodological, and Political Observations by an Insider." *Social Problems* 27, no. 2, 209–19.

Bourgois, P. (1988). "Conjugated Oppression: Class and Ethnicity among Guaymi and Kuna Banana Workers." *American Ethnologist* 15 (May), 328–48.

Bridges, Lee. (1973). "Race Relations Research: From Colonization to Neo-Colonialism? Some Random Thoughts." *Race* 14, no. 3, 341–441.

Ghose, Indira. (1998). *The Power of the Female Gaze. Women Travelers in Colonial India*. Delhi: Oxford University Press.

Government of India. (1999). *India's Ninth Five-Year Plan*. New Delhi: Planning Commission.

———. (N.d). *Project Plan, Mahila Samakhya Program*. New Delhi: Ministry of Human Resource Development.

Government of Karnataka. *Human Development Report*. Bangalore, India: Planning Commission, 1998.

Hill-Collins, Patricia. (1986). "Learning from the Outsider Within: The Sociological Significance of Black Feminist Thought." *Social Problems* 33, no. 6, 514–32.

Horowitz, Ruth. (1983). *Honor and the American Dream: Culture and Identity in a Chicano Community*. New Brunswick, NJ: Rutgers University Press.

Human Rights Watch. (1999). *Broken People: Caste Violence Against India's "Untouchables."* New York: Human Rights Watch.

Joshi, Barbara R. (1986). "Introduction." In *Untouchable! Voices of the Dalit Liberation Movement*, edited by Barbara R. Joshi, 9–14. London: Zed Books.

Krieger, Susan. (1991). *Social Science and the Self: Personal Essays on an Art Form.* New Brunswick, NJ: Rutgers University Press.

Lal, Jayati. (1996). "Situating Locations: The Politics of Self, Identity, and "Other" in Living and Writing the Text." In *Feminist Dilemmas in Fieldwork,* edited by Diane L. Wolf, 185–214. Boulder, CO: Westview Press.

Mahila Samakhya Karnataka. (1996). *Beacons in the Dark. A Profile of Mahila Samakhya Karnataka.* Bangalore: Mahila Samakhya Karnataka.

Mani, Lata. (1990). "Multiple Mediations: Feminist Scholarship in the Age of Multinational Reception." *Feminist Review* 35, 24–41.

Mendelsohn, Oliver. (1998). *The Untouchables. Subordination, Poverty and the State in Modern India.* Cambridge: Cambridge University Press.

Mendelsohn, Oliver, and Marika Vicziany. (1994). "The Untouchables." In *The Rights of Subordinated Peoples,* edited by Oliver Mendelsohn and Upendra Baxi, 64–116. Delhi: Oxford University Press.

Merton, Robert. (1972). "Insiders and Outsiders: A Chapter in the History of the Sociology of Knowledge." *American Journal of Sociology* 78, no. 1, 9–47.

Miller, Eleanor. (1986). *Street Woman.* Philadelphia: Temple University Press.

Mohanty, Chandra. (1987). "Feminist Encounters: Locating the Politics of Experience." *Copyright* 1, special issue, 30–44.

———. (1991). "Introduction. Cartographies of Struggle: Third World Women and the Politics of Feminism." In *Third World Women and the Politics of Feminism,* edited by Chandra Talpade Mohanty, Ann Russo, and Lourdes Torres, 1–47. Bloomington: Indiana University Press.

Moore, Joan. (1991). *Going Down to the Barrio: Homeboys and Homegirls in Change.* Philadelphia: Temple University Press.

Pettman, Jan. (1991). "Racism, Sexism and Sociology." In *Intersexions: Gender/Class/Culture/Ethnicity,* edited by G. Bottomley, Marie de Lepervanche, and J. Martin. Sydney, 187–202. Australia: Allen and Unwin.

Pierce, Jennifer. (1995). *Gender Trials: Emotional Lives in Contemporary Law Firms.* Berkeley and Los Angeles: University of California Press.

Purkayastha, Bandana, Mangala Subramaniam, Manisha Desai, and Sunita Bose. (2005). "The Study of Gender in India: A Partial Review." *Gender & Society* 17, no. 4, 503–24.

Rayaprol, Aparna. (1997). *Negotiating Identities. Women in the Indian Diaspora.* Delhi: Oxford University Press.

Reinharz, Shulamit, with the assistance of Lynn Davidman. (1992). *Feminist Methods in Social Research.* New York: Oxford University Press.

Sanchez-Jankowski, Martin. (1991). *Islands in the Street: Gangs and American Urban Life.* Berkeley and Los Angeles: University of California Press.

Stacey, Judith. (1991). *Brave New Families.* New York: Basic Books.

Stacey, Judith, and Barrie Thorne. (1985). "The Missing Feminist Revolution in Sociology." *Social Problems* 32, 301–16.

Stack, Carol B. (1983). *All Our Kin: Strategies for Survival in a Black Community.* New York: Basic Books.

Stanley, Liz, ed. (1990). *Feminist Praxis: Research, Theory and Epistemology in Feminist Sociology.* London: Routledge.

Subramaniam, Mangala. (2001). *Translating Participation in Informal Organizations into Empowerment.* PhD diss., University of Connecticut.

———. (2006). *The Power of Women's Organizing: Gender, Caste, and Class in India.* Lanham, MD: Lexington Press.

Wainwright, David. (1997). "Can Sociological Research Be Qualitative, Critical *and* Valid?" *Qualitative Report* 3, no. 2 (July). Available at www.nova.edu/ssss/QR/QR3-2/wain.html (accessed April 20, 2006).

Ward-Schofield, J. (1993). "Increasing the Generalisability of Qualitative Research." In *Social Research: Philosophy, Politics & Practice*, edited by M. Hammersley, 200–25. London: Open University/Sage.

White, William F. (1993). *Street Corner Society: The Social Structure of an Italian Slum*, 4th ed. Chicago: University of Chicago Press.

Wolf, Diane L., ed. (1996). *Feminist Dilemmas in Fieldwork.* Boulder, CO: Westview Press.

9

Perils of Witnessing and Ambivalence of Writing: Whiteness, Sexuality, and Violence in Rio de Janeiro Shantytowns

Donna M. Goldstein

I want to use the space provided to me in this collection to reflect critically on my own insertion into the urban milieu of Rio de Janeiro, a site where the rule of law is thin, where racism is expressed in popular culture through the linkage of race/color and crime, where the police are brutal and are considered by the poor to be their mortal enemies, and where the possibility of being in the wrong place at the wrong time is high. The women I worked with struggle to maintain a sense of dignity and a sense of humor in the face of both police and gang-based brutality in their neighborhoods, and they use tough love as a deterrent on their young children in order to keep them off the streets and distant from the gangs' promise of easy money. These are women who are doing the best they can to keep themselves and their children out of the way of violent, male-dominated institutions. In the context of Rio de Janeiro, there are two factions at war: the police versus the drug-trafficking gangs that are embedded in local communities.

In my ethnography *Laughter Out of Place: Race, Class, Violence and Sexuality in a Rio Shantytown* (Goldstein 2003), I devote a great deal of the prose to documenting and analyzing the cyclical nature of poverty, violence, and revenge that characterizes the everyday lives of women living in the urban shantytowns of Rio de Janeiro, Brazil, where I carried out fieldwork in the early 1990s. While I addressed some of the reflexive issues that most immediately required clarification when writing *Laughter Out of Place*, I have not yet had an opportunity to reflect more fully on my own coping strategies in this particular fieldwork context—a context that required constant negotiating of my own identity not only in relation to the people I worked with most directly, but also in relation to the society at large that informed our interpretations of one another, in particular our understandings of race.

Nor have I had the opportunity in writing to explore more fully the profound personal effects that this kind of research produces on the soul.

In this chapter, then, I want to write more explicitly about my own imperfect choices of racial and sexual identification while in the field. I would like to reflect on some of the more submerged aspects of fieldwork behavior—on the time I spent dressing and presenting myself and on the ways in which my own whiteness, perceived femininity, and foreignness worked mostly to privilege me in this setting. It is through these reflections that I have also become even more acutely aware of the power dynamics existing in this particular field site. This essay thus addresses the ways in which this form of long-term engagement throughout years of fieldwork affected my psyche, my research, and the kinds of intimacies I was ultimately able to develop.

THE CONTEXT

Some time ago I was able to view the quite remarkable 2002 documentary film titled *Bus 174*, directed by the *Carioca* (from Rio de Janeiro) director José Padilha. The film's focus is a bus hijacking that took place in a middle-class Rio de Janeiro neighborhood in June of 2000, in which a twenty-one-year-old man named Sandro do Nascimento took several passengers hostage. The documentary draws from the actual footage of the event, filmed by television journalists who arrived on the scene at the same time as the police. The event was broadcast live for more than four hours on Brazilian television as approximately 35 million viewers nationwide tuned in. Most importantly, however, the film documents the cruel and harsh life of the lone hijacker Sandro, interspersing footage of the live hostage standoff with interviews from individuals who had known the perpetrator intimately over the course of his life.

Sandro had grown up as one of Rio's numerous street children. His early life was marked by movement in and out of juvenile and adult correctional institutions. As a young man, he was one of the few survivors of the famed Candelária massacre that took place in Rio de Janeiro in 1993. This was an internationally publicized event during which hooded members of a death squad—later discovered to be off-duty police—killed seven homeless boys and wounded two others, spraying them with gunfire as they lay sleeping in front of the Candelária Church in the commercial center of Rio de Janeiro. The Candelária massacre—as it was called at the time—transfixed the Brazilian nation in 1993, causing the country to question its treatment of street children, poverty, cyclical violence, and the flawed nature of Rio de Janeiro's police forces. The June 2000 bus hijacking documented in *Bus 174* was connected to the Candelária massacre through the emergence of Sandro as both a survivor of Candelária in 1993 and the lone hijacker of *Bus 174* in 2000. If there had been any uncertainty that the cycles of violence and revenge taking place in Rio were deeply connected to the collective despair of Rio's angry and impoverished young men, the second event—now shockingly told in this documentary film—extinguishes that doubt.

The documentary challenges its audience to look closely at Sandro's life and at the various ways in which young men like Sandro are ultimately excluded from social life and condemned by Brazilian society. The audience learns that at a young age, Sandro was a witness to the brutal murder of his mother and soon after wound up living on the streets. The audience also learns that although Sandro, like many street children, had developed a serious and chronic drug-use problem, he was not regarded by his peers or the professionals in either the juvenile or adult correctional system as an organically violent individual. The audience also learns that much of what Sandro is performing in front of the live television cameras—threatening each of the hostages with a bullet to the head—is undone privately as survivors later reveal that Sandro is calmly reassuring the hostages that he does not want to harm them; that he just wants to be able to escape alive from this situation. Personally traumatized by the violent events in his own life—namely, the death of his mother and of his friends at Candelária—Sandro has a particularly contentious relationship with the police with whom he finds himself in negotiations. His repeated hysterical outbursts to the police are revealing: He berates them for being cowards and for killing his sleeping comrades at the church; he chastises them for later killing witnesses who were scheduled to go to court to identify the police responsible for the Candelária massacre. All 35 million Brazilians watching know—as does Sandro himself—that no matter what happens to the hostages in his control, the likelihood that Sandro will emerge alive from this event is practically nil. As a young, dark-skinned Afro-Brazilian man from the Rio shantytowns with no education and with a long life on the street, there is little hope for his long-term survival or success in Rio's hierarchized structures of class and race.

I am grateful to the filmmakers for putting together this remarkable document and for once again stimulating discussion among middle- and upper-class Brazilians about police violence and the relationship of this violence to impoverished, racially marked young men. This film speaks to some of the central tensions in contemporary Brazilian society: that is, how to think about violence, race, human rights, and justice in a society with a long history of colonialism, racial inequality, and class bifurcation. Despite the viewing audience's generalized sympathy for the hostages, a number of other issues surface and become defining as the film heads toward its tragic climax: in particular, the irreversibility of Sandro's life circumstances and the structure of police brutality and incompetence.

The police remain poised outside of the bus until eventually Sandro tires of his situation and emerges with his pistol pointed at the head of one of the hostages, a girl named Geísa. A "sharpshooter" of the police forces comes within shooting range of Sandro, fires, and misses him, accidentally shooting Geísa instead. According to the official autopsy, Sandro's gun had also fired into the head of the hostage before he was "neutralized" at the scene. In spite of the fact that there are numerous opportunities throughout the event for the police to shoot Sandro—sharpshooters are within range at all times—there seems to be an unspoken agreement that Sandro should not be murdered in front of 35 million television viewers. In the last few scenes, the police are shown holding back the lynch mob that forms to kill Sandro. Sandro makes it alive into the back of a police car, only so that minutes later the police can smother and murder Sandro themselves, off camera. Unfortunately, as my work and that of other scholars interested in extralegal violence in Latin America have shown (e.g., Caldeira 2000; Goldstein 2003; Holloway 1993; Holston and Caldeira 1998; Huggins 1991; Leeds 1996; Pinheiro 1991; Zaluar 1994), the policing institutions in the region have remained problematic from the colonial period through to the present.

FIELDWORK INTERLUDE

In the course of my fieldwork in Brazil, I met many men like Sandro do Nascimento because the "subjects" of my research were their mothers. Glória, a dark-skinned Afro-Brazilian woman in her late forties who worked as a domestic worker her entire life and who is the central character in *Laughter Out of Place*, had raised one of the most notorious drug gang leaders in Rio de Janeiro, Pedro Paulo, who I had the opportunity to meet and interview during an overnight visit at Ilha Grande (Big Island) Prison (also known as the Devil's Cauldron) in September of 1992. Glória planned the weekend trip and insisted that I accompany her, her boyfriend at the time, and her two youngest children in exercising this family visiting privilege. We cooked food all night long and then early in the morning made our way to the ferryboat landing and paid for our voyage on the boat that makes the trip between the mainland and the island. When we docked on the island, it was about nine o'clock in the morning, and a female security guard employed by the prison was waiting at the pier to greet us. At that hour, most of the passengers on the boat were coming to the island to visit imprisoned loved ones, alongside a few tourists and residents. There on the pier, in full public view, the security guard began to match her list—the prisoners—with those of us who had come as their visitors. After she marched us briskly to a security headquarters especially for visitors and divided the men from the women, I found myself waiting with Glória and about thirty other women for the next eight hours. Everyone in our room was placing towels or small blankets they had brought with them on the floor, attempting to claim precious space for lounging and a possible nap. They all seemed to know the routine and were prepared for the long day of waiting. One woman, who saw me standing and waiting patiently for the process to begin, called out to me, "Ohh, *Neguinha* [Little Blackie, a term of endearment], sit down," in a thoughtful attempt to let me know that it would be a lot more comfortable to claim a space to park myself in for the rest of the day instead of standing the entire time. There were a few chuckles when she called me *Neguinha* because I was one of only two or three whiter-skinned women in the room, and I definitely stood out. One by one we were called into a tiny office, where we were asked to strip completely naked. Then flashlights were beamed onto all our private parts to make sure we had not smuggled in a prohibited object, such as a knife. Glória was not the only one who had brought gifts and pots of food; the inspection of everything we had brought with us then commenced and took hours, and I was forced to leave my camera and tape recorder in the security area. Finally, at about five o'clock, a minivan from the prison came to pick us up, and we all piled in, exhausted by the long day of waiting and anticipating the reunion with loved ones. The climb to the prison seemed long and treacherous—more than a half hour of rugged driving through thick tropical vegetation. The curves on the road were sharp and dangerous and fed the anxiety quietly brewing in my stomach.

Upon arriving at the prison, we were led to what was known as the *área de lazer* (recreation area) and served a sweet drink similar to Kool-Aid. Pedro Paulo had not been certain that we were coming, and he had to be summoned to the area, which was actually a long, narrow hallway with twenty to twenty-five small rooms spread out along two sides. Iron bars were welded onto the padded doors of the rooms, but the doors were left swinging open at this time of the day, and one could peek in and see that some of the rooms were quite spruced up, with television sets and throw rugs on the floor. Unfortunately we were issued one of the worst cubicles, one that was quite dirty and had years' worth of tropical fungus growing in every corner. There was a set of bunk beds, a sink, and a little cooking area where we were able to set our pots to warm.

In our room that night was Amélia, another guest at the prison, a young woman who was there on her birthday to visit her long-lost brother, Adhmar. She claimed that she had not seen him since they were children of three or four years of age, more than two decades ago. According to Amélia, she and Adhmar were separated as children when, after the death of their mother, she was given to one family, and he to another. Adhmar was a heavyset, soft-spoken man who grew up on the streets and was now serving a long prison sentence. I never asked what his crime had been; it would have gone against the prevailing etiquette. Amélia brought to mind the images I had stored in my mind of Catholic novitiates, young nuns-in-training I had known in other Latin American contexts; she appeared innocent to an extreme, almost otherworldly. I doubted that she actually was Adhmar's sister. I had heard about women who were drawn to and eventually became involved with men in prison from women in Felicidade Eterna (Eternal Happiness, the name of the Rio shantytown I did my fieldwork in) who knew of such cases. Glória's daughters, Soneca and Anita, believed that a certain kind of woman—and they even hinted that it might especially be common among women who had recently become *crentes* (literally: believers, religious converts)—hope that through their faith they can redeem another person from a criminal life. Likewise, I had read an abundance of popular articles that spoke of the sweeping religious conversion movement within Rio's prisons. Thus, I wondered whether Amélia was really related to Adhmar or whether perhaps she was one of the women I had heard about. She kept repeating clichéd phrases such as "When a woman loves, she really loves, and it is one person." Somehow I did not believe that they were siblings, but this was a story I would not be able to confirm in either direction. In any case, Amélia's optimism and faith in the goodness of human nature, as well as her seemingly spiritual approach to the world, made an interesting contrast that night to the combined cynicism of Pedro Paulo and Adhmar.

Having been informed at the last minute that he had visitors, Pedro Paulo arrived at the recreation area from the bowels of the prison. Pedro Paulo was a young man of about thirty, extremely tall and muscular, and the most articulate of Glória's children. She introduced me to him as her *filha branca* (white daughter), and this puzzled him for a moment and made him pause, I believe because he was wondering whether it was possible that Glória actually gave birth to someone as white as me. Perhaps because he had been out of touch with her for so many years, he thought anything was possible. After letting him wonder for a bit, Glória laughed loudly and explained that I was like a daughter to her, and that I was in fact an anthropologist writing a book about women in the shantytowns of Rio de Janeiro. Pedro Paulo immediately understood my presence as a chance for him to be remembered and perhaps even immortalized in my book. He seemed like a young man who was used to being listened to, and he had much to say. Unfortunately, we were all exhausted. None of us had eaten more than a few salty crackers during the entire day, and I felt dizzy with hunger. The children, Zeca and Félix, were even too tired to wait for the beans and rice to be heated, and they opted for bed before dinner. They were all too used to days like this, when one's body becomes tired and ultimately disinterested by what often turned into an all-too-long and familiar wait between meals.

Pedro Paulo was a fan of reggae music, and one of the first things he requested from me was to find him a Jamaican-colored *boné*, or cap, similar to the one Bob Marley wore. He seemed to have an affinity not only for the music but also for the politics that reggae music represents. Compared with the many other friends I had known in the shantytowns who were of Pedro Paulo's generation, he seemed far more politicized and aware of the absurd nature of the poverty in Rio. One could see in his body language and hear in his monologues that Pedro Paulo was a young and energetic man, filled with anger. He had recently learned that his "woman" in Rocinha (the largest *favela* or urban shantytown in Brazil), Josilene, was pregnant with his child and was considering having an abortion. Pedro Paulo threatened that if she aborted his child, the first thing he would do upon leaving prison would be to kill her: "*Ela matou o meu filho. Agora vou ter que matar ela.* [She killed my child. Now, I am going to have to kill her.]" He felt that when a woman has sex with a man, she ought to know the consequences, a comment that forced the women in the room out of their listening mode and into verbal battle. Glória and Amélia countered that men ought to take part in birth control as well—that it should not fall only within the domain of women. Soon, however, Pedro Paulo launched into another long harangue, this time about Rocinha's Comando Vermelho (Red Command, the most well-known imperialist drug gang in Rio de Janeiro) and how this particular gang acts to preserve "family values." Pedro Paulo connected his own personal position on abortion to his sense that Red Command, as a group sharing a set of core values, promoted his particular sense of right and wrong. He told us how much he hated abortion and equally despised women who were not monogamous. For Pedro Paulo, the job of "the man" is to put the food on the table for his family, and as long as this is taken care of, it is fine for that man to have as many women as he wants—as long as they "don't lack anything," of course. I was surprised by how well he was able to articulate the male double standard on fidelity, making it sound as if it were a unique, well-developed doctrine emanating from Red Command rather than a more generalized cultural norm.

At midnight, the visitors are locked into the cubicles together with the prisoners, a fate that seemed daunting to me after having spent the evening chatting with Pedro Paulo and Adhmar. I was forced by Glória into taking a section of the bottom bunk bed; she was concerned that her "white daughter" sleep comfortably. Meanwhile, she and her boyfriend, Zezinho, unrolled some blankets and spread themselves out on the floor. Shortly after the lights went out and as I was dozing, I noticed the smell of cigarettes close to me and felt a man attempting to place his hands on my body. It was extremely dark in the room, and I was guessing that the hands were Pedro Paulo's. I whispered to the transgressor that I was "like a sister" to him and that he should treat me with a little more respect.

Finally, I threatened to wake Glória and tell her what he was doing, at which point he immediately pulled away and moved back sheepishly to the other bed. I was momentarily giddy for having thought of using Glória as a threat against Pedro Paulo, but I realized early in the morning that the intruder actually had been Adhmar! Nevertheless, I am guessing that through his friendship with Pedro Paulo, he had understood that Glória was not someone to cross, and my threat to expose him had indeed functioned almost magically. I decided, wisely, I believe, to refrain from telling Glória about the episode until we were safely in the minivan heading back down the road from the prison, so as not to disturb the rest of our visit. Her response was what I had suspected. She would have liked to "break his face" for trying something like that with me, and she probably would have wanted to cut short our visit—or worse, she might have entered into some kind of violent physical battle in that tiny room. In any case, I was glad I did not ruin the trip, and I made her swear and promise never to mention the incident to Pedro Paulo either, since I did not want Adhmar to suffer any for his momentary transgression.

Upon his release from prison in 1995, Pedro Paulo went back to his gang and his old life in Rocinha. Josilene, the woman Pedro Paulo had referred to as his "woman," had not followed through with the abortion, and Pedro Paulo returned to her and responsibly took over his fatherly obligation to his son, Raul, which included teaching him how to distinguish between different kinds of guns. During our brief prison visit, Pedro Paulo had made it clear that he was not interested in working for slave wages, as his mother had done her entire life. He openly scorned Glória's definition of "honest" work and quite articulately described the impossibility of any self-respecting man supporting a family on a Brazilian minimum wage (which at the time hovered around $100 U.S. per month). He was angry and impulsive, but I found his analysis of minimum-wage work to be quite accurate. In 1995, only a few months after being released from prison, he was killed in a shoot-out with police in Rocinha. Glória had no tears left to shed over Pedro Paulo, perhaps because she had tried so hard over the years to reason with him and had come to accept their differing perspectives of the world.

Over the years, Glória's lament about Pedro Paulo had been constant. She tried to understand why her firstborn had turned out to be a *marginal* (marginal person, criminal). She considered him the most intelligent of all her children—he had completed his secondary schooling and could read and write at a relatively sophisticated level. But, according to Glória, early in life he exhibited his love for "the street," and this tendency, finally, was the strongest influence on his character. In many of the life stories of the women in Glória's network of friends and family, the women had worked in the homes of others, raising the children of strangers but being forced themselves to leave their own children with an older sister, a grandmother, or "the street." Glória herself was raised by her grandmother while her mother worked in Rio de Janeiro to earn enough money to move the entire family. In reflecting on her own work-filled life, she also attributes the loss of Pedro Paulo to "the street" and its violence to the fact that she was too busy to keep track of him as much as she would have liked.

According to Glória, Pedro Paulo spent a good portion of his youth in and out of the state's child correctional institution—Fundação Nacional do Bem-Estar do Menor (FUNABEM). He seemed to have emerged from that experience even angrier than when he went in, and upon finishing his time there, he quickly returned to Rocinha and became involved with the infamous Red Command. From that time on, Glória knew that his life would be a short one. She had always told her children, using Pedro Paulo as a negative role model, that *"bandido não tem amigo* [bandits have no friends]." Pedro Paulo was known to sleep restlessly, with a gun under his pillow in constant expectation of trouble.

Pedro Paulo had watched Glória and her entire generation slave away as domestic workers in the homes of the wealthy in the Zona Sul (South Zone, signifying the wealthy neighborhoods of Rio de Janeiro) for barely subsistence wages. He was not moved, either, by the men he knew in Rocinha who worked at honest jobs. Men like Pedro Paulo felt they had been cheated out of their own futures. Further, Pedro Paulo had figured out early on that those of his class and background do not have a great deal of social mobility. Those whom he knew in "honest" professions—domestic workers, construction workers, security guards, and so forth—struggled their entire lives, working hard but still barely making a living for themselves and their families. My sense is that what marks Pedro Paulo's generation is the recognition, although in some ways inarticulable, of the impossibility of "the good life" for those of his race and background. In places like Rocinha, gang leaders and some "successful" gang members have built large houses for themselves and have been able to acquire a piece of "the good life" that is so central to Carioca identity. More than anyone else, Pedro Paulo had a sense of the riches and the good life of the *bacanas*, those who lived on the asphalt streets, the wealthy people in the Zona Sul, as he referred to them. His descriptions of apartments he had robbed were filled with details about electronic devices, clothes, and other elements of "the good life" that he believed these people inhabited. His anger seemed somehow justified to me because I knew of few cases of social mobility out of the *favela* and safely into middle-class existence. It surely did happen, but the route was treacherous and reserved for a lucky few. As an intelligent young man growing up in Rocinha, Pedro Paulo found the allure of gang life to be irresistible. It seemed to offer an alternative to backbreaking manual labor, at the same time promising a decent wage and offering instant economic improvement.

THE SPACE OF FIELDWORK

The fieldwork space that proved to be most challenging for me was the *favela* I came to know through Glória and her family, Felicidade Eterna, situated some fifty kilometers from central Rio de Janeiro. During my extended stays with Glória, I would nestle in with her family at night in their tiny shack, sleeping, as they did, on my side, curled up like a spoon so as to make enough room for anywhere between eight and fourteen of us on the makeshift bed, a foam mattress thrown on the floor with bedding. I had chosen this kind of personalized fieldwork because, after carrying out a great deal of survey research on the spread of HIV/AIDS and women's sexual culture in the shantytowns, I felt the need to go further and get closer. I wanted to find out how the working poor experienced living within the social apartheid that characterized Rio de Janeiro—how they understood it, tolerated it, and even, at times, made fun of it. I wanted to know how these working women organized their lives in communities that were known by the middle classes for high levels of violence. Getting that close, however, also required some compromise on my part: a willingness to follow the myriad and specific cues to what my friends would see as appropriate behavior. In fact, much of the behavior my young women friends advocated to me at the time, particularly appropriate "female" behavior, got them into trouble with their boyfriends, their spouses, and sometimes with the local gang. One among the many challenges I faced, then, was to fit in within the boundaries of good ethnographic practice known as participant observation—that is, to do as others do—and yet to stay safe at the same time.

During my first extended period of fieldwork I experienced Felicidade Eterna as a remarkably safe place. My experience there was similar to that of Janice Perlman, whose classic work about three Rio *favelas*, *The Myth of Marginality: Urban Poverty and Politics in Rio de Janeiro* (1976), describes them as "internally safe and relatively free from crime and interpersonal violence" (136). As a foreign researcher, I felt safe in a small shantytown where everyone knew who I was. Nevertheless, in the years that followed, I realized that the peaceful moment I had experienced in Felicidade Eterna during the early 1990s was not necessarily a stable one. Felicidade Eterna experienced distinct cycles of calm and violence that were not immediately perceivable in any one time period. In those later years, residents described to me their feeling that their own situation was deteriorating. They referred to what they perceived as an inability for the honest worker to remain outside the cycles of violence between warring and territorially based drug gangs as well as between those gangs and the police that regulated daily life in these areas. Residents felt that the violence of the 1990s was becoming increasingly unpredictable, drawing in targets and victims who had nothing to do with drugs or violence. In fact, Glória had moved her entire family away from Rocinha to another shantytown in the late 1980s because she saw that her son Pedro Paulo was gaining notoriety in the Red Command. She wanted to shield the rest of her family from his ongoing battles and prevent his lifestyle from seducing her younger boys into the gang life. A later move from this second home was precipitated by a robbery and the rape of her two daughters, which she took as evidence that the situation in that neighborhood too was deteriorating.

During return visits to Brazil in 1995 and 1998, I discovered that there were many sorts of relationships that had to be precariously balanced in order to achieve periods of peacefulness such as the one I had experienced in the early 1990s. For one thing, having a local gang that was led by a reasonable person was key to the stability and safety of Felicidade Eterna residents. Later, when the boss of the *favela* was killed and replaced by younger men, there was less predictability and stability. These poorest working-class sectors experience levels of everyday crime and violence that are in a completely different realm from those experienced by the middle and upper classes. Such everyday experiences of violence have compelled these populations to embrace solutions that seem paradoxical but upon closer examination make good sense, given the absurd situation residents find themselves in—a situation characterized by stifling poverty, profound class inequities, alarming levels of domestic violence, and racism.

THE RULE OF LAW AND ITS EMPTINESS IN CERTAIN SPACES

Although talk about violence and crime proliferates across classes, the forms and levels of daily violence and suffering in the city of Rio de Janeiro are experienced differently according to class, race, gender, and location. As Anthony Pereira (1997) explains, the rule of law, so often touted as the measure of a consolidated democracy, is applied differentially in Brazil.[1] One of the reasons such a wide gap exists between the universalism of formal legality and the actual extension of citizenship rights is due to the country's hugely inequitable economy, statistically represented in its extraordinarily high Gini coefficient (0.63), which surpasses those of both South Africa and India.

Pereira (1997) dubs the differential application of the rule of law "elitist liberalism," or "the granting of the right to civil liberties on a differential basis depending on some aspect of the person's social status and identity (be it neighborhood, profession, skin color, gender, or something else)" (9). This elitist liberalism is not merely some conspiracy of the middle and upper classes against the poor to hold back the consolidation of democracy; deeply rooted (hegemonic) historical and structural factors make a transition to a more inclusive liberalism difficult to achieve.

During the early 1990s, when I was carrying out my initial fieldwork in Rio de Janeiro, Felicidade Eterna had no more than a few hundred residents, and the gang consisted of a man named Dilmar and four young men. Very soon after I started visiting Glória in the shantytown, she insisted on bringing me by Dilmar's tiny shack and making the appropriate introductions. His name was often spoken in a whisper, as if to mention him at all was to ask for trouble. In his mid-thirties, Dilmar was tall, charming, and handsome, with olive-colored skin. He seemed to hang around the shantytown most days, making many *pssssssiu* sounds to passersby with whom he had business. Dilmar, like many in Felicidade Eterna, shuffled around the hardened dirt alleyways, which turned to mud during the rainy season, in his trademark yellow flip-flops. The only sign of wealth I could see was the expensive-looking watch on his wrist, and I was surprised to find that his shack was almost as bare as Glória's—it had a stove, a bed, and a slightly better television and stereo system, but not much else. If Dilmar was making money from his position as a gang leader, he was not investing it in his daily life in Felicidade Eterna. Because I had seen the homes and sensed a different kind of wealth among the members of the larger, more imperialist drug-trafficking gangs in Rocinha and Vidigal—mostly members of Comando Vermelho—I had expected him to be better off economically. His wife was younger than he was and pregnant when I first met him, but if I had not been told that he was the *chefe* (boss), I would never have guessed it from his appearance and his home.

I was encouraged—or, more accurately, obliged—by Glória and my other friends in Felicidade Eterna to introduce myself to Dilmar right away, as nobody wanted me to be mistaken for somebody I was not. My friends wanted to make sure that Dilmar knew that I was a friend and a person to trust who was not connected to the police in any way. Of course, the most compelling reason to meet with Dilmar was to gain permission to live in Felicidade Eterna and to gain some form of protection as a citizen of the shantytown. After introducing myself as an anthropologist and outlining, however feebly and inadequately, what anthropologists do, I explained to Dilmar that I was interested in writing about how the poorest segments of the working classes in Rio live. I told him that I was especially interested in the lives of women like Glória. Dilmar thought this was a fine project. He gave me the names of some of the elders who had participated in the first land invasions in Felicidade Eterna and who could provide me with some "local history." He also asked that I not take pictures of him or his *turma* (group), a request I readily agreed to. He seemed to be pleased to help me in my request to "hang out" in the *favela*, and because I spoke mostly with women, he was satisfied that I was not a snoop or a spy for the police. Both Dilmar and the residents of Felicidade Eterna understood the complicated nature of police-gang relations and wanted to be careful that my presence would not upset the balance that they had achieved during this period. At the time, I had little perspective on how violent the situation could become in these seemingly out-of-the-way areas, and I had readily dismissed the warnings from middle-class friends about the potential dangers of this kind of work.

What was in fact most shocking to me about the shantytowns of Rio de Janeiro was just how fragile the rule of law really was—that is, how empty these spaces were of any tangible rule of law as I had known it. I was profoundly reminded of how "raced" and "classed" the legal system is, not just in Brazil, but in my own country, the United States. I found that political scientist Guillermo O'Donnell (1993) was correct in codifying this idea of a differential rule of law into his notion of zones, color coded according to the degree of the rule of law and state presence. In his taxonomy, "blue" zones are areas that have a high degree of state presence, effective bureaucracy, and a properly functioning legal system; "green" zones are those with a high degree of territorial penetration and a lower presence of the state in functional and class terms; and "brown" zones are those with a very low or negligible state presence in both dimensions. O'Donnell's analysis of democratization suggests that the brown zones are characterized by a number of distinct properties: "personalism, familism, prebendalism, clientelism, and the like" (1359). In these brown areas, O'Donnell points out, the state is unable to enforce its legality, so while it may be possible for an individual to vote freely in elections and have one's vote counted, one cannot expect proper treatment from the police or the courts. Accordingly, these zones, represented by shantytowns in urban areas or by rural areas where feudal relations predominate, offer a kind of "low-intensity citizenship" (1360). The state is unable to enforce its legality and therefore it is expected—even predicted—that it will use extralegal force against the populations in these areas. This is what makes such populations so vulnerable to abusive elements within the police forces. This creates a situation whereby large segments of the population experience the police forces as oppressive, or, even more pointedly, as the other team in a long, drawn-out battle for justice in the homeland.

In the absence of a reliable state presence, the drug gangs have evolved over time to fill a role beyond simple trafficking in illegal goods. They are called upon to right the wrongs of everyday life, and in this role they are tolerated and sometimes even venerated. Further, because they provide favors and help in times of emergency, they are often perceived as "good bandits" or "good criminals." The low-intensity citizenship of the residents in the brown zones means that they must depend on the gangs not only to provide an alternative rule of law but also to fill in whenever the state is absent or even oppressive. Residents depend on their local gangs for protection from outsiders of all kinds who, like many invading armies, do not respect the citizens of the locale they hope to conquer. I was often surprised that friends of mine in the shantytown would fear the demise of their own local gang, not so much out of any kind of affection for its members, but rather out of fear of what it means for a community to be without protection. Invading gangs are believed to be disrespectful of residents, conducting illegal business in inappropriate places and engaging in shootouts with police without first warning residents.

The fragility of the rule of law and the gross violation of human rights that inevitably accompanies this context is less visible to the middle and upper classes, who live in central urban settings and who are more likely to be able to use their class position to intimidate or to buy their way out of inconvenient rules enforced by police, such as traffic violations. Partially it is their class position and place of residence that immunizes them from experiencing what it means to live in an area ruled by adolescent boys. The situation of the poor and working classes is made visible only through events such as those represented in the film *Bus 174*, where the public comes in touch with, or is reminded of, the incompetence and corruption that characterizes the police forces. In 1997, for example, the people of Brazil were able to watch a video recording of a middle-class motorist being harassed and eventually shot by a policeman who was trying to extort money from the driver for no apparent reason.[2] The scene, played repeatedly on television, caused a stir throughout the country. I was not in Brazil at the time, but I tried to imagine how different segments of the population might have viewed this event. Given the experiences of my friends in Felicidade Eterna with local police over the years, the broadcast must have been received as quite familiar. The poor and working classes are routinely criminalized by the middle and elite classes and by the police forces. In these brown zones that are removed from the benefits of economic well-being and the institutions and organizations that make up "civil society," a different set of actors are gaining local powers of their own. The absence of the state in such areas means that these local gangs provide a parallel or alternative rule of law that deals with all kinds of "private matters"—theft, domestic violence, infidelity, rape—that the state is unable and unwilling to address.

BEING ABLE TO LEAVE

My fieldwork situation involved living for extended periods of time in regions that were ruled by gangs and frequented by policing forces. Often they were calm and stable places with minimum violence; at other times they were unpredictable, highly violent, and tense. My greatest privilege, in contrast to my friends in the shantytown, was being able to leave Felicidade

Eterna and sleep in a comparatively secure middle-class neighborhood whenever I felt there was a potential for violence. During my return visit to Rio de Janeiro in 1998, Glória's son-in-law, Adilson, was shot and killed in Felicidade Eterna in a revenge killing, an event that sent Glória, her family, and some of her neighbors to find refuge among relatives living in other places. I rented a hotel room for the month and heeded Glória's warnings to stay away from Felicidade Eterna for a while. Throughout this time I was faced with specific ethical questions. I had my suspicions regarding who might have been involved in the murder, but, like my friends in the shantytown, I had become completely disillusioned with the "authorities" and chose to keep quiet. I had come to believe that police involvement usually made things worse for residents. Many of my friends from the shantytown came to visit me in my hotel room, and it was in the private interviews I conducted there, far from Felicidade Eterna, that I was able to piece together a more complete picture of the effects of urban violence on the women I had known. I was often asked to turn off my tape recorder whenever anyone would bring up events or themes related to the gangs, as most of my interviewees adhered to the *favela*'s law of silence about gang activities. If not for the privacy of the hotel room in the distant South Zone of the city, far away from the problems of the brown zone, the friends I had come to know over the years might never have felt safe enough to share their narratives about gangs and police in such intimate detail.

IDENTITY NEGOTIATIONS

The women I worked with in Felicidade Eterna had to develop strategies to keep themselves safe and out of range of warfare between opposing gangs and between gangs and police. Sometimes this involved fleeing for a time and waiting until things cooled down. But I have witnessed other strategies as well, such as becoming a *crente* or religious convert—that is, declaring loyalty to one of the many evangelical religious denominations that are highly visible in these communities. As a *crente*, an individual is motivated to dress more conservatively: women with long skirts and men with button-down white shirts, jackets, and ties. These visual cues communicate to both the gangs and the police that the person has decided to exit the game and have nothing to do with any of the activities that motivate these warring factions—drugs, alcohol, infidelity. While conducting fieldwork in the shantytowns of urban Rio de Janeiro, I too had to make some decisions, some of which were conscious, about how to present myself in these public arenas in order to remain safe. Early on in my fieldwork I had made a decision not to discuss two important aspects of my personal identity that were meaningful to me in the United States: my cultural/religious background and my sexual orientation. The people I knew in the shantytowns therefore assumed that I was Catholic and heterosexual, as those are the default categories of identity operating there. At the time, I was preoccupied with fitting in and not drawing attention to myself.

My relationship with Glória and her family stood somewhat apart from this early self-inflicted edict. When I first met Glória, she had been a domestic worker for many of the AIDS activists living in the South Zone of Rio de Janeiro, most of whom were gay men and lesbians. Glória knew that these were my friends and that there was probably a good chance that I was a lesbian too, but she was always careful to ask me about my "boyfriend." In the beginning stages of our friendship, I let her know that the "boyfriend" I was mourning after a long-distance breakup had been a woman, but she was not really interested in that, nor did she want to pursue the topic. In other words, I took it for granted that Glória long knew "the truth," but was choosing to ignore it for various reasons that I will discuss momentarily. It seemed that she very much wanted to engage with me publicly as a heterosexual; if I was something else, it was not necessarily something she needed to acknowledge publicly or talk about with others. Glória was my friend, but she was also my vital link to everyone else in the community, and above all else she wanted me to be respectable. Had I been adamant about sharing the details of my lesbian partnership with Glória, I might have put her in an awkward position vis-à-vis her friends and all of the people with whom she put me in contact.

Having once been heterosexual, I was able to amply participate with my friends in their romantic pleasures and pains, but I could not honestly share the gender of my partner with them, nor any of the details of that aspect of my life in the United States. I imagine that this is not a huge issue when the research involves short-term interviewing intimacy, but because my fieldwork was one of immersion and long-term engagement, I had to be at peace with denying this particular aspect of my identity, even among people who were extremely curious about my life. Glória communicated to me her need to keep my sexual identity an unacknowledged secret between us by continually ignoring all of my attempts to tell her the truth. I believe now that this was Glória's way of protecting both of us. Being perceived as a lesbian would have depleted my status as a privileged white North American woman. It would have put Glória and myself in a kind of danger that would have been subtle yet palpable. Perceived as a deviant of sorts, I would have opened myself up to the psychological and physical risks of those who are considered less worthy and whose bodies and persons might be more easily transgressed. It is perhaps too culturally specific to call this homophobia, but both of us understood the danger nonetheless of admitting to my lowly place in the Brazilian sexual hierarchy.

When asked about my personal life at home in the United States, I tried to answer as honestly as I could within the boundaries of the context I was participating in. This was complicated at times because there were two *travesti* (transgendered men) living in Felicidade Eterna who were the subjects of constant jokes and teasing, as well as a lesbian mother who, after having been beaten various times by her husband, had run away with a policewoman and left all her children behind. I therefore felt dishonest at times for not standing in some kind of solidarity with these other "deviants," but convinced myself that this was the best thing to do given my situation. By staying "closeted" and allowing others to think of me as heterosexual, I was able to maintain a higher degree of respectability. But it has also occurred to me that Glória and my other dark-skinned Afro-Brazilian friends might have felt their own respectability compromised if it had become widely known that I was sexually different. Part of my safety and my place in the hierarchy of social relations in Felicidade Eterna was built around my whiteness and foreignness. To have been known as a lesbian would have compromised my relatively high position in this hierarchy and quite possibly my safety, as well as the safety of my friends.

Similarly, it also seemed more "respectable" to leave my cultural/religious background as a Jew out of my self-presentation. I had learned throughout my travels that there were incredible ideas about Jews, some of which were simply strange, others of which bordered on anti-Semitism. Throughout the many years I spent in and out of Brazil, I had found that Glória, her family, and her network of friends had changed religious affiliations various times and that religious affinity was dependent on a number of factors. Many of them had become devoutly religious and had temporarily become members of evangelical denominations. Somehow, because of the fluidity of this identity, my own religious affiliation seemed like an easy aspect of my own identity to refrain from talking about. While my friends assumed that I was a secular person without strong religious convictions, they also assumed that I shared a working knowledge of Catholicism and other forms of popular religion that are part of the everyday fabric of Felicidade Eterna.

These sorts of reflections on fieldwork and on ethnographic production have gained a visible and important place in anthropology, drawing force from both feminist theory[3] and the first two volumes associated with the crisis of representation that were published in the mid-1980s (*Anthropology as Cultural Critique: An Experimental Moment in the Human Sciences* and *Writing Culture: the Poetics and Politics of Ethnography*). The flurry of discussion surrounding these two volumes coincided with my entry into graduate school, and I incorporated some of the suggestions offered by these critiques and those that followed them into *Laughter Out of Place*. But I have always been reluctant to enter into "agonistic confession" (Pels

2000) without a clear ethnographic purpose. As I was writing this essay, I heard a fascinating lecture by Haitian-born and U.S.–trained anthropologist Gina Ulysse, who carried out fieldwork in Jamaica. Her project is to harness the power of reflexivity in the service of furthering the analysis of power relations in localized contexts, which she discusses as the "political economy of reflexivity" (Ulysse 2004). In particular, she writes about her own experiences as a black woman in the field—for example, how her race, class, nationality, and dress affected her interactions with the people she worked with—in order to illuminate the hierarchical structures that function in Jamaican society. Her work solidifies the necessity for certain kinds of reflexive engagements for approaching difficult-to-grasp racial power dynamics. I had for a long time been aware of the privilege my white foreign status afforded me in this particular fieldwork situation, but in hearing her presentation, I further recognized the analytical importance of writing about these relations as part of a broader power dynamic.

One of the most profound lessons I learned in the course of my fieldwork in Rio de Janeiro is how closely race or color is aligned with class, and how both are tied into underlying notions of sexuality in the Brazilian context. In *Laughter Out of Place*, I examine the idea of black female sexual allure and its relation to the maintenance of racism in Brazil. Specifically, I explore the ways in which Glória and her friends harness their sexual capital and fantasize about certain forms of race-based social mobility. As a white North American woman carrying out research in Brazil, my range of movement within the highly "classed" Brazilian society was extraordinarily broad, ranging from contacts with elite intellectuals and AIDS activists (the majority of whom were white) living in security-guarded condominium complexes to infamous drug gang leaders living in high-security prisons (many of whom were not white). My foreignness and whiteness proved to be a cloak of privilege in a range of contexts. As the shantytown was filled with a good proportion of white immigrants from northeast Brazil (as well as Afro-Brazilians from Rio and from nearby states), I was able to "blend in" quite easily as a light-skinned person from the northeast. Glória enjoyed having me in her company and telling everyone we met that I was her "white daughter," a comment that drew many double-takes and follow-up questions, but which also, it seems, lent her a good deal of status in Felicidade Eterna.

My whiteness also carried specific benefits to Glória in the society at large. When Glória needed to apply for an identity card for her son Félix, for example, I was a useful person to have along. In those situations, I appeared to be a white middle-class woman either of Carioca or foreign origin in a line of poor darker-skinned women, all of whom were hoping that by obtaining an identity card for their child, they would be buying a bit of protection. The identity card proved to the police that the carrier was a member of a legitimate household and was under the age of eighteen. It was something that a gang member probably would not have. Glória, for example, understood the code and the need for the identity card very well. Félix had always been a bit sloppy with his dress and was also tall and very thin; most important, he was very dark-skinned, a characteristic that made him particularly vulnerable to police harassment. From the perspective of the police, Félix had the look of a young scoundrel, and Glória worried about his fate. The identity card served as an added bit of protection. In many instances, so did I. Glória often asked me to accompany her children to various places around town, knowing that my white phenotype was assurance that nothing bad would happen to her children.

My whiteness afforded me a kind of automatic "respectability" in middle-class Rio, no matter what clothes I was wearing. Often during this period of fieldwork, my dress consisted of tight spandex shorts, a T-shirt, and flip-flops—a standard uniform for both middle-class beachgoers and young women from the shantytown heading in to the South Zone to work in middle-class homes. But as I eventually understood it, the exact same outfit on a young dark-skinned woman would be enough to cause suspicion in the upscale South Zone boutiques and in some cases even prevent entry. Nobody ever told me that my whiteness worked to erase such suspicions, but I experienced it everywhere, especially in daily interactions that took place in middle-class communities.

Once I invited a few of Glória's children with me into a McDonald's restaurant after a day at the beach. While the majority of patrons in the restaurant were also entering in slightly sandy beach clothes, all eyes were on us. This restaurant is generally out of the economic reach of the poorest classes. While beach clothes signify a day at the beach for a white person, they signify poverty for young, dark-skinned Brazilians. Because of this, Glória's children had rarely been to the beach because she feared what could happen to them. They could be mistaken for street children, for instance, and wind up in a difficult situation. In this context then, my white presence functioned as protection against the police.

My whiteness also enabled me to conform easily to casual forms of white femininity and respectability, as long as I wore long hair and tight-fitting jeans. During a preliminary research visit to Brazil in 1988, I arrived in Rio de Janeiro with the short haircut that was stylish at the time in Berkeley, California. In Rio, however, this haircut was read as unfeminine, boyish, and possibly lesbian, and I abandoned this style during subsequent field trips. At the beginning of my fieldwork I wore American-style, loose-fitting jeans, which quickly marked me as an outsider and was also perceived as unfeminine, unattractive, and decidedly not sexy. I eventually bought a few pairs of Brazilian jeans. I made sure I used appropriate make-up for different occasions, which proved to be particularly important across classes for going out in the evening. Being "not sexy" in Rio is the last thing one wants to be, because attractiveness functions as a protection of sorts—people want to be more polite to you, men want to help you, and even potential robbers might treat you better. In the early 1990s, for instance, I was robbed in broad daylight with a friend in Copacabana, a neighborhood in the wealthy South Zone of the city. Two men pointed a gun at our stomachs, where our money belts were, and asked us to give over everything to them, a request we hurriedly aquiesced to. Not long after this incident, the same friend was robbed in her own apartment in Leblon, another wealthy South Zone neighborhood. As a linguist, she was amused by the fact that the robber had called her by the name *Gatinha*, a term that translates as "Little Cat" but that is also a form of address for an attractive woman. Although the robber forcibly locked her into a bedroom closet, she knew that she would not be harmed by an intruder who found her attractive.

Basically, the women in Felicidade Eterna, much like myself, attempted to keep themselves "safe" from the various forms of urban violence encountered in everyday life. Glória and her daughters would always advise me about appropriate places to hide my money when we entered a public bus. They had been robbed on public buses numerous times, and they were especially careful on paydays to take the more expensive bus that made fewer stops. In the beginning of my fieldwork, I thought my friends were exaggerating their stories of theft on public buses, but I later learned that this was one of the most routine forms of theft. The women I knew who worked hard all month long as domestic workers in the homes of the wealthy were not happy to lose their monthly pay in this predictable manner.

Theft was not the most upsetting crime, however. Over time I discovered that many of my closest informants had been raped in territorial or drug gang wars, and that this was far more common than I had earlier thought. Some of these young women were attached to gang members as a form of protection. They felt that being the wife or girlfriend of some "big man" would protect them from harm (i.e., they could always threaten their assailants with revenge), but in fact it probably made them more vulnerable as targets in the endless quest for territory and power. In my own case, I found it prudent to present myself as a woman who was working in Brazil temporarily, and who was in a serious relationship back home and therefore not interested in having a Brazilian boyfriend. I wore a ring and sometimes claimed to be married.

Presenting myself as a serious social scientist embedded in my work and disinterested in romance provided its own kind of shield from much of the violence that took place in Felicidade Eterna. So much of the violence between civilians in the shantytown—not necessarily even between gang members—had to do with romantic affections and affiliations. Both men and women hated to be cuckolded or dumped by a partner, and many of the violent scenes that took place during my time in the field had to do with failed romance of one kind or another. The women I knew would often engage in making offerings or obtaining the advice of a practitioner of black magic in order to bring bad luck, bad health, or even death to a rival woman. But men would often take the next step of confronting a romantic rival with physical violence, which in turn sometimes meant getting the local gang—and occasionally even the police—involved. Men would call in the local gang—and the violence system it offered—in order to punish an adulteress. As I have described in detail in *Laughter Out of Place*, there is a great deal of complicity in the shantytown that what the gang metes out as a form of justice is better than what the police could or would do.

Brazilian state and municipal authorities are emphatically detached from addressing an entire host of problems that people living in Felicidade Eterna must deal with on a daily basis. In countries that have far-reaching social service systems, sexual abuse and violence are often addressed from within the system. But in the shantytowns of Rio de Janeiro, such affairs are considered to be private issues and therefore outside of the purview of the public legal system. Nevertheless, without the intervention of social service institutions and a reliable policing system, these kinds of problems create their own cycles of revenge and involve the gangs as on-hand substitutes.

In concluding this set of reflections on my fieldwork in Rio de Janeiro in the 1990s, I want to return for a brief moment to the Bus 174 incident. Some of the images of events captured in the documentary film have stayed with me. Early on in the standoff with the police, Sandro allowed the men on the bus to exit but kept six women as hostages. In his rantings, Sandro urged the police to give into his demands for a safe exit and to not force him to blow the head off of a pretty young woman. I could not help but notice that all of the women Sandro kept hostage on the bus were young and light-skinned, somewhere further up the Brazilian hierarchy of race and class than Sandro himself, but not quite white enough within the Rio race and class hierarchy to be driving in their own cars. I wonder whether the police noticed this as well, and were therefore less careful about placing the hostages in further danger. I thought again about my own whiteness and how my friends in Felicidade Eterna on occasion used it and their relationship with me in order to protect themselves and their children.

In one of the most haunting scenes of the film, the camera enters one of the prisons where Sandro had spent some time, providing the viewer a glimpse of the crowded and inhumane conditions that typify these institutions. The entire filming of the prison, including the faces of the inmates, are altered by switching the camera into "negative" mode, thus preserving the anonymity of the prisoners while providing a ghostly representation of their existence. The prison is filled with angry young men like Sandro—men like Glória's son Pedro Paulo—all of whom had been taken hostage in an undeclared civil war fueled by poverty, racism, and anger. My foreign and white presence in the neighborhoods that nurtured these young men and their police enemies served as a temporary safety charm for the women I came to know. These women both love and fear these angry young men and often find their own bodies as pawns on the urban battlefield. As an anthropologist, I tried to understand their ambiguous emotions and act as a witness to their struggle, never losing sight of the fact that I could exit their lives and this war at any time.

NOTES

1. I draw here from Pereira's (1997) working definition of the rule of law:

> The ideal of the rule of law is not simply that the actions who control the state are legal in some technical sense. Instead, it is that law forms a complex and interlocking pyramid of rules in which the state itself is bound, and in which the constitution is the ultimate authority to which subordinate statutes, regulations, administrative rules, and judicial sentences are in compliance. State power is exercised within this pyramid of rules, from which it derives its legitimacy. Laws are clear, publicly available, and consistently applied, and they reflect some degree of popular consensus and normative allegiance. Rather than being merely the rationalization of the prerogatives of those who rule, the rule of law represents a fusion of and compromise between the "peoples" and the "state;" law. (2)

2. See *New York Times* (1997).
3. See Mascia-Lees, Sharpe, and Cohen's (1989) insightful article on the contributions of feminist theory and the erasure of this body of work from consideration by the new ethnographers.

REFERENCES

Caldeira, T. (2000). *City of Walls: Crime, Segregation, and Citizenship in São Paulo*. Berkeley and Los Angeles: University of California Press.

Clifford, J., and G. E. Marcus, eds. (1986). *Writing Culture: The Poetics and Politics of Ethnography*. Berkeley and Los Angeles: University of California Press.

Goldstein, D. M. (2003). *Laughter Out of Place: Race, Class, Violence and Sexuality in a Rio Shantytown*. Berkeley and Los Angeles: University of California Press.

Holloway, T. H. (1993). *Policing Rio de Janeiro: Repression and Resistance in a Nineteenth-Century City*. Stanford, CA: Stanford University Press.

Holston, J., and T. P. R. Caldeira. (1998). "Democracy, Law, and Violence: Disjunctions of Brazilian Citizenship." In *Fault Lines of Democracy in Post-Transition Latin America*, edited by F. Agüero and J. Stark, 263–96. Coral Gables, FL: North-South Center Press at the University of Miami.

Huggins, M. (1991). *Vigilantism and the State in Modern Latin America: Essays in Extra Legal Violence*. New York: Praeger.

Leeds, E. (1996). "Cocaine and Parallel Polities in the Brazilian Urban Periphery: Constraints on Local-Level Democratization." *Latin American Research Review* 31, no. 3, 47–83.

Marcus, G. E., and M. M. J. Fischer. (1986). *Anthropology As Cultural Critique: An Experimental Moment in the Human Sciences.* Chicago: University of Chicago Press.

Mascia-Lees, F. E., et al. (1989). "The Postmodernist Turn in Anthropology: Cautions From a Feminist Perspective." *Signs: Journal of Women in Culture and Society* 15, no. 1, 7–33.

New York Times. (1997). "Outcry Over Police Brutality in Brazil." April 2, A3.

O'Donnell, G. (1993). "On the State, Democratization and Some Conceptual Problems: A Latin American View with Glances at Some Postcommunist Countries." *World Development* 21.

Pels, P. (2000). "The Trickster's Dilemma: Ethics and the Technologies of the Anthropological Self." In *Audit Cultures: Anthropological Studies in Accountability, Ethics, and the Academy,* edited by M. Strathern, 135–72. London and New York: Routledge.

Pereira, A. (1997). "Elitist Liberalism: Citizenship, State Violence, and The Rule of Law in Brazil." Paper presented at the XX International Congress of the Latin American Studies Association, Guadalajara, Mexico, April.

Perlman, J. E. (1976). *The Myth of Marginality: Urban Poverty and Politics in Rio de Janeiro.* Berkeley and Los Angeles: University of California.

Pinheiro, P. S. (1991). "Police and Political Crisis: The Case of the Military Police." In *Vigilantism and the State in Latin America: Essays on Extralegal Violence,* edited by M. Huggins, 167–88. New York: Praeger.

Ulysse, Gina. (2004). "Mediating Stigma: Gendering Class and Color Codes in Jamaica." Lecture presented at the University of Colorado Department of Anthropology Colloquium Series, March 12.

Zaluar, Alba. (1994). *Condominio do Diabo.* Rio de Janeiro: Revan/UFRJ.

10

Power, Safety, and Ethics in Cross-Gendered Research with Violent Men

Lois Presser

A concern with power and its reach has feminist scholars attending to the ways in which they might dominate or exploit the women who are their research participants (Cotterill 1992; Oakley 1981; Stacey 1988; Wolf 1996). According to Wolf (1996), feminist scholars "have sought to break down the hierarchical and potentially exploitative relationship between researcher and researched by cultivating friendship, sharing, and closeness that, it was felt, would lead to a richer picture of women's lives" (4). Increasingly, though, research studies conducted by feminists involve male informants, including men who are marginalized by class and race. This trend problematizes feminist methodological choices (Huggins and Glebbeek 2003). Gestures of intimacy counteract the already precarious acceptance of women as professionals and may be seen as indicating sexual interest (Easterday et al. 1977; Horn 1997; Huggins and Glebbeek 2003; Hunt 1984; Schwalbe and Wolkomir 2002). A show of vulnerability may also undermine the female researcher's safety while interviewing men. Clearly, female researchers benefit from "being in charge" in cross-gendered research settings. How is such power achieved? And how do we reconcile the necessary hierarchical relation with feminist ethics? To begin to address those questions, I consider power dynamics during interviews I conducted with men from April 1999 through February 2002 in the United States. The men had perpetrated serious violent crimes including rape, murder, assault, and robbery.

Before, during, and after the research, I heard often—from institutional review board members, colleagues, and friends—that it was very risky for me to meet with these men alone. While doing the interviews, though, I rarely felt threatened. I took practical steps to present myself as an unsuitable target of violence or sexual pursuit. I avoided mentioning where I lived and the fact that I lived alone. When one early research participant—with a history of rape, attempted murder, and aggravated assault—phoned me at home, I changed my home telephone number and had it unlisted. If someone assumed that I was married, I did not correct him. In fact, I wore a gold ring on my left hand during the interviews to suggest that I had a husband, a protector. I also dressed conservatively for the interviews. These are some of the defenses that Western women routinely employ (Stanko 1997). However, the ways in which I gained control went beyond these "mundane" tactics. Two additional dynamics contributed to my sense of safety.

First, I was aligned with institutional and usually (in fifteen cases) government authority. I was introduced to most of the research participants through social service organizations working with convicts, ex-convicts, and homeless people in New Jersey, New York, Ohio, and Pennsylvania. My contacts at these organizations were friends or former colleagues. I interviewed twenty-two of the twenty-seven research participants exclusively on the premises of these organizations. Whereas these interviews were held in vacant rooms with doors closed, the institution was palpably "present." Several participants made reference to what I might report to organizational administrators, usually at the close of interviews. Thinking that the men thought they were under the "gaze" of an institution with sanctioning power made me feel safe.

After a while, I interviewed men away from direct formal control, such as in coffee shops and university classrooms. By this point, I had become aware of a *second* power dynamic. The men were using the interviews to present themselves as decent. They were resisting their classification as problematic persons (Loseke 2003; Presser 2004). All of the men spoke of themselves as morally good in the present moment. In launching these claims to goodness, the men were frequently quite sexist and bossy. Still, they did not resort to violence, and, moreover, I had the feeling that they would not. I recognized violence as a *symbolic resource*. I believe, and believed during the interviews, that violence functions to substantiate some claim about the perpetrator's character (Athens 1997; Katz 1988; Luckenbill 1977; Toch 1969). The fact that the interviews with me did not demand violence as a resource, because I did not dispute the men's definitions of self, made me feel safe. In other words, I felt that I had influence as long as I allowed them to demonstrate a certain persona.

The notion that violence ultimately defends identity claims was inchoate while I was conducting the interviews. I suspect that this notion—and hence, ideas about what might provoke or forestall violence—get assimilated into heuristics learned early by girls (Stanko 1997). As a woman, the female criminologist already has experience in discerning potential dangers posed by men. Our defensive strategies may not "really" keep us safe, but they increase our *sense* of safety and thus allow us to go about our everyday activities, including scholarly activities.

Presently I will describe specific exchanges with three research participants in my study. Before turning to those data, I will further consider why my interviews precluded the "need" for violence. That is, I will discuss in more detail the theoretical grounds of my sense of safety during interviews with violent men.

SIGNIFYING MASCULINITY—VIOLENCE AND THE INTERVIEW

Violence champions the moral position of its perpetrator (Toch 1969). It is a ploy in a struggle for standing. Diverse "types" of violence share this quality of signifying something about its perpetrator's value, whatever else the violence does, or, more precisely, is *meant* to do. Thus, Katz (1988) considers armed robbery as a means to achieving "*moral superiority*, where the temptation and the challenge to self-confidence concern not simply what may be taken but the prospect of 'taking' or making a fool of the victim" (242; italics in original). Of so-called senseless murders, Katz writes: "The key emotional dynamic on the path to these murders is a play with moral symbolics in which (1) the protagonist enters as a pariah, (2) soon becomes lost in the dizzying symbolics of deviance, and then (3) emerges to reverse the equation in a violent act of transcendence" (290). Luckenbill (1977) analyzed seventy homicides and found that killing was a final stage of a dynamic "character contest" (Goffman's [1967] concept). Each homicide began with the offender interpreting the victim's statement or action as intentionally communicating insult, insolence, or disobedience. The offender "retaliated" in order to save face.

Macro-level power relations frame the power dynamic that is the violent act. Feminist theorists conceptualize rape as a political crime, "the act of a conqueror" (Brownmiller 1975, 35), which is supported by women's economic and political subordination (Box 1983, 132). Systematic torture and killings ordered by a government or other social group assert a reality about the moral positions of the individual perpetrator and of the group vis-à-vis that of the victim (Cohen 1955; Huggins, Haritos-Fatouros, and Zimbardo 2002; Keane 1996). Riots, Toch (1969) observes, are "morality plays" (206) that contest the indifference of a mythic oppressor. Whether the violent offender is an individual or a group, and whatever the broader history and thus significance of the violence, identities are being protested or accomplished through it.

Messerschmidt (1993) puts in gendered terms the phenomenological perspective on violence, proposing that violence is a common resource for identifying oneself as *masculine* where other resources are blocked. In the

Western context, hegemonic masculinity "emphasizes practices toward authority, control, independence, competitive individualism, aggressiveness, and the capacity for violence" (Messerschmidt 2000, 10). Thus, violence, of itself, conveys the "right" identity for many men. According to Messerschmidt (1993, 2000), "masculine resources," as well as situational opportunities, affect *how* one will present oneself as masculine, violently or otherwise.

> Masculine resources are contextually available practices (e.g., bullying, fighting, engaging in sexuality, and acting like a "gentleman") that can be drawn upon so that men and boys can demonstrate to others they are "manly." Resources appropriate for masculine construction change situationally (2000, 12).

Messerschmidt discusses various constraints on masculine resources. In his 1993 book, *Masculinities and Crime*, he emphasized *structural* constraints on the achievement and maintenance of economic success. The "violent men" I interviewed were mainly poor. Messerschmidt's theory of violence as masculine action may be valid for these informants. But the question of my immediate safety during research encounters with men orients me to their *physical marginalization*—specifically, their incapacitation by the state—as constraining demonstrations of masculinity.[1]

The men I interviewed were, for the most part, confined to an institution or under community supervision, and thus their contacts with "regular" people were limited. As Schwalbe and Wolkomir (2002) observe: "[S]ituations that make it difficult to signify control, autonomy, rationality, and sexual desirability may be especially anxiety provoking for men wedded to displaying hegemonic masculinity" (205). Schwalbe and Wolkomir are especially interested in the challenge that research interviews pose to masculinity. They state: "to sit for an interview, no matter how friendly and conversational, is to give up some control and to risk having one's public persona stripped away" (206). Research interviews may thus prompt insistent displays of masculine control among male informants (see also McKeganey and Bloor 1991).

If the research interview is a challenge to male informants' masculinity, it is also a potential masculine resource. Schwalbe and Wolkomir (2002) write: "It is an opportunity for signifying masculinity inasmuch as men are allowed to portray themselves as in control, autonomous, rational, and so on" (205). Self-construction is ostensibly "up for grabs," especially in the open-ended interview as opposed to other formats (cf. Pool 1957). Given that most of my research participants were incapacitated in men-only facilities, the open-ended interview *with a woman* was a handy platform for masculine self-portrayal. After all, *male* needs its opposite, *female*, for vivid demarcation.

In most cases I was the sole audience for whatever presentation the informant might make.[2] What sort of audience was I? I was surely not physically threatening. Nor did I threaten the men's self-statements. I did not ask challenging questions. My concern was the construction of identity. I was not especially concerned with the validity of the men's accounts. Moreover, my training in qualitative interview methodology had cautioned me against challenging informants for the sake of data collection (Schatzman and Strauss 1973; Spradley 1979). Thus, I seldom disputed what a research participant said about himself. My responses to the men's accounts were largely tolerant. I posed no "surplus threat"—over and above the threat posed by my built-in control as interviewer—to the informants' narrated identities as *manly* men (Schwalbe and Wolkomir 2002, 206).

The men's narratives commonly posited the state as an enemy that had wrongly characterized them as essentially criminal. Throughout the research, I distanced myself from the state in speaking with the men. I insisted that I was an independent researcher collecting confidential data, despite any acquaintance with someone at the agency. I gave the appearance of agreeing with what the men said about their crimes and their victims, sympathizing with their treatment by the criminal justice system, and in one case advocating for clemency. In fact, my persona as a representative of the state—or at least of respectable society—coupled with my support for their stories, is likely to have made me a desirable sounding board on matters of being misunderstood.

My simultaneous reliance on the state for a sense of safety raises ethical dilemmas, including support for the state's project of controlling those marginalized by class and race, and deception as researcher and activist. I will return to these ethical issues at the close of this chapter. Here I wish to emphasize that, having been granted discursive resources (e.g., a deferential audience) for establishing honor and resisting marginalization, my research participants had no particular *need* of violence. The interviews allowed alternative means for conjuring oneself as a man of integrity. In short, whereas interviews risk discrediting the informant's masculinity (Schwalbe and Wolkomir 2002), overall, my interviews invited nonviolent masculine self-construction and performance.

In this chapter I focus on three informants from my study: Ralph, Dwight, and Kevin (all pseudonyms). They were not the most serious offenders in my sample, though Kevin was sentenced the most harshly of anyone. Ralph and Dwight are African American. Kevin (since executed) was white. When I first met them Ralph was thirty-four, Dwight was forty-one, and Kevin was thirty-seven. I selected these three men for close analysis because together they offer a rich view of the uses of power in interviews between female scholars and marginalized men. My analytic focus is on the complementary uses to which the men and I put power, and the implications of these power relations for safety and ethics.

RALPH

I interviewed Ralph twice in a minimum-security, treatment-oriented correctional facility where he was sent following a year in prison. The treatment he received there was cognitive in its orientation, seeking to make "clients" aware of their crime-conducive thinking errors (Yochelson and Samenow 1976) so as to spot them in the future. Ralph had been convicted of robbery, though the original charges also included sexual assault. He explained that he had simply taken the rent money due him from an evasive female tenant; he denied having sexually violated her. Ralph's criminal record included various property offenses. He also told me about his experience selling and using marijuana, for which he had not been arrested.

Ralph resisted his correctional treatment. He posited himself as a nonoffender. In claiming essential decency, Ralph relied heavily on "proving" to me his innocence of rape. He sought my opinion for the purpose of confirming that he was, in fact, no rapist. My assumed clinical expertise and my female gender were equally important aspects of my assignment as evaluator. In the exchange presented below, Ralph asked me to verify how I felt being in the interview room with him, which would support his claim that he is not "really" a rapist.

> *Ralph*: Now, I don't know—based on me having this interview, or—How do you feel? Do you feel comfortable? Do you feel like you in here with some nut? (chuckle)
>
> *Lo*[3]: (shake head)
>
> *Ralph*: Huh, okay. (laughing) You know wha' I mean. I'm—people have a sense of understandin' and feelin' comfortable with people. You know wha'm sayin'? They know when a person is—sincere or they know when a person is real or they know when they around somebody that just ain't got all they scruples.

Ralph involved me as a partner in his clinical assessment of self, reasoning that I would have felt uncomfortable with him if he were a rapist. He called on my intuition to make that assessment ("people have a sense of understandin'"). I supposedly could intuit the presence of a "real" rapist. In a later exchange, Ralph summoned more professional competencies on my part:

> *Ralph*: Would you bring him [a hypothetical rapist] to this facility, knowin' you got women work here? Would you? On a *personal* basis, would you do it?

Lo: Well, it's uh—it's the treatment services or whatever over—maybe—I'm just—like—well I'm not really [unclear]—

Ralph: No. Honestly.

Lo: Yeah I don't really know.

Ralph: As a doctor's point of view.

Lo: I don't—well I'm not a doctor *yet*. I don't really know—

Ralph: I know, but you studying to be a—okay, as a—

Lo: Yeah, I mean—(pause) uh—it—uh—I don't really know, because I don't know—maybe there's nothing lik—I don't know New Jersey that well. Maybe there's nothing like it in New Jersey.

Ralph: Okay. Where you from?

Lo: New York City.

Ralph: New York? Same thing. New York and New Jersey the same thing. We right over the bridge, girl! You—you—you right there!

Here, Ralph contended that no clinicians would allow a real rapist into a facility with female staff, as he had been. Ralph bid me to support that logic. I was rather uncooperative.

The previous exchange can be analyzed in terms of the following conversational "moves." Ralph asked my opinion of him, which I declined to give. He referred to my expert authority, which I denied having. Ralph rejected my denial. Then I claimed lack of knowledge because I am from a different geographic area. I thus took myself out of the assigned structural position, instead speaking as a layperson. Adroitly, Ralph moved to personalize the exchange by asking me where I am from, then bridging the distance between us as laypersons. He was warm and familiar ("We right over the bridge, girl!"), even while dismissing my position.

I clearly tried to remain neutral—to avoid evaluating him. My efforts only led Ralph to a succession of alternative ways for narrating his "decent"—that is, "nonrapist"—identity. Whereas I denied things about myself, I neither asserted nor denied anything about *Ralph*. If I was unhelpful, I was also unprovocative. The transaction confirmed a certain passivity on my part. I would not actively threaten Ralph's version of who he was. The exchanges with Ralph also indicate—and indicated to me at the time—that he would *gently* try to get me on his side. He ardently exploited my female gender and other social locations, including my ascribed role as clinical expert, to accomplish his self-presentational goals. Yet he did not force the issue of his goodness; to do so would have undermined the whole effort.

DWIGHT

Like Ralph, Dwight used the interview to demonstrate his goodness. Dwight was in many ways a more fearsome character to me, based on the lengthy and serious criminal record he himself described. By age thirteen he had committed burglary, car theft, and robbery, and was using cocaine and heroin. At fourteen, he was arrested and incarcerated for larceny. His case was waived to adult court, and he served a year and a half in adult prison. Soon after, at age sixteen, he was arrested for armed robbery. This case too was waived to adult court, where Dwight was sentenced to prison for ten years. While incarcerated, he stabbed a fellow inmate who had allegedly thrown hot water on him.

Dwight's recent prison sentence reflected two distinct criminal charges. The first charge was for the rape of a female acquaintance who, earlier the same evening, wanted to have sex with him. He had declined, but hours later he raped her forcibly. He described the rape as a power struggle. He was "playin' her game," something he attributed to socialization into a certain subculture: "When a person live out in the street, they play so many games." Ironically and tragically, while the court case for the rape was pending and Dwight was at home awaiting trial, his girlfriend's teenage daughter was raped. After hearing of it, Dwight found and shot the neighbor who had raped her. The man survived, and Dwight was charged with aggravated assault. Dwight pled guilty to both the rape and the aggravated assault and served fifteen years in prison. I asked if he felt he had a choice regarding the shooting, and he answered that he very much loved his girlfriend, whose daughter had been victimized. He also stated: "I was the man of the house so I had to do what I had to do."

I met Dwight following his prison release. He was on a two-year parole term and living in a halfway house. Dwight emphasized that he had changed while most recently in prison. He shared with me autobiographical writings from prison treatment programs, in which his Muslim name is recorded. Dwight commented that many men knew him in prison and they assigned him a name that suggested sensitivity. Offering an example of his humane prison persona, he said that he would often advise a new young inmate on how "to keep his manhood." Dwight also participated in treatment programs for sex offenders. He came to believe that rapists are "sick" but also that men generally need to respect women's wishes and feelings.

In describing the crimes he had committed over the years, Dwight—like Ralph—tended to focus on past sexual violence. Dwight had obtained gratification living up to a tough image and dominating women. He frequently bought women alcohol until they were inebriated and then had sex with them; he admitted that the women often did not know what they were doing. In Dwight's narrative, he has been socialized to withhold feelings and to disrespect women. Both emotional repression and disrespect for women led to offending.

Lessons in changing his thinking and errors and reconnecting with his feelings have purportedly instilled a more respectful attitude toward women. Dwight now lives peacefully with people, women in particular. He provided several examples of coming to women's assistance. He advised one woman to leave a neglectful boyfriend; he advised another to pursue a college degree in defiance of her husband's wishes and family demands. He enjoyed nothing more than to talk to women about his new sensitivity. He told a woman he recently encountered at a social service agency: "When I went in, ya know, I thought all females was a sex object. Yeah I say, now no woman out here on the street got to worry about me puttin' a hand on 'em." These days, Dwight struggles to be recognized as the good man that he is.

Like Ralph, Dwight used "me" to tell his story. Unlike Ralph, Dwight recalled a former criminal/bad self. During the first of our two interviews, he described his pattern of sexual exploitation, casting me as a would-be victim:

> *Dwight*: Let's say for instance. Me an' you out. Okay. We're havin' fun. Okay? Uh, I know you. I know you like to drink. Right? OK, now I'm gonna feed you all this alcohol, right?. . . . Once I got you so intoxicated—y'know wha'am sayin'?—that you don't know where you're at—you don't know where your mind at.

> *Lo*: Right. So you're saying you did *that*, but—but—and you *do* consider that rape.

> *Dwight*: Yeah. . . . See, I didn't look into that type behavior, until I started—uh—see I finished the [Name] Program. I graduated from it. An' it's given me a more—it give me a lot of insight. Ya know it give me a lot of tools, insight about what women—what they all about

In the foregoing exchange, I exemplify one who would have been at risk with Dwight in the past, but who is no longer at risk. His own change safeguards me. The question I posed ("You *do* consider that rape?") clarifies the "data" but also gives me reassurance that Dwight has morally distanced himself from the kind of menacing behavior—behavior that could menace *me*—he has just described.

Dwight was one of several men who seized an opportunity to advise me on something specifically related to their criminal pasts (Presser 2004). This too marked his reform. He advised me to hold onto personal power and satisfaction in romantic relationships with men:

> *Dwight*: Ya know, you a good person. So, I'm hopin' that you don't get—you're stuck with some [unclear] guy—you know wha'm sayin'—

Lo: (chuckle)

Dwight: —don't want you for—don't want you for you.

Dwight's sexual protectiveness may be seen as the accomplishment of a chivalrous masculinity—"acting like a 'gentleman'" (Messerschmidt 2000, 12). Of course, his chivalry is also an assertion of authority. Later in the same interview, Dwight and I struggled for control. He instructed me on helping him to violate the rule against smoking inside the house.

Dwight: See? Then I started uh—understandin'—under—Did he [halfway house director] come back? Did he come back?

Lo: No. Why—?

Dwight: Did he come back?

Lo: No.

Dwight: S' anyway, 'scuse me, I got to have a cigarette.

Lo: Oh.

Dwight: You see a car comes, just say: "Y'all put it out!"

Lo: Oh, 'cause you're not supposed to smoke?

Dwight: Not here.

Lo: Oh, y—you don't want to go out there?

Dwight: No, it's t—too wet out there.

Lo: It's too what?

Dwight: Too wet.

Lo: Oh.

Dwight: Been rainin'! You been in here all—it been rainin'!

Lo: Oh, it has been raining. Are you sure? Maybe you should.

Dwight: No! I'm straight!

Lo: Really? 'Cause if it's a rule, you know, and you just finished saying how you like people to keep you on the straight track.

Dwight: Mm-mm!

Lo: All right. I'm gonna let you do what you want to do. (looking out the door to the small backyard) You know what, that kitty has got to go to a vet!

This exchange captures the interactional nature of the power dynamic. Dwight enlisted me as his accomplice in breaking a house rule. I acted on behalf of the halfway house administration, conveying their rules ("Maybe you should"). When Dwight resisted, I tried to convince him to change his mind by presenting myself as one who might help to keep him out of trouble ("You like people to keep you on the straight track"). Finally, when I could not gain his compliance in this way, I gave in by agreeing not to contest the rule violation ("I'm gonna let you do what you want to do"). Thus I reasserted some authority, albeit of a passive sort: *I* am the one to *let* him do as he wishes. To ease tension after the power struggle, I acted in a stereotypically feminine manner by conveying empathy for a small animal ("You know what, that kitty has got to go to a vet!"). Just as quickly as I had assumed the position of the halfway house—of authority—I assumed a gentler position. As *either* a person of influence *or* a female helpmate, I tried subtly to sway Dwight without angering him and jeopardizing my safety.

I was not conscious of my own assertiveness in situ. Only upon analysis did I recognize the challenges I sometimes posed, such as in the foregoing exchanges with Ralph (concerning the placement of a rapist in his facility) and Dwight (concerning in-house smoking). While the research was underway, I perceived myself as passive. It is within this context that I felt safe from aggressive action by the men.

KEVIN

Kevin was not referred to me institutionally, as Ralph, Dwight, and most of the other research participants were. Instead, I found *him* through activist channels. I met Kevin's sister at a meeting of a death penalty abolition group. I gave her my phone number to give to Kevin. He was the last person I interviewed for this study. Kevin had been on death row for eighteen and a half years as of our first phone interview. His execution was scheduled to take place approximately two months later. When our contact began, his legal appeals had all but run out. In the course of robbing a convenience store, he was alleged to have fatally stabbed the store clerk. Kevin maintained that an accomplice stabbed the clerk. The murder was a matter of frequent discussion in local news outlets as well as the anti–death penalty meetings I attended. Kevin and his family maintained his innocence of the murder. The details of his legal appeals were familiar to me and to many others in the region.

For eight months I interviewed Kevin via telephone and mail—never face-to-face, since he was only allowed visits from family members and his lawyers. Kevin was limited to placing collect phone calls to me, each lasting a maximum of fifteen minutes, at times designated by correctional officers. The telephone interviews with Kevin were supposedly monitored by the prison administration; a recorded message—a male voice—at the start of our calls said as much. Altogether I conducted nine phone interviews with Kevin. I typed notes on these interviews immediately after our calls. I attempted to recall as many direct quotes from the interviews as I could. Kevin phoned me a total of thirty-four times, but I was usually not at home when he called, especially during daytime hours. In addition to our nine phone calls, I sent Kevin three letters with questions and he replied with four letters.

Kevin asserted a positive, even superior sense of self, and chastised the politicians and journalists who stigmatized him. He depicted himself as an enemy of corrupt authority. In a letter Kevin sent me in Month 7, he described himself as being "under constant attack." Kevin understood that the battleground was as much discursive as it was pragmatic. He resented that the media had depicted him as "this monster" (second interview). He mentioned his intent to file a slander suit against the local newspaper for "calling [him] a punk and a coward for 18½ years," thus "attacking [his] character." Kevin's acquaintance with me affirmed his "true" character. In Month 9 I asked Kevin how he wanted to be remembered. He responded: "I think you've known me long enough and spoken with me long enough to know that I'm not some kind of uneducated monster like they make me out to be."

By his own account, Kevin's character was virtually unimpeachable. He referred to his principles on a number of occasions. His alleged "codes of honor" kept him from betraying people, even to save his life. He contrasted his integrity with that of the accomplices who had informed on him. In one story, recounted in a letter (Month 7), a female partner urged him to live less by his principles than by practical concerns, but he could not. The coherence of Kevin's self-identification as an especially upstanding person was served by sparse detail of what he had done to harm other people.

I tried several times to obtain a complete account of Kevin's past actions, including crimes. He did not ignore these requests but, rather, was artfully vague in responding. I wrote him in Month 2 and listed several questions, which he answered in his letter of Month 3. What follows is an extract from that letter, where he transcribed my questions (italicized here) exactly before responding to them:

What was your life like before you entered prison?

Well, I played hard. I loved beautiful women and parties in the bars a bit to [*sic*] much. I hustled etc. . . . For the most part though, I was staring [*sic*] to turn my life around and started working as a roofer.

What is your criminal history?

My criminal history. . . . Well I grew up around real gangsters. Not these wannabe clowns that have no morals nor honor. They were good hearted people—but business was business and not to be talked about. My criminal record is very limited. Truthfully I pretty much don't have a record. Not in the sense of anything serious. I once got popped with a controlled substance. And made a no contest plea. I once got popped with a stolen truck. I pled out to that as well.

Through narrative—here, written—Kevin was able to construct a good, manly self. He relegated his misconduct to a romantic world of good-hearted gangsters. In that world, both secrets and principles are kept. Like a number of other research participants, Kevin's offending was allegedly not so serious insofar as his criminal record was short.

Kevin was aware of my activism against the death penalty and my specific concern about his case through the circumstances of our meeting. My advocacy for Kevin was not especially active. I organized a campus petition drive on his behalf, wrote letters to political figures, and attended several sign-holdings. Regardless of my actual efforts on his behalf, Kevin *positioned me* as his advocate. At the start of our third interview (Month 2), Kevin asked, "Did you go to the meeting last night?" taking for granted that I knew about a meeting concerning the status of his appeals. In Month 8 Kevin's mother phoned me to relay a message, as Kevin had been trying to call me unsuccessfully. He told his mother to tell me: "Pass the documents that I mailed to you around campus. Have people write or e-mail the governor to order a federal investigation into my conviction and the Somers County prosecutor's office." Clearly, Kevin cast me as a partner in his struggle against a corrupt justice system. But he *directed* me in this effort; it was not an equal partnership.

I communicated to Kevin that I opposed criminal justice coercion. I literally began the research with Kevin with a critique of the prison administration, which I launched in our very first exchange:

Lo: Wow—glad we were finally able to get in touch. So is your situation now that they don't tell you when they're going to let you out to use the phone?

Kevin: Yeah. It's that people are pretty lazy. It's such a stressful job, being a CO [correctional officer].

Lo: Yeah.

Kevin: You sit around on your butt all day. [laugh]

My comment about Kevin's lack of control over telephone access suggested empathy for Kevin and objection to how he was being controlled. Kevin interpreted my advocacy for him in stereotypically gendered ways. He positioned me as a victim of his execution inasmuch as he believed I had come to care for him. As such, he assumed the role of my protector—an emotional helpmate. At the close of most of our phone conversations and in his letters to me, he urged me to "stay strong." During our eighth interview, seventeen days prior to his execution, Kevin shared this exchange about feelings:

> *Lo*: Has a date been set?
>
> *Kevin*: February 19.
>
> *Lo*: Wow.
>
> *Kevin*: Don't sound so down about it!
>
> *Lo*: It's depressing. You don't think it's depressing?
>
> *Kevin*: Nah. It's part of life, baby girl.

Concerning his looming death, Kevin renounced his own feelings, a typically masculine feat that may impede understanding of the informant's emotions (Schwalbe and Wolkomir 2002), but here exposes the research as a venue for Kevin's construction of an empowered self. Kevin cast me as sensitive and assigned himself the complementary masculine role as my hero. My gender positioning served him well. During our next phone call, which would be our last, Kevin again raised the topic of my feelings: "Lo, now the last time I spoke with you it was kind of hard on you." Apparently it was a fond impression. Kevin protected not just any person but specifically a sensitive female ("baby girl").

Kevin also explicitly positioned me as a romantic/sexual partner. My manner was friendly and familiar, which Kevin used as a basis for sexualizing the relationship, as in the following exchange from Month 2 (third interview).

> *Lo*: How long have you been in prison?
>
> *Kevin*: Eighteen and a half years. . . . Yeah, I was a good-looking young guy when I came in here. Now I'm old, fat and balding.
>
> *Lo*: How old are you?
>
> *Kevin*: I'll be thirty-eight in December.
>
> *Lo*: Oh, you'd better not call yourself old 'cause you're not much older than me.
>
> *Kevin*: How old are you?
>
> *Lo*: How old am I? Um, 35.
>
> *Kevin*: Oh, you're a baby. You're a minor gettin' old guys arrested.

Kevin's overtures eventually increased in frequency and intensity. At the close of our fourth phone interview (Month 3), Kevin bid me goodbye with "sweetheart." He used terms of endearment regularly after that time. In his letter of Month 7, Kevin addressed me as "Dearest Lois" and wrote: "I enjoyed talking with you the other day. I enjoy the conversation of a [*sic*] intelligent woman." Kevin met his wife of fifteen years only *after* having been incarcerated on death row. Thus I suspect that he saw our phone encounters as a normal avenue to achieving romance. Pollner and Emerson (1983) observe: "In some situations the time collaboratively spent in research activities may be viewed by persons as time spent in the cultivation of a potential sexual relation" (241). The fact that the state threatened to end his life within months would only have hastened the perceived courtship.

Kevin's flirting became more aggressive toward the end of his life. Our seventh interview (Month 8) had Kevin comforting me about the near prospect of his execution: "Don't worry. I'll be out there stalking you before too long! I like you college girls." Amiably I replied: "I can tell," thus attending to Kevin's more benign statement about liking college girls and ignoring the prior threat. Kevin joked in the same way during our very last talk: "I'll come back and stalk you. I'd make a good stalker. Then you'll say, 'Mommy, Daddy!' [mimicking a young female voice]" In light of Kevin's claims to moral decency, I was unsure just how to evaluate this stalking threat. Was he playing with—resisting—his categorization as evil? Since he had already established himself with me as righteous, it seemed unlikely that he would feel the need, now, to assert that claim ironically. Instead, I believe that Kevin was conveying a message of power over me. The state, Kevin's master for more than eighteen years, was to control his life even to the point of terminating it. Finally, he was left with virtually no resources for "being" a dominant male. Kevin constructed a fantasy of hegemonic masculinity through posthumous aggression.

I did not ask Kevin to stop making sexual remarks. I may have been concerned that he would terminate our contacts if I challenged him, a risk other women researchers acknowledge (Easterday et al. 1977; Horn 1997; Huggins and Glebbeek 2003). Of course, I could screen his calls—letting my answering machine play—and I sometimes did. But I felt that to defy the threats outright and redefine the nature of the relationship would have infringed on my data collection efforts. Had Kevin harassed me out in the "free" world, I would likely have felt it necessary to terminate our research relationship, and the study would have suffered as a result. Thus I gained something from his confinement and my dishonesty. I was beholden to the state for my safety during productive research.

DISCUSSION

Feminist social scientists have paid considerable attention to the research-er's power relative to the research participant, and particularly the ethical problem of dominating female, minority, and postcolonial informants. But female researchers also use power while interviewing *men*. These male informants may undermine our authority on account of gender, but they can never completely usurp it. Clearly, social positions other than gender impact research dynamics (Brown 2001; Horn 1997; Hunt 1984; McKeganey and Bloor 1991; Treviño 1992). For one thing, many of the men we study are marginalized in ways that we are not. This was certainly true of the participants in my project. They were mostly poor people of color, the typical captives of the criminal justice system. Even men who once held positions of power may now be under physical constraint, like the rapists interviewed by Scully and Marolla (1985), who were incarcerated in Virginia. Physical marginalization of male offenders translates into power and a sense of safety for the researcher—male or female.

The circumstance of marginalization shapes what informants make of the research opportunity, with implications for power *and* safety *and* ethics. In the present case, the state's thoroughgoing control of labeled offenders created identity problems that made the research a handy site for self-identification processes. I pulled weight as a necessary collaborator in the men's artful constructions of moral identity. Gender (masculine) identity was also problematic for these men. They used my female gender to demonstrate masculinity in the interviews.

Actively, if not consciously, I made the interview a hospitable site for my informants' identity projects. I did not contest their exculpatory accounts of their crimes and statements about their victims. Nor did I call negative attention to propositions and other sexual remarks. These were not deliberate safety maneuvers on my part. If anything, they were deliberate data collection strategies. Though effectively gendered—an aspect of hegemonic femininity—a tolerant demeanor is a standard tool of qualitative research. Clearly, the research interview comes with its own mechanisms of informal social control. Informants want us to think well of them; they use our social positions to construct a positive impression/persona. To my mind, this nonviolent variety of social control is not *in itself* unethical.[4] As women researching men, we should use our informants' desire to appear good. It allowed me to listen to stories of brutality without worrying that I would be brutalized next. I was able to concentrate and to gain intellectual purchase on how men's violence gets scripted as good, necessary, and normative, and thus how it gets perpetuated.

Of course, nothing—no micro-level process—works *in itself*, divorced from political context. The identity politics of the interview were articulated to state power over low-status offenders, and thus to injustice. Political forces hone a preoccupation with safety from the interpersonal violence of such offenders, as the late Steven Box (1983) observed:

[T]he powerful commit devastating crimes and get away with it, whilst the powerless but "potentially dangerous" commit less serious crimes, but get prison. Thus prisons function not only to demoralize and fracture potential resistance to domination, but they also supply ideological fodder by way of providing a massive legitimation to the portrait of crime and criminals so artfully and cynically constructed by legislators and those who influence them. In providing this service, they also further weaken potential working-class resistance by instilling in them a fear of "conventional criminals," which is not entirely irrational. In turn, this leads to an increased demand for more and more state imposed "law and order." In this way the powerless are manipulated to look upward, like children for protection. (222)

A concern with interpersonal violence, to the virtual exclusion of corporate and state violence, is nurtured by the state in order to distract us from systemic harms, which thus maintains ruling relations (Box 1983; Reiman 2001). Yet elites, including corporations and governments, cause more overall harm than those conventional offenders who get arrested and convicted—labeled—as such. Further, conventional offending seems to be a complex result of economic despair and thus of structural inequity. The status quo contributes to *and* maintains itself through "crime."

Even those who view state criminal justice as a mechanism for controlling the poor, like Box (1983), take for granted that women need the state to control men for the sake of safety. A fear of these men is "not entirely irrational," given the prevalence of conventional violence and especially violence against women by men whom they live or work with (222). Whereas conventional male criminals are foils for capitalism, they still they use what power they have to do harm (Lea and Young 1986). And thus it is understandable that we might support the state's project of maintaining control over *relatively* powerless criminals—"looking upward" for protection during research. I am implicated in state control of men of low status.

Two other interview dynamics are ethically troubling to me. First, the men's self-constructions effectively reproduced binary distinctions between men and women, victims and offenders, and good and evil. In fashioning himself as my hero and our relationship as one of romantic struggle—"we against the world"—Kevin substantiated hegemonic gender positions *and* a moral opposition of good versus evil. Such constructed differences lay the basis for social injustice, violence, and inequality. They threaten safety. I participated in this "difference-making" process. It benefited me to the extent that, in the short run, it seemed to *ensure* my safety: The men were "doing" goodness with me in the interviews. My consolation in all this is that I obtained rich data on how social difference is constructed situationally and collaboratively. In the nonresearch world, such as that of clinical work, where change is the *explicit* aim, I would have more difficulty rationalizing my collusion in talk that maintains the ruling relations (see, for example, Orme, Dominelli, and Mullender 2000, 95).

Second, I am uneasy about my dishonesty during the interviews. I presented myself as sympathetic to the men's claims of being misunderstood and mistreated; in several cases my sympathy was false. An unsettling example is how I deceived Kevin by acting like an advocate when I had lost much of my heart for it. To act in such a way may have reassured Kevin—and my empathy for him was certainly at play—but it was also intended for hassle-free data collection. Now, as I protest legally ordered executions, I recall how the prospect of Kevin's execution was a comfort and a help to me not very long ago. I can no longer treat "state injustice" as a monolith, something I do not participate in. What I can and feel I *must* do is to make such power relations more visible.

I would encourage scholars to adopt a similar stance of strong reflexivity (Harding 1991), whatever aspect of social life they are investigating. The context of the interview, including the resources that allow our studies to take place at all, provide data on social life and especially how power is accomplished.

NOTES

1. In a more recent work on male youth, the *body* constrains masculine action (Messerschmidt 2000), which gets me closer to the local context of action that is the concern of this chapter.

2. I interviewed Wayne, a deaf man, three times in the presence of a sign language interpreter. My phone interviews with Kevin were supposedly monitored by the prison administration. Finally, James was interviewed in the context of a class I was teaching, with eight others present. As I show presently, in all cases, the role of the "audience" was active and thus more interlocutor than audience.

3. The author is known as "Lo."

4. Nor, Goffman (1959) teaches us, is it avoidable. From a very different standpoint, Foucault (1983) posits a contemporary form of power that regulates definitions of self. This form, which he calls "subjection," is a historical phenomenon. Power relations are inherent in social life; this particular technique of power is not.

REFERENCES

Athens, L. (1997). *Violent Criminal Acts and Actors Revisited*. Urbana: University of Illinois Press.
Box, S. (1983). *Power, Crime, and Mystification*. London: Tavistock.
Brown, S. (2001). "What Makes Men Talk about Health?" *Journal of Gender Studies* 10, 187–95.

Brownmiller, S. (1975). *Against Our Will: Men, Women, and Rape.* New York: Simon and Schuster.

Cohen, A. (1955). *Delinquent Boys: The Culture of the Gang.* New York: Free Press.

Cotterill, P. (1992). "Interviewing Women: Issues of Friendship, Vulnerability, and Power." *Women's Studies International Forum* 15, 593–606.

Easterday, L., D. Papademas, L. Schorr, and C. Valentine. (1977). The Making of a Female Researcher: Role Problems in Field Work. *Urban Life* 6, 333–49.

Foucault, M. (1983). "Afterword: The Subject and Power." In *Michel Foucault: Beyond Structuralism and Hermeneutics,* edited by H. L. Dreyfus and P. Rabinow, 208–26. Chicago: University of Chicago Press.

Goffman, E. (1959). *The Presentation of Self in Everyday Life.* Garden City, NY: Doubleday.

———. (1967). *Interaction Ritual.* New York: Pantheon.

Harding, S. (1991). *Whose Science? Whose Knowledge? Thinking From Women's Lives.* Ithaca, NY: Cornell University Press.

Horn, R. (1997). "Not 'One of the Boys': Women Researching the Police." *Journal of Gender Studies* 6, 297–308.

Huggins, M. K., and M. Glebbeek. (2003). "Women Studying Violent Male Institutions: Cross-Gendered Dynamics in Police Research on Secrecy and Danger." *Theoretical Criminology* 7, 363–87.

Huggins, M. K., M. Haritos-Fatouros, and P. G. Zimbardo. (2002). *Violence Workers: Police Torturers and Murderers Reconstruct Brazilian Atrocities.* Berkeley and Los Angeles: University of California Press.

Hunt, J. (1984). "The Development of Rapport Through the Negotiation of Gender in Field Work among Police." *Human Organization* 43, 283–96.

Katz, J. (1988). *Seductions of Crime.* New York: Basic Books.

Keane, F. (1996). *Season of Blood: A Rwandan Journey.* London: Penguin Books.

Lea, J., and J. Young. (1986). "A Realistic Approach to Law and Order." In *The Political Economy of Crime: Readings for a Critical Criminology,* edited by B. MacLean, 358–64. Scarborough, ON: Prentice-Hall.

Loseke, D. R. (2003). *Thinking about Social Problems: An Introduction to Constructionist Perspectives,* 2nd ed. New York: Aldine de Gruyter.

Luckenbill, D. F. (1977). "Criminal Homicide as a Situated Transaction." *Social Problems* 25, 176–86.

McKeganey, N., and M. Bloor. (1991). "Spotting the Invisible Man: The Influence of Male Gender on Fieldwork Relations." *British Journal of Sociology* 42, 195–210.

Messerschmidt, J. W. (1993). *Masculinities and Crime: Critique and Reconceptualization of Theory.* Lanham, MD: Rowman and Littlefield.

———. (2000). *Nine Lives: Adolescent Masculinities, The Body, and Violence.* Boulder, CO: Westview.

Oakley, A. (1981). "Interviewing Women: A Contradiction in Terms." In *Doing Feminist Research,* edited by H. Roberts, 30–61. London: Routledge and Kegan Paul.

Orme, J., L. Dominelli, and A. Mullender. (2000). "Working with Violent Men from a Feminist Social Work Perspective." *International Social Work* 43, no. 1, 89–105.

Pollner, M., and R. M. Emerson. (1983). "The Dynamics of Inclusion and Distance in Fieldwork Relations." In *Contemporary Field Research: A Collection of Readings,* edited by R. M. Emerson, 235–52. Prospect Heights, IL: Waveland Press.

Pool, I. de Sola. (1957). "A Critique of the Twentieth Anniversary Issue." *Public Opinion Quarterly* 21, no. 190–98.

Presser, L. (2004). "Violent Offenders, Moral Selves: Constructing Identities and Accounts in the Research Interview." *Social Problems* 51, 82–101.

Reiman, J. (2001). *The Rich Get Richer and the Poor Get Prison*, 6th ed. Boston: Allyn and Bacon.

Schatzman, L., and A. L. Strauss. (1973). *Field Research: Strategies for a Natural Sociology*. Englewood Cliffs, NJ: Prentice-Hall.

Schwalbe, M. L., and M. Wolkomir. (2002). "Interviewing Men." In *Handbook of Interview Research: Context and Method*, edited by J. F. Gubrium and J. A. Holstein, 203–19. Thousand Oaks, CA: Sage.

Scully, D., and J. Marolla. (1985). "'Riding the Bull at Gilley's': Convicted Rapists Describe the Rewards of Rape." *Social Problems* 32, 251–63.

Spradley, J. P. (1979). *The Ethnographic Interview*. Fort Worth, TX: Holt, Rinehart and Winston.

Stacey, J. (1988). "Can There Be a Feminist Ethnography?" *Women's Studies International Forum* 11, no. 1, 21–27.

Stanko, E. A. (1997). "Safety Talk: Conceptualizing Women's Risk Assessment as a 'Technology of the Soul.'" *Theoretical Criminology* 1, 479–99.

Toch, H. (1969). *Violent Men: An Inquiry Into the Psychology of Violence*. Washington, DC: American Psychological Association.

Treviño, A. J. (1992). "Interviewing Women: Researcher Sensitivity and the Male Interviewer." *Humanity and Society* 16, 504–23.

Wolf, D. L. (1996). "Situating Feminist Dilemmas in Fieldwork." In *Feminist Dilemmas in Fieldwork*, edited by D. L. Wolf, 1–55. Boulder, CO: Westview.

Yochelson, S., and S. E. Samenow. (1976). *The Criminal Personality: A Profile for Change*. New York: Jason Aronson.

11

Negotiating the Muddiness of Grassroots Field Research: Managing Identity and Data in Rural El Salvador

Jocelyn Viterna

Researching violence raises a number of personal and ethical difficulties for female social scientists; the most common is perhaps balancing personal safety and well-being with effective and equitable research relationships. This chapter adds an additional set of concerns: How studying violence affects the types and quality of data available. A central danger in my field research revolved around the challenges associated with encouraging "memories" and assessing the "truth" of respondents' memories, all within a social system structured by gender, by asymmetrical personal power, and by globalized economic power. These issues posed a number of challenges to learning about women's past involvement in El Salvador's recent (1980–1992) grassroots civil war.

The rural Salvadorans I interviewed in 2000–2001 had survived twelve years of civil war; I wanted to learn about their wartime experiences. Because few written records existed, I relied upon interviews with war survivors. Yet I suspected that such complicating factors as interviewee memory, literacy, and trust, combined with the intensity of the violence that most interviewees had experienced, would severely limit the amount and type of information that I would obtain. How accurately could prospective interviewees remember a civil war that had ended nearly ten years before I began my interviews? How willing would they be to recount these memories to me, an outsider from a nation considered hostile to their past war efforts? Would I be able to hear and understand the accounts that they shared with me, accounts that would undoubtedly be far different from my own life experiences? I was initially quite unprepared for the extent that my position as a woman researcher from a powerful first world country might shape interviewees' narrative accounts.

271

In this chapter, I discuss conducting research in postwar El Salvador, beginning by "Situating the Research" within El Salvador and within the lives of that country's grassroots activists—the "regular" people (as opposed to the leaders) who were the rank-and-file rebel army during the country's civil war. I then explore, in "Important Actors; Absence of Voice," the relative lack of written documentation and academic scholarship on the Salvadoran grassroots in general, and on grassroots women in particular. In the third section, "Negotiating Muddy Terrain," I describe the challenges associated with data gathering in rural Salvadoran communities, where memories of the war, actors' participation in it, and whether and how they narrated such information to me, was structured by temporality, by gender, and by personal and global economic power differentials. In addressing these considerations, I discuss in the chapter's fourth section—"Wading the Murky Waters of 'Memory' and 'Truth'"—how memory and truth are shaped in retrospective interview accounts. In the fifth section, "Memory Challenges; Challenging Memory," I identify the tactics I developed to overcome the dangers of remembering. Among the most important dangers were those related to gender and power, the subject of the sixth section. The chapter concludes with "A Qualitative Methodologist's Toolbox."

SITUATING THE RESEARCH

The Farabundo Martí National Liberation Front, the FMLN,[1] was a rebel army that waged guerrilla warfare against El Salvador's ruling military dictatorship from 1980 to 1992. An umbrella organization comprised of five smaller militant groups and many nonviolent political groups, the FMLN battled against the Salvadoran Armed Forces largely in El Salvador's rural areas. The United States, embroiled in a Cold War with the Soviet Union, was a fervent supporter of El Salvador's military government. They labeled the FMLN "communist" and provided the Salvadoran state with billions of dollars to defeat the FMLN (LaFeber 1993). The United States continued to give aid to the military dictatorship in El Salvador even when it was clear that the Salvadoran government was responsible for terrible human rights abuses against its own people (Danner 1994).

Even though the Salvadoran Armed Forces were better funded, better equipped, better trained, and had more soldiers, the FMLN were not easily defeated. For twelve years, the FMLN successfully challenged the Salvadoran Armed Forces in military combat, and in 1992 they forced a UN–brokered peace agreement between themselves and the Salvadoran government. The resulting peace accords brought a dramatic social and political transformation to El Salvador: the FMLN obtained legal status as a political party, democratic elections became regular for the first time in El Salvador's history, the military was reduced in size and in power, and more than thirty-six thousand previously landless received small properties (Álvarez and Chávez 2001). Many formerly quiescent men and women developed into social and political activists (Wood 2003). Women in particular—said to have increased their political power as a result of their unprecedented high levels of militant FMLN revolutionary participation—became active in postwar civil society struggles (Kampwirth 2004; Luciak 2001). Yet these positive outcomes had come at a high price: Approximately eighty thousand Salvadorans had lost their lives, more than 1 million had been displaced from their homes, and the infrastructure of the nation had been heavily damaged by twelve years of violent conflict.

Before discussing my own research, I first define two terms used in this chapter—"grassroots" and "guerrilla." By grassroots, I mean the "regular" or "typical" people (as opposed to the "leaders") who constituted the majority support for the FMLN political and military movement. In the FMLN, the leaders often came from middle-class urban backgrounds and were fairly well educated (Dunkerley 1982; Wickham-Crowley 1992). By contrast, the "grassroots," the people who filled the ranks of the guerrilla army, were typically poor people from rural areas who had little or no formal education (Wickham-Crowley 1992; McClintock 1998, 266–67; Goodwin 2001, 164–65). In addition to the grassroots in the FMLN rebel army, the FMLN also had grassroots supporters in the rural areas where the rebel army operated. These people, called "collaborators," often provided FMLN guerrillas with food, information about the location of Salvadoran military troops, and safe houses in which to hide. Without a doubt, these thousands of grassroots participants and supporters, who together are the focus of my chapter, were instrumental to the overall success of the FMLN.

A "guerrilla" is a fighter in a small, irregular army (as opposed to a state's army) that relies on surprise and "guerrilla" tactics (ambush, raids, snipers, mines, etc.) to attack a larger, stronger enemy. The aim of guerrilla warfare is to inflict maximum damage on the enemy with minimum time and casualties for their own forces.[2] I focused on guerrillas who lived and worked in rural FMLN guerrilla camps for a period of at least six months.[3] Over the course of my interviews, I learned that the FMLN guerrilla camps were—like most social organizations—stratified by occupation. Some people had the primary job of fighting, others were largely responsible for cooking, others for radio communication, and still others made grenades, or carried messages, or treated the wounded, or recruited support from surrounding communities. I initially considered labeling and studying only those "guerrillas" who were combatants, yet I found that nearly all men and women in a camp had been trained to use a firearm, and most carried guns whenever they were available. Even those whose primary occupation was not combat sometimes had to engage in battle. Moreover, people frequently started out in one job and then moved to another, with a person who had begun as a cook later becoming a full-time combatant. Because of the need for all those living in an FMLN camp to be trained and ready to fight, and because all people living in a camp had given up their "normal" lives to support the FMLN full-time, 24/7, 365 days a year, I decided that a grassroots person's residence in a guerrilla camp was sufficient for me to study them as an FMLN guerrilla.

IMPORTANT ACTORS; ABSENCE OF VOICE

Many social scientists conclude that the FMLN insurgency would not have lasted for twelve years, nor would it have wielded such power in the peace negotiations, if it had not had extensive popular support. Yet even given the critical role of the grassroots in this and other peasant-based revolutionary movements, scholars note that grassroots participants are seldom given voice in scholarly analyses (Bermeo 1986; Kriger 1992; Wood 2003). Most studies rely on official or elite sources, in part because these sources generate archival data. By contrast, grassroots activists are less likely to document their experiences, or to have their experiences documented by others.[4] Moreover, even when scholars rely on retrospective interviews instead of written records, they tend to talk to leaders rather than the grassroots. The theoretical justification is that leaders matter; their decisions and actions determine the strategies that a political organization will use, the ideologies that a political organization will adopt, and whether and how the regular folk will join the movement or organization (Morris and Staggenborg 2004). I also suspect that leaders are interviewed because, as a group, they tend to be more visible, more educated, more likely to live in urban areas, and therefore are generally more accessible to scholars. As a result of the academic focus on leaders, there are few micro-level explanations of why regular people have engaged in extraordinary revolutionary actions, even at great personal risk.

Other explanations of grassroots participation argue that macro-level political or economic changes create a situation that is particularly conducive to large-scale mobilizations. Yet these accounts cannot tell us why some people joined a movement, while other people—who hear the same messages from leaders and live in the same political and economic context—decide not to join. Answering this question requires comparing the experiences of grassroots activists with nonactivists (Viterna 2006).

As I began preparing for my dissertation research in 1998, I knew that I wanted to give voice to the FMLN grassroots for several reasons. First, I wanted to compare whether and how the leaders' reports of the movement differed from those of nonleaders. Second, social movement theory tells us that participating in a high-risk movement is likely to have a strong impact on participants' future activism, political ideologies, and life choices (McAdam and Paulsen 1993). If this holds true for El Salvador, then nearly fifteen thousand FMLN guerrillas, and an even larger number of FMLN collaborators, may have experienced life-altering changes through their participation. I wanted to know whether and how past participation might influence present-day involvement in local politics and activism. Third, I wanted to understand the experiences of the nearly 30 percent of the FMLN rebel army that was female.[5] Since waging war is a largely masculine endeavor in all societies (Wechsler Segal 1995), it seemed particularly surprising that some (but not all) poor, rural women from highly patriarchal El Salvador rejected traditional gendered norms, picked up automatic weapons, and took mortal risks for social change. Knowing that very few women had reached leadership positions in the FMLN (Vázquez, Ibáñez, and Murguialday 1996), I was certain that most women in the FMLN were grassroots participants. Like most studies of activism, however, the few scholarly investigations of FMLN women guerrillas focus on women who were typically more educated and urban dwellers, and not likely to be very representative of grassroots FMLN women.

Perhaps another reason that there is little written on grassroots activists from El Salvador's war period is that trust and safety during times of violence complicated data gathering. In El Salvador a few government agencies and researchers had conducted surveys of rural *campesinos*, but respondents were often unwilling to provide information to unknown questioners during a politically violent time (Wood 2003, 32). Moreover, the grassroots often lived in isolated rural areas that were dangerous for investigators.[6]

Understanding FMLN grassroots experiences during the Salvadoran civil war would therefore be largely dependent upon my gaining interviews from individuals in the present who had experienced the war between ten and twenty years earlier. I would need a plan for identifying a representative group of interviewees who had lived in the 1980s in the war zone, and I would need a reliable local contact to help me connect with and establish trust within these communities. I would also need to hire and train local assistants to help conduct surveys and interviews, and I would need a reliable means of transportation to get me to the isolated villages that I was hoping to study. This far-from-easy set of requirements took me into the "muddy terrain" of field research.

NEGOTIATING "MUDDY" TERRAIN

Choosing Villages

In an ideal research setting, ensuring a representative sample would have been relatively simple. I would simply seek out a list of former FMLN guerrillas and randomly select the names of those I wished to interview. However, such ideal conditions rarely exist with research on grassroots populations, as other research in this volume demonstrates. Given the absence of such a list, I sought to create a representative group by first selecting three *municipios* from across El Salvador. (A *municipio*, similar to a U.S. county or parish, includes a number of smaller villages within it). Each *municipio* was chosen for its being on a United Nations list of the twenty-five municipalities most violently disputed during the country's civil war and for its representing a different geographic region of El Salvador.

I then selected six villages from within these three *municipios* as the sites of my research. Although *municipio* boundaries themselves were not altered by the war, the geographical map of villages had changed dramatically. Many villages that existed before the war were either destroyed or abandoned, while new villages were created under the peace accords' land redistribution program. Groups of guerrillas demobilized together under UN supervision and groups of civilians returning together from refugee camps were typically given plots of land near one another. Often, the people who received land in the newly formed villages were associated with the same ideological branch of the FMLN guerrilla army, and so certain communities came to be identified not only as FMLN supporters, but also as supporters of a particular faction of the FMLN.[7] A primary concern for my village selection was to have representation from each of the five factions of the FMLN. Other concerns were that villages would vary in size, histories, and economic resources.

I decided to seek the advice of knowledgeable locals to help me find the villages that met my selection criteria. Having spent the 1998–1999 academic year in El Salvador on an academic fellowship, I already had a network of friends and acquaintances in the not-for-profit sector that could help me identify and select villages and perhaps even indicate contacts within these villages. The villages in my final sample ranged in size from about three hundred to one thousand people; their primary economic activities ranged from growing coffee, beans, corn, and sugar cane to mining salt or raising shrimp. Only one of the six villages I chose (the largest) had existed before the war. The other five were "repopulations." In each village, I had the name of someone on the village council, or another respected community leader, to whom I would direct my request for research.

Entering Villages

I decided to rent a room for my home base in El Salvador's capital city of San Salvador—a place with electricity and Internet access and nearby copy centers, university libraries, and archives. Knowing that I would need to spend a great deal of time living in villages, I had to seek reliable transportation between San Salvador and the selected communities. During my previous time in El Salvador, I had learned that travel in rural areas was exceedingly difficult. One of my communities was not accessible by bus; a three-hour bus ride from the capital would deposit me on a narrow dirt road and, after two hours of walking, I would finally arrive at the community. Given that I would be carrying many papers, recording devices, drinking water and clothing for several weeks, and some food to share with the families where I stayed, I decided bus travel and the long trek to the village was not a viable option. Moreover, even where buses or pickup trucks ran regularly from the capital to villages, the transport was slow, cramped, and not very reliable, especially considering that I had only ten months to conduct 150 interviews. I thus decided I needed to purchase a car to facilitate my interviewing in the villages. With the luxury of a vehicle,[8] I was able to get to villages with relative ease.

My next task was to begin integrating myself into each community. During my first trip to a community, I asked around after my contact, introduced myself as a friend of the person who helped me to select that community, and told my contact, a local woman, about my project. I then asked when the next village council meeting was, and if I might speak at that meeting. I would typically hang out for a while longer with the contact or I would buy a Coke at the local *tiendita* (a small store, generally within a local family's home) and chat with the people nearby, and then leave until the council meeting.

My contacts in the first three villages were all women; all were excited by my project and exceedingly generous about sharing their time and skills with me. I was a bit surprised, therefore, when my contact in the fourth village, a man, was less than cooperative. My attempts to explain my project to him were continually interrupted by his sharing his war experiences with me: He wanted to make sure that I included his narrative in my book. My attempts to solicit an invitation to the village council meeting were rebuffed as "unnecessary." After more than an hour of listening to my contact's war stories, I left with an appointment to return at a later date. I hoped I would be more convincing at a second meeting with this man and that he would facilitate my explaining my research to the village council.

Early in the second meeting, the man proposed marriage to me, with a clearly stated goal of using our marriage to earn passage to the United

States. I was dumbfounded. The man lived with his *compañera* (a female life partner) and their two children, was significantly older than I, and had barely let me say more than a few words in either of our two meetings. I immediately began to review our interaction in my head: What had I had done to provoke this disaster of miscommunication? What had I said? Was my dress appropriate? Had my polite laughter at his jokes or my solo visits to his home been culturally inappropriate? Then another question emerged: Why was I blaming myself for his lack of propriety? My instinct was to exit the situation immediately, so I turned and walked out the door. Once on the porch and in the public eye, I explained to the man that I felt our working relationship had been compromised, and that I would not be returning to his community anymore, but that I was grateful for his time and attention, and that I was sure the wartime experiences he had shared with me would be excellent contributions to my eventual book. I then made a quick exit to my car and did not return to his village. I chose another community in the same *municipio*, with the same factional ties, but at a distance from the original community.

After this experience, I decided that all my initial contacts in rural communities should be women. I did not feel that working with men would put my person in danger, but I worried it would endanger my chance of having productive and trusting working relationships with women, and I was especially interested in women's experiences. My only interactions would be with the men I interviewed.[9] During my second visits to the selected villages, I typically met with the council, explained my project, and solicited formal approval for its implementation. I emphasized that there would be no financial benefit for the community, but suggested that my project would provide a service by documenting the experiences of village residents. I made clear that interviews were voluntary and that I would leave a copy of the interview tape with the respondent if he or she so desired. I suggested other nonfinancial ways that I could "give back" to the community. I could collect the names of the community members' friends and families who had died in the war and submit them to a group that was building a monument in San Salvador to honor civilian casualties (this monument has since been built, and the names I collected are inscribed). I promised to share a copy of my book with villagers. Over the course of the investigation, community leaders would sometimes approach me with additional ideas for "giving back": a donation and teaching. I donated to a local monument fund, taught youth the basic rules of basketball, and discussed with a women's group the background of U.S.-Afghanistan relations in the context of 9/11.

After I received permission to conduct my research, I began to seek housing arrangements. In the first two communities, my initial community contacts offered me a place in their homes. In the third community, I began living in a nearby town with a friend and commuted about fifteen minutes each morning to the village. After about one week of commuting, I received an invitation from a local woman, a leader in the community, to stay with her family. In the fourth community, the council encouraged me to stay in a tiny, three-room hotel that had been erected for visitors; this would generate income for the community—my cost was about $1.30 per night. Even in that town, however, I soon received an offer to stay with a family. In the fifth and sixth communities, I shared a home with internationals living there. Once in each village, I made sure to attend community meetings, celebrations, and work gatherings. I would often help carry water, and on one occasion I accompanied a family while they picked corn and coffee. This helped me get a feel for their lives outside the home. I was almost always invited to share my meals with someone in the community. (Sometimes I ate four times in one day so as to not appear rude by refusing offered food). I typically spent about two months in each community. During these months, I would live in the community for a week, then return to San Salvador for a few days to drop off completed questionnaires and pick up new supplies, and then return to the community for another week.

Identifying and Selecting "Representative" Actors

I hoped to make generalizations about why grassroots men and women joined the FMLN, and how being in the guerrilla army affected their present day ideas and activities. Such generalizations would be more reliable, I assumed, if I interviewed individuals who were relatively representative of those who actually participated in the FMLN. I had already selected villages that captured an array of geographical, economic, and ideological factors, so if I were to interview a relatively representative group of men and women within these villages, I reasoned, then I would get a strong sense of which characteristics were shared by women guerrillas, and how they differed from women who did not join the guerrillas. It would also allow me to understand the different experiences of men and women.[10]

In order to select a pool of respondents who represented most former grassroots FMLN guerrillas and nonguerrillas, both men and women, I needed to obtain basic background information on village residents. I accomplished this by hiring teenage assistants from local schools to complete a very basic survey of village residents. I chose teenagers because they had learned to read and write at a far higher level than most adults in the community, and because they were often interested in and excited about my project. I paid them each a small amount for their labor, and, given that many villagers live in poverty, I did not turn away any teen who wished to participate. Happily, this arrangement never got out of control, given the small population of teenagers in each village. We would travel door to door in the community[11] in groups of two or three asking a few simple questions: What was the family name? How many adult men and women lived in the home? What were their ages? Which of those adults, if any, had lived in an FMLN guerrilla camp during the war?

Using this data, I created a master list of all women and men in the village who *had been* in an FMLN guerrilla camp, and all of those who *had not*. After ranking each person on my household list from youngest to oldest, I then selected from each community fourteen women (seven guerrillas and seven nonguerrillas), and six men (three guerrillas and three nonguerrillas) to interview. The guerrillas were selected at random from the age-arranged list; I then matched this sample with nonguerrillas who were closest in age to the selected guerrillas. We allowed people to self-define what was meant by "living in a guerrilla camp," so sometimes someone on the list who I expected to be a "nonguerrilla" actually qualified as a guerrilla, and vice versa. (At that point in my research, I had not decided how I would define a "guerrilla." This definition arose through the process of data analysis.) In the end, using the definition of "guerrilla" stated earlier in this chapter, I obtained a sample from all six villages of 120 interviewees: 38 guerrilla women, 46 nonguerrilla women, 20 guerrilla men, and 16 nonguerrilla men.[12]

After identifying a relatively representative group of grassroots guerrillas and nonguerrillas, I then had to convince selected respondents to take part in an interview. Not only was I an outsider hailing from the very country whose government had funded the corrupt Salvadoran government's efforts to wage war against the FMLN, but I was also asking potentially sensitive questions about the interviewees' past and present political stances and other such potentially sensitive subjects as their wartime sexual activities, their involvement in warfare itself, and their life in El Salvador during a time of extreme violence.

Educational Disparities; Interview Questions

Not only did my advanced education highlight differences between myself and my interviewees, but it also generated communication problems. This affected interviewees' testimonies and how I interpreted them. For example, in my initial interviews, I sometimes used words that interviewees did not understand. Interested in interviewees' present-day political attitudes, I borrowed a question from a survey previously conducted in El Salvador, asking if interviewees thought that "democracy was the best form of government." Yet when I asked this in my interviews, I quickly discovered that the rural Salvadorans did not know what "democracy" meant. This created awkward moments; I was unsure whether to proceed after offering a definition, or just pretend that the problem was with my Spanish and then move forward. After having definitional problems with ten straight interviews, I decided it was time to rewrite my questionnaire. The new version avoided words that had proven difficult or, in some cases, provided a definition for each interviewee. I then retested my instrument on Salvadoran friends to make sure it flowed smoothly, and asked for lots of suggestions on what was the best way to ask about a particular topic. My goal was to avoid any additional situations where someone might acutely feel our differences in education.

A particularly difficult problem emerged out of my questions about whether there had been "sexual harassment" in guerrilla camps. Previous research had suggested that women guerrillas, in addition to being subjected to the dangers of warfare, were also subjected to dangers from their male FMLN colleagues. Reports from women who had been leaders in the FMLN suggested that men frequently pressured women, especially grassroots women, to have sex with them (Luciak 2001, 15; Kampwirth 2004). My interviews made clear that women often joined the FMLN at fourteen or fifteen, with some joining as young as eleven. Given that men outnumbered women in guerrilla camps by more than two to one, and that most women in the FMLN camps were young and not under parental control, it is easy to believe that sexual pressures were present.

My first hurdle in attempting to access such information was finding ways to talk about sexuality between men and women. Asking if men had "pressured" women for sex promoted an immediate negation: "There was no rape in guerrilla camps." The rural Salvadoran women seemed to relate directly to the most extreme form of inappropriate male sexual violence against women—rape, as violent force in penetration—but they did not seem to recognize and have words for the "lesser" forms of sexual domination. These potentially inappropriate sexual pressures or harassments were nameless; were they seen as men's "natural" behavior? Did such a view render this male behavior invisible to a woman?[13] Overall, Salvadoran ex-guerrilla women insisted that they had never had as good "protection" from men before or after the war as while living under the strict rules of the guerrilla camp. Although I take very seriously their arguments about the camp providing additional protections against rape, especially in comparison to their lives today, I had a nagging feeling that these women may have faced situations that I would define as sexual pressure (harassment), but that they themselves did not.

Anonymity

Interviewees could see that I was writing down what they said, but they generally were unable to read. I worried that this might raise questions about their anonymity and cause them discomfort because, during the civil war, having one's name on a list often resulted in murder by a death squad.

I thus made certain to tell each interviewee that I would not write down his or her name, only notes from our "conversation." I made sure they could see what I was writing at all times, with the hope that they would at least recognize the absence of their name. A few insisted that I write down their names, demonstrating the pride they felt in sharing their testimony with me. I told all interviewees that if they wanted to remember our conversation, I would make them a copy of the cassette tape. A few took me up on the offer; most seemed uninterested.

MURKY WATERS OF "MEMORY" AND "TRUTH"

Faced with a paucity of historical written documentation from the viewpoint of the Salvadoran grassroots regarding their involvement in their country's civil war, and the role of women guerrillas among such actors, I knew that I would need to conduct retrospective interviews with these former participants. But how might actors who had been part of a politically charged struggle remember and recount their experiences? Obviously, their political and personal beliefs would influence the tone of their recollections; would it also influence the type of information they were willing to share? How would my status as an outsider from the United States—the nation that had funded the Salvadoran military fighting against the FMLN—affect what people were willing to tell me? And at the most basic level, what will people have forgotten over the last decade?

I began to read what researchers have learned about interviewees' ability to remember a past. In general, psychological studies of memory demonstrate that humans are generally able to correctly remember the broad outlines of their past experiences (Schacter 1996). In particular, memories of past *events* are more reliable than memories of past *attitudes* (Markus 1986); highly intense events are particularly well remembered in the short and the long term (Bradley 1994; Witvliet 1997). People often fail to remember the source of knowledge or the details of a particular past event (Schacter 1996). Since one of my research interests was how past events and experiences affected present-day attitudes and activities, I had some confidence that interviewees would remember past events, even if they were fuzzy on details. One challenge was how to tap into such details.

As a sociologist, I knew that remembering and recounting past experiences and their details is a social as well as cognitive exercise. Indeed, scholars of social memory have demonstrated that although individuals may remember well the occurrence of an event, other aspects of remembering—if and how it is reinterpreted, the value ascribed to it, and details about it—are malleable (Schwartz 1997; Olick and Robbins 1998; Auyero

1999). Zerubavel (1996) argues that what a person decides to remember, what is deemed appropriate to forget, and the tone or feeling ascribed to each memory are all dependent upon a person's present-day social context, or "remembrance environments" (see also Huggins, Hairtos-Fatouros, and Zimbardo 2002). For example, how a person feels in the present about a political group will influence how he or she portrays the group's past actions (Auyero 1999). In addition, memories of the past may incorporate elements of memories held by other associates at the time. Through such associations people share and confirm the past and create (re-create) memories through conversation (Zerubavel 1996). Halbwachs (1992) has demonstrated that memories can be used to either tie a person to, or create distance from, collective others. In my case, for example, people who were dissatisfied with the FMLN in the present may have underreported their past relationship with the FMLN as a way of distancing themselves from that organization.

Memories can be manipulated to achieve a particular end. For example, a person or group may consciously attempt to legitimate a present action or interest by how they discuss it.[14] Or a person may attempt to reconcile past experiences with his or her present day identity, such as when past torturers justified their past actions through present-day discursive explanations (Huggins et al., 2002). In my research, I had to continually assess the ways that interviewees' "remembrance environment" might be shaping what they shared with me.

MEMORY CHALLENGES; CHALLENGING MEMORIES

I entered the field knowing what past research had to say about "memory" and then had to put such information into interview practice. I decided to focus on three kinds of challenges to memory: (1) *Information decay*: how accurately could interviewees remember what had happened to them up to twenty years earlier? (2) *Remembrance environments*: how might interviewees' current social context, or "remembrance environment," influence their recall of the past? (3) *Violence*: would past violence shape whether and the way that past experiences were recounted to me?

Information Decay

My first questions were designed to re-create, with as much detail as possible, an interviewee's experiences before and during the civil war, since these "events" are thought to be the most reliably remembered. I began by

identifying where a respondent had lived before the war and soliciting information about her prewar family situation.[15] By identifying the many places
a woman had lived before and during the war, I was able to reconstruct a
woman's wartime actions.[16] I then asked marital and birth questions: When
did she first take a partner, when did she first get pregnant, number of
children, their ages, and so on. Finally, I asked questions about her activities within and outside the home over those years. I used a number of cues
to develop a timeline of past events with the interviewee. For example, if
the respondent was unsure what years she had participated in a particular
organization, I would ask her if she remembered which children she had
with her when attending the organization's meetings. I could then use the
age of the children to estimate the dates of her attendance. Knowing local
history was also critical. For example, if the respondent did not remember
the date when she joined the guerrillas, I could ask if she joined before or
after the assassination of the archbishop, the paving of the highway, or a
particular peasant massacre. I also knew which organizations had operated
in an area so that I could ask specifically about their actions. My hope was
that these cues would help an interviewee link an important, concrete event
like childbirth or a massacre to potentially less memorable events like the
dates of certain meetings. The time line helped me to feel more confident
that I was not missing events that were critical to my analysis.

Once I had established the "facts" of an interviewee's life, I followed with
questions intended to elicit narrative accounts of each individual's wartime
experiences. For example, after re-creating the environment under which
a woman had joined the guerrillas in the past (where she lived, who she
lived with, how many children she had, what activities she was involved
with, etc.), I would then ask the more subjective question of *why* a woman
decided to join the FMLN. I continued this rotation of asking a series of
concrete, life experience–rooted questions followed by more narrative
questions. For example, next I asked about the woman's life in an FMLN
camp: What work did she do when she first arrived at the camp? Was she
assigned that task? Did she ever move to another task? Would she walk me
through a typical day in a guerrilla camp? Did she take a partner in the guerrilla camp? Did she get pregnant while in the camp? Where did she have
her baby? These questions were then followed by the more subjective questions about how women felt about their experiences in the camps. In this
way, every respondent was first encouraged to think about the same broad
outline of past events, and then each individual respondent decided which
of those events would take center stage in *her* narrative of why she joined
and how she felt about her experiences. I hoped that by mixing questions
about concrete events with open-ended questions that sought subjective
memories, I could reduce memory inaccuracies.

Remembrance Environments

Understanding whether and how the present-day environment affects the way that things are remembered was a formidable challenge. It seemed to lessen this problem that I was primarily concerned with how past *events* had affected present-day *attitudes*, since events are generally better remembered than attitudes. Yet I worried that a person's present-day relationships with, and attitudes about, for example, the FMLN political party might shape how that former guerrilla remembered past involvement with the FMLN guerrilla movement. Because I had a relatively representative pool of interviewees, I decided to look for patterns in present-day characteristics that may explain how individuals remember the past. When these patterns exist, I hypothesized, I could then examine how the present-day environment seems to be shaping the past. When these patterns do not exist, it would provide stronger support that what women report in the past is a fairly accurate approximation of what "really" happened. To continue with the above example, I hypothesized that former guerrilla women who continued to associate with the FMLN political party, and who positively assess this political party in the present, would also be more likely to speak positively about their past guerrilla mobilization experiences. I was surprised to discover no correlation between a woman's present-day attitudes about the FMLN political party (her "remembrance environment") and currently stated reasons for having joined the FMLN, suggesting relatively accurate accounts of the past in this instance (Viterna 2006).

Violence

Some scholarship suggests that extreme violence can complicate remembering (Jelin 2003; Wieviorka 1999): Traumatized interviewees might lack the desire to relive the past through memory or lack words to describe a horror of the past. Other research has found that intense events are remembered with more accuracy than less intense events (Bradley 1994; Witvleiet 1997): Trauma—because of its emotional intensity—is remembered with particular accuracy (Schacter 1996; Wagenaar and Groeneweg 1988). Still other research on memory finds that violent crises can force a reevaluation of one's past: A "remembrance environment" can be created that reshapes explanations about a traumatic past.

Would interviewees be able to talk with me, a young graduate student, about past violence? And what consequences might my probing into interviewees' experiences with violence have for their lives, especially given that poverty left them with few if any resources for effectively dealing with trauma? I thus decided that I would seek to uncover reports of past violence, but that I would only push for the most basic outline of an occurrence; I would leave additional details to the interviewees' discretion. Sometimes a respondent answered questions about past violence with short, precise answers. I would typically probe briefly, sometimes by repeating what he or she told me or just by sitting in silence and allowing the interviewee a great deal of time to decide if he or she wanted to offer more details. If the person did not appear willing to talk after one or two probes, or after a weighty silence, I would simply move on. Sometimes, however, such probes would launch respondents into a long and tearful description of the past experience. These descriptions were often filled with vivid details, yet lacking in organization and difficult for me to follow. To illustrate, when I asked a sixty-one-year-old woman to tell me how her seventeen-year-old daughter and twenty-two-day-old granddaughter had died, she replied:

Interviewee: Look . . . my daughter . . . she died . . . in a massacre.

Viterna: In Copapayo? (I knew that most of the survivors of the Copapayo massacre—the ones who escaped before the soldiers arrived and trapped the rest—were living in this woman's village in the present day.).

Interviewee: Yes . . . no! No, in San Nicolás

Viterna: Too many massacres.

Interviewee: Yes, in San Nicolás, that's where it was . . .

Viterna: A massacre.

Interviewee: Yes, a massacre.

Viterna: Soldiers came?

(silence)

Interviewee: They put in everyone that they could one on top of the other. When I went there, they told me where my daughter had stayed. I went . . . , I entered the door thinking I was going to take her out alive, that she was alive. I opened the door [to the house]: The dead that were there. Look, it was a very horrible thing. I screamed and I was all alone, seeing this . . . and it was as if God showed me my daughter, in life, the little piece of her dress . . . a little dress that had a little green floral print . . . . Ay, I said to myself, here is my daughter . . . and, how was I supposed to find her . . . [there was] this huuuge . . . . mountain of people, some were underneath, others on top of others. . . .

As I listened, I had many questions: How had her daughter died? Was she shot? Knifed? Or simply suffocated by the pile of dead bodies? Was she raped first? What happened to her baby? Was the pile of bodies mostly women and children, or mostly men, or a combination? Yet in this and similar cases, I did not interrupt with questions. When the interviewee finished her story, both she and I were in tears. I turned off the recording device and just sat in silence with the interviewee for a few moments. I thanked the woman for sharing the story with me, telling her that I could not begin to comprehend this experience, but that I was glad that I could at least tell the story of her daughter and the other victims in my book. Thinking over my decision to not press for the details of an interviewee's experiences with violence, I realized that it would have felt ugly to press for details, and then sit and meticulously take notes, record a person's sobs, and then move "professionally" to the next question. It would have felt like I was taking a woman's profoundly personal story and turning it into a commodity.

Ironically, when an interviewee reported violent events to me in a matter-of-fact tone, a stance much more common among the men,[17] I felt much more comfortable probing for more details. If the interviewee set such a tone, I would use that tone in my follow-up questions. Ironically, these interviewee narratives did not generate the depth of details derived from the more emotional interviews, usually delivered by the women interviewees. One consequence, however, was that the matter-of-fact interviewee responses fit rather neatly into my event-based questionnaire framework, while the richer and more emotional narratives were more difficult to "quantify."

GENDER AND POWER

Gender played a part throughout my field research, with three of the most consistent and perplexing gender-related issues identified below: "Downplaying; Pumping Up," "Sexualizing Interviewer," and "Leveling Power; Living with Asymmetry."

Downplaying; Pumping Up

I quickly discovered that gaining access to interviewees was gendered. When I first visited a prospective female interviewee's dwelling, I was typically welcomed without hesitation into her home. Inviting me to "take a seat," she typically offered me a drink or a snack. However, when I suggested an interview, about half the women demurred—giggling nervously and averting their eyes as if they were embarrassed at the thought of an interview. These women often insisted that they really did not know anything that would be of value to me, and tried to explain away their past participation in the FMLN as inconsequential, saying: "I only lived in the guerrilla camps for a short while," or "I only worked as a cook," or "I don't know anything about politics." The other half of the female interviewees, by contrast, happily and readily agreed to be interviewed at my first request.

I found that the best way to convince a woman who was reluctant to take part in an interview was by offering to help make the day's supply of tortillas, a traditional female activity. The presence of a foreigner trying to form cornmeal into round circles and cook them on an open fire without burning her fingers often seemed very comical to the women, leading to much laughter at my expense. The women would come to my assistance with advice and helpful hands, guiding my clumsy efforts. The lesson in tortilla making illustrated that I was out of *my element* and *in theirs*—in effect, at the mercy of the local experts who could teach me aspects of their lives. This collaborative act had brought me—a foreigner—into *their world*, and in the process leveled the power differentials between us in their favor. This leveling of power ultimately helped me to gain a woman's trust. When I returned to interview these woman at a later date, always couching my request for an interview with, "You have a great deal to teach me about what it means to be a woman in El Salvador," I was in all but one case granted an interview.

Conversely, however, the village men seldom needed encouragement to grant me an interview. I would ask for an interview and, in nearly every instance, I would have immediate acceptance. I had to ask myself if this was due to the prestige men gained by being interviewed by a young foreign woman, or due to the kudos derived from telling "manly" wartime exploits? To explore the possibility that information was made-up or amplified, I frequently cross-checked an interviewee's claim to have been an FMLN guerrilla with other community members. For example, before I even began the interviews, I asked the family with which I was staying, and/or the family of my initial contact, to list for me those in the community who had been guerrillas. I asked town council members similar questions. This allowed me to check an interviewee's self-reported participation[18] in the civil war with other community members' information about an interviewee's participation. Obviously, the small size of the communities, plus the fact that everyone knew I valued talking to both participants and nonparticipants, made this informal check possible. In my many attempts to check narratives against the store of community knowledge, I only once found a man who might have overstated his FMLN involvement.

In the case of the thirty-six male interviewees, and related to the impact of gender on interview process and outcomes, I quickly took control of the interview process by suggesting we sit outside the house for the interview. I wanted to portray myself as a social science professional, so I worked to ensure that we were in plain sight of the community. On several occasions, the children of a household where I was living would follow me to an interview. As a social scientist, I knew that I should interview individuals in private to secure the confidentiality of the interview, but when children followed me to interview a man, I made an exception. Playing nearby as

I interviewed a man, I felt the children's presence lent me research legitimacy, a valuable counter to the alternative designation of me as a "spouse-stealer." I found myself highly conscientious about my body language during these interviews. I sat up straight and maintained physical distance, rather than leaning forward, as I did with the women. I avoided all physical contact with the men, while with the women I often found myself patting a shoulder or squeezing a hand when they shared their painful memories. Likewise, I used my "official," educated voice with men, and my "conversational," more colloquial voice with women.

Even given the care that I took to maintain a highly professional dialogue with male interviewees, there were still some awkward personal situations: I received two additional marriage proposals, each explicitly mentioning the value of marriage for securing "a green card." One man who propositioned marriage also wanted to know more about "sexually free" U.S. women, asking me if it were true that U.S. men trade wives for a night, "just for fun?" I said very clearly and firmly, without any hint of a smile, that "I would be returning to the United States with interviews, no husbands," adding that a man in the United States might request a wife swap, but that I was quite certain that he would quickly find himself in divorce court and with no chances of ever finding a wife again. I then immediately asked the next interview question and moved forward as if the interruption had not happened.[19]

Sexualizing Interviewer

An especially important aspect of the field research surrounded the intersection of gender and power. Before even beginning my interviews, I felt that I would be judged by women and men alike in terms of the ubiquitous stereotype that U.S. women are sexually promiscuous. I further suspected that speaking with a *chelita*—a young white female—would give the male interviewees some prestige among other men in the community. I knew of some of the sources of such perceptions: Men's places of employment—feed stores, car repair shops—were replete with scantily-clad Western women on calendars and posters. "Girlie pinups" were pasted on the inside walls of buses or hung from taxi mirrors. Televisions, even in the most isolated rural communities, featured Saturday night Hollywood films with blonde heroines taking off their clothes. In contrast, the weeknight *novelas* portrayed pious *Latina* heroines guarding their virginity until marriage.

Given that earning the women's trust was most important for my research, I decided I would have to behave in a manner that did not promote a promiscuous image, even if it meant distancing myself from the male interviewees. In general, I worked to develop warm relationships with women and kept my distance from men in the villages except when interviewing them. At community gatherings, I would stand with the women and away from the men. When I attended a community dance, I only danced with young children. I always wore conservative slacks and shirts in the villages. On those occasions where I would need to bathe in a relatively public place (a fairly common occurrence in El Salvador, where water supplies are publicly shared), I would bathe while wearing a T-shirt and shorts (washing my clothes as well as my body). I changed to dry clothes when I was in a private place.

Leveling Power; Living Asymmetry

In general, *my taking steps* to enter the private household spaces of women's work leveled my power vis-à-vis village women. As I have said, this was crucial for gaining many women's permission to conduct an interview. In contrast, however, while power differentials were also leveled in the case of village men, it could be argued that the *men initially* took the lead in elevating their power vis-à-vis mine: By defining me as a *chelita*, a young white female, I felt they designated me an object of the men, thus enforcing the men's power relative to my own. This had the potential to define my role relationship with male interviewees as social rather than professional. I countered this by exaggerating professionalism, as the previous discussion illustrates.

I also confronted challenges created by Salvadoran men's power over "their" women; this sometimes influenced my ability to secure an interview with a woman. In one case, a woman I had selected from my sampling list initially raised my curiosity when she did not invite me inside her house for a drink or treat me in the friendly manner to which I had grown accustomed. She then demonstrated her husband's power by addressing my request for an interview by first looking at her husband and then saying, "no." I did not push for an interview with this woman because I was concerned that I might endanger her, assuming that an interview would draw her husband's further disapproval. I asked my village contact whether she thought that it was worth a second attempt and was told that "it was better not to return," adding that the woman's partner could "get very angry." I heeded her advice and did not return to that household.

My gender, and locals' assumptions about it, had to be negotiated throughout field research. By back-staging any aspect of my sexuality that might have been construed as mirroring that of a *typical* "sexually promiscuous" Western woman, I gained the trust of village women and enjoyed some measure of protection from the designs of some poorly behaved village men. I negotiated the Salvadoran patriarchal system in a manner that gave traditional village women greater control over me through my insertion into their cooking and thus into traditional gender norms. Relying on "professionalism" reduced some of my "exoticness" to the village men and reduced their opportunities to sexualize me. The upshot was that by immersing myself in local gender norms, a system that traditionally favors the men, I was perhaps more likely to obtain from male villagers less exaggeration of their masculinity and greater narrative honesty in their recollections about wartime activities.

Economic Inequities

While economic inequalities cannot be totally separated from gender, as I learned, my assumed and real income privilege relative to those I was studying created some challenges of its own. In many respects, I was largely helpless to lessen the most obvious economic differentials between informants and myself: I was a (presumably) rich Westerner; they were poor *campesinos*. My decision to purchase a car, while greatly increasing the number of interviews I could complete during my time in the country and improving my sense of personal security on the road, was a powerful illustration of the economic disparities between us. Were people agreeing to participate in interviews because they expected something in return? Assuming that this might occur at least in some cases, I attempted to reduce some interpersonal economic differences by beginning each interview with the statement that I was a student and in El Salvador on a scholarship. Salvadorans were familiar with this term because many former combatants had received scholarships through the peace accords for educational training. I also made clear that there were no material rewards for participating in the study, only the "personal reward" of the satisfaction that comes from having your experiences documented so that others can learn from them.

Perhaps generating the impression that there were some rewards for participating in my study, I occasionally used my car for the benefit of the community, an act that I framed as "community participation" rather than direct "payment" for an interview. When a young woman broke her arm in a soccer game, her sister and mother found me and asked me to drive her to the hospital, which I did. I also once made several trips from the village to the church in a nearby town so that villagers could attend the funeral of a young boy who had died from electrocution while picking fruit in a tree tangled with electrical wires. I aimed to be generous with the community whenever I could, but I worked hard never to privilege one individual over another with a material gift, particularly by providing transportation in *direct exchange* for an interview.

Global Economic Power

Global economic power differences were salient in my day-to-day research activities. My status as a citizen of the United States highlighted glaring asymmetries—both perceived and real—between myself and the interviewees. The most immediate was that El Salvador's grassroots had experienced "foreigners bearing gifts." Shortly after the war had ended in 1992, hundreds of international aid workers had descended upon Salvadoran war zones with the objective of providing aid for El Salvador's postwar reconstruction. As part of the peace accords' war "demobilization" package, those who registered with the United Nations as (retiring) FMLN guerrillas were given either land for farming, education, or training. Former guerrillas often received a small plot of land for a home, as well as assistance in building a house. Through the course of my interviews, I learned that some had managed to access other "gifts" from the international community—tables, chairs, farming implements, and sewing machines. Those who had not fought with the FMLN, or who had fought and left before the peace accords were signed, often resented that they were not given the material goods that FMLN combatants had received. Clearly, an important message to the beneficiaries of such international support was that "foreigners like to assist men and women who had fought with the FMLN."[20] One outcome of this expectation was that I had to be alert to the possibility that FMLN interviewees could pledge allegiance to, or exaggerate their past collaboration with the FMLN, with the hope of receiving tangible economic benefits from a "first world" outsider.

In only two instances, both at the end of the interview phase of my field research, was I approached by women asking if I would keep them in mind if I heard of any opportunities for funding a "project" in their community. When I asked what these women, whom I had interviewed a year earlier, meant by a "project," they said funding for a "collaboration" (a joint project) between their village and outsiders for a project to raise chickens or "teach a skill." In another instance, three women, also previously interviewed, needed assistance filling out an application for a development project—"a milk cow for every woman in the community," and wanted me mail the application in the United States. Since the projects were slated to benefit communities rather than individuals, I agreed to both requests. I was in their village saying "good-bye," so these women's requests may have been an attempt to keep a "piece of me" with them through "collaboration."

A QUALITATIVE METHODOLOGIST'S "TOOLBOX"

I propose six tools for analyzing retrospective oral data, as these tools emerged from my research on social movement activists in El Salvador.

Tool 1: Retrospective research—An archaeology of memory. Incorporate the existing research on memory into your research design.

Tool 2: Bracket interview questions with history. Use knowledge of local history and events to present an interviewee with a concrete past, as a means of "bracketing" the more distant event and feelings in a question.

Tool 3: Triangulation. Using more than one research technique, in order to increase the confidence in one's emerging data, is the essence of triangulation. This can be difficult to employ on grassroots movements and actors, where a lack of formal and even informal documentation exists. However, I practiced triangulation by comparing interview testimonies with statements of past behaviors, comparing past *with* present actions, interviewing actors associated with the interviewee, conducting community surveys, and employing my own knowledge of history to "check" interviewee statements.

Tool 4: Recognize power. It is not always possible to eliminate power differentials between researcher and researched, although these can be lessened, albeit often within the boundaries of an existing system of patriarchy. Power is dynamic and negotiable; it is most effective and honest to openly acknowledge power differentials. Researchers must be alert to power within the research dynamic if they are to effectively negotiate it within a research setting.

Tool 5: Collective and Personalized Memories. Social movement researchers need to separate "collective scripts" provided by social movement activists from such activists' "personalized" narratives. For example, in my research, in contrast to the women's more stock collective narratives about their wartime lives in guerrilla camps, were their highly personal stories. These personal stories each had their own flavor, protagonists, and rhythms. While both the "collective scripts" and "personalized narratives" are valuable to the study of social movement activism, the activists, and a movement's "knowledge production," social movement researchers will very likely find the "personalized narratives" perplexing: Scripted collective narratives are easy to categorize and code, while personalized narratives often seem to defy codification and yet are essential to understanding the experiences of the grassroots.

Tool 6: Writing and rewriting. Research does not end with data organizing, coding, and the search for analytical patterning, for the processes of knowledge production continues as results are written. In writing and revising and subjecting one's ideas to collegial review—through presentations, seminar papers, and submissions to refereed journals—new ideas emerge, some original ones may fade away, and existing ones will become more precise.

NOTES

1. FMLN is an acronym for the "Frente Farabundo Martí para la Liberación Nacionale." For more information see Armstrong and Shenk 1982; Dunkerly 1982; Montgomery 1995.

2. This definition is based loosely on Mao Tse-tung's (1937) *On Guerrilla Warfare*, a text that also informed the actions of the FMLN command.

3. Six months is a figure developed from the time distribution in my data. I found that a few individuals went to the guerrilla camps for only a week or two and then exited, and so I did not want to count them as guerrillas. Most common, however, was that once an individual had stayed for a few months, he or she tended to stay for many years. The more permanent individuals who left the camps after the shortest period of time (approximately nine months) tended to be those who joined close to the end of the war and were forced to exit when the peace accords were signed.

4. As I found in my research, one reason that little is written about the grassroots FMLN participants is that they were often illiterate or only slightly literate. Those few who knew how to write were not likely to keep records: paper and pencils were not readily accessible and free time at a premium when living in a civil war. A few diaries from a few literate guerrillas had made their way into museums, but since my research questions required answers as representative as possible, I wanted a larger group of grassroots interviewees than those leaving diaries.

5. This percentage is documented by UN statistics on postwar demobilization processes (Luciak 2001).

6. Isolation made these areas useful for hiding guerrilla fighters, with much of the military violence thus taking place in these areas.

7. The five organizations that came together in 1980 to form the FMLN still maintained a great deal of autonomy in their actions, finances, and ideologies during and after the war. They varied in their historical development, their orientations toward warfare, and (to a lesser extent) their organizational structures and their political ideologies. Most of these factions were geographically distinct as well, with certain areas of the country being associated with certain factions.

8. Using the funds from selling my car in the United States, I spent several weeks in El Salvador finding and purchasing a used car. Again, my previous connections helped—a Dutch aid worker returning to the Netherlands after several years in El Salvador wanted to sell her vehicle, a 1989 Suzuki Samurai. (Negotiating the Salvadoran paperwork for registering the vehicle and having the police accuse me of driving a stolen vehicle and impounding my car are associated stories that are at times deeply funny, and at times deeply frustrating, and far too long to elaborate in this chapter). Learning to drive stick shift in the tangled traffic of El Salvador was also a challenge.

9. It is worth noting that I broke this agreement with myself in my fifth community. There, an exceedingly bright and well-read young man in high school was one of a group who helped me with my surveys (described in the text). I had come to know this young man better through my relationship with his mother and older sister. When I was running low on time, I asked his help in conducting the last three interviews with men in the community. He proved himself an excellent interviewer. However, I did remain firm in insisting that all my initial contacts were with women.

10. I do not suggest that breadth of numbers, or representation, is always more important than the depth gained in fewer and longer interactions with informants. I simply argue that for this particular research question, a representative group of informants was necessary. To illustrate, in past research, scholars studying women guerrillas talked only to women guerrillas. Because most of the women they interviewed had family members in the guerrilla movement before they joined, they reasoned that these family connections were critical for encouraging most women

to join the guerrillas. In my research, I found that women who did *not* join the guerrillas *also* had family members active in the guerrillas. Because this characteristic is shared by both guerrillas and nonguerrillas, it therefore cannot by itself be used to explain why some women joined the guerrillas and others did not.

11. In the four smallest communities, we surveyed each household (usually about one hundred). In the two largest communities, we selected a subset of households using a community census.

12. Initially, I had hoped to conduct interviews in three more villages from a fourth *municipio*, but given time and funding constraints toward the end of my fellowship year, I decided not to pursue interviews in the last *municipio*. Instead, I decided to return to each of the communities I had already investigated and do additional interviews, this time just with community leaders and their daughters. I felt these additional interviews would provide necessary comparisons that would help me understand why some women continued their activism after the war, and others retreated from public life. This additional group of twenty women leaders and ten daughters brought my total number of interviews to 150.

13. I reworked the questions about power and sexual relations throughout the research, soliciting advice from feminists in women's organizations who worked with rural Salvadoran women. With their help, I learned to ask questions like, "If a man was interested in a woman, but the woman was not sure if she was interested in him or not, what might the man do to get her to have relations with him?" I would also give some specific examples, such as, "Would he say things like, we may die tomorrow, so let's enjoy tonight together?" Questions, based on concrete actions, words, and examples gave a better picture of what happened in the camps (see Viterna 2003).

14. U.S. civil rights activists in the 1960s often recounted "sit-in" protests as "spontaneous" eruptions of disobedience (Polletta 1998). In reality, these protests were well-planned and highly coordinated events, but framing them as "spontaneous reactions" helped to further the movement by helping to present their cause as so "naturally right and universal" that actors "erupted" spontaneously against it.

15. Such questions included: number of brothers and sisters, how her family earned its living, where did she go to school, how many grades did she complete, who lived in her household.

16. Did she go directly from her family home to a Honduran refugee camp and then not return to El Salvador until the war had ended? Or did she report living in "the mountain" for six years in the middle of the 1980—a sign that she was likely living in a guerrilla camp?

17. I suspect the primary reason men expressed little emotion in recounting violence was because of masculine expectations that men be strong and unemotional. Assuming that this might be the case, I was more likely to probe men about the outlines of a violent episode than I was a woman. In the case of women, I feared that such probing would be perceived as rude or inconsiderate.

18. When an opportunity presented itself for informal conversations with other members of an interviewee's family, I would often solicit information about the war experiences of the interviewee.

19. These inappropriate occurrences with men were uncommon. Of the thirty-six men interviewed, only two made inappropriate comments. Most men treated me with professional respect. However, the uncomfortable experiences, in addition to

my daily experiences with sexism—catcalls on the street, girlie pinups in taxis—created a hypersensitivity about regulating my relationships with men.

20. Although the U.S. government funded the Salvadoran army in its fight against the FMLN, many international citizen groups gave various kinds of support to the FMLN, who were seen as the champions of the poor and the defenders of the civilian population against the abuses of its own and the U.S. government. The FMLN worked hard to garner international aid throughout the war and these connections continued to pay off in the war's aftermath.

REFERENCES

Álvarez, Antonio, and Joaquín Mauricio Chávez. (2001). *Tierra, conflicto y paz*. San Salvador: Asociación Centro de Paz CEPAZ.

Armstrong, Robert, and Janet Shenk. (1982). *El Salvador: The Face of Revolution*. Boston: South End Press.

Auyero, Javier. (1999). "Re-membering Peronism: An Ethnographic Account of the Relational Character of Political Memory." *Qualitative Sociology* 22, 331–51.

Bermeo, Nancy Gina. (1986). *The Revolution within the Revolution: Workers' Control in Rural Portugal*. Princeton, NJ: Princeton University Press.

Bradley, Margaret M. (1994). "Emotional Memory: A Dimensional Analysis." In *Emotions: Essays on Emotion Theory*, edited by Stephanie H. M. van Goozen, Nanne E. Van de Poll, and Joseph A. Sergeant, 97–134. Hillsdale, NJ: Lawrence Erlbaum Associates.

Danner, Mark. (1994). *The Massacre at El Mozote*. New York: Vintage.

Dunkerley, James. (1982). *The Long War: Dictatorship and Revolution in El Salvador*. London: Verso.

Goodwin, Jeff. (2001). *No Other Way Out: States and Revolutionary Movements, 1945–1991*. Cambridge: Cambridge University Press.

Halbwachs, Maurice. (1992). *On Collective Memory*. Translated and edited by L. A. Coser. Chicago: University of Chicago Press.

Huggins, Martha, Mika Hairtos-Fatouros, and Philip Zimbardo. (2002). *Violence Workers: Police Torturers and Murderers Reconstruct Brazilian Atrocities*. Berkeley and Los Angeles: University of California Press.

Jelin, Elizabeth. (2003). *State Repression and the Labors of Memory*. Minneapolis: University of Minnesota Press.

Kampwirth, Karen. (2004). *Feminism and the Legacy of Revolution: Nicaragua, El Salvador, Chiapas*. Athens: Ohio University Press.

Kriger, Norma. (1992). *Zimbabwe's Guerrilla War: Peasant Voices*. Cambridge: Cambridge University Press.

LaFeber, Walter. (1993). *Inevitable Revolutions: The United States in Central America*, 2nd ed. New York: W. W. Norton.

Luciak, Ilja A. (2001). *After the Revolution: Gender and Democracy in El Salvador, Nicaragua, and Guatemala*. Baltimore: Johns Hopkins University Press.

Markus, Gregory B. (1986). "Stability and Change in Political Attitudes: Observed, Recalled, and 'Explained.'" *Political Behavior* 8, 21–44.

McAdam, Doug, and Ronnelle Paulsen. (1993). "Specifying the Relationship between Social Ties and Activism." *American Journal of Sociology* 99, no. 3, 640–67.

McClintock, Cynthia. (1998). *Revolutionary Movements in Latin America: El Salvador's FMLN and Peru's Shining Path*. Washington, DC: United States Institute of Peace Press.

Montgomery, Tommie Sue. (1995). *Revolution in El Salvador: From Civil Strife to Civil Conflict*, 2nd ed. Boulder, CO: Westview Press.

Moser, Caroline, and Fiona Clark, eds. (2001). *Victims, Perpetrators, or Actors? Gender, Armed Conflict and Political Violence*. New York: Palgrave.

Morris, Aldon D., and Suzanne Staggenborg. (2004). "Leadership in Social Movements." In *The Blackwell Companion to Social Movements*, edited by David A. Snow, Sarah A. Soule, and Hanspeter Kriesi, 171–96. Malden, MA: Blackwell.

Olick, Jeffrey K., and Joyce Robbins. (1998). "Social Memory Studies: From 'Collective Memory' to the Historical Sociology of Mnemonic Practices." *Annual Review of Sociology* 24, 105–40.

Polletta, Francesa. (1998). "'It Was Like a Fever . . . ' Narrative and Identity in Social Protest." *Social Problems* 45, no. 2, 137–59.

Schacter, Daniel L. (1996). *Searching for Memory: The Brain, the Mind and the Past*. New York: Basic Books.

Schwartz, Barry. (1997). "Collective Memory and History: How Abraham Lincoln became a Symbol of Racial Equality." *Sociological Quarterly* 38, 469–96.

Tse-tung, Mao. (1937 [1978]). *On Guerrilla Warfare*. Translated by Samuel B. Griffith II. Garden City, NY: Anchor Press.

Vázquez, Norma, Cristina Ibáñez, and Clara Murguialday. (1996). *Mujeres-montaña: vivencias de guerrilleras y colaboradoras del FMLN*. Madrid: Horas y Horas.

Viterna, Jocelyn S. (2003). *When Women Wage War: Explaining the Personal and Political Consequences of Women's Guerrilla Participation in El Salvador*. PhD diss., Department of Sociology, Indiana University, Bloomington.

Viterna, Jocelyn S. (2006). "Pulled, Pushed and Persuaded: Explaining Women's Mobilization into the Salvadoran Guerrilla Army." *American Journal of Sociology* 112, no. 1, 1–45.

Wagenaar, Willem A., and Jop Groeneweg. (1990). "The Memory of Concentration Camp Survivors." *Applied Cognitive Psychology* 4, no. 2, 77–87.

Wechsler Segal, Mady. (1995). "Women's Military Roles Cross-Nationally: Past, Present and Future." *Gender and Society* 9, 757–75.

Wickham-Crowley, Timothy. (1992). *Guerrillas and Revolution in Latin America: A Comparative Study of Insurgents and Regimes since 1956*. Princeton, NJ: Princeton University Press.

Wieviorka, Annette. (1999). "From Survivor to Witness: Voices from the Shoah." In *War and Remembrance in the Twentieth Century*, edited by Jay Winter and Emmanuel Sivan, 125–41. Cambridge: Cambridge University Press.

Witvliet, Charlotte van Oyen. (1997). "Traumatic Intrusive Imagery as an Emotional Memory Phenomenon: A Review of Research and Explanatory Information Processing Theories. *Clinical Psychology Review* 17, no. 5, 509–36.

Wood, Elisabeth Jean. (2003). *Insurgent Collective Action and Civil War in El Salvador*. Cambridge: Cambridge University Press.

Zerubavel, Eviatar. (1996). "Social Memories: Steps to a Sociology of the Past." *Qualitative Sociology* 19, 283–89.

IV

ETHICS AND SECRECY

12

Secrecy and Trust in the Affective Field: Conducting Fieldwork in Burma

Monique Skidmore

OPEN SECRETS

The 2005 tsunami that struck Southeast Asia took two hundred thousand lives, leaving in its wake an ocean of grief. Yet this natural disaster made relatively little impact upon the coastal communities along the Bay of Bengal. Burma (Myanmar), one of the areas largely spared the tsunami's violent wrath, is situated on the western side of Southeast Asia, with China and Thailand to the east, Bangladesh and India to the west, the Andaman Sea to the south, and the Bay of Bengal to the southwest. In Burma, with its rocky coastline, a much smaller number of people lost their lives as compared to such neighboring countries as Thailand. The Burmese people, masters of black humor, tell a story of why the country suffered so much less devastation than others:

> When the first waves were about to hit the shores of the Irrawaddy Delta, three giant fish[1] suddenly rose from the waters. The three fish—Nga Shwe, Nga Htwe and Nga Mann—stopped the waves and ordered them to turn back. The tidal waves were surprised by the abrupt appearance of the three huge fish but insisted on striking the shore anyway. Again, the fish commanded the waves to turn back immediately. The tidal waves asked why. One fish answered: "This is enough. We have already destroyed the country." Sympathizing with the people of Burma, the colossal waves receded and Burma was saved the tsunami's full fury. (Irrawaddy, 1/31/2005)[2]

The *Irrawaddy*, an online magazine, explains:

> This [kind of] political satire is wildly popular among Burmese in Rangoon these days. The three fish . . . [represent] the country's top leaders, Senior

301

General Than Shwe, Deputy Senior General Maung Aye, and General Thura Shwe Mann. The destruction the fish refer to, of course, is the destruction that the [Burmese] military junta has inflicted on the nation.

Burma has the world's longest surviving military dictatorship of modern times, having begun in 1962, when General Ne Win usurped power from Burma's postcolonial fledgling democracy. The forty-plus-year destruction of Burma by subsequent military regimes is one of the Burmese people's longest and most poorly kept "open secrets." This "open secret" includes anger about the military government policies that have deepened poverty, suppressed virtually all civic freedoms and public forms of resistance, and enriched the pockets of the powerful.

Government propaganda, the "official story," seeks to drown the populace in fanciful and implausible explanations for their poverty and the lack of civic freedoms. Denial, a matter of course for the Burmese state, results in the military regime disowning the existence of, and its responsibility for, everything: AIDS, prostitution, earthquakes, fires, floods, epidemics, heroin production, corruption, and money laundering. Even bad weather is given an official spin: "Today is fine and sunny," an account that serves the state very well when rain falls on important days in the military calendar. The Burmese people believe that rain can be a bad omen on such days.

The Burmese recognize as an "open secret" that such official political discourse bears no relationship to their political desires, motivations, actions, and indeed to any "reality" as they know it. However, the political and social costs of challenging official stories are too great for the vast majority of Burmese to attempt. This does not change the fact that in Burma, truth is a commodity that does not need to be openly voiced to be known and to exist—it is the essence of the open secret and it is conveyed through, rather than in spite of, a pervasive public silence.

In the minds of the regime's leaders, too much silence is threatening: continual affirmation of the regime's legitimacy and its nation-building programs is required through participation in pro-government mass rallies, antidemocracy forums, and by enforced membership in such parastatal organizations as the Union Solidarity and Development Association (USDA). On the other hand, silence is absolutely necessary when the government is spinning its propaganda: At mass rallies people must sit in silence for several hours while listening to speeches against the pro-democratic opposition, the National League for Democracy, and such rights groups as Amnesty International and the International Labor Organization.

However, for the Burmese people, silence does not equal consent. The truth is spread through clandestine videotapes, gossip, and rumor. Videotapes of the 2005 tsunami's destruction of Burmese coastal communities circulate through private homes in the cities and video huts in the villages, demonstrating a truth that is hidden from them by the military. The price of being caught with, or for viewing, a video is sizable: Those who watch and distribute tsunami videos are jailed.[3] Behind the video representations and people's grieving is the hope that natural disaster is an omen that presages political change. To counter the potential impact of the video pictures of the tsunami disaster, the Burmese military offers superficial banter about the disaster, initially making statements denying the need for aid and downplaying the damage (Irrawaddy 2005). The tsunami became subsumed in official media in Burma, mentioned as part of "World Meteorological Day celebrations" and an excuse to tour hospitals and for the generals to be seen giving "necessary aid and assistance" (Myanmar Information Committee 2005). Truth and trust are never even considered in the "official stories" penned by the Burmese Information Ministry and the Department of Psychological Warfare.

Burma's most important "open secret" is the desire of the vast majority of the population for an end to military rule and for the ushering into their country of democracy, peace, and respect for human rights. These secrets are almost impossible to keep from bubbling over, particularly when joy, anger, or fatigue lead Burmese people toward a liberating recklessness. This occurred among the Burmese in 1996 attending the pro-democracy leader (and 1991 Nobel Peace Prize winner) Aung San Suu Kyi's roadside speeches. They were unable to mask their joy at her unflinching rejection of nondemocratic rule. Military intelligence agents were on hand to photograph the tears that ran down the faces of Aung San Suu Kyi's loosely assembled streetside audiences. On one particular day, I saw four monks being beaten with umbrellas (it was the monsoon season) as they attempted to make their way along University Avenue to Aung San Suu Kyi's home. People walked, took a taxi (with license plates removed) or a bus to the pro-democracy leader's house, ensuring that the regime's agents could not follow them back to their dwellings. All participants in this particular drama were well aware of the risks they were running by making public their support for the pro-democracy movement and its leader.

Thus, in spite of the Burmese military banning all forms of public association involving more than four persons, and forbidding the freedoms of expression and speech, there is still public activism in Burmese cities, towns, and sometimes even villages. Ironically, it is precisely during such moments when the people's secrets must be kept at all costs, that their anger and fatigue at military rule often spills over into open protest. Even though so much depends on their silence—personal and family safety, a livelihood, and perhaps even sanity—some Burmese feel strongly that it is their duty to resist the regime, despite the consequences if they are caught. In such circumstances, protestors can be charged with high treason and even sentenced to death.

Just the same, the Burmese people's "open secrets" are passed carefully, through word of mouth—in tea shops, on the streets, and in village tea circles. Their "treacherous" secrets sometimes take the form of rumors—such as a widely held belief that the military regime engages in occult practices while pretending to be practicing Buddhism (Keiko Tosa 2005, 154–73); sometimes of wordplay—the military council's name in Burmese is given a one-letter change so that it reads "Cow's Committee"; sometimes as humor—as we saw in the story about the three giant fish saving Burma's coastline from the 2005 tsunami; and sometimes as cartoons—in a few leisure and sports magazines, cartoons obliquely and cautiously point to the absurdity of the military regime and its corrupt inefficiency (Skidmore 2004, 120–46). As an anthropologist it is thus possible to track some of these "open secrets" about military rule; they help to create what I have labelled an "affective field site" (Skidmore 2003), with special challenges for research practice and ethics.

WORKING IN THE AFFECTIVE FIELD

Wherever and whenever terror, political violence, and propaganda are at work and fear is thus pervasive, the field site becomes primarily an "affective" one. In an affective field site, danger and fear are experienced differentially according to the gender, ethnicity, nationality, and social position. Looking back at how I, as a field researcher, experience and negotiate the perceived and real dangers of my affective field sites in urban and village Burma, my gender has constrained my ability to conduct fieldwork in certain Burmese locations. On both an emotional and professional level, I decided very early in my research career that the systematic rape of minority women, girl children, and infants in Burma's eastern war zones made these areas too risky for me, since this deliberate war strategy has been reserved largely for women.[4]

As a white-skinned woman in Burma, I stick out like a sore thumb, especially in areas off-limits to foreigners. While such a fact at times increases my fear of the field, at the same time, being short, plump, and female is an advantage for me as a foreign researcher in Burma. My build makes it less likely that, to Burmese, I appear menacing or particularly shifty. Indeed, Burmese people say that I look like the "idyllic version" of a respectable, middle-class married Burmese woman. Coupled with my Burmese language skills and knowledge of Burmese habits and customs, I have repeatedly gained permission from the Burmese regime to conduct in-country fieldwork. I have, however, never been so naive as to assume that this tacit permission translates into feelings of safety—either for my personal safety or that of my informants and their families.

Indeed, such outward physical symbols of "acceptability" would be very quickly nullified if I were seen by Burma's military regime as acting against it. This danger has been frequently driven home to me by the arrest, beating, and torture of foreign journalists and Western human rights activists over the decade that I've worked in Burma (Mawdsley 2002).[5] Even members of the foreign national and diplomatic communities in Burma have been arrested and tortured, and have died in prison (Aye 1998). Most troubling from the perspective of being able to predict who is safe and who is not, the arrest in late 2004 of the head of Burma's military intelligence organization, Prime Minister Khin Nyunt, is proof positive that no one is safe, despite military rank, wealth, political lineage or heritage, or any other markers of state loyalty or service. By demonstrating that no one is safe, this arrest amplified and hardened Burma's climate of fear. This, of course, made securing and conducting interviews with Burmese very difficult, a frequent by-product of working in an affective field site, where secrecy and caution are the people's best weapons against authoritarian repression.

In the affective field site, where normal geographic familiarity is overlaid by a topography of *emotionally experienced* locations, the familiar routines and assumptions about personal safety are revealed to be comforting fictions that can no longer provide a psychological refuge. By this I mean that we all have ways of dividing up our local environment according to beliefs about personal safety. Women, for example, in Western societies rarely wander alone late at night. Similarly, in urban Burma there is this kind of geographic division of space for each individual or group, but it is overlaid by a continually shifting map of emotionally dangerous places. Buildings that house the apparatus of the state and its military hardware (and spyware) are tacitly avoided by pedestrians. When arriving at and leaving the psychiatric hospital, one of my field sites, it was necessary to pass a major military installation on Pyay Road. At times of unrest, several tanks would line its entranceway. Near these kinds of places, civilian traffic is sparse and hurried, and I was almost completely unaware of the many such sites that I avoided. Like other residents of Rangoon, I scurried away down alternate alleyways and thoroughfares, avoiding the gaze of the military eye. At other times, these sites seem innocuous, part of the familiar landscape. Most of the time, the state is unaware of the different emotions it is engendering. There is no doubt, however, that fear is the dominant emotional ethos mandated by the state, because it is widespread fear that stops Burmese people from rising up against the military regime. It is very important, therefore, for Burmese people to present a public persona that shows a "credible harmony" between one's emotional life and appropriate submission to government policies.[6] Any other reactions are met with a malicious suspicion.

This is the emotional climate that I unknowingly entered in 1996 when I began my fieldwork in Rangoon. As a graduate student committed to social justice I was opposed to any regime that was not democratically elected and that committed human rights violations. Conducting interviews with Burmese over the years had only hardened these political attitudes. The sheer volume and ubiquity of everyday misery, inadequate food, and suffering due to a lack of basic health care are elements of Burmese life that compete with ongoing repression to make me determined to continue writing about Burma and conducting fieldwork in-country. From the outset of my field research I resolved to be completely honest with potential interviewees about my own critical political position regarding Burma's military government. In almost all cases, they and I agree politically. Sometimes, however, I discover an interviewee who positively supports the Burmese government. In my latest research, for example, I am interviewing former military officers who tortured pro-democracy activists and students. Again, I am honest about the research project and my difficulty in understanding how the informant can hold such pro-regime views. We engage in discussions so that the informant can help me to comprehend the context and motivations behind his or her actions.

I learned during the December 1996 and January 1997 pro-democracy "hit-and-run" student demonstrations in Rangoon that the city residents seemed to feel great personal pressure to tell their "open secrets" about military rule, despite the politically dangerous climate. Yet I also saw that their secrets did not flow easily: in interview conversations, these interlocutors let out huge shuddering sobs and choking sounds; low moans often escaped from their mouths. Such was the degree of internalized and embodied resistance uttering their secrets out loud, a situation certainly fueled by the dangers known to be associated with "betraying" the military. Perhaps, as a result of such a looming threat, the Rangoon interviewees would tell me their "open secrets" only on their own terms, in a manner that would help them keep control over their coveted information. Interviews had to be conducted in a location, and at a time, that they considered safe. They carefully edited their interview disclosures. They exercised their "right" after an interview to request that I "revise" or destroy my notes.

In one example of an interviewee's control over her information, a female interlocutor told me during an extended interview that she knew Aung San Suu Kyi's phone number, and she proceeded to recite the number. The next day, the interviewee admitted to me that this revelation has resulted in her "being unable to sleep," a problem that she said would not change until I had torn up the field note I had written containing Aung San Suu Kyi's phone number (Skidmore 2004, 40). She watched as I destroyed the notes I had made. After I had interviewed the woman two more times, she came to me asking that I rewrite the notes that I had taken during my interviews with her. Then, as if this had not been sufficient, the woman returned yet another time to beseech me to tear up my (now rewritten) field notes. Eventually she allowed me to write field notes of this whole process, including her knowledge of Aung San Suu Kyi's phone number, and to take the field notes out of the country. This woman's desire for the world to know the depth of the Burmese people's fear under dictatorship was strong, but so too were her years of conditioning about the need for silence and secrecy in social life.

Most of my interview strategies, and the researcher positionalities that accompanied them, grew out of my being in an affective field site. This required constant attention to how I would negotiate danger and fear, the research process, and fieldwork ethics. Where fear is pervasive, as I have said, conversations and questions *about fear* tend to heighten the emotion of fieldworker and informant alike (Skidmore 2003). What further complicates fieldwork within such a setting is the secrecy that surrounds and permeates every research moment, as my research in a Burmese village will illustrate shortly.

SECRECY

After fear, and directly related to it, another defining characteristic of an affective field site is the interaction between secrecy and silence. Secrecy, a subject of some sociological and anthropological inquiry, has been explained by anthropologist Beryl Bellman (1984), in his introduction to *The Language of Secrecy*, through the sociology of Georg Simmel (1950). Simmel saw "secrecy" as a "sociological form," less understood as an individual's concealment of certain information than as a *relationship* involving the reciprocal control and management of information. Bellman argues that secrecy relies for its power upon the *potential consequences* of disclosure: revealing the content of a secret "provides grounds for a different interpretation of the social reality" (3–5). According to such thinking, secrecy can be seen as "a strategy for behavioral adaptation [that involves] the coping mechanisms that humans display in obtaining their wants or adjusting their lives or purposes" (Tefft 1980, 321).

Sociologist of secrecy E. A. Shils (1956) views secrecy as a category of action involving the management of social life. Secrecy involves voluntarily withholding information from certain individuals or groups, and he gives the example of national security policy where various "national interests" determine who is given access to information (intelligence). Shils argues that secrecy is an impossible condition: it cannot be maintained in the face of real and imminent threats, and certainly the efficacy of torture rests on this belief. If secrecy is, as Shils argues, such a ubiquitous social category, but ultimately an implausible or ineffective one, why is it so important in authoritarian societies?

Although most academic researchers have focused their explorations of secrecy on the strong narrative cues that *initially establish* secrecy among group members, and upon the criteria that define who may enter the secret group, my fieldwork ended up working with and discovering secrecy as an ongoing dynamic: a *micro-level* interpersonal *relationship* structured *in part by macro-structural* realities;[7] *a process* that involves *research and ethical challenges* for both researcher and researched; a set of *outcomes* for those who hold and for those who want secrets.

As a micro process it involves the managing of information between intimates. Until a field researcher is considered to be an intimate "insider," this level of knowledge is withheld from him or her. The ethnographic record is littered with accounts of informants lying, obfuscating, and deliberately omitting material critical to an understanding of the subject of the field research. Perhaps the easiest group of informants I have worked with in Burma are the young women working in the sex industry. A brothel can hardly be disguised as a different kind of workplace—it is immediately obvious the kind of employment in which the young women are engaged. There is an immediate level of intimacy involved in knowing the illegality of the work and the social stigma attached to such work. Some of these women remained impervious to my questions, in the sense that they remained emotionally detached from the content of their narratives. With perhaps half of my informants, events in their life histories invited an emotional attachment with me, and the women and girls willingly allowed me to enter their affective landscape.

In one woman's case, her husband had recently died, leaving her to support four children, the eldest being eight years old. She was willing to tell me about the taunts and cruelty of her neighbors, who routinely threw rocks upon the thatched roof of her house and screamed abuse at her in front of her children. It was a horrible story, and her eyes beseeched me to identify with her as a victim. When she realized that I could see her emotional pain, she went on to tell me that the local security officer had issued stern warnings to her neighbors. He told them that she was engaged in a very noble act—supporting four children from starvation, and that it took great courage on her part to do what she did for her love of her children. This shared emotional story not only allowed me to see the "not-so-black-and-white" nature of the individuals who enforce power at a daily level in Burma, but it also created access for me to other honest accounts of the sex workers' daily lives. The woman providing for her four children was treated with respect by the other women in the brothel, and by telling me her story she made it possible for other women to divulge their secrets to me as well.

Within Burmese society today, peoples' secrets—and the relationships developed to protect secrets and secret holders—are clearly structured by Burma's authoritarian politics. Burmese peoples' "open secrets" about government rule, particularly its negative effects on them and on their country, cannot be openly voiced without severe consequences. If a powerful group's secrets are exposed as false, then the reality that their secrets help to fortify can change. Revelation of secrets can lead to a "new definition of the situation," to a new alignment of power, and a shift in the locus and content of "truth." Given the macropolitical realities behind secrecy in Burma, secrecy about almost everything is mandatory.

Even knowledge of the democracy leader Aung San Suu Kyi's phone number is a mandatory secret. My friend's knowledge of the secret was difficult for her to bear, and the process by which she repeatedly divulged and then tried to take back her secret from me is a good example of the ongoing *process* of secrecy. Initially my friend saw the information as highly dangerous. In an evolving *relationship* with the information itself, my friend came, over time, to view the information as less potentially dangerous. The laws governing this kind of information remained the same, but her involvement with me, a foreigner, and many conversations about the political reality of Burma and new insights into the way the rest of the world viewed Burma, all contributed to her changing relationship with the subversive piece of information. My friend needed to go through this process herself—ethically, all I could do was acquiesce to her requests to destroy my field notes of our conversations, and then rewrite them as she changed her mind. Over the past decade, however, she has helped me collect data, persuaded her friends and acquaintances to talk openly with me, and become a regular listener to the BBC's outlawed Burmese-language news on shortwave radio. Revealing her secret has led her to define her situation differently, and new modes of action have become possible.

MANAGING DANGER AND SAFETY

In the affective field site, danger and the need for secrecy influence choice of a fieldwork location, choice of informants, and modes of data collection and storage. From my perspective as an interviewer, it is important to conduct fieldwork in spaces where I and my informants can be safe. While the risks for me as a foreigner are substantially lower than for Burmese people, and it is not possible to completely eliminate them, it is nonetheless crucial to minimize the risks of conducting research as much as feasible. I have learned that in practical terms this means staying away from military-controlled areas and trying to hold conversations out of the earshot of others. This includes the potential for informers eavesdropping in tea shops, and of surveillance of phone lines and bugging of hotel rooms or offices. In other affective field sites, anthropologists have, for example, conducted interviews and sheltered in the relative safety of their cars (Green 1999), and in a later section I show the ways I went about data collection in a rural village by hiding in the open.

In fact, danger is ubiquitous in Burma, making interview site selection critical. Burma's fixed topography of danger—bombed markets and shopping centers, interrogation centers, army barracks, military parade grounds and headquarters, as well as any location where Burma's democracy movement was violently crushed in the failed 1988 pro-democracy uprising—sets some of the parameters for interview site location. My challenge in selecting an interview site location did not end with avoiding such fixed and known locations of danger: field site affectivity also has a temporal quality. Danger is often dramatically created on certain formally designated days of these military council's celebration calendar—military "security" tightens during the run-up to major military parades on Independence Day, the date renamed by the military council as "Armed Forces Day." Military security can become tight on days known for past government repression—on the anniversary of Burma's brutally suppressed August 8, 1988, pro-democracy uprising. During such days, tanks, barricades, checkpoints, bayoneted soldiers, the dreaded riot police and their covered vans sequester areas previously considered safe. Such sudden, temporary alterations in the Burmese landscape can reshape the boundaries of "the field" and increase interviewees' perception of the dangers associated with areas once considered affectively neutral and thus "safe."

For my part, as a researcher I have come to recognize that what I once considered "safe" (i.e., "an acceptable level of risk") as field research in Burma can change over time and within place. At the beginning of my academic research career, there were some potentially dangerous risks that I was willing to take. As a childless doctoral student living in Rangoon, I reasoned that research activities that might land me in jail temporarily or lead to my deportation—for example, discussing politics with Burmese people—were "acceptable risks" for conducting research about the Burmese government's war against its own people.

As the years rolled on, and my personal life as well, what had once been an "acceptable" level of fieldwork risk became "unacceptable." I returned most years over the next decade to conduct more fieldwork and carried with me pictures of my wedding, then my first child, and eventually my second child. Now, a mother of two, I can no longer enter Burma without defining safety and danger in terms of my children. They need their mother, and I have a responsibility to conduct research in a manner that doesn't endanger me. Certainly, I recognize that one reason for studying health in a Burmese village may have been that, because Burmese women identify with my multiple roles of mother, professional, advocate for social justice, wife, and comanager of a busy household, I might have "respectability" and "approachability," which might provide some measure of safety in the process.

Just as my definition of an "acceptable" personal research risk changed substantially over my own life course, it also changes during the period that I am in the field. I often felt no fear of the state when first entering Burma. The field site did not become fully affective for me until I began to see its dangers in personal terms. My own transformation did not occur until I started to record and witness interlocutors' accounts of repression and of human rights violations and be accepted as having solidarity with all those in Burma who sought to resist military rule. It is not possible to remain outside of this affective domain when one is creating personal links with informants as part of the research process. In the words of one interlocutor, "I know this is a dictatorship and I know well what a dictatorship is. . . . Sometimes our phone gets tapped. They can just come and take you away. This is what dictatorship is, and I hope by now, Monique, you know it too."

Not only did political repression control the level of danger associated with an interview location, but I came to recognize that by creating a closed, presumably safe research space, I was very likely increasing the affectivity of a field site for both researcher and interviewee. In affective field sites conversations and interview questions in fact often heighten the emotions of both fieldworkers and informants (Skidmore 2003, 5–21). For example, when almost all of a researcher's questions can entail being viewed by the government and its supporters as "the enemy"—as conspiring with those who challenge the state by thought, word, or deed—the fieldworker and her interviewees, as well as their family and friends, can be placed in peril.

Since, in the affective field site, feelings of danger and vulnerability can be experienced by fieldworker and interviewee alike, it was common for me to feel many of the same emotions as my informants and it was simply not possible during, for example, the pro-democracy "hit-and-run" student demonstrations in late 1996 and early 1997 to set aside these feelings. In fact, no matter what I did to reduce danger to myself, I could still become just as paranoid and fearful as my interviewees. Particularly during times of political crisis, their feelings of fear impacted upon me and my field research, field insights that are seldom mentioned in field-work methodology manuals.

By the time I finished my doctoral fieldwork, I was using the same strategies that Burmese people use to deny, dampen down, and try to ignore fear. Rumors, propaganda, and visible signs of the regime's weapons of crowd control and repression became elements of my daily landscape that I needed to consciously work against in terms of mounting a resistance to paranoia, exaggeration, and fear. For their part, my Burmese interlocutors also seemed to see danger in different ways, with their vision of danger changing during our research relationship with one another. I was initially perceived as a great risk, but eventually I was seen by many of my

informants as much less of a risk as time has passed and no adverse consequences have occurred through their association with me.

Knowing that affective field sites can militate against getting interviewees
to disclose just about anything, as my fieldwork will continue to illustrate,
one might ask how a field researcher most effectively works in such a
setting. As I have already illustrated, by assuming the interacting roles of
"activist-by-proxy" and of "co-conspirator," I could negotiate information
with interlocutors on terms favorable to them and to myself. In the remainder of this chapter I elaborate more fully the relational intimacies between
co-conspirators in an affective field site, particularly as these related to
information gathering.

The backdrop for the analysis is a Burmese village where I sought to
create the relational intimacy necessary for interviewer and interviewee to
feel safe and develop trust in one another. In the case example, I consider
the broader implications of establishing these relationships, including
continuing to explore the methodology and the ethical responsibilities of
working in cultures of secrecy. I examine the forms of secrecy and trust that
are culturally available and accessible in authoritarian Burma and how my
knowledge of these cultural currencies enabled the eventual collection of
quality field data.

A VILLAGE'S SECRET

The river ferry—an optimistic Burmese term for an overcrowded, leaky,
narrow-hulled boat with a dodgy outboard motor—veers sluggishly
into a receding mud bank at the edge of a village in lower Burma. I am
accompanied by my civilian research assistant[8] and a member of the
Myanmar Traditional Medicine Department (an official chaperone). To
work outside Burma's large cities, I needed military government permission, which included the condition that one of its representatives would
travel with me. It had helped me secure the government's approval of my
project focusing upon indigenous medical knowledge and practices. This
has been consistently viewed by Burmese military and health officials as
laudatory; my presence in Burma has thus been considered by the military
an "acceptable" risk.

Military permission for my fieldwork far from protected me from military repression: There was always a risk of coming across someone willing
to inform against me. Yet at the same time, being a researcher from an
Australian university may have offered a modicum of protection: At odds
with other Western nations that had imposed foreign policy sanctions on
Burma's military government, the Australian government has not. One upshot of this is that the Burmese government does not routinely deny visas

to Australians. Such guarded acceptability certainly could give potential interlocutors every reason to associate me with the military itself.

Setting aside that worry, after a four-hour trip from Rangoon, I arrived in an unremarkable riverine village. Setting foot into a new field site—a rural village where I had no existing contacts—I soon realized how blasé I had become about getting quality fieldwork material in Burma. For years—since first beginning research in Rangoon in 1994, I have relied successfully on my network of urban friends and acquaintances, a network painstakingly created and maintained. Its slender threads are continually threatened by the heavy tension created for myself and informants alike by fear and the vulnerability that comes from being a foreigner or knowing one, and knowing that military agents know of these taboo associations, but this network has served me well.

Now, as I embarked upon my first day's research in the village—with no available contacts or knowledge about existing networks—I decided to begin with something useful and relatively safe for all concerned: a village survey. Knowing that this would be a surefire method of getting to know who's who in a short period of time, I felt relieved: Speed was of the essence because I might not get permission from the Burmese government to stay in the village for more than a few weeks.

I already knew certain things about Burmese villages: Until about the mid-1960s, most such villages comprised approximately five hundred people and were grouped into tracts, with each tract governed by a headman or headwoman. Since the 1960s, significant forced internal displacement throughout the country has meant that village tracts can now contain from one to eleven villages. The village headman/woman is now in a kind of power-sharing arrangement with a local village tract's secretary of the State Peace and Development Council (SPDC), the latter representing the lowest level of administration within Burma's military regime.

Striking out to conduct the village survey, I calculate that with some of the village partially submerged under water and thus unreachable, there are 116 accessible houses. Dividing the village into manageable sections, I begin knocking on doors. The first house I visit has a large blackboard tied to one side of the house. It announces the presence of a *payawga saya*, a master of evil spirits; the blackboard indicates the times the healer will be available and the kinds of services he performs.

As I walk further into the village I see large, shallow metal bowls underneath several trees, always at the intersections of village paths. I note that in Burma this is a common indicator of witchcraft, and I look for other evidence of medical and magical phenomena. In the center of the village I see a small, enclosed wooden platform that contains a shrine to the Indian goddess Kali. This Kali shrine is raised on stilts and surrounded by a newly painted, low picket fence.

Off to my right I see a large pavilion. The pavilion has an overhanging palm-thatched roof that reaches almost to the muddy ground, an aspect of its construction that I discover is not accidental. Squinting to look inside the pavilion, I can just make out an elaborate shrine, the far wall covered with symbols I know to be associated with Buddhist sects. These sects are considered to have revolutionary potential because they use knowledge of the occult to achieve everyday power, and this also antithetical to more or-thodox Buddhists who see it as a deviation from Buddhist teachings. They have been banned in Burma since 1979.

Moving just a little further along a path, I come across further signs announcing "astrological services," and near these I see a Buddhist *dham-mayoun*—the latter a resting building for Buddhist pilgrims and the main village gathering place. What I have seen so far is as visible to the village's secretary of the SPDC—the lowest-level military power in such a village—who would be likely to declare the occult, its representatives, and their prac-tices, and those involved with the occult, illegal "subversives." I am curious as to how the illegal occult activity can be so visible, with an obvious village following, and survive military repression.

It is clear that the villagers are very uncomfortable about my interest in the evidence of occult practices. That's not surprising, considering many practitioners of the occult are considered to be potential political enemies. What I mean by this is that, as early as 1979, the military regime realized that occult practitioners were natural leaders, whose power derived partially from their alleged mastery of occult law but also from their charismatic per-sonalities that allowed them to draw large numbers of followers. Freedom of association does not exist in this military state and the regime makes illegal all of the ways that Burmese people may band together. Buddhism is therefore a potential problem for the regime and it has spent millions of dollars and many years controlling and suborning Buddhist monks (the Sangha). Offshoot groups from Buddhist orthodoxy are called sects, or *gaing*, and these combine Buddhism with the occult. These are illegal and pose a particular threat to the regime, but even witchcraft doctors and those who practice religions other than Theravada Buddhism (such as Kali wor-ship) are viewed with suspicion.

I note the villagers' heightened tension, but nevertheless I am feeling ex-cited. I have traversed a great number of hurdles to be able to conduct field-work in a Burmese village. This particular village is clearly rich with a variety of healing modalities, and I am anxious to begin interviewing. This is the point at which things head downhill very quickly. At the first house—it has been designated publicly as where the "master of evil spirits" (*payawga saya*) lives—I ask if the healer lives there. A young married woman, the matriarch of the household, tells me:

"No, there's no one like that here."

"Um, okay then, what about that great big sign on the side of the house advertising a *payawga saya?*"

"Oh, that old thing? It's been there forever."

Now, I grant you that my language skills aren't as good as I'd like them to be, but even I can spot a big fat lie in Burmese.

Undaunted, next I move to the houses that I suspect contain the astrologers and perhaps an alchemist or two. I explain my reason for being in the village and ask if anyone in the household practices any kind of medical, healing, religious, or spiritual practices. "No, there's nothing like that here." "No, we don't do any of that here, we're all good Buddhists. We just work and go to the monastery." It is becoming clear that this is the village people's mantra (as well as that of two other villages that I later visited). Frustrated, I walk to the middle of the village and inspect the Kali shrine. I then knock on the doors of the houses closest to the shrine, asking the villagers in each house about the shrine that stands just outside their front entry. They responded: "What shrine?" "Oh, that old thing. I don't know anything about it." "That thing there? It's been there for years; it's not used anymore."

With little more than a litany of lies and obfuscations to carry my fieldwork forward, I trudge around the village for three days more and hear nothing different. I visit the village's Buddhist Abbott—the *Sayadaw*—whose small monastery is located to the west of the village. I also make calls at the village office of the secretary of the SPDC, and I visit the village's health clinic, where I speak briefly with its practical nurse, called "Sister." Finally, I speak with the owner of the village's only shop. Receiving little more than guarded courtesies from these village actors, I decide to retreat to Rangoon to assess my marked lack of progress in fostering rapport between myself and my informants.

Something that happened at the end of that day had given me a lot to think about. As I stood waiting for the ferry to Rangoon, I decided to go over and chat once more with the village's SPDC secretary. Looking across the way, I saw that my research assistant, Daw Phone Phone—a sharp and diplomatic woman—had begun a quiet woman-to-woman chat with the hospital clinic's "Sister." As the two women huddled together in muted conversation, the "Sister" whispered village rumors to Phone Phone, an act that suggested her interest in initiating a co-conspiratorial relationship with me—albeit initially through my Burmese research assistant. On our way back to Rangoon that evening, I learned the content on this conversation, as recounted to me by Phone Phone. The "Sister" had told her that "there is a madman in the village but he is being kept from us." This man is "staked to a metal post in the rice fields and held in place by a twenty foot-long rope." The co-conspiratorial posture that the "Sister" had adopted with my research assistant forced me to look squarely at how being associated with a representative of the military, my chaperone for the village research, might be affecting my field research.

I had much to think about back in the relative comfort of Rangoon: Should I even return to the village to conduct research? Must I reconfigure in the minds of prospective interviewees my relationship with the military? How could this be accomplished? How could I get villagers to be more open? From working in urban Burma I had learned how to keep a low profile with regard to the security forces: I meet with people in out of the way places, or alternatively, in very crowded places like markets. I am never seen publicly with the same person more than about once a year. I don't use the telephone to set up meetings. I stay in the public eye and I stick to banal topics, waiting for the moment when my informant steps over that line and we begin to take the conversation along pathways forbidden by the military regime. What I needed to do was to find a way to translate this urban mode of trust building into an appropriate and feasible rural one.

The most immediate consequence of my night in Rangoon was to resolve to find a way to return to the village without the Ministry of Health functionary from Rangoon. I was relieved when this man informed me that while he was keen to obtain information about traditional medicine in rural Burmese villages, he understood my need to talk to villagers outside of his presence. He would drink tea with the village SPDC secretary or the clinic "Sister," the latter my new co-conspirator, while I conducted interviews. The military functionary's new willingness to separate himself from me, of course, doesn't alter the fact that I had already been seen in his presence and, in the eyes of the villagers, I had some favored relationship with the military regime. It seems to me that it is largely this perception that caused the villagers to spin lies in the hope that I'll go away.

Undaunted by such doubts and enthusiastic that this day's interviews were going to be fruitful, I arrive once more in the village the following morning. Accompanied this time only by Phone Phone, I edge along the raised bamboo walkway to the thatched pavilion that houses the shrine of the village's Buddhist sect. I am met halfway along the rickety narrow path by a mixed group of men and women who demand to know my business and tell me to turn around and go back. They line up along the bamboo path, blocking my access to the pavilion. It's not the ideal place to have a conversation. From my point of view, it's too open and, we could be seen by the government officials. But this is precisely why the villagers want to be seen talking to me here. They will be able to explain, if the village secretary should ask them to, that they refused me any information. I tell the small group: "I would like to talk to you, but first, I'm going to go and look at the shrine."

It's a bit of a standoff: I can't push past them, because the board we're standing on is only four inches wide, so I stand stiffly—Burmese bodily code for "resolute." In this way I signal, in Burmese terms, that I'm going to stand here all day if necessary, but I'm not going to turn back. Faced with my resolute body language and scratching the back of their heads— Burmese bodily code for "angry"—the group turns and trudges along the walkway until we reach the pavilion with its occult shrine inside. Relieved, I assume that I have "won" this opening sortie—but will our confrontation block building rapport?

I decide to approach these villagers through "co-conspiratorial" discourse— a strategy I would not recommend without exercising great care. As I sat squatting on the ground with the small group of alarmed villagers in front of the pavilion, I explain:

> I am not with the government and I do not support it. I had to come with the military guy otherwise I would not have been given permission to work in villages. I know how things work here. I know you are frightened and I appreciate that. I promise I will cause you no trouble. I want to write about the kinds of medical and magical healing that still exist in Burma because I know that there is almost no health care provided by the government. I have worked in Burma for a long time and anything you tell me will be kept away from the government. I will not write down your names, and I will not take my notes with me when I leave Burma—I will destroy them. Whatever you tell me will be safe, I promise you. You know that I have permission to be here and to talk with you. If you want to tell me about life here in the village, I would like to hear about it and tell others about it. But if you are too worried about me being here, then of course I'll leave. I don't want to cause you trouble.

I then sat back on my haunches, feeling darn proud of that long speech in Burmese. I was even more pleased with the immediate repositioning of the barriers of secrecy:

> Oh, well, why didn't you say that in the first place? We assumed you worked for the government. We've never had a foreigner here before. What do you want to know? Do you like our shrine? Let us tell you about it . . .

CONCEALMENT AND REVELATION

My co-conspiratorial disclosures to the small group of villagers in the Buddhist sect's pavilion about own my political sympathies and the relationship of these to my research in their village helped to incorporate me into their "double frame." According to Goffman (1974), a "double frame" exists when being the holder of a group's secrets simultaneously designates one as an "insider" and forbids telling the group's secrets to "outsiders." Once I had demonstrated that I had the correct "insider" knowledge and perspectives, the small group of villagers became more open with their disclosures that day. Besides the amount of direct information that I gained, I could see from the "we-see-you-as-an-insider" inflections in their voices and their use of "we-are-insiders-together" lowered tones, accompanied by their strategic silences, that I had become a provisional insider. They seemed to have made the decision to believe that I could be trusted to maintain their secrets from the military regime.

Along the way, a series of relational intimacies were being created between myself and these villagers, leading them to share, for the first time, knowledge about their daily lives with a complete stranger. I, for example, demonstrated my in-depth knowledge of the many Buddhist *gaing* in Burma, their aims and rituals. I used Burmese and Pali words and phrases that demonstrated my proficiency with the occult in particular, and with Burmese culture and history in general. In this way the villagers came to sense my considerable affiliation with Burma. This prompted them to speak to me as a fellow initiate, and our conversations began to range widely, covering a great many aspects of Burmese life and village concerns. In this respect, the clinic "Sister" remained a strong ally, being seen talking with me about medicine and plants, and our conversations covered much ground under the umbrella of village "well-being."

Another important aspect of this relational intimacy was reciprocity: Over the course of my stays in the riverine village, the residents extracted as many secrets from me as I did from them. Often when conducting interviews throughout both rural and urban Burma, I asked if I could use a tape recorder, and my informants responded by also wanting to tape our interviews. Most importantly, villagers—beyond the few that I had directly introduced myself—knew that I had initiated the exchange in front of the pavilion by speaking against the regime in a way that pulled those there into my "open secrets" about it. It was almost as if the village as a whole had evaluated me through that encounter and decided that I constituted an acceptable risk.

Of course, the villagers had no guarantee that what they told me would not be used against them, or in what ways it might be used. Time had taught them that keeping secret as much of their life as possible lowered the risk of adverse consequences to them and their families. The burden of fear that individuals bear depends upon many different factors and it was impossible to satisfy all of the villagers of my good intentions and my ethical conduct. The *payawga saya*, for example, was determined not to meet with me and lived in his temporary hut out in the rice fields whenever I was in the village. For some people, fear is simply too deep to overcome and trust is too difficult to manage under conditions of authoritarianism.

Through actively seeking induction into the secrets of this Burmese village—which pulled me and my work into an affective field site—I had knowingly placed an ethical burden on my field research. I believe that this ethical burden is beyond that experienced by fieldworkers in more traditional field settings. For example, the consequences for informants even being seen with a foreigner are potentially significant. Their vulnerability was ratcheted up by discussing and disclosing information about subjects considered politically "taboo." Consequently, interviews had to be conducted with utmost caution, with initial contact and interview locations specified by informants themselves (Skidmore 2003). In the cities this is a strategy that can involve visiting people's homes late at night, taking a walk in an open space, or meeting, supposedly by chance, in busy open places such as markets. But in the village there was nowhere to hide, so I adapted my city methodology of hiding in the open. I asked all the elders of the village to meet with me in the Buddhist pavilion, the *dhammayoun*. We began by drawing maps of the village, and they marked on them events over an eighty-year period. We then moved out in small groups around the village so that they could show me these places and we also began to venture further afield looking for various herbs and medicinal plants. The government officials found these activities very reassuring and further relaxed their surveillance of my activities. These activities allowed both space and time for conversations and the gathering of life histories. We routinely returned to the *dhammayoun*, which as a Buddhist building it represented the natural village meeting place and became the "safest" place to meet informants.

Beyond conducting a careful methodology, however, there exists an ethical burden related to the psychological well-being of one's informants. To give one prominent example—during those first days when the villages resolutely lied to me, the evidence of their occult activities was all around: in the tattooed bodies of rice harvesters seeking magical protection against snakebites; in the shrines dedicated to magical healing through the occult; in the Kali shrine; and in other non-Buddhist practices such as witchcraft, astrology, alchemy, and black magic. It would have been impossible for the village monk (*Sayadaw*) and the SPDC secretary to have been ignorant of the villagers' "deviant" beliefs and practices, but clearly they turned a blind eye so long as it did not alter the existing power structures. By asking about these visible signs of occult practices, I caused fear. Was this ethical?

Many young researchers start out with a belief in the necessity of documenting examples of repression and of human rights violations. There is a voluminous literature on human rights abuses in Burma, but almost nothing about the routine misery, suffering, and ill health that constitutes the broadest and most pervasive form of human rights abuses in Burma. I made it clear to the villagers who confronted me on that rickety bamboo walkway leading to the Buddhist sect's pavilion that I would go away and take my questions with me if that is what they wanted. I had no desire to add to their burden of fear. Always in conditions of fear, in affective field sites it is necessary to allow informants to initiate conversations that induce fear or that cause painful memories to surface. It is not ethical to do otherwise.

During my years of research in Burma I have learned that people's self-censorship can be seen on one level as adding an additional layer of protection—perhaps if they do not actively voice their "open secrets" about illegal occult activities and the military's punishment of these, these believers will escape military repression. However, on a more basic level, silence is an ingrained habit: The Burmese people live under the world's longest-surviving military dictatorship, where secrecy has been a prominent feature of public life for a very long time. Perhaps, the best that I could expect as a field researcher was that villager interlocutors and myself could share information through a "co-conspirational" relationship. The ties that bound were our shared condemnation of—and secrecy about—Burma's military government. Undoubtedly they withheld much information about their lives, hopes, and fears, but in those several weeks I learned an enormous amount about rural life in Burma, and I laughed, cried, and sympathized with these villagers, and they in turn learned through my stories and photographs of my life in Australia. My methodology continually worked toward decreasing fear through increasing the content of my half of the co-conspiratorial relationship and in not asking the questions I most wanted to ask but allowing villagers to speak about their concerns, in their own time, at a place of their own choosing.

LEAVING THE AFFECTIVE FIELD

What happens when researchers leave the affective field? Just as my Burmese interviewees had learned to "edit" their thoughts and disclosures, being in the field in Burma had conditioned me along these lines as well. After spending just over a year in Rangoon when conducting my doctoral fieldwork in 1996 and 1997, I found that it then took me more than another year after returning home to stop covering my mouth with my hand when speaking about Burma's military regime. I also needed time to stop sliding my eyes toward street corners to see who might be loitering before I entered and left buildings. Each time I leave the "affective field" I need to consciously stop using secrecy as a methodology for living.

I also found that my experience in the affective field, where "good" and "bad" and "safe" and "dangerous" were clearly dichotomized by place and person, followed me home. Dudwick and De Soto (2000, 4) argue that in postsocialist societies, fieldworkers continue to live with long-held demarcations developed in the field, where they had learned to adopt a "Manichean" vision of the field as containing a few intimates who could be trusted and "the rest of the world" that was not trustworthy. Even to think of writing about my field experiences caused fear, and now, a decade after that initial doctoral fieldwork was conducted, I continue to feel the weight of the regime's implicit threats of violence toward me as I write this chapter and I have started to type one-handed as I use the other hand to cover my mouth, a subconscious defence against the military regime finding out that I am an opponent actively working against it.

In "Secrecy and Fieldwork," Richard Mitchell (1993) stresses that a researcher's relationships with his or her informants are "inseparably and simultaneously both cognitive and affective" (12). Indeed, I learned that an emotional process occurs when the enforced psychological intimacy between co-conspirators is abruptly ended through the researcher's departure from the affective field. Often when I leave Burma, informants revert to their tactics of denial and use distancing strategies to cope with the feelings of loss that occur when an intimate co-conspiratorial relationship becomes international and occasional. My informants have seen pictures of my children and understand well why I am leaving, but the weight of the secrets they have told me, and the emotions spent in revealing them, result in some informants never being able to accept my departure. When I am not present, the close emotional relationship between myself and other members of what has become our "in-group" can no longer be continually reaffirmed; after a period in which their methodology of secrecy as a way of living, it has become untethered. When I return for the next research trip, I find that many of my previous informants feign surprise at our earlier topics of conversation; they seem to wish to speak of "less sensitive" issues. Once again, I must begin to slowly and carefully immerse myself in the affective field by seeking access to the group's "open secrets" as a fellow co-conspirator, who as an "activist-by-proxy" will also assume the burden of concealing these from the state.

NOTES

1. "Giant Fish Save Burma from Tsunami," *Irrawaddy*, January 31, 2005, www .irrawaddy.org/aviewer.asp?a=4347&z=153.

2. Ibid.

3. "Burmese Authorities Ban Tsunami Disaster News and Images from Asia," *Democratic Voice of Burma* (DVB), January 18, 2005, www.english.dvb.no/news .php?id=3913.

4. Betsy Apple and Veronica Martin, *No Safe Place: Burma's Army and the Rape of Ethnic Women* (Refugees International, 2003), www.refugeesinternational.org/

files/3023_file_no_safe_place.pdf; Shan Human Rights Foundation (SHRF) and Shan Women's Action Network (SWAN), *License to Rape: The Burmese Military Regime's Use of Sexual Violence in the Ongoing War in Shane State* (Shanland.org, 2002), www.shanland.org/shrf/License_to_Rape/license_to_rape.htm; Women's League of Burma (WLB), *System of Impunity: Nationwide Patterns of Sexual Violence by the Military Regime's Army and Authorities in Burma* (WLB, 2004), www.womenofburma. org/Report/SYSTEM_OF_IMPUNITY.pdf.

5. "U.K. Activist Plans New Burma Mission," BBC Online, November 8, 1999, http://news.bbc.co.uk/1/hi/uk/509225.stm.

6. See, for state construction of affect, Mary-Jo Delvecchio Good and Byron Good, "Ritual, the State, and the Transformation of Construction of Emotional Discourse in Iranian Society," *Culture, Medicine and Psychiatry* 12, no. 1 (1988); Janis Jankins, "The State Construction of Affect: Political Ethos and Mental Health among Salvadoran Refugees," *Culture, Medicine and Psychiatry* 15 (1991); Skidmore 2003.

7. Moving to a more macro level, research on privacy has led to debates about the right of the state to know the affairs of individuals and nongovernment groups and to the privileging of "national security" over civilian rights to privacy. In the wake of al-Qaeda terrorist attacks around the world, the right to voluntarily withhold information (that is, exercising privacy), has significantly decreased in many societies. However, even before the international "War on Terror," secrecy was a suspicious social form because of its use in concealing illegal materials and activities.

8. It is crucial for the existence of research assistants to remain anonymous when working in authoritarian states. The research assistant could be held responsible for the fieldworker's actions and could be charged with a myriad of charges regarding violation of the various secrecy acts. It is equally important that the research assistant be carefully chosen: He or she must understand the ethics of working with repressed populations, must be unaligned to the security forces, and must be able to psychologically adapt to the heightened vigilance that is needed when working with foreigners in contemporary Burma.

REFERENCES

Aye, Moe. (1998). "The Last Days of Mr. Leo Nichols." In *Tortured Voices: Personal Accounts of Burma's Interrogation Centres*, edited by All Burma Students' Democratic Front. Bangkok: All Burma Students' Democratic Front.

Bellman, Beryl L. (1984). *The Language of Secrecy: Symbols and Metaphor in Poro Ritual*. New Brunswick, NJ: Rutgers University Press.

Dudwick, Nora, and Hermione G. De Soto. (2000). "Introduction." In *Fieldwork Dilemmas: Anthropologists in Postsocialist States*, edited by Hermione G. De Soto, 4. Madison: University of Wisconsin Press.

Goffman, Erving. (1974). *Frame Analysis*. New York: Harper and Row.

Government of Myanmar. (2005). Myanmar Information Committee, Information Sheet No. D-324 (I). January 18.

Green, Linda. (1999). *Fear as a Way of Life: Mayan Widows in Rural Guatemala*. New York: Columbia University Press.

Irrawaddy. (2005). "Giant Fish Save Burma from Tsunami," January 31. Available at www.irrawaddy.org.

Keiko Tosa. (2005). "The Chicken and the Scorpion: Rumor, Counternarratives, and the Political Uses of Buddhism." In *Burma at the End of the Twenty-first Century*, edited by Monique Skidmore, 154–73. Honolulu: University of Hawai'i Press.

Mawdsley, James. (2002). *The Iron Road: A Stand for Truth and Democracy in Burma.* New York: North Point Press.

Mitchell, Richard G., Jr. (1993). *Secrecy and Fieldwork. Qualitative Research Methods,* vol. 29. Newbury Park, CA: Sage.

Shils, Edward A. (1956). *The Torment of Secrecy: The Background and Consequences of American Security Policies.* Glencoe: Free Press.

Simmel, Georg. (1950). *The Sociology of Georg Simmel.* Translated by Kurt Wolff. New York: Macmillan.

Skidmore, Monique. (2003). "Darker than Midnight: Fear, Vulnerability and Terror-Making in Urban Burma (Myanmar)." *American Ethnologist* 30, no. 1.

———. (2004). *Karaoke Fascism: Burma and the Politics of Fear.* Philadelphia: University of Pennsylvania Press.

Tefft, Stanton K. (1980). "Secrecy as a Social and Political Process." In *Secrecy: A Cross-Cultural Perspective*, edited by Stanton K. Tefft, 321. New York: Human Sciences.

13

The Veiled Feminist Ethnographer: Fieldwork among Women of India's Hindu Right

Meera Sehgal[1]

In the late 1990s I conducted twenty-one months of ethnographic research in North India on women's participation in the Rashtra Sevika Samiti (National Female Volunteers' Association), a core women's organization in the Hindu nationalist movement. As an Indian feminist from a Hindu cultural background, I wanted to understand why and how women became involved in India's violent right-wing Hindu nationalist movement. In this article I use my experiences in the field to illustrate how the principles of feminist ethnography both did and did not work for me within a field-work situation in which I was a feminist "researching up"—that is, where I was studying a dangerous group with more power than myself. Some of my greatest personal and research challenges occurred within a research context theoretically favorable to utilizing feminist ethnographic methods; however, the larger sociopolitical context made such methods dangerous and inadvisable.

My analysis in this chapter is divided into four parts, with the first, "Women and Hindu Nationalism," describing the Hindu Nationalist movement and women's roles in it. In the next section, "Feminist Research and Right-Wing Women," I evaluate feminist ethnographic research principles in terms of their practicality and utility for studying a violent, right-wing women's organization. In the third section, "Power, Positionality, and Emotional Dynamics," the core analytical component of this chapter, I introduce three factors that most immediately structured my field research process: power, positionality, and emotions. In the fourth section, "Veiling in the Midst of the Hindu Right," I illustrate how these factors and the processes that they generated played out during three phases of my field research: entering the field, working in the field, and leaving the field.

WOMEN AND HINDU NATIONALISM

The focus of my research—the Rashtra Sevika Samiti—a group hereafter labeled the Samiti, is a hierarchical, militarized, cadre-based Hindu nationalist women's organization that plays an important role within the larger Hindu nationalist movement. The Samiti ranks as one of the most powerful agenda-setting and institutionally well-established organizations within the range of women's organizations in the Hindu nationalist movement. The Samiti has its own clearly demarcated boundaries, codified rules, regulations, goals, functions, and office bearers. Characterized as "an intensive physical and ideological training-center," the Samiti provides "a small group of hand-picked cadres" for leadership positions within the larger Hindu nationalist movement (Sarkar 1996, 199), In fact, most of the women in Hindu nationalist movement leadership positions are trained by the Samiti before they circulate to other movement organizations. Indeed, the Samiti's training is a necessary step toward these women ultimately circulating into leadership positions within the larger Hindu nationalist movement.[2]

The Hindu nationalist movement, which has existed in India since the late nineteenth century, mobilizes "Hindus" to propagate an exclusivist, right-wing Hindu nationalist ideology referred to as *Hindutva* (literally, "Hindu-ness") by it's proponents. It aims to establish a Hindu state in the territory currently occupied by the modern nation states of South Asia (i.e., Pakistan, Afghanistan, Bangladesh, and Sri Lanka). Their preferred state would relegate all non-Hindus to second-class citizenship. However, given that India's Hindu population is, in fact, divided among itself by caste, class, ethnicity, region, language, and culture, the Hindu nationalist movement appeals to a "Hindu-first" sensibility and mobilizes anti-Muslim hatred as a powerful glue with which to unite the fractured Hindu polity.

The discourse of Hindu nationalism constructs the Hindu community as vulnerable and beleaguered, constantly under attack from various enemies, with the most reviled of these being the Muslim community. Hindu nationalists promote the idea that, despite being an overwhelming numerical majority in contemporary India, Hindus are a persecuted group. In contrast, Muslims, who are India's largest numerical minority, are framed as a "pampered group" that enjoys special privileges. This narrative of Hindu victimhood is fueled by fears that Muslim "infiltrators" from Pakistan and Bangladesh will combine with Indian Muslim nationals to form a powerful political force within India, with the Indian Muslim nationals forming a formidable voting block and usurping power from Hindus.

Associated with this contemporary discourse is a historical narrative that portrays India as the "motherland," the "Nation of the Hindus" since the ancient Vedic period (approximately 1500–500 BCE, preceding the birth of the Buddha). Hindu nationalists paint this Hindu motherland—imagined as having flourished hegemonically across Afghanistan, Pakistan, Nepal, Bangladesh, Myanmar, and Sri Lanka—as the victim of repeated incursions by outsiders, most egregiously by seven centuries of Muslim conquest and followed by three centuries of British colonial rule. The problems now faced by contemporary India are blamed primarily on Islam, and secondarily on Christianity and Westernization. According to such a worldview, Muslims were never, and never will be, "true" Indians, as their first loyalty is toward Islam, Mecca, and Medina—the latter, Islam's holy sites. Hindu nationalists argue that the Islamic "fifth column" has weakened Hindu national identity and hinders establishment of a Hindu state. Consequently, Hindu nationalists see their programmatic mission as having to "rid" India of "Muslim infiltrators," inform the world of Pakistan's terrorist conspiracies, and increase India's defense against Pakistani and Muslim terrorism, all while working toward fostering a homogeneous Hindu identity among India's divided Hindus.

Violence is crucial and integral to Hindu nationalist discourse and practice. It is connected to the movement's very identity as a movement of Hindus, historically "victimized" by the Muslims, who need to demonstrate to themselves and others that Hindus are strong, virile, and united enough to take "revenge" for the imagined historical injustices perpetrated on them by the Muslims. Hindu nationalist violence often takes the form of large-scale "communalist," anti-Muslim riots that are systematic, preplanned, recurrent, and highly gendered in the distribution of violent roles. That is, while large groups of armed Hindu nationalist men have targeted Muslim neighborhoods, burning and looting homes and businesses, murdering Muslim men and sexually brutalizing Muslim women, Hindu nationalist women have facilitated this violence by providing auxiliary services.[3] Powerful female leaders have given fiery, inflammatory speeches before "communalist" attacks (Basu 1995, 1996); rank-and-file women have provided backup services to their "frontline" men by "breaking down houses, helping wash away the blood of those killed" (Butalia 20001, 107). These women have also prevented other women from helping the victims of such violence, who are predominantly women and children. Within the framework of this "gendering" of Hindu nationalist violence, I came to focus on women's roles in the Hindu nationalist movement.

FEMINIST RESEARCH AND RIGHT-WING WOMEN

Given the Samiti's politico-organizational status and operational mission as a right-wing Hindu nationalist women's organization that supports and facilitates violence against Muslims, how could I, a secular-left Indian feminist from a Hindu cultural background, conduct "honest" feminist field research on this organization? The long and short answers are that, while my research design was informed by the frameworks of feminist ethnography and standpoint epistemology, I soon found that the power dynamics involved in studying women of the Hindu right made adhering to these principles extremely difficult. One of the most critical issues debated in feminist ethnography concerns power and inequality in the production of knowledge. Feminist theorists like Sandra Harding (1991), Dorothy Smith (1993), Nancy Hartsock (1998), and Patricia Hill-Collins (2000) have shown how social, political, racial, economic, and other power dynamics influence the production of knowledge, privileging certain knowledge producers, designating some research and discourse as more legitimate than others, and often silencing the voices of the marginalized. Feminists emphasize the importance of women's lived experiences as the basis of knowledge and position women as subjects of analysis, rather than its mere objects.

Feminist epistemological principles, based on the assumption that the researcher is usually more powerful than the researched, encourage honesty, empathy, trust, and rapport in research, with the aim of diminishing power imbalances between researcher and researched. Some feminist researchers have also recommended—as research strategies for diminishing power imbalances between researcher and researched—employing such research techniques as "self-reflexivity," "disclosure" (about one's own location in hierarchies of power), rigorous honesty, and "dialogical interviews." To promote the ethics of research, feminists have suggested guaranteeing strict confidentiality by articulating and/or receiving written consent of the researched. For promoting equality in the production and analysis of knowledge, feminists have argued for soliciting and incorporating the research subject's input into the research process itself, engaging in analytical collaboration with the researched, and even engaging in multiple authorship with those studied (see, for these recommendations, Collins 1999; Devault 1999; Gluck and Patai 1991; Gottfried 1996; Harding 1996; Hartsock 1998; Naples 2003; Smith 1993).

Judith Stacey (1991) questions whether feminists might not be deluding themselves that they can ever equalize the power imbalances between themselves and those they study.[4] In any case, as valid as these feminist research recommendations are for most research situations, I found the assumptions underlying some of these principles problematic during my fieldwork. Transparency and self-disclosure, both based on the assumption that the researcher is typically more powerful than the researched, was not the case in my research. My research subjects were embedded within a significant power structure based upon the hegemony and influence of the Hindu nationalist movement in India and its documented proclivity toward violence. When researching violent right-wing movements that, in the first place, strenuously resist being studied and, in the second place, view feminist researchers as traitors to their ideals, these prescriptions of honesty and the full disclosure of information about onesself and the research project, rather than equalizing power imbalances, might make the research impossible to do or limit the quality of the data produced, and would very likely make the researcher and her family physically and emotionally vulnerable to reprisal.

Methodologies based on rapport and empathy assume some degree of ideological compatibility between the researcher and researched. Recent scholarship on what Nigel Fielding (1993) has termed "unloved groups" (i.e., violent right-wing groups) highlights the problematic nature of this assumption (see Blee 2002; Ellis 1995; Kleinman and Copp 1993; Lee 1995; Mitchell 1993; Nordstrom and Robben 1995). Reflecting on her fieldwork with women in organized racist groups in the United States (such as the Ku Klux Klan, Christian Identity groups, and neo-Nazi Skinheads), Kathleen Blee (1998) observes that

> [i]t is one thing to understand the world through the eyes of an informant with whom you have some (even a little) sympathy, but a very different matter to think about developing rapport with someone—like racist activists—whose life is given meaning and purpose by the desire to annihilate you or others like you. (388)

The Hindu nationalist movement indoctrinates activists with a violent hatred against what it labels "anti-national traitors to the Hindu motherland." Such "traitors" include feminists, leftists, secular Hindus, Muslims, and Christians. Under such circumstances, when a feminist "researches up"—studying dangerous groups that have more power than she has—she might have to negotiate power differentials in unconventional ways and reimagine ideological incompatibilities as complexities that are sometimes best left veiled. However, even then, the secrecy involved in the veiling of the ethnographer is never absolute and shifts according to the context. As sociologist Richard Mitchell (1993), who conducted covert research on a right-wing paramilitary survivalist group in the Pacific Northwest of the United States, has pointed out, secrecy in social action and social science research is relative, rather than absolute. It is context specific, rather than universal. I would add that secrecy is partial rather than complete and it is "always embedded in," as Mitchell has pointed out, "and interpreted through cultural contexts, meanings and practices" (6). In the end, as social actors as well as researchers, we ourselves are always partial: We perform and present contradictory and shifting identities that are culturally contextualized and circumscribed by the power dynamics within a particular setting. These insights about power, "truth," secrecy, and context guided my field research in India.

I would argue that feminist epistemology and research methods, centered as they are on social justice and activism, have a place among researchers who study "unloved groups," albeit a place not yet systematically explored and explicated. For my part, in this research, I discovered the necessity to go beyond the fixed, monolithic, unidirectional notions of power that frame researchers as all-powerful, potential exploiters and see research subjects as relatively powerless victims. Therefore, in my field research—rather than discarding feminism as a guide for fieldwork—I found that feminist research paradigms, being based on critical theory (Guba and Lincoln 2004), provided me with an avenue for navigating the existing top-down power dynamic that seemed initially to be complicating my research. Guba and Lincoln observe that paradigms based on critical theory aim at critiquing and transforming structures that "exploit humankind" (30). In such paradigms, "advocacy and activism are key concepts" and "the inquirer is cast in the role of instigator and facilitator" (30). I wanted to produce knowledge that would help resist an Indian variant of fascism, to look for the contradictory spaces and fissures that could potentially crack open the fundamentalist facade of imagined Hindu unity, and to identify the potential for dissent and resistance within the ranks of the movement.[5] I became convinced that critical theory's aim of knowledge production for critique and emancipation, with the researcher positioned as a "transformative intellectual," as "advocate and activist" (Guba and Lincoln 2004, 29), could provide me with an effective route toward achieving these research outcomes.

POWER, POSITIONALITY, AND EMOTIONAL DYNAMICS

Power: The Complexities of Studying Up

I faced a number of methodological difficulties during and after my fieldwork, most arising from an uneasy interaction between two different methodological and research contexts: situations where applying feminist ethnography might be a viable option, yet where using its principles was inadvisable. It was precisely where these two contexts intersected—creating in the process an ethnographic "borderland"—that I faced some of my greatest fieldwork challenges.[6] Typically, settings in which the application of feminist ethnographic principles are viable are where the researcher has power relatively equal to or greater than that of the researched and/or when there is some ideological compatibility between researcher and researched. Contrasting with this are those research contexts of right-wing movements in which the researcher is "researching up," particularly on groups that are powerful, dangerous, and secretive and who view the researcher's worldview as inimical to theirs.

I realized very early in my research that applying the principles of feminist ethnography would be inadvisable in situations where I was "researching-up" and/or within "borderland" research contexts, where applying the principles of feminist ethnography could have been a viable option, yet was not recommended for reasons of my own safety. I was repeatedly struck, when working within such research contexts, by Judith Stacey's observation about "the difficult contradictions between feminist principles and [the often divergent] ethnographic methods" that are often required in a not-feminist-friendly research environment (1991, 114).

Positionality: Partial, Shifting, and Strategic

By positionality, I mean a researcher's location within existing hierarchies of power and the ways in which the researcher's identity and affiliations are positioned among and by others. Ethnographic identities develop in relation to the interaction between three different kinds of positionalities: ascribed positionality (as is generally the case with gender), selective positionality (when one *opts for* a particular position), and enforced positionality (where one's position is *forcibly defined* by others in ways contrary to one's self perception; Franks 2002). However, these three kinds of positionalities are not fixed or static; they interact and change through negotiation, making "identity relative to a constantly shifting context, to a situation that includes a network of elements involving others, [and to] the objective economic conditions, [and to] cultural and political institutions and ideologies" (Alcoff 1997, 349). Pointing to the dynamic nature of positionalities, Mitchell (1993) argues that "ethnographic identities are not so much given roles to be played as they are emergent products of fieldwork itself, forthcoming as researchers and subjects explore each other's cognitive and affective revelations and concealments" (4).

Central to the development of an ethnographic identity is the extent to which a researcher discloses to those she is studying the relevant facts about herself and her research. This disclosure depends upon interactions between ascribed, selective, and enforced positionalities in the field. Such disclosure can range on a theoretical continuum from "full disclosure" to "total nondisclosure," with "partial disclosure" and "partial secrecy" falling between these two poles. In this middle region of selective disclosure, the researcher foregrounds certain aspects of her identity and research and veils other aspects. The evolution of my ethnographic identity underscores the argument that identities are constructed, staged, contextual, partial, contradictory, and strategic (Visweswaran 1994).

My front-stage field research identity evolved through my use of "strategic essentialism," in which I tactically presented myself as the underinformed daughter of a retired Indian army officer from a Punjabi Hindu background, whose paternal family had migrated to Delhi from Peshawar (now in Pakistan) during the 1947 Partition of British India (into the independent nation states of India and Pakistan).[7] Based at the time of my field research inside the United States as a doctoral student, I had married in the United States as well. I explained to prospective interviewees that I was doing my PhD fieldwork on "status of Hindu women in Uttar Pradesh," a northern Indian state. While basically all of these identities and facts are true, of course, I am a good deal more than these things, as I shall illustrate shortly within the research dynamic itself.

Emotional Dynamics

Increasing numbers of qualitative research scholars have pointed out that "emotions" are in one way or another present in most field settings, whether the researcher wants them to be or not (Blee 1998; Campbell 2001; Ellis 1995; Kleinman and Copp 1993; Lee-Treweek 2000; Mitchell 1993). However, even though affect clearly intrudes itself into many research settings, impacting upon the researcher and researched alike (Campbell, 2001), researchers are taught to ignore their "feelings" along with any potential data that is associated with the emotional dynamics of research. Thus, despite the fact that a researcher's relationships with the people she studies are simultaneously and inseparably both cognitive and affective (Mitchell 1993, 12), the dictates of empiricist, dispassionate social science force many researchers to focus exclusively on the cognitive and to disregard the affective and embodied. Elaborating on the shortcomings of the latter, Geraldine Lee-Treweek (2000) argues that qualitative social research should be seen as emotional labor—an ethnographer needs to recognize her own emotions, seeing them as "data," in order to gain insight into the social life of the research setting. Blee (1998) goes a step further to suggest two ways that attention to emotional dynamics can facilitate the research itself: First, by analyzing the emotional dynamic between respondent and researcher, the researcher can more effectively assess how a particular interview relationship might be influencing her data interpretation and analysis. Second, the emotions evoked in the researcher during data collection are in themselves a useful source of data (382).

In the next section, I illustrate through the richness of case examples, the interactions of power, positionality, and emotional dynamics at each of three periods of my research: entering the field, becoming ensconced in the field, and leaving the field.

VEILING IN THE MIDST OF THE HINDU RIGHT

Entering the Field

The north-central Indian state of Uttar Pradesh (UP) is part of India's Hindi-speaking heartland and is its most populous state with 80 percent of its population Hindu and just over 15 percent Muslim. UP, one of India's lesser-developed states economically, has one of the country's lowest literacy rates. Best known internationally for being the location of the Taj Mahal and Varanasi (Benares), UP is much frequented by tourists. A stronghold of the Hindu nationalist movement, UP contains Ayodhya City, where, in 1992, Hindu nationalists demolished a seventeenth-century Muslim mosque.

New to my field site in UP, my first task was to gain access to Hindu nationalist women. I had assumed that as an Indian woman from a Punjabi Hindu cultural background, with a Hindu name and proficient in the Hindi language, that I would have no problem accessing the movement and its activists. I was focused on the ascribed components of my positionality vis-à-vis those I was hoping to study: Since we were Hindu women, I had assumed that arranging interviews would be relatively simple. It never occurred to me that I might have to "prove" my insider status, something that is more expected, I assumed, among researchers who bring primarily "selective" (for example, "outsider") positionality into an interview setting. My assumptions about having easy access to those I wanted to study was also based on a "cooperative model" of field research, in which I assumed that, as a researcher, I could just walk into the setting and carry out research among supportive research subjects (Douglas 1976, 167).

I was mistaken: The movement was profoundly suspicious of me, particularly my being a "student from a Western university." They viewed me as an outsider, possibly even a "Westernized" feminist traitor to the "Hindu nation." I experienced emotionally for the first time what I already knew intellectually and politically: that the movement did not subscribe to secular notions of Indian nationhood and citizenship. For Hindu nationalists, India is peopled by "true citizens"—Hindu nationalists striving toward the establishment of one Hindu nation—and "pseudocitizens"—those who do not subscribe to the Hindu nationalist worldview and need to be taught to accept second-class citizenship rights.

My initial plan had been to locate some prominent leaders from the Hindu nationalist movement—its "gatekeepers"—explain my research objectives to them, and get their consent to conduct participant observation in settings where women were involved. I would then ask these women to introduce me to rank-and-file and other lower-level activists. I assumed that I would be able to work with the Hindu nationalist women, irrespective of their status and rank, in an honest, upfront, and consensual manner. After all, these women and I had come from similar backgrounds—Hindu, upper caste, middle class, north Indian—and would probably share a number of gender interests in common, or so I assumed. All of this was, of course, based on my false assumptions about a shared universal sisterhood among women in general, and among women with ascribed positionalities similar to my own in particular. I was all set to acknowledge the power imbalance between us and disclose my biases to them on the assumption that, as the researcher, I was more powerful than they, my research subjects.

Finding a Research Strategy

Although I had fundamental disagreements with Hindu nationalist ideology and with the movement's goals, I imagined that my worldview would not be an obstacle to the research process. As I saw it, this worldview represented my own personal and political beliefs, which I intended to bracket in order to keep an open mind toward the right-wing women I was going to study. I planned to foreground the Hindu nationalist *women* and their *gender interests* as a way of keeping at bay my aversion toward the movement's ideology and practices. Little did I realize that my real and assumed beliefs and behavior would be an object of intense and incessant scrutiny by movement activists. In hindsight, I now speculate that in my construction of myself as a feminist researcher, I had fallen into what Stacey (1991) has termed "the delusion of alliance" (116), a belief that flows from the assumption that empathy and identification are possible between feminist researchers and the women they study, which led to a good deal of soul searching on my part.

All my attempts at finding a direct, neutral strategy for approaching Hindu nationalist leaders were met with stiff resistance by movement members. This resistance brought me face-to-face with two issues relating to the movement's resistance to my research. The first was that although Hindu nationalist discourse proclaimed Hindus as homogenous and united, in fact, Hindu nationalist leaders knew full well that Hindus were not as the movement's discourse described. There were Hindus who strongly disagreed with the ideology and practices of the movement. The movement is suspicious of such "traitors," who, in movement leaders' perception, have been corrupted by Western ideologies of secularism, Marxism, and feminism. I, all my self-presentations to the contrary, could very well be such a traitor. I found, as Jeffery Sluka (1995) and many others have found, that "no neutrals are allowed" when conducting ethnographic research in communities involved in political conflict and violence: "Whether or not you take sides, those actively involved in the situation are going to define whose side they think you are on. They will act toward you on the basis of this definition, regardless of your professions of neutrality" (287). Clearly, such enforced positionality plays an important role in the field.

The second issue related to the Hindu nationalist movement's resistance to me is the movement's need to protect itself from dangerous outsiders. Comprised of several centralized, hierarchical organizations that function in highly secretive ways, the movement's leaders resist documentation of their organization's activities. No doubt, leaders did not want me documenting their practices or finding a female activist who might provide me with an internal critique of the movement. My research design had not taken into account "that the actors might deliberately manipulate and obstruct the gathering of ethnographic knowledge" (Robben 1995, 87). I soon realized I'd have to find ways to get around these two sources of resistance to my research if I wanted to do ethnographic fieldwork.

I had three options before me, each involving varying degrees of secrecy with impacts on the data that I produced, on me as a researcher, and on my research subjects. My first option would entail presenting myself to the movement as a neutral, dispassionate researcher, keeping my leftist feminist values a secret. But I had tried this and found it unsuccessful. Even if members of the movement had allowed me to research them, I am convinced they would have treated me as a reporter and given me only the information they deemed fit for public consumption. I would have received a "hard sell" promotion of their agenda cloaked in a benign facade of Hindu tolerance and gentility. The second option available for carrying out the research would be to conduct completely covert research by infiltrating the movement as a potential recruit. The data I would be able to produce would be a more accurate representation of the inner workings of the movement; I would be able to access its strategies, activists, behaviors. This strategy would very likely produce information not meant for outsiders. The third option would involve complete honesty and self-disclosure ("Yes, I think you're all fascists—could I please study you?") and hopefully obtaining the movement leaders' consent to research the movement. Even with such consent, there would have still existed some degree of deception and certainly a great degree of hostility, mistrust, and constant efforts to "prove" the accuracy of their political agendas. This was not the kind of ethnography I wanted to do, nor would it enable me to understand the worldview of ordinary Hindu nationalist women. I would have had to limit myself to a discursive analysis of publicly available documents, media, and interviews of prominent leaders, rather than participant observation among the rank and file.

CONDUCTING FIELDWORK: THE "OVERT/COVERT" DICHOTOMY

Veiling: Creating Partial Invisibility

The point of laying out the above hypothetical choices is to argue that the prevailing hegemonic view of ethnographic research as either "fully overt" or "totally covert" establishes a false dichotomy. I would argue, following

Mitchell (1993), that there are degrees of covertness—a continuum of deception—in social life as well as in social science research because

> [t]o keep no secrets, to be totally honest, to totally disambiguate each component of symbolic communication, to define each word, to provide historical and contextual qualifiers for each component of symbolic communication, to define each word, to provide historical and contextual qualifiers for each statement, and to spell out all motivations for and implications of the content and assertions in any interaction is a near-infinite task. (7)

My veiling or covertness started off on a relatively small scale. During the initial stages of fieldwork, I realized the necessity of "faking it" (Klein 1983), giving socially desirable responses rather than honest ones, the necessity of "crafting a persona consonant with the expectations of those" I wanted to study "in order to gain entrance and acceptance in nonpublic action" (Mitchell 1993) of "impression management" (Goffman 1966). Dress, physical gestures, facial expressions, and ways of making eye contact and shaking hands are all part of a presentation of self that influences the social interaction between ethnographer and interlocutor (Agar 1980). All of this evolved, on hindsight, into an "investigative field research model" similar to the kind advocated by Jack Douglas (1976). Using a combination of cooperative and investigative techniques, the investigative research model is based on the assumption that "profound conflicts of interest, values, feelings and actions pervade social life," requiring the use of covert participant observation coupled with infiltration (wherever necessary) as one of its tactics (Douglas 1976, 55–82). As Mitchell, a proponent of the investigative research model, argues:

> If the front door isn't open, try the back. If they don't like you as Twiddle Dum, then go as Twiddle Dee. Successful empirical sociology depends on understanding the ways social actors, including researchers of all kinds, manage secrecy and disclosure of their motives, identities and practices. (1993, 31)

My fieldwork identity ended up being based on partial disclosure and partial secrecy, in which I strategically "front-staged" essential aspects of my identity and veiled or "back-staged" other aspects of my biography, my ideological alignments, and my political standpoints. My "front stage" emphasized a strategic essentialism in which I presented myself as a Hindu daughter and wife from a valued class and caste position doing PhD fieldwork on the status on Hindu women. My married identity helped mitigate the activists' suspicions about my identity as a researcher from a Western university and reduced some of their anxieties about an upper-caste, middle-class Hindu woman traveling alone and independently across India. I used personal familial contacts to obtain access to lower-level activists, who then provided me with referrals to other local rank-and-file activists. Once I had developed a rapport with them, I worked my way up to national-level leaders. They viewed me as an activist in training who they could use to start a branch of the movement in Wisconsin, where I was attending graduate school. My playing into the assumptions of Hindu nationalist leaders that I was a potential recruit is similar to Nigel Fielding's covert approach in his study of Britain's racist National Front Party, in which Fielding adopted the role of a potential recruit and promoted the image of being sympathetic to the party and its principles, which allowed him an insider's view of membership (Fielding 1982).

My construction of a strategically essentialist identity did not appear full-blown at the beginning of my fieldwork. It evolved as I went through different phases of my fieldwork. Initially, my strategically essentialist identity was based on my ascribed positionality: a middle-class, upper-caste, educated, urban Hindu Punjabi female—a set of status designations that were expressed through adherence to specific ways of self-presentation (which included clothing style, jewelry, symbolic adornments, body language, and mannerisms). Of course, my presentation of an "acceptable" self, as I assumed this to be defined by conservative Hindu nationalist women, was neither always fully believed nor unconditionally accepted by these women. Subscribing in my research to what Mitchell (1993) has called "the myth of cosmetic identity"—a belief that with skill it is possible to pass unnoticed among attentive strangers, even though protected from "detection only by a few items of disguise" (43)—I resolved to conduct research mainly wearing *saris* and *salwar kameezes* (the latter, long haremlike pants and long shirt with a scarf worn by north Indian Punjabi women and increasingly by urban middle- and working-class women all over India). I combined this dress with a few subtle markers of my married Hindu status, assuming that such markers would announce my female "correctness" to my interlocutors. However, I was taken aback when, midway through my fieldwork, I was confronted by an older female member of the movement who vehemently informed me that wearing a *salwar kameez* "is a Muslim way of dressing." The woman asserted that "good Hindu women always wear *saris.*"

My clothing style apparently suggested to this interlocutor that I could be a Pakistani spy. Mitchell illustrates, with an example from his covert fieldwork on a paramilitary survivalist group, that when he and his research partner tried to blend in and "hide behind our costumes," rather than blending in, their disguises were keenly observed and classified by the survivalists as a sign of naive enthusiasm (1993, 50). Rebecca Klatch has also pointed out that a researcher's best-laid plans for presenting the "appropriate" self—by doing whatever it takes to not bring on unwanted attention—does not guarantee anonymity. Although Klatch was not covert in her 1980s study of U.S. women of the New Right, she still had to consider the image of her presentation of self to others. Recounting a story about attending a right-wing conference, Klatch (1988) remembers being approached at the gathering by a feminist "spy" of the New Right: She had "never met this woman before, and ha[d] no reason to believe [that this feminist spy] . . . knew the few other 'spies' [that] I had met." Klatch found being recognized as an outsider troubling: "I didn't know whether to laugh or be distressed that I apparently was not as invisible as I thought!" (80).

In the case of my covert research on Hindu nationalist women, having just been told by an older nationalist woman that my wearing a *salwar ka-meez* indicated that I might be a Muslim spy led me to interrogate myself about this woman's reaction: Was this the idiosyncratic view of one extremist woman, or did it represent the "common sense" view of the movement? How could anyone view a dressing style emblematic of and hegemonic among large sections of urban Indian and traditional Punjabi Hindu women as "Muslim" or as Pakistani? This woman's very negative reaction to my clothes reminded me of the communicative power of the gendered body: It is, as Visweswaran (1994) astutely points out, "(ad)dressed intimately by history and culture, age and class"; I would include by religious nationalism as well. In any case, "what we female (as opposed to male) ethnographers wear has some bearing on how we are received as social actors and anthropologists" (14). The Hindu nationalist woman's rejection of any traditions that she did not consider "exclusively" Hindu reinforced for me the movement's investment in controlling Hindu women's bodies and its desire to use its women as symbolic barriers and border guards against Muslims, Christians, or others.

Since essential aspects of my fieldwork identity had to be announced by what a conservative movement "saw" as "appropriate" dress, I made sure that I carried out the rest of my fieldwork "dressed up" in a *sari* and adorned with emblazoned markers of my married Hindu identity.[8] What the "Pakistani spy" episode underscores is that at no point during my fieldwork could I assume the security of my insider status with the movement activists. I had to repeatedly perform that identity in contingent, partial, contradictory, and strategic ways under the continual scrutiny of movement activists.

I quickly learned in the course of field research that covertness is a two-way street. I began to see that my own covertness was matched by that of the Hindu nationalist interlocutors. Furthermore, it was clear that each of us was subtly and covertly "bargaining" for our interests on the basis of what we perceived to be the identity and social location of the other. Within such a dynamic, I discovered that the Hindu nationalists and myself each held assumptions about, and goals for, the other that were not always totally true and usually not fully explicit. I had needed open access to high-level national and regional Samiti leaders; these leaders perhaps granted me such access because they hoped to use the "me" that they "saw" to expand their movement into the United States. Likewise, later on, it probably helped me gain entry into the Samiti's paramilitary camp that Samiti leaders assumed that, as a "Hindu" doctoral student in sociology at a prominent public American university, I could be used to spread and strengthen the movement inside the United States. This fiction seems to have "worked," in part, because I neither said that I would do so nor indicated that I would not.

Questions That Resonate

Of course, how I dressed was not the only thing that could mark me as "safe" to Hindu nationalist women. I had to be very strategic about how I posed questions to these women and how I interpreted their responses. It was a constant challenge because, as other researchers have found, right-wing informants have a vested interest in communicating partial, distorted, and misleading accounts. Blee, for example, argues that "accounts by those who have participated in campaigns for racial and religious supremacy . . . often are laced with deceptive information, disingenuous denials of culpability, and dubious assertions about their political motivation" (1993, 597). This is not to say that the informants are deliberately lying, indeed, they may really believe their distorted and partial versions of reality that are "often indistinguishable from the stories manufactured and disseminated" by the right-wing movement itself (1993, 599; 2002).

I attempted to get around such obfuscation by structuring my questions around issues relevant to upper-caste, middle-class, urban Hindu women. Such issues include their views about the status of Hindu women, the problems faced by contemporary Hindu women, and the ways to resolve these problems. Approaching interviews through the perspective of gender interests viable to these women helped me shift activists' responses from formal and almost programmed, defensive, and deceptive postures about their complicity and culpability in violent anti-Muslim pogroms, toward being comfortable speaking about what they perceived to be more neutral women's themes. Their answers to these questions invariably brought out the extent to which they had internalized the movement's larger ideology and their own interpretation of that ideology. For instance, nearly all the interviewees talked about the status of Hindu women across two periods: in the "pre-Muslim era" and in the "post-Muslim era." The pre-Muslim era, according to them, was the golden "Vedic Age" of the Hindus, when the "great Hindu nation, one of the greatest civilizations of the world, flourished." Then, both men and women were equal in status. Women, they asserted, were free, independent, educated, and had a "great character." The Muslim era began with waves of invasions by "barbaric" Muslim hordes from Central Asia (Turks, Afghans, Mongols, Mughals, and Persians). These invaders, according to my interviewees, destroyed the Hindu civilization by pillaging temples, forcibly converting Hindus to Islam, and brutalizing Hindu women. To protect their daughters, Hindu parents started restricting them to the home and putting them in *purdah* (the veil). These necessary reactions to the Muslim incursion progressively eroded the status and freedoms of Hindu women.

While the similarity of the various female interlocutors' responses alerted me to their unexpectedly strong awareness about, and their anger with, gender inequity—which they rooted discursively in past Muslim domination—I also wondered whether their anger toward Muslim men had been learned through their participation in the Samiti. Allowing their responses to one set of questions to suggest another set, I then pursued the more sensitive issue of what they had learned in the Samiti within the context of their previously developed gender narrative. Each such set of questions was, of course, posed within a particular material context. A particularly important turning point during my fieldwork came when I was given permission by a national-level Samiti leader to attend a paramilitary training camp run by the Samiti. This camp was one of the fifty camps conducted by the Samiti every year in different parts of India. The camp I attended drew 135 participants and thirteen instructors from seventeen north Indian cities. The overall atmosphere of the camp, and of Samiti camps in general, is rigid, authoritarian, and strict. They feature harsh and intense indoctrination of the Samiti's Hindu nationalist ideology. Run in a militarized fashion, with a strong emphasis on forcibly inculcating discipline, a typical day at the camp at which I participated included four hours of physical training; five hours of ideological indoctrination via lectures, group discussions, rote memorization; and two hours of indoctrination through cultural programs. The physical training ranged from martial arts and fighting with daggers to yoga and games, and included an emphasis on how to organize neighborhood units, all ostensibly in the interest of teaching women self-defense. Regardless of the format of the program, the lesson put forth was a Hindu nationalist version of the history of India and its contemporary sociopolitical situation highlighting its purported supporters and enemies, and the integral role of the Samiti in restoring the Hindu nation's greatness. Here the Samiti's instructors constructed history lessons that highlighted the historic and contemporary rape of Hindu women by Muslim men (kings and commoners alike in times of peace and strife). The Samiti's physical training was justified as self-defense and a facet of "women's empowerment" on the basis of this sexualized history lesson.

Emotional Dynamics

Fear was a dominant emotion that intensified before, during, and after fieldwork: fear of being targeted for violence if my leftist-feminist identity was discovered and fear of reprisal for the "betrayal of the Hindu nation" after publishing my research.[9] These are not an imaginary fears or groundless paranoia, but related to the power of the movement and its documented human rights abuses. I had started my fieldwork with the warnings from other Indian feminists who had studied the movement about how the movement was maintaining computer files on people they considered their opponents and monitoring their movements. I remembered my conversation with an American academic who had researched the Hindu right; she warned that her Indian feminist friends who had given her a place to stay had received anonymous letters threatening rape after the Hindu nationalists realized the academic had stayed with them while conducting her research. I saw how an Indian CNN reporter (a woman with a Hindu name, living adjacent to my parents' home) had to have 24/7 police protection due to the death threats she had received from the movement for her "false and biased" coverage of the movement. All this was over and above my review of reports by Indian civil liberties groups documenting the extreme violence perpetrated by Hindu nationalist activists against Muslims and opponents of the movement. I had started my fieldwork with a tremendous sense of trepidation and fear; this continued to penetrate my consciousness during the field research itself.

Recently, Hindu nationalists threatened a group of Indian women that included a U.S.–based Indian feminist researcher, Indian judges, and human rights activists with public stripping and rape just for researching and conducting a tribunal on Hindu nationalist and upper-caste violence (Williams and Poch, 2005). The upshot of this threat was that, despite having obtained the consent of all those she taped, the group's researcher was forced to publicly destroy her taped interviews with Hindu nationalist activists.

Yet another fear dogged me: I feared being judged by my own friends and colleagues: What if those I respected came to see me as co-opted by Hindu nationalism? One particular incident illustrates the ideological tightrope that I walked and exemplifies the participation required of the researcher if she really wishes to fully understand the world of interlocutors. Well into my research, I went to a Hindu nationalist rally, being videotaped by the movement's TV station, to hear a speech by an impassioned popular female ascetic whom I had interviewed earlier. As she was going to start her speech, the speaker spotted me in the audience and insisted (on the microphone) that I join her on stage; I was to sit behind her with other high-level Hindu nationalist dignitaries and organizers. She made everyone raise their fists and chant various Hindu nationalist slogans, all the while looking over at me to see if I was participating in a sufficiently impassioned manner. I managed my behavior on stage to suggest support for her Hindu nationalist message, all the while having nightmarish visions of being broadcast on the Hindu nationalist cable channel—"outed" as an apparent Hindu nationalist to the Indian progressives monitoring the movement.

I would argue that immersion into the feeling worlds of subjects is always problematic and risky, but especially so when the researcher is unsympathetic with her subjects' worldviews. Such immersion has an emotional impact on the researcher: Believing in the value of being collaborative with and loyal to women, I found it difficult to study Hindu nationalist women because they neither deserved my feminist loyalty nor my appreciation. Yet, at the same time, I sometimes found myself "understanding" and even liking some of my interviewees on a personal level. When such dissonance occurred, it could have immobilizing consequences.

Like other researchers of right-wing movements, I was surprised and pained to discover that I liked some of the activists I studied (Blee 1998, 2000; Klatch 1988; Koonz 1987; Mitchell 1993; Robben 1995). Blee points out that it is common for scholars of "loathsome political groups" to feel "painful emotional dissonance of discovering that participants in some of history's most horrific social movements can be charming and engaging in interview situations" (1998, 392). I formed close bonds with many teenage participants in the Samiti's paramilitary camps, who came to see me as a role model. Though I felt pride at being seen as a role model, I also felt conflicted about my veiling (i.e., pretending to be someone I was not). Yet while such a situation could have lent itself to employing feminist ethnographic methods (e.g., my being honest and disclosing my biases and political standpoints), it would have been dangerous for me to do so. Thus, although I found myself within a fieldwork situation theoretically compatible with feminist ethnographic principles, I could do little more than employ the "emotional labor" necessary for creating the image that I was a supportive role model, a position compatible with how the adolescent interlocutors saw me. Feeling guilty at pretending to be something that I was not, I resolved this, as Sluka had done in his covert research on the IRA in Northern Ireland, by reassuring myself that my only field option was being covert if I intended to capture the inner workings of a secretive right-wing group. This meant abandoning straightforward moves toward feminist ethnography, based as it is on a paradigm of truth and openness among researchers and interlocutors. The most I could do was resolve to avoid any action that would cause emotional or physical damage to interlocutors.

When confronted with a range of contradictory emotions (fear, revulsion, and anger to pride, bonding, camaraderie, and guilt), I often handled these by trying to suppress my feelings (Kleinman and Copp 1993), especially if they arose in the midst of an interview or a participant observation setting. Other strategies for continuing to hear and see things that evoked emotional contradictions were to discuss my experiences and feelings with trusted feminist friends, to intellectualize the emotional contradictions, and to focus on aspects of my data in order to downplay the emotional side of my research experiences (Lee-Treweek 2000). Perhaps, as a result of these combined strategies, I was better able to back-stage my research-related emotions and transfer to the front-stage academic strategies for devising more effective interview strategies. I attempted to intellectualize what I was hearing and seeing, in part, by focusing on the interview as a "technique" and, in part, by explaining to myself sociologically what I was seeing and hearing. Such strategies, of course, complicated the interview itself: I had to think fast to ask the right question, while at the same time processing my troubling feelings about the interlocutor's responses and developing a follow-up question to the person's response. When all these techniques failed, I would become physically ill and/or feel intellectually paralyzed, unable to look at and analyze my field notes and interview transcripts.

In his discussion of "ethnographic seduction,"[10] in which the researcher bonds emotionally with individual interlocutors and is sometimes "led astray unawares," Antonius Robben (1995) argues that such seduction "is a dimension of fieldwork that is especially prominent in research on violent political conflict because the interlocutors have great personal and political stakes in making the ethnographer adopt their interpretations" (83–84). Perhaps it is partially a result of such a dynamic that covertness comes to be two-sided—the researcher must be covert to get what interlocutors have and interlocutors need to use secrecy to control what they give out (see Huggins, Haritos-Fatouros, and Zimbardo 2002). At the center of such covertness, in the case of the researcher, at least, ethnographic seduction can be rooted in an immersion into the feeling worlds of one's subjects. Mitchell points out that such immersion is possible only through a researcher's being able to wash away the belief that a "cosmetic self" with its "fabricated affect," can exist behind a "real, dispassionate, objective self" (Mitchell 1993, 51). Yet, as Mitchell and others have pointed out, immersion into interlocutors' subjective worlds requires researchers to recognize that they cannot be "pure observers" who have no effect on the research subject. Rather, researchers are necessarily implicated in the production of the action and discourse that they study.[11] Such a research reality, observes Mitchell, is nonproblematic to researchers who are sympathetic to those they study. However, as my research and that of others has demonstrated, the role of a researcher in the production of knowledge becomes very problematic when studying those whose politics, values, and norms the researcher finds objectionable.

LEAVING THE FIELD: SHAKING OFF TRAINING

Deprogramming

After two weeks of veiled participant observation at the Samiti paramilitary camp, I had unwittingly internalized elements of the Hindu nationalist worldview that required considerable time and energy to neutralize once I had left the field. At these camps, physical training for women is justified as a way to empower women by helping them defend themselves against male violence. I had come to believe that the "self-defense" techniques being taught at the paramilitary camps were empowering for women. I was indignant about the seeming organizational inability of Indian feminist groups to reach women and girls to teach them self-defense. I felt that the Hindu nationalist movement genuinely filled the vacuum in a highly contested political arena by providing services sorely needed by urban middle-class Indian women.

It took many hours of postcamp discussions in my parents' home with my feminist secular historian husband to shake off the Samiti's camp indoctrination. My husband had spent hours debating with me the meaning of "empowerment" for women. He insisted that I compare the self-defense program taught by the Samiti to the feminist self-defense programs that I had taught in the past. He reminded me of the secular interpretations of Indian history that challenged the anti-Muslim ones being promoted by the Samiti. We examined together the reports by Indian civil liberties groups of human rights violations by the Hindu right. By the end of this process I began to see how deep the movement's hook had lodged within me. Having regained reflexive balance, I could begin rereading my field notes from the ideological indoctrination sessions at the Samiti's paramilitary camp.

The movement's Hindu nationalist, hate-filled, anti-Muslim ideology was transparent in these lectures.[12] This helped me understand how one's worldview is mediated through one's body and emotions, with embodied experiences perhaps having a more profound impact on our worldview than knowledge cognitively obtained. The important point is that if this was the impact that participating for twenty-one months in Samiti programs had on me—a secular-left feminist with extensive resources for obtaining critical analysis of Hindu nationalism—then one can imagine the impact of such experiences on a woman from a Hindu nationalist background with minimal access to similar resources.

False Dichotomies

Just as research methods are simplistically dichotomized into overt and covert, the emotional and intellectual elements of research are also wrongly separated. I started the research with a very simplified, polarized, emotional view of the movement—one was either for or against it. I was very clear about "whose side I was on," and convinced that the movement's activists were "wicked" or "insane." I therefore approached them with a considerable degree of revulsion and anger, in addition to the fear mentioned above. By the end of the fieldwork, things no longer seemed so simple and had moved to issues of "shifting identities." I better understood why there were outside supporters of the movement and why I came across Hindu nationalist activist women that I liked and could relate to. I had moved away from my earlier view of the movement as primarily a form of irrational extremism, having a tenuous contact with reality. I now considered it analytically and politically compelling to understand the Hindu nationalist movement as a critique of an existing situation and an attempt to propose an alternative (albeit a revolting one), as addressing ordinary people's desires and needs in ways that resonated with their daily concerns in a rational way, as grounded in the material conditions of reality.[13] For example, many Samiti women attended the camp because they were aware of violence against women and believed that they would learn self-defense techniques at the camp.

When I began this research I didn't have a clear idea about the "psychological costs" (Klatch 1988, 83) and the "emotional dangers" (Lee-Treweek 2000, 115)[14] involved in this type of a study. As Klatch puts it, "the desire to become emotionally involved and personally interested, as well as the fear of being 'found out' as a non-believer, are pushed to an extreme when studying a community which represents beliefs and values in opposition to one's own" (1988, 83). When one adds covert research to the above mix, the emotional dangers are intensified manifold. However, I did not fully prepare myself for the emotional repercussions of undertaking this study; my emotions in the field and after fieldwork came as quite a shock. The emotional aspects of research are rarely considered or planned for during mainstream methodology training.[15] Lee-Treweek points out that researchers need to think of and develop strategies to cope with "emotional dangers" because the emotional experience of research can turn out to be highly threatening to the self.[16]

I had started my fieldwork disagreeing with those feminists who characterized right-wing women as victims of false consciousness, unable to identify and act upon their gender interests (Dworkin 1983). I began the study aligning myself with those feminists who viewed right-wing women as rational, self-conscious actors, capable of analyzing and organizing around their interests (Bacchetta 1996; Basu et al. 1993; Blee 2001; De Grazia 1992; Klatch 1988; Koonz 1987; Sahgal and Yuvul-Davis 1992; Sarkar 1991). These remained intellectual and cognitive alignments. However, at the same time, I was unable to shake off the emotional belief that right-wing women are "brainwashed lackeys of patriarchy," an emotional positionality that runs counter to seeing such women as powerful agents who were collectively struggling for their interests. The alignment of my cognitive feminism and my emotional beliefs did not occur until the end of my fieldwork.

Another consequence of conducting covert research was the great stress that I endured as I tried to maintain the facade of a sympathetic participant of the movement. I used my married status as an excuse to leave and reenter the field,[17] in order to recuperate from the stress and fear brought on by the research. When I ultimately stopped collecting data, my decision to leave the field had been strongly influenced by the emotional costs of my covertness.[18]

AFTERWORD: LESSONS LEARNED

In the process of negotiating and debating the research methodology that would best serve my research goals, I had to grapple with ethical considerations. As I worked to veil aspects of my identity, issues about ethics became more and more visible to me. I took a number of steps before, during, and after the research to protect my informants and to ensure their confidentiality. I have changed names of people, places, dates, and identifying characteristics that might connect specific individuals to my work. I held off publishing my work for a while (which might arguably be due to a combination of fear and ethical issues), in order to most successfully separate myself from the field and its actors.

As for my recounting the violent, hate-filled, right-wing ideology of Hindu nationalism, different branches of the movement (including the Samiti) openly communicate their ideology in writing, speeches, and through the media. With respect to the violence committed by movement members and their facilitators, I relied exclusively on investigative reports published by human rights and civil liberties groups, on newspaper accounts, and published and unpublished studies of the Hindu right. I did not see any acts of violence or hear of any specific plans to carry it out. Had I been party to plans of violence, I would have had a very compelling ethical need to report it, with consequences for my continuing the research. My interviewees went out of their way to emphasize the peaceful nature of their organization and movement. I did not cross-question activists about their participation, planning, or witnessing of Hindu-Muslim riots because that would be contrary to their portrayal and performance of a nonviolent, victimized Hindu female self. It would have signaled to them that I didn't really believe them and was basing my questions on what they saw as the biased reports of secular media and human rights commissions. My experience underscores Sluka's caution that those conducting research on politically conflictual groups need to be sensitive to what sort of questions may be asked and what sort are taboo. While conducting research amongst IRA guerillas in Belfast, Sluka avoided asking questions about arms and violent operations (1995, 287–88).

The most ubiquitous ethical quandary that I faced was danger to myself: Just how much danger, be it physical or emotional, should a researcher realistically subject herself to? This question is particularly important for those directing student research in dangerous zones or groups, as one of the anonymous referees for *Women Fielding Danger* pointed out. I was frequently reminded at the paramilitary camp of the physical dangers associated with working undercover in an ethnographic "borderland" where feminist ethnographic openness collides with the field conditions that make such methods inadvisable and dangerous. If I had been fully open about myself and my research to camp participants, this would have posed great physical danger to myself, my family, and my friends in India. The fear of being "found out" never fully left me at any point during my field research.

In conclusion, we need to reconfigure the principles of feminist research to go beyond cooperative models of research to include investigative models, particularly when "studying up." We must consider how ethnographic identities are multiple, partial, shifting, staged, contradictory, and strategic, with the ethnographer "herself represent[ing] a constellation of social, linguistic and political forces" (Visweswaran 1994, 50). As feminists, we need to recraft the binary of overt-covert methodologies into a continuum of secrecy based on power dynamics within the field itself. Though the ideals of feminist researchers may be inspired by a commitment to social justice, strict adherence to such methods can preclude researching certain topics—particularly where the research subjects are more powerful than the researcher—and may rule out investigative research models. As feminist scholars we should be willing during and after fieldwork to focus on our emotions as repositories of data and include emotional labor as part of the cost of doing research, particularly on right-wing movements.

NOTES

1. I wish to thank Myra Marx Ferree, Kathy Blee, Martha Huggins, Michelle Rowley, Parna Sengupta, and Brendan LaRocque for their critical commentary and support in writing this article.

2. The Hindu nationalist movement has diversified branches of which the following are prominent: a parliamentary party (the BJP—Bhartiya Janata Party, the Indian People's Party), mass sociopolitical organizations (primarily the RSS—Rashtra Svayamsevak Sangh, National Volunteer's Association; and the VHP—Vishwa Hindu Parishad, World Hindu Council), women's wings (Mahila Morcha—Women's Front, Durga Vahini—Durga's Soldiers, and the Rashtra Sevika Samiti—National Female Volunteers' Association), and a paramilitary wing (Bajrang Dal). The movement refers to itself as the Sangh Parivar (Sangh Family) to emphasize its joint familial structure and lineage deriving from the RSS, the patriarch of the movement. The movement has expanded into party political process, civil society, and institutions of local and state governance with organizations in most arenas of civil society: education, labor, social services, policy-oriented think tanks, and mass media (owning publishing companies, a cable TV channel, and studios where audio-video programs are recorded for dissemination through a national distribution network).

3. For examples of women's participation in Hindu nationalist violence, see S. Hameed, R. Manorama, M. Ghose, S. George, F. Naqvi, and M. Thekaekara (2002), *How Has the Gujarat Massacre Affected Minority Women? The Survivors Speak,*

Fact-Finding by a Women's Panel, Citizens Initiative, Ahmedabad, April 16; People's Union for Civil Liberties and Shanti Abhiyan (2002), "Women's Perspectives on the Violence in Gujarat," in *Gujarat: Laboratory of the Hindu Rashtra*, ed. Indian Social Action Forum (New Delhi); P. Advanni, N. Hussain, R. Nayyar, E. N. Rammohan, A. Ahmed, P. Anand, R. Rajput, V. Dhagamvar (2002), *Report of the Committee constituted by the National Commission for Women to assess the Status and Situation of Women and Girl Children in Gujarat in the Wake of the Communal Disturbance* (Delhi: National Commission for Women).

For documentation of Hindu nationalist violence in anti-Muslim pogroms February/March 2002 in the state of Gujarat, see the following reports by national and international human rights organizations: K. M. Chenoy, S. P. Shukla, K. S. Subramanian, and Achin Vanaik (2002), *Gujarat Carnage 2002: A Report to the Nation* (New Delhi); K. M. Chenoy, V. Nagar, P. Bose, and V. Krishnan (2002), *Ethnic Cleansing in Ahmedabad: A Preliminary Report*, SAHMAT Fact Finding Team to Ahmedabad, March 10–11; National Human Rights Commission (2002), *Gujarat Carnage: A Report* (New Delhi: Popular Education and Action Center).

4. Stacey highlights what she calls "the feminist ethnographer's dilemma," in which the ethnographer inevitably betrays (and, Kamala Visweswaran adds, is betrayed by) a feminist principle. See Stacey 1991; Viswesvaran 1994.

5. This is not an uncommon goal for feminists in other parts of the world. For instance, Rebecca Klatch (1998) documents how she unexpectedly discovered the existence of an underground network of feminist and leftist activists "spying" on the right wing in the United States in her study of women in the New Right. On feminist research facilitating social change, see Naples 2003; Devault 1999; Gottfried 1996.

6. On the concept of a borderland, see Anzaldua 1999.

7. The Hindu nationalist movement has an elaborate narrative around the Partition of British India. Belonging to a family with paternal grandparents who migrated to India with their entire family because of the partition and having a father who spent his life in the Indian army fighting in India-Pakistan wars carries cultural legitimacy with the Hindu nationalists, which was why I foregrounded those aspects of my positionality.

8. Markers of marriage for women among upper-caste north Indian Punjabi Hindus typically include the following: *Sindhur*, red vermillion powder in the hair parting; a red *bindi*, a dot painted or stuck on forehead; gold and glass bangles; and a *mangalsutra*, a black-and-gold bead necklace.

9. The Hindu nationalists have a Web site called Hinduunity.org that maintains a "hit list" (now called "blacklist" because of people's threats to sue them) complete with a graphic of a hanging noose dripping blood that lists the names, addresses, phone numbers, e-mail addresses, and sometimes photos of people they regard as the "enemies of Hinduism." Included here are the names of several U.S.–based academics, along with famous people like Arundhati Roy and Pervez Musharraf (the military dictator of Pakistan).

10. Robben's definition of ethnographic seduction is based on Devereux (1976, 44–45), who defined seduction as emotional allurement rather than conscious manipulation. However, Robben uses seduction exclusively in its neutral meaning of "being led astray unawares" rather than as allurement or entrapment (1995, 83–84).

11. Mitchell's view is based on Camus' and Sartre's notion that "feeling is formed by the acts one performs."

12. My participant observation at the movement's paramilitary camps for women enabled me to challenge Indian feminist speculations that physical training at these camps could lead to women's empowerment that could potentially be used in the home against domestic violence. As I analyzed the physical training programs at the camp, I came to realize that the main emphasis was not on how to teach women to defend themselves in practical situations but rather to reinforce in them a visceral fear of the enemy Muslim male. For more information on how problematic was the idea of empowering women through physical training at the Samiti camps see Sehgal 2004, 2007.

13. I have Mary Layoun to thank for this insight.

14. Lee-Treweek defines emotional danger as a "serious threat to a researcher's psychological stability and sense of self derived by negative states induced by the research process" (2000, 115).

15. For instance, simple things like Klatch's advice about keeping two separate sets of field notes—one set on emotions and another set of "regular" field notes.

16. My primary concern during and after fieldwork was the physical danger my research might pose to me and to my family. Such thinking was influenced in part by contemporary attitudes in the research community that *physical* danger is the primary and most commonly experienced form of danger in ethnographic research. Very few research scholars have elaborated the emotional dangers associated with physically dangerous fieldwork. Indeed, it complicated my handling and openly addressing such emotional dangers because I felt that including material on my emotions in my field reports was risky because it could influence how others judged the validity of my research accounts. See how, for instance, Lee's *Dangerous Fieldwork* (1995) only mentions psychological or emotional distress a few times; the bulk of the book focuses on a research world of gangs, thugs, drugs, and physical danger. Also see Campbell 2001.

17. My coming and going was accepted by the Hindu nationalist women because I was viewed as a married woman who, within the Indian context, is seen as having primary duties toward their husbands and their husband's families. They assumed I had constraints on my time imposed by my husband and in-laws (I did nothing to correct that misconception).

18. Each interview meant traveling long distances by trains and buses to far-flung towns, and then a two-to-three-day commitment per interview during which I had to develop a relationship with the woman's family and repeatedly answer innumerable questions about my background and motivations before I was allowed to interview. They often invited me to stay with them for the duration of my visit to their town (which would have eased my financial strain), but the thought of being on guard so as not to blow my cover continuously for three or four days generally made that a terrifying proposition.

REFERENCES

Advanni, P., N. Hussain, R. Nayyar, E. N. Rammohan, A. Ahmed, P. Anand, R. Rajput, and V. Dhagamvar. (2002). *Report of the Committee Constituted by the National Commission for Women to Assess the Status and Situation of Women and Girl Children in Gujarat in the Wake of the Communal Disturbance*. Delhi: National Commission for Women.

Agar, Michael H. (1980). *The Professional Stranger: An Informal Introduction to Ethnography*. New York: Academic Press.

Alcoff, Linda. (1997). "Cultural Feminism versus Post-Structuralism: The Identity Crises in Feminist Theory." In *The Second Wave: A Reader in Feminist Theory*, edited by Linda Nicholson. New York: Routledge.

Anzaldua, Gloria. (1999). *La Frontera/Borderlands: The New Mestiza*. San Francisco: Aunt Lute Books.

Bacchetta, Paola. (1996). "Hindu Nationalist Women as Ideologues: The 'Sangh,' the 'Samiti' and Their Differential Concepts of the Hindu Nation." In *Embodied Violence: Communalizing Women's Sexuality in South Asia*, edited by Kumari Jayawardena and Malathi de Alwis. New Delhi: Kali for Women; London/Atlantic Highlands, NJ: Zed Books.

Bacchetta, Paola, and Margaret Power, eds. (2002). *Right-Wing Women: From Conservative to Extremists around the World*. New York: Routledge.

Basu, Amrita. (1995). "Feminism Inverted: The Gendered Imagery and Real Women of Hindu Nationalism." In *Women and the Hindu Right: A Collection of Essays*, edited by Tanika Sarkar and Urvashi Butalia. New Delhi: Kali for Women.

———. (1996). "Mass Movement or Elite Conspiracy? The Puzzle of Hindu Nationalism." In *Contesting the Nation: Religion, Community and the Politics of Democracy in India*, edited by David Ludden. Philadelphia: University of Pennsylvania Press.

Basu, Tapan, Pradeep Dutta, Sumit Sarkar, and Tanika Sarkar. (1993). *Khaki Shorts and Saffron Flag: A Critique of the Hindu Right*. Tracts for the Times, vol. 1. New Delhi: Orient Longman.

Blee, Kathleen M. (1993). "Evidence, Empathy, and Ethics: Lessons from Oral Histories of the Klan." *Journal of American History* 80 (September), 2.

———. (1998). "White Knuckle Research: Emotional Dynamics in feildwork with Racist Activists." *Qualitative Sociology* 21, no. 4.

———. (2000). "White on White: Interviewing Women in U.S. White Supremacist Groups." In *Racing Research, Researching Race: Methodological Dilemmas in Critical Race Studies*, edited by France Winddance Twine and Jonathan W. Warren. New York: New York University Press.

———. (2002). *Inside Organized Racism: Women in the Hate Movement*. Berkeley and Los Angeles: University of California Press.

Campbell, Rebecca. (2001). *Emotionally Involved: The Impact of Researching Rape*. New York: Routledge.

Chenoy, K. M., S. P. Shukla, K. S. Subramanian, and Achin Vanaik. (2002). *Gujarat Carnage 2002: A Report to the Nation*. New Delhi.

Chenoy K. M., V. Nagar, P. Bose, and V. Krishnan. (2002). *Ethnic Cleansing in Ahmedabad: A Preliminary Report*. SAHMAT Fact Finding Team to Ahmedabad, March 10–11.

De Grazia, Victoria. (1992). *How Fascism Ruled Women: Italy, 1922–1945*. Berkeley and Los Angeles: University of California Press.

Devault, Marjorie L. (1999). *Liberating Method: Feminism and Social Research*. Philadelphia: Temple University Press.

Douglas, Jack D. (1976). *Investigative Social Research: Individual and Team Field Research*. Beverly Hills, CA: Sage.

Dworkin, Andrea. (1983). *Right-Wing Women*. New York: Perigee.

Ellis, Carolyn. (1995). "Emotional and Ethical Quagmires in Returning to the Field." *Journal of Comtemporary Ethnography* 24, 68–98.

Fielding, Nigel. (1982). "Observational Research on the National Front." In *Social Research Ethics*, edited by M. Blumer, 80–104. New York: Holmes and Meier.

———. (1993). "Mediating the Message: Affinity and Hostility in Research on Sensitive Topics." In *Researching Sensitive Topics*, edited by Claire M. Renzetti and Raymond M. Lee. Newbury Park, CA: Sage.

Franks, Myfanwy. (2002). "Feminisms and Cross-ideological Feminist Social Research: Standpoint, Situatedness and Positionality—Developing Cross-Ideological Feminist Research." *Journal of International Women's Studies* 3.

Gluck, Sherna, and Daphne Patai. (1991). *Women's Words: The Feminist Practice of Oral History*. New York: Routledge.

Goffman, Erving. (1966). *Behavior in Public Places: Notes on the Social Organization of Gatherings*. New York: Free Press.

———. (1969). *The Presentation of Self in Everyday Life*. London: Allen Lane.

Gottfried, Heidi. (1996). *Feminism and Social Change: Bridging Theory and Practice*. Urbana: University of Illinois Press.

Guba, Egon G., and Yvonna S. Lincoln. (2004). "Competing Paradigms in Qualitative Research: Issues and Approaches." In *Approaches to Qualitative Research: A Reader on Theory and Practice*, edited by Sharlene Nagy Hesse Biber and Michelle Yaiser. New York: Oxford University Press.

Hameed, S., R. Manorama, M. Ghose, S. George, F. Naqvi, and M. Thekaekara. (2002). "How Has the Gujarat Massacre Affected Minority Women? The Survivors Speak." Fact-Finding by a Women's Panel, Citizens Initiative, Ahmedabad.

Harding, Sandra. (1991). *Whose Science? Whose Knowledge? Thinking from Women's Lives*. Ithaca, NY: University of Cornell Press.

Hartsock, Nancy. (1998). *The Feminist Standpoint Revisited and Other Essays*. Boulder, CO: Westview Press.

Hill-Collins, Patricia. (2000). *Black Feminist Thought: Knowledge, Consciousness, and the Politics of Empowerment*. New York: Routledge.

Huggins, Martha, Mika Haritos-Fatouros, and Philip G. Zimbardo. (2002). *Violence Workers: Police Torturers and Murderers Reconstruct Brazillian Attrocities*. Berkeley and Los Angeles: University of California Press.

Hutalia, Urvashi. (2001). "Women and Communal Conflict in India: New Challenges for the Women's Movement in India." In *Victims, Perpetrators or Actors? Gender, Armed Conflict, and Political Violence*, edited by Caroline Moser and Fiona Clark. New Dalhi, India: Kali for Women.

Klatch, Rebecca E. (1987). *Women of the New Right*. Philadelphia: Temple University Press.

———. (1988). "The Methodological Problems of Studying a Politically Resistant Community." *Studies in Qualitative Methodology* 1, 73–88.

Klein, Duneili. (1983). "How To Do What We Want To Do. . . ." In *Theories of Women's Studies*, edited by Gloria Bowles and Renate Duelli Klein. London: Routledge.

Kleinman, Sherryl, and Martha Copp. (1993). *Emotions and Fieldwork*. Newbury Park, CA: Sage.

Koonz, Claudia. (1987). *Mothers in the Fatherland: Women, the Family and Nazi Politics*. New York: St. Martin's Press.

Lee, Raymond M. (1995). *Dangerous Fieldwork*. Thousand Oaks, CA: Sage.

Lee-Treweek, Geraldine. (2000). "The Insight of Emotional Danger: Research Experiences in a Home for Older People." In *Danger In the Field—Risk and Ethics in Social Research*, edited by Geraldine Lee-Treweek and Stephanie Linkogle. London: Routledge.

Mitchell, Richard G., Jr. (1993). *Secrecy and Fieldwork*. Qualitative Research Methods, vol. 29. Newbury Park, CA: Sage.

Naples, Nancy. (2003). *Feminism and Method: Ethnography, Discourse, and Activist Research*. New York: Routledge.

National Human Rights Commission. (2002). *Gujarat Carnage: A Report*. New Delhi: Popular Education and Action Center.

Nordstrom, Carolyn, and Antonius C. G. M. Robben, eds. (1995). *Fieldwork under Fire: Contemporary Violence and Survival*. Berkeley and Los Angeles: University of California Press.

People's Union for Civil Liberties and Shanti Abhiyan. (2002). "Women's Perspectives on the Violence in Gujarat." In *Indian Social Action Forum*, edited by Gujarat. New Delhi: Laboratory of the Hindu Rashtra.

Robben, Antonius C. G. M. (1995). "The Politics of Truth and Emotion among Victims and Perpetrators of Violence." In *Fieldwork Under Fire: Contemporary Studies of Violence and Survival*, edited by Carolyn Nordstrom and Antonius C. G. M. Robben, 81–103. Berkeley and Los Angeles: University of California Press.

Sahgal, Gita, and Nira Yuval-Davis. (1992). "Introduction: Fundamentalism, Multiculturalism, and Women in Britain." In *Refusing Holy Orders: Women and Fundamentalism in Britain*, edited by Gita Sahgal and Nira Yuval-Davis. London: Virago Press.

Sehgal, Meera. (2004). *Reproducing the Feminine Citizen-Warrior: The Case of the Rashtra Sevika Samiti, a Right-wing Women's Organization in India*. PhD diss., University of Wisconsin–Madison, Department of Sociology.

———. (2007). "Manufacturing a Feminized Siege Mentality: Hindu Nationalist Paramilitary Camps for Women in India." *Journal of Contemporary Ethnography*, Special Edition on Racist Right-Wing Movements, 36, no. 2, 165–83.

Sarkar, Tanika. (1991). "The Woman as Communal Subject: Rashtra Sevika Samiti and the Ram Janmabhoomi Movement." *Economic and Political Weekly*, August 31.

———. (1996). "Heroic Women, Mother Goddesses: Family and Organization in Hindutva Politics," In *Women and the Hindu Right: A Collection of Essays*, edited by Kali Sarkar and Urvashi Butalia. New Delhi: Kali for Women.

Sluka, Jeffery A. (1995). "Reflections on Managing Danger in Fieldwork: Dangerous Anthropology in Belfast." In *Fieldwork under Fire: Contemporary Violence and Survival*, edited by Carolyn Nordstrom and Antonius C. G. M. Robben, 276–94. Berkeley and Los Angeles: University of California Press.

Smith, Dorothy. (1993). "Knowing a Society from Within: A Woman's Standpoint." In *Social Theory: The Multicultural and Classic Readings*, edited by Charles Lemert. Boulder, CO: Westview Press.

Stacey, Judith. (1991). "Can There Be a Feminist Ethnography?" In *Women's Words: The Feminist Practice of Oral History*, edited by S. B. Gluck and D. Patai, 111–19. New York: Routledge.

Visweswaran, Kamala. (1994). *Fictions of Feminist Ethnography*. Minneapolis: University of Minnesota Press.

Williams, Mark, and Jehangir Poch. (2005). "San Francisco Professor Fears Hindu Retaliation." *San Francisco Chronicle*, June 23.

14

Studying Violent Male Institutions: Cross-Gender Dynamics in Police Research—Secrecy and Danger in Brazil and Guatemala

Martha K. Huggins and Marie-Louise Glebbeek[1]

To promote discussions of methodological issues associated with cross-gendered research in social science, we each will elaborate our field research on Latin American police—Glebbeek on Guatemala and Huggins on Brazil. This chapter, which is divided into six parts and a conclusion, begins with a synthesis of some feminist theoretical discussions about intra- and intergender interviewing, "Feminist Research: Women Interviewing Women and Men," followed by our own initial experiences locating and interviewing policemen in our own field sites, "Women Researching Men." In the body of this chapter we explore "Contextual Backgrounds," "Confronting Secrecy," "Soliciting and Hearing Atrocities," and "Tackling Ethical Dilemmas." Our conclusion, "Listening, Believing, Surviving," reviews the principal challenges of our research.

Having explored the commonalities of our two research projects—each of which was separated from the other in time by five years—we present five working propositions about women studying organizations dominated numerically and structurally by men. First, feminist scholarship provides some guidelines for such research, but its applicability is neither direct nor immediate. Second, for example, much cross-gender research requires negotiating and maintaining power differentials between researcher and researched. Third, particularly in cross-gender research on secrecy and danger, intergender dynamics can thwart some research objectives and often serendipitously promote others. Fourth, intergender dynamics can complicate the ethical dilemmas associated with research on powerful agents and agencies of the state. Finally, the emotional flexibility associated with such intergender research is epistemologically relevant for understanding research outcomes.

FEMINIST RESEARCH:
WOMEN INTERVIEWING WOMEN AND MEN

Feminist methodology provides useful guidelines for women researching women, a case of intragender research. One important objective of such research methodology is to eliminate or reduce power differentials between researcher and interviewee. In Pamela Cotterill's words, "This model aims to produce non-hierarchical, non-manipulative research relationships which have the potential to overcome the separation between the researcher and the researched" (1992, 594). Stanley and Wise (1983) find unjustifiable women researchers treating their interviewees as "object." Yet Stanley and Wise (in Cotterill 1992, 603) suggest that a respondent is always vulnerable—whether a woman or a man—suggesting limits to reducing power differentials between researcher and researched.

In response, many feminists argue that the only honest approach is for a researcher to make herself just as vulnerable. The goal for some feminist researchers is to develop a "friendship" with female interviewees, because as Diane Reay (1996: 64–65) argues, "Distancing of the researcher from the researched results in their inscription as 'other.'" This can presumably be eliminated by an interviewer's investing her own identity in the research relationship and "by answering respondents' questions, sharing knowledge and experience [with them], and giving [them] support when asked" (Cotterill 1992, 594). In her study of "motherhood," Ann Oakley (1981), for example, was open to interviewees taking the initiative in defining her relationship with them; she encouraged and was asked personal questions, a process that established "a relatively intimate and non-hierarchical relationship." Oakley argues that this fostered the success of her study (47). For Oakley, therefore, the goal of feminist research is "progression to friendship . . . [because] . . . the pretense of neutrality on the interviewer's part is counterproductive: participation demands alignment" (46).

For Rapoport and Rapoport (1976, 9), this alignment can be accomplished through "collaborative research . . . [that] engages both the interviewer and respondent in a joint enterprise" of forming a relationship with one another such that research methods are jointly chosen, objectives are identified, and the researched assists in interpreting data. Some feminist critics of such a "collaborative progression toward friendship" have pointed out that women's relationships that are structured by more than gender, class, ethnic/racial, and age differences may in fact complicate a "progression toward friendship." There are a number of other drawbacks for the researcher in becoming an interviewee's friend, for friendships too can be exploitive and manipulative on both sides. And the interviewer-as-friend can be pulled into the interviewee's discursive universe in a way that hinders going beyond surface presentations and appearances (see Cain 1986; Cotterill 1992; Gelsthorpe and Morris 1990; Phoenix 1994; Reay 1996).

But while it may be valuable in research "by, on, and . . . for women" (Stanley and Wise 1983, 17) to reduce power differentials between researcher and researched, is this strategy practicable, productive, or safe in women's research on men? Lorraine Gelsthorpe (1990, 92) maintains that it is quite one thing to break down power differentials between women researchers and their female interviewees and quite another to do this when a female investigator's interviewees are men. Developing this critique, Maureen Cain (1986, 262) argues that while some people are "'entitled' to become research subjects," others should legitimately remain "objects" of research. Cain explains that if she were to interview members of the International Association of Chiefs of Police (IACP) about their organization and its activities, it would be neither productive nor useful to engage these men in feminist "collaborative research." As Martha Huggins (1998) found in several interviews with IACP members, allowing these police officials to guide the subject and course of her research and structure how their involvement in Latin American police training was to be written (something that they very much wanted to do) would have produced a version of IACP police assistance to Latin America that privileged their keeping their secrets over Huggins's discovering them. Cain is correct that some interviewees must remain objects of study, with hierarchy in such cases being necessary and legitimate.

But does hierarchy shift in the process of conducting research? Many feminists (see Cotterill 1992; Gelsthorpe 1990; Oakley 1981; Phoenix 1994; Reay 1996) have pointed out that over the course of a research project, power relations between researcher and researched may change such that at some points the researcher has more power over the researched, while the interviewee may have more power at other points. This is as true for intragender (Cotterill 1992; Reay 1996) research as for cross-gender research (Cunningham-Burley 1984; Gelsthorpe 1990), as some scholarship in this volume demonstrates and to which this analysis may contribute as well. Leveling power relations between researcher and researched could in fact disguise power as interactive and negotiated and as shifting throughout an interview, a fact not to be disguised for those wanting to learn about the richness of fieldwork settings.

The ways in which cross-gender interviewer/interviewee power negotiation can complicate ethical and safety issues and affect a woman's conducting research have seldom been explicitly elaborated for cross-gender research. Some aspects of this were considered in Lorna McKee and Margaret O'Brien's (1983) research on fatherhood and in Gelsthorpe's (1990) study of men's prisons. However, neither of these explicitly elaborated the implications of gender and gendered power for research ethics and for a researcher's affective relationship to interviewees, to herself, and to the research project. Reflexivity that combines subjective emotional feelings with "objective" data is often seen as unscientific—a premise of positivism roundly criticized by many feminist methodologists.

Feminist critics of positivism (Campbell 2001; Jaggar 1989; Krieger 1991; Reinharz 1979) maintain that "feelings, . . . beliefs, and values . . . shape . . . research and are a natural part of inquiry": "Emotions influence our research, and our research can affect us emotionally" (Campbell 2001, 15). Consequently, feminist researchers explore their own research experience, including feelings and emotions, rather than dismissing these as unscientific and irrelevant. Their objective is to "record the impact of the research on themselves" (Gelsthorpe 1990, 94), a strategy used by Rebecca Campbell in an analysis of women interviewing female rape victims. Recognizing that scholarship on some "topics—trauma, abuse, death, illness, health problems, violence, crime [can touch] . . . emotional nerves within the researcher," Campbell (2001, 33) argues that these subjective responses are legitimate aspects of research, as our analysis here hopes to demonstrate through its discussions of intergender power, struggles over secrecy, management of danger, and negotiated ethics.

WOMEN RESEARCHING MEN

Within the context of a study about danger, violence, and secrecy, in 1993 Martha Huggins, together with Mika Haritos-Fatouros and Philip Zimbardo (2002), began conducting interviews with Brazilian police who had been torturers or assassins during Brazil's twenty-one-year military period (1964–1985). A middle-aged U.S. academic and principal and primary interviewer for the team's study, she had already explored violence and crime in Brazil for eighteen years.

In 1998 Marie-Louise Glebbeek (2000, 2001, 2003) launched her study of Guatemala's newly organized Civil Police force. As a young female doctoral student from the Netherlands, her objective was to examine the impact of democratization on political state police organizational climate and operations. When Glebbeek's research began, her exposure to Guatemala and its police was primarily academic.

Setting aside the obvious differences between us—e.g., age, experience, length of time previously in the particular field—we actually shared a number of important status characteristics in common: Both of us were academic women and Caucasian foreign nationals within our Latin American research settings. We were either primarily (Glebbeek) or exclusively (Huggins) interviewing men. We sought information on things held secret and therefore had to overcome difficult research hurdles before our study could even begin. The most central of these hurdles was discovering how to penetrate the sheath of secrecy that stood between ourselves and our research objectives. Along these lines, before entering the field we each prepared—as far as we could predict or imagine them—for the problems associated with securing interviewees and getting them to tell their stories. However, once in the field, our problems expanded far beyond our initial expectations.

As research complications mounted, we each tended to personalize our data collection problems, assuming they were unique to place, situation, interview technique, and specific interviewer/interviewee dynamics. It was only after our research had ended—as a result of exchanging information about each other's research experiences—that we recognized that a number of problems we had considered purely personal stumbling blocks or advantages were very likely general correlates of secrecy compounded by gender and its intersection with age, nationality, class, and race/ethnicity. While we still recognize that the impact of gender on research and on research outcomes cannot be established outside a comparative analysis of male and female researchers (see Gelsthorpe 1990), our initial discoveries suggest the role of various sociocultural constructions of female gender on research processes—a subject that certainly deserves future comparative analyses and incorporation into methodologies about cross-gender research.

CONTEXTUAL BACKGROUNDS

Glebbeek in Guatemala

In 1998 I began a four-year study (1998–2002) of the newly established Guatemalan National Civil Police (Policia Nacional Civil, PNC), created after the December 1996 peace accord[2] between the Guatemalan government and the former guerrilla group Unidad Revolucionaria Nacional Guatemalteca (URNG). I was launching my anthropological investigation at a historic moment of democratization in Guatemala, with the goal of documenting the objectives, implementation, and consequences of Guatemalan police reform from a variety of perspectives. It complicated my research that, besides needing to penetrate a police wall of silence, I had to interview police and nonpolice groups with conflicting ideologies and practices.

One set of interviewees, the Civil Police, had members who had violated or were currently violating human rights. Another set, the nongovernmental human rights organizations along with MINUGUA, the United Nations Verification Commission supervising the Guatemalan peace process, were documenting and denouncing these and other Civil Police illegalities. A third set of interviewees, the Spanish Civil Guard (Guardia

Civil Espanola) that was training Guatemala's new Civil Police force, was professionally beholden to a fourth set of interviewees, the European Union officials who were funding and monitoring Guardia training. A final group of interviewees, the general population, could be or might have been victims of police violence.

One result of interviewing such potentially disparate and incompatible groups, organizations, and interests was that, on any given day, I would hear accounts that severely clashed with one another. One day, for instance, I interviewed a representative from MINUGUA who described democratic policing as demonstrating respect for human rights—e.g., using dialogue and mediation to solve conflict rather than violence and repression. Later that same day, a Spanish Guardia police trainer explained that contemporary democratic Spain was "worse off" than it had been under Franco's dictatorship—when criminality was repressed by hard-handed authoritarianism. The police trainer considered this old-style policing as positive, an attitude he may have communicated to his Guatemalan trainees. Because of the necessity to give each group's position equal time, I always felt pressured to choose between each group's different worldview, with each believing that its version of "reality" was correct and that the other groups' were distorted.

Getting into the Field

Before my first research trip to Guatemala, doubting that officials of the new Civil Police force would let me study their institution, I secured what seemed a valuable research contact, set up through the University of Utrecht in the Netherlands, where I was preparing my doctoral dissertation proposal. However, I learned very quickly that this Guatemala City contact was useless: Because the Guatemalan research institute had not studied the Civil Police organization, it asserted that it could not help. Left with no advance contacts, I searched for an individual or organization that could arrange a meeting with a Civil Police official. However, one of my first contacts was with MINUGUA, an organization unlikely to provide any introductions to a Civil Police official: The Civil Police were as critical of MINUGUA as MINUGUA was of Civil Police reform.

The first big break came from Dutch Embassy officials who were in contact with Spanish Guardia officials. Through the Embassy's local associates at the European Union, an interview was granted with a Spanish Guardia official. But, perhaps because this official had been "strongly encouraged" to facilitate my research, he initially resisted doing anything for me: Feared by most NGOs, the Guardia colonel let me know that my Spanish was terrible, that I was naive and ignorant, and that the project would be a disaster. Yet despite the colonel's uncooperative bluntness, he eventually facilitated my research at the Civil Police Academy and at a Civil Police precinct.

At my first meeting with the Spanish Guardia colonel, I had explained that I hoped to conduct research at the Guatemalan Civil Police Academy. I wanted to start my Civil Police "career" where every Guatemalan policeman begins it. The Spanish Guardia colonel introduced me to police academy staff, who then introduced me to the academy's director. With everything apparently in order, I went to the Civil Police Academy for my first day of fieldwork: I was to become a "student" in the academy's fifth class of new recruits. Arriving at the academy's gate—bolstered by the confidence that I had properly prepared for this day—I was stopped and told that I could not enter. After some minutes of talking and explaining, I was escorted to an education department official who solved the misunderstanding by providing a letter authorizing my research. This experience drove home to me once again the power of others over my research.

In theory, at the academy I had ample opportunities to observe and interview recruits. In fact, fitting interviews into my and the recruits' daily schedules was difficult. As a full participant in many academy training activities—marching to breakfast, lunch, and dinner and attending the theoretical, practical, and self-defense classes—I had trouble fitting interviewing and observation into my and other students' schedules.

Interviewing the female recruits[3] was much easier than obtaining and conducting interviews with male recruits, instructors, and officers. During the afternoon siesta, I rested in the female barracks and chatted informally with the women, reducing formal differences between myself and them as they styled each other's and my hair and talked about common interests, an example of Oakley's (1981) "progression to friendship." From these informal conversations, I then segued into formal interviews—asking about the women's motives for joining the Civil Police, their experiences at the academy and their professional aspirations.

Getting these same questions answered by male recruits, instructors, and officers was much more difficult because the academy's intergender interaction rules prohibited men and women from getting to know one another outside official learning settings. Since I did not want to break academy rules, it was only possible to build rapport with the males when such interaction was officially permitted—at a formal meeting outside of class. But such meetings did not lend themselves to establishing the kind of rapport that I had with the female recruits.

As a result, most interviews with the males that I had known at the academy had to be carried out after my police academy fieldwork had ended. It was then that I learned that, as inhibiting as the intergender interaction rules had been for establishing the rapport necessary to carry out my police academy research, these rules had shielded me from unwanted personal advances by male police and officials. Such advances would seriously complicate my postacademy police precinct research, a gender-related problem exacerbated by my need to penetrate a police wall of silence about abuses.

Indeed, the road to further research was far from clear. Being foreign, young, and a woman made me feel extremely vulnerable at the predominantly male police academy and precinct. Likewise, Gelsthorpe (1990, 95) and her female research associate remember feeling "quite out of place" at a Birmingham, England, men's prison. It magnified my own feelings of vulnerability that I was unable to think of any way to protect myself if a research situation got out of hand. One idea was to hire a male research assistant, but I thought the police would be more trusting—and tell more confidences—if I worked alone. In the end, the main precaution that I took was to enroll in self-defense classes and purchase a mobile phone—apart from trusting luck.

Gender Opens and Shuts Doors

While physical danger was ubiquitous during my fieldwork, the most pervasive daily challenge was simply having prospective interviewees take me seriously. It was extremely difficult to get the director of the Civil Police to give me an interview; it took several weeks just to get in to see him. It took months to make appointments for interviews with government and political and police officials, only to find these canceled or the official failing to show up. Male researchers had recounted similar experiences, but certain routes for getting interviews may be more available to men than to women. For example, one male researcher confided to Martha Huggins that he gets interviews with police and political officials by inviting them out for a drink. As this scholar explained, "I just get a few drinks under a man's belt and he tells me all that I need to know." This option was not available to us without risking an increase in the problems that could threaten our professional status and personal safety.

Yet one problem I struggled with constantly—the lack of seriousness accorded to me and my study—actually opened some avenues to information. I could just show up at officials' offices without an appointment—something that presumably a naive young foreign woman "would do"—take them by surprise, use a little charm—something they expected a young woman to do—and get an interview on the spot. Somewhat later, after I had gained access to a police precinct, I was allowed to navigate relatively freely, perhaps because, as a young woman with imperfect Spanish, I was considered unthreatening.

Still, at the same time, a series of ongoing complications were associated with my being young and a woman. Most interviews had to be held, for privacy reasons, during a policeman's off-duty hours, often resulting in an evening appointment. Such meetings were frequently misunderstood as "dates." Especially the middle-rank police officers made remarks about my personal appearance or "availability": "What is the color of your eyes?" "Are you a natural blonde?" "What are you doing later today?" "Do you like to dance?" I was unprepared for such comments in my professional role. Over and over again, I had to explain that I was not "available" and that I was solely interested in the interviewee as a civil policeman. Yet because my study also dealt with the person behind the uniform, I had to ask personal questions—resulting in my having to balance a thin line between an interviewee's personal and strictly professional interests. Nonetheless, police interviewees construed my personal questions as wanting to be romantic.

Huggins in Brazil

For several reasons, my experiences with male torturers and assassins worked out differently from what Glebbeek encountered in Guatemala. The most challenging overall aspect of my research was secrecy—their keeping it and my wanting it. My research challenges were not primarily associated with interviewees' interpreting my behavior as an opportunity for romantic contact. I assumed that this was due to my being middle-aged in an extremely youth-oriented culture, or a combination of this and my having secured some key interviewees through a university course I was teaching on comparative policing, or through another interviewee who was a prospective interviewee's trusted friend. Perhaps, as an academic known to have studied Brazil for decades and in a position of authority because of this and due to my teaching course on policing, male power was somewhat reduced. In the process, a distribution of asymmetrical power developed in my favor that I was not willing to abandon for a collaborative research agenda with these men.

Getting into the Field

Initially, the greatest stumbling block to my research was locating torturers to interview. In 1993, when Mika Haritos-Fatouros, Phil Zimbardo, and I met in São Paulo to seek police who had tortured or murdered during Brazil's military period, several unexpected realities of the field made it clear that our sample "wish list" would be exceedingly difficult to obtain and pursue. Not only were others reluctant to identify former "violence workers," as we labeled our prospective police interviewees, but when we did find them, these police did not want to be interviewed. Trying to be as invisible as possible, the violence worker perpetrators sought to put that part of their lives behind them.

Before entering the field, my research colleagues and I had worked out a method for indirectly finding serially violent police. It was assumed that there was no direct way of securing police interviewees who had tortured and murdered. Our team's indirect strategy for netting possible violence workers was to limit the sample to police who had been in units known to have carried out the heaviest repression during Brazil's military period.[4] It was reasoned that a policeman who had been in such a unit, in a country dominated by a national security ideology, would have either himself committed extreme violence or been present when violence was taking place.

But the police whose names were actually already on human rights groups' published lists of known torturers and murderers were simply unwilling to be interviewed, exercising their unchallengeable power over a researcher wanting to learn about them and their misdeeds. Most of these men, successfully retired, certainly had good reasons to feel abandoned by a police institution that had failed to come to their defense against human rights groups' and journalists' "persecution" of them. But by self-censoring their disclosures about violence, they seemed to protect the very police institution that had "abandoned" them. Having already experienced public exposure and socially and sometimes even professionally negative censure for their violence, these former police feared new problems if their interviews somehow became public, even though they were assured that any reference to their interviews would maintain their anonymity.

Suspecting that those who did not identify as strongly with their police organization might talk more openly about their violence, I also sought interviews at a prison for incarcerated police—even though such police had not been incarcerated for having tortured or murdered during Brazil's military period. It was my initial assumption that those no longer in policing would talk more openly about their own and others' atrocities. In fact, an interviewee's openness did depend upon how he had left his last police position—successfully retired or humiliatingly expelled.[5] However, overall, there was equally great reluctance among interviewees—whether in the police, retired from policing, or in prison—to disclose their own and their organization's secrets. Police who talked most openly tended to have moved farthest away from their prior police identities. For example, Jorge, an imprisoned "born-again" former executioner, wanted to be interviewed about his past because he now saw himself as "a different person under the Lord." In contrast, Vinnie, although expelled from his militarized police force and also incarcerated but not a Pentecostal, was very guarded about his participation in hundreds of death squad executions.

Gender Opens Doors

While the need to maintain secrecy clearly had a great impact upon interviewees' willingness to disclose hidden information, I also wondered if being a woman, along with other related status characteristics, might be interacting with secrecy to simultaneously grease some tongues and silence other ones. I discovered that a combination of my gender, "insider knowledge," professional status, class, color, and temporary residence in

Brazil—the latter making me a cultural "outsider"—very likely combined to help secure some interviewees and to produce among them some greater openness and some silences. For example, it very likely contributed to interviewees' openness that I was not Brazilian and therefore would presumably be taking their interview disclosures away to the United States. While the interviewees were assured that I would not use their real names in any research report, it could have increased interviewees' confidence that before any book could be written, I had to spend a good deal of time in my own country, rather than staying in Brazil where I could come into contact with Brazilian journalists or human rights activists who would want my information immediately. In other words, my status as a cultural outsider may have made interviewees more willing to open up to me. Yet some interviewee information very likely came more slowly because of concern for my "feminine sensibilities," as defined in Brazil, than if I had been a man. It is possible that the relative absence of graphic descriptions of scenes of torture or murder resulted from the male policemen's belief that a woman should not hear such things. At least one interviewee said so explicitly. However, at the same time, being a woman may have led me to be seen as more "forgiving" and "nurturing," possibly inviting some interviewees to express stronger emotions about their violence (e.g., crying) that they might not have shared with a male interviewer. This seems to have been one of Gelsthorpe's (1990, 97–98) experiences in her study of male prisoners.

By contrast, my nongendered academic "insider knowledge" about policing, both in Brazil and elsewhere, may have led to my acceptance into interviewees' work worlds as a partial professional "insider." In a variety of cultural settings it has been found that if those interviewing police are recognized as "insiders" (with police, of course, considering themselves the most legitimate insiders), the interviewer will be more readily accepted by prospective police interviewees. While an academic specialist on the police may not ever be a "real" insider, having any kind of respectable insider knowledge was perceived by Brazilian interviewees as preferable to being a total "outsider." Just the same, whatever academic knowledge of policing I could demonstrate to my police interviewees, as a woman researching a predominantly male institution I still may have been limited in how much I could ever be considered a full occupational insider.

Nevertheless, the fact that I was primarily an academic, rather than a human rights activist or a journalist, clearly opened some doors: At least half of the interviewees remarked that they would accept being interviewed because, as an academic, I was "objective," while journalists and human rights activists "are not." This greater trust in university academic interviewers was also found in Payne's (2000) research on men in Latin American "uncivil movements." However, if an academic is willing to use journalistic exposé methods that confront interviewees with talking or suffering even greater stigma in an article that they have not had a chance to influence, some information might be gained that "value-free" academic research would not be able to secure. Of course, this is precisely why interviewees said that they did not trust journalists (see Huggins et al. 2002, chap. 4). Therefore, I did not employ such methods with my interviewees, selecting instead presumably more ethical and subtle interview strategies.

Color differences and Brazilian definitions of color "respectability" very likely structured my acceptability and nurtured interviewee openness. But while much of Brazil's population is "Black" by U.S. definitions of racial descent and generally accorded lower social status, in fact, of my interviewees all but two (neither of them atrocity perpetrators) were white or light to medium brown. Therefore, it is not clear how the color differences between interviewees and me might have affected interview outcomes. But it is probable that my own pale Anglo-whiteness—in a sociocultural system that values light skin and associated physical characteristics above the darker ones—may have reinforced my presumed higher status relative to that of the interviewees. The impact of such a color difference in and of itself on interviewees' willingness to participate in the study, and their openness during the interview itself, is clearly a matter of speculation at this point, though certainly of great interest.

In the end, I assume that a combination of characteristics associated with my status—being female, foreign, an academic whose work was known to some prospective interviewees, of a higher social class than most interviewees, and of a socially valued skin color—helped me secure interviewees and promoted somewhat greater willingness among them to disclose valued secrets about theirs and others' police atrocities. Much like a bartender or beautician, I was in the role of a "friendly stranger"—a relatively unthreatening outsider to whom interviewees felt they could disclose their feelings, complaints, and deepest secrets. Whether their assumptions were correct or not, believing them apparently led interviewees to open up to a "friendly stranger" in ways they might not do otherwise. While in the end I could not assess precisely how gender, insider occupational knowledge, status as an academic, and the combined variables of class and color, along with my position as a cultural outsider, influenced interviewees' willingness to be interviewed and shaped the amount and types of disclosures they made, the combination of these factors mostly affected interview outcomes positively.

CONFRONTING SECRECY

Glebbeek: Cautiously Approaching Guatemalan Police Secrets

I entered the Guatemala City police precinct where I was to conduct interviews filled with doubts and ominous questions. Would police be open about things normally held secret? How could I be objective with police whose organization had been responsible for great atrocities—murders, mutilations, torture, disappearances? Would the police be objective? I recognized that entering secret police worlds would require strategy, stealth, perseverance, and focus. I would have to be keenly aware of the interview atmosphere and the timing of questions. Whether an interview was formal and structured or informal and ad hoc would depend upon the situation. On several occasions, I had prepared a formal interview, but discovered that informality was more appropriate: A few jokes and "chitchat" offered a greater possibility of getting my questions answered. When an interviewee felt at ease, he opened up more, and this contributed to a successful interview. These extensive preliminaries were just one more reminder of the interviewees' power over an interviewer.

In order to ensure the success of an interview, at the beginning I tried to avoid asking sensitive questions, and concentrated instead on the technical aspects of police work. When I later turned to questions about corruption or human rights violations, I was careful not to coax statements that an interviewee would later regret or that might make me uneasy about knowing something that I was "not supposed to know" at that time (Sluka 1995). An important interview strategy was being sensitive to what I was "supposed" to know and when I was "supposed" to know it. Of course, I wanted such information eventually, but at a time "appropriate" for both interviewee and me. This seemed to buy me the opportunity to ask more sensitive questions later, when my discretion had time to be established. Within this implicit power negotiation, I kept my eyes and ears open and made mental notes of any illegal things that I witnessed or learned about in interviews or casual conversations.

Most of my information about police irregularities came from a group of male police cadets whom I had known at the academy. At regular meetings after their academy graduation, these confidential informants spoke freely about abusive colleagues and police corruption, including, but not limited to, the purchase of ranks and paying to pass academy exams. One student in particular provided me with a wealth of such information; he had been transferred from precinct to precinct because of his refusal to participate in extortion and bribery—disaffection greased this interviewee's tongue.

In all interviews, I tried to be as honest as possible about my study, but I still felt manipulative. For example, to gain an interviewee's trust and establish rapport, I had to be sensitive to the interviewee's expectations. When I noticed that an interviewee liked to display his knowledge, as if he were a teacher speaking to a young student, I became an eager pupil. When I recognized that an interviewee was probing my academic knowledge of policing, I adopted the role of an expert, showing that I had good academic knowledge about police institutions. When an interviewee was authoritarian, I became subordinate. When I discovered that someone was sensitive to "female charms," I used them. In other words, in order to secure cooperation from the men I was interviewing, I had to adhere to their patriarchal notions about women, something discovered by Gelsthorpe (1990) in her study of men in prison and by McKee and O'Brien (1983) in their examination of "fatherhood."

Yet, just the same, as time passed (months and even years), I was amazed at how freely some policemen came to speak about the sensitive topics they had considered taboo at an earlier point in my research. After a long research association, and up to fifty cups of coffee together, interviewees had apparently ceased to be concerned about me writing a book about their Civil Police institution, perhaps one of the benefits of spending years in the field. However, one drawback is that the more time I spent with an interviewee, the greater the probability of his making inappropriate sexual advances toward me, an outcome that increased interviewee's relative power over me.

Huggins: Cautiously Approaching Brazilian Police Secrets

Spending only three months conducting interviews, and carrying out only one interview with each interviewee, I tended not to experience problems with sexual harassment. My biggest problem was that the majority of prospective interviewees would not grant an interview if I began by informing them that the team was studying police torture and murder. I told an interviewee that we were conducting a comparative study about policemen's lives in times of conflict and crisis, which was indeed the case. I then explained that our team was examining the careers of Brazilian police who had been in service between the 1950s and the 1980s. This too was correct because the study required information from the periods before, during, and after Brazil's military regime. Only after I had established rapport with a police interviewee—usually some two hours into a three- to four-hour interview—did I ask about a policeman's involvement in brutality, torture, and murder. Even then, these issues had to be handled with great care or the interviewee would refuse to proceed further.

Recognizing that an interviewee's memory about atrocity could not be probed until the dynamic of silence that was controlling both researcher and interviewee had been penetrated, I became part of a secrecy interaction that contained four elements: security measures, espionage, entrusted disclosures, and post hoc security precautions (see Tefft 1980a, 1980b). The interviewees used "security measures" throughout an interview to protect sensitive information and personal identity and to guard against my efforts to secure their secrets. A common "security strategy" employed by the police denounced by human rights groups was to flatly refuse to be interviewed and then to suggest another policeman who had supposedly carried out definitively evil deeds. Throughout the process, I had a nagging feeling that these police assumed that I was so gullible, perhaps because I was a woman, that I believed their stories. They may have assumed that as a foreigner, I had not read Brazilian press accounts of their public exposure by human rights groups. In fact, I had read such accounts, but naturally assumed it would be counterproductive to disclose this. By contradicting a potential interviewee, I might encourage him to exercise his power to pull out of the interview.

A common security strategy that enhanced an interviewee's power relative to mine was for him to delay revealing secrets until my bona fides had been established: They would ask me about my family—"Are you married?" "Do you have children?"—about my interest in studying the police, and about my plans for publishing the study. Once the interview began to progress past this point, I used "espionage" to penetrate an interviewee's defenses. Espionage involves finding what a secret-holder will exchange for partial or complete revelation of his information. Because money or other material goods were not going to be offered in exchange for information, I had to come up with ethical forms of what Pierre Bourdieu (1977) terms "symbolic capital." This included continually reminding interviewees about the importance of their insider knowledge of policing and their unique opportunity to contribute to an understanding of Brazilian police. A more subtle form of symbolic capital was to acquiesce in interviewees' digressions, including listening to long autobiographies and unfocused self-analyses. I learned very quickly that cutting off an interviewee in the middle of one of his seeming digressions resulted in a flash of anger and threats to cease the interview, something that is possibly more common when a woman takes charge of redirecting an interview than when a male interviewee does so. In any case, by allowing an interviewee to adorn some part of his answer—usually in response to questions about violence—in a way seemingly off the subject, I could "purchase" the trust necessary for securing other secrets later on.

At first I was concerned that interviewees' long digressions would never get back to the policeman's hidden stories. Indeed, Simmel (1950) argues that the function of "symbolic adornment" is to distract from the hidden. However, rather than an interviewee's adornments wasting my time, they signaled that I had come close to his most precious secrets: It became clear that interviewees' digressions were really a form of "entrusted disclosure," a process of the interviewee himself setting up his account in a way that provided a favorable background for what was to follow. Sounding like pure and simple prevarication, "entrusted disclosure" was used to influence my view of an interviewee as a "professional" who had "appropriately" carried out torture and murder. The interviewees' "entrusted disclosures" were used to neutralize the possible negative image of their past conduct and to maintain or even enhance their power relative to me. In the process, I learned what interviewees considered a culturally acceptable explanation for atrocity (see Cohen 1993; Crelinsten 1993; Huggins et al. 2002, chap. 11).

Interviewees used "post hoc security" measures to neutralize shame, guilt, or punishment, or to incorporate me into the secrecy process. For example, after one torture trainee–turned-murderer had spoken openly about the killings that he had committed in a notorious state-organized murder squad, he began looking for some poetry he had written. After presenting it as a gift to Haritos-Fatouros and me, the two females in our research team, this former policeman continued to explain the violence that he had committed. He had briefly deflected attention from his bad side and used gift giving and the social reciprocity associated with it to introduce my colleague and me to his more positive side, an illustration of Robben's (1995) "ethnographic seduction," defined as employing "personal defenses and social strategies . . . [that lead the researcher] astray from an intended course" (83).

SOLICITING AND HEARING ATROCITIES

Huggins: Deposing Atrocity

Personal and social memory about atrocity cannot be constructed until the dynamic of silence that controls both researcher and interviewee has been neutralized. For the researcher, this requires becoming conscious of the interviewee and interviewer identities that can reinforce certain kinds of silences. For example, if a violence worker is to speak truthfully about his career, he must be willing to become open and public, at least to the interviewer, about his past deeds. This often means squaring past violence with the current sociopolitical climate and the interviewee's own, usually changed, status (Huggins 2000; Huggins et al. 2002).

At the same time, the interviewer must be conscious of bearing witness to atrocity and recognize the ways that, in working to expose atrocity, an interviewer can inadvertently promote an atmosphere of silence and secrecy. For example, moral sensitivity to difficult topics can keep researchers from pursuing or probing atrocity testimonies in the first place; Marie-Louise Glebbeek, however, strategically delayed exploring sensitive information in order to secure such information later. Furthermore, the pain of listening to violent histories can lead interviewers to distance themselves emotionally from disturbing material, something Inga Clendinnen (1998) argues hampered research on Nazi atrocity perpetrators. And "hierarchies of credibility" can make the assertions of violence perpetrators appear illegitimate, as Howard Becker (1967) has argued for deviants in general, and Reay (1996) discovered for race, gender, and class hierarchies. Together, the factors identified by Clendinnen and Becker could lead an interviewer to fail to solicit atrocity perpetrators' stories or to misread and interpret their silences and responses.

But of course even soliciting violence workers' accounts far from guarantees their disclosing past atrocities. One strategy for breaking the secrecy surrounding state-linked violence, a method that I (2002) label "deposing atrocity,"[6] involves an intentional play on words. It suggests simultaneously the two meanings of depose—in legal terminology, "to testify," and in political terms, "to remove from a position of authority." Accomplishing the first version of deposition leads the interviewer to solicit deponents' explanations, justifications, and accounts of atrocity—getting them to testify about what they have done, how they did it, and why they carried it out.

To accomplish these goals, deposing atrocity also requires overthrowing the authority of secrecy that silences interviewer and interviewee. For the interviewer, this is facilitated by taking the role of an "onlooker witness," a phrase coined to indicate that the researcher is simultaneously inside and outside the interviewee's account. Thus, as Robben (1995, 84; see also Nordstrom and Robben 1995) argues, ethnographic researchers "need to analyze [violence perpetrators'] accounts and be attentive to [the ethnographers'] own inhibitions, weaknesses, and biases [in order to] better understand . . . both victim and victimizer." This is essentially Rebecca Campbell's (2001) argument in *Emotionally Involved*: To understand painful subjects, a researcher needs to recognize and understand the unpleasant emotions and self-doubts generated by soliciting unsettling accounts. An onlooker witness deposing atrocity must mediate between each of two pairs of research approaches—listening without moral acceptance and empathizing without condoning—a process that begins when an interviewee account raises questions about the interviewer's own values and identity.

TACKLING ETHICAL CHALLENGES

Glebbeek: Ignore Some; Anger at Others

I felt constantly that I had to betray my own personal and research ethics to carry out my research. In one example, during a surprise visit to a police precinct building, a man rushed up to me and began screaming in my face. Initially assuming that this was an angry policeman challenging my unannounced visit, I suddenly noticed that the man's hands were cuffed at his back—an arrestee who had escaped from the precinct's makeshift detention area. When a precinct policeman saw what was going on, he grabbed the arrestee and hit him violently in the face with the butt of his revolver. I was profoundly shocked and disturbed, but there was little that I could do about it. I felt that ethically I should have taken the side of the mistreated prisoner, but also recognized that this would harm my research relationship with precinct police. I thus ignored the situation and left the building, but resolved to incorporate this incident into my assessment of Guatemalan Civil Police reform.

In another example, having received permission from a high-level Guatemalan police official to move to another phase of my research, I left his office feeling positively about this man. Later that day, I read in a newspaper that in the 1980s the man had headed a death squad. I was stunned: How could I have had any positive feelings for such a man? These painful doubts were exacerbated when, just a few hours later, I interviewed a person whose family member had been killed in the 1980s—either by that policeman himself or by a man just like him. Such conflicting situations and feelings made it sometimes difficult to ignore my anger and remain impartial. These issues bubbled up when, on my way to a police conference hosted in one of the Guatemalan police departments, the car in which I was traveling stopped for villagers protesting along and across the road. In the dirt at the side of the road was the body of a man, shot and killed by a policeman unwilling to yield to protestors. The policeman was on his way to the same police conference that I was traveling to attend. Thoughts raced through my mind: Could I still go to the conference? Would it be possible for me to pull myself together and be a "professional"? Could I back-stage my negative feelings about such police long enough to conduct interviews with them?

These challenges to my research ethics were everyday occurrences. Even far away in the Netherlands, writing about Guatemalan police illegalities, I felt as if I were betraying police informants' trust—an irrational way of thinking that illustrates the conflicts inherent in adopting "progression to friendship" in research on violence perpetrators. Continually I had to ask myself how someone studying a police institution with a long history of violence and repression could become in any way partial to that institution. I had not anticipated that objectivity itself—that is, seeing interviewees as people first and listening openly to their accounts—would pull me into the interviewee's point of view. If, as researchers, we could simply objectify and demonize the violent police we study—as they have done to their victims— this would certainly provide a check on developing feelings of humanity toward them. But, of course, demonizing and objectifying those we study would violate the most basic rules of research and ethical practice.

Reflexive Introspection

In the end, the most important check on becoming either too partial or too negative about any of the groups that I was studying was to engage in reflexive introspection. I questioned myself about the correct moral or ethical research course in each given situation. Such questioning was often nurtured by my own silences during interviewee testimonies that

I found morally repugnant. During such silences that such repugnance generated, I would ask myself what my silences meant ethically. Did they suggest approval of an interviewee's disclosures? What did my role switching during an interview imply about my own positions relative to an interviewee's testimony?

If researchers work alone, such personal self-examinations are frequently the only way to overcome the anxieties associated with emotionally charged interviewing, whereas researchers in a team can meet and discuss interviews and explore their feelings and reactions to interviews, as Campbell (2001) did in her research on rape victims. However, even within such a supportive group context, Campbell's team of female researchers still felt a great deal of fear and anger about rape perpetrators—emotions that Campbell describes as rooted in the experience of being a woman in a "rape culture" where all women are rendered vulnerable to violence.

Huggins: Anger, Transference, Complicity

One of the most difficult things about hearing painful and anger-producing accounts is that the interviewer must find ways of keeping her own anger out of the research setting. In my interviews with Brazilian violence workers, I discovered that these feelings could not be allowed to creep into the interview situation if the interviewees were to continue their disclosures. I had to push negative feelings about interviewees to the back-stage and deal with them later—alone in my hotel room. One way of coping with my anger and paranoia was to become analytical about interviewees, my role with them, and their accounts about violence. By becoming analytical, I could more effectively process what I was hearing. I learned to see an interview as including real-but-shifting—as well as fictional—identities on the part of both interviewer and interviewee. I recognized that an interviewer cannot express all that she really feels and expect an interviewee to give up what she needs. Likewise, interviewees cannot disclose everything that they are and still protect their hidden identities and secrets.

Yet knowing all this academically did not completely shield me from feelings of moral and ethical compromise. For example, in an interview with Bruno, who was on a human rights group's list of known torturers, he maintained that he had never tortured anyone: "I could not have done so because I was then warden of a prison outside the urban areas"; Bruno alleged that most torture had occurred in urban areas. I knew that this claim was unlikely, because many facilities for political prisoners were in hard-to-reach locations precisely because their isolation afforded protection against exposure. Yet I did not feel it within my research role to contradict Bruno. However, by not challenging Bruno's positive presentation of himself, was I validating his positive presentation of self? Was this torturer's testimony sufficiently important to warrant me becoming part of, and therefore promoting at least to some degree, albeit temporarily, Bruno's fictional identity? Was I compromising my research ethics because I knew that a failure to support Bruno's identity narrative could suspend the interview itself?

Reflexive Introspection

These nagging ethical questions pointed to an even more formidable one: What is the appropriate role for an interviewer who deposes atrocity—"objective" observer, maintaining distance from subjects and subject matter, or "subjective" participant in the ethnographic worldview of an atrocity perpetrator? By encouraging Bruno to continue, I had allowed myself to be incorporated into what Erving Goffman (1961) would call Bruno's "face maintenance." This established a dynamic that moved the interview toward discovering more of Bruno's secrets through a new collaborative synthesis between myself and Bruno, an example of what Habenstein (1970) labels "research bargaining" and an illustration of how power is negotiated in the course of an interview. It is quite clear that once the new interview equilibrium with Bruno had been established—with this troubled torturer's identity implicitly validated—Bruno was able to talk more openly about his past (see Huggins et al. 2002).

But Bruno did not get off without his own turmoil: The day after my interview with him, Bruno arrived midmorning—two hours late—to drive me to the Civil Police Academy. In a sweat on a cool day, highly agitated, smelling of alcohol, and on the verge of tears, Bruno stated that the interview had left him nervous, upset, and depressed. He said that his life was falling apart: His marriage was failing, his job was boring, and he had no reason to live. When I asked what had happened, Bruno said that looking at his present life through the eyes of the past had made him wonder who he is today. This created an ethical dilemma: Bruno needed help, but I could not tell his colleagues at the police academy all that he had shared with me the day before to explain his present condition. However, the problem was resolved when one of Bruno's colleagues confided that Bruno had "been very upset and troubled" for some time. Bruno's colleague had already intervened to get his friend psychological help. It was not the interview disclosure that had precipitated the emotional turmoil; it had merely refocused it.

Just the same, when I recount this interview to criminal justice scholars and students in the United States, there is often moral outrage about the ethics of conducting research that so deeply upset an interviewee—even if he is a torturer. Conversely, when I describe Bruno's breakdown to Latin American faculty and students—whether or not they have been themselves, or have had a family member, victimized by security force abuse—their response is exactly the opposite: "Such a man gave so much misery to others that he deserves whatever he gets." This polemic notwithstanding, just looking at how Bruno's grief structured my interview with him, by sharing his discomfort with me—something that this very strictly masculine police-man would not likely do with a male interviewer—Bruno incorporated me into his ongoing disclosures.

CONCLUSION: LISTENING, BELIEVING, SURVIVING

In the end, nagging questions remain about whether an interviewer can trust the accounts of police, especially those guarding secrets about their own and other police abuses of power. Does skepticism about the ability of perpetrators to be honest, along with real fear of them personally, influence what scholars research and write about them? How does the emotion-ally devastating impact of atrocity stories shape research narratives about state violence? Yet while seeking answers to these important questions, the researcher must carefully and persistently chip away the wall of secrecy surrounding illegal police activities.

In sharp contrast to the permissibility of research on survivors of atrocity—where an interviewer can morally accept taking simultaneously the role of interviewer, observer, and victim (see Campbell 2001; Gunn 1997) and be morally transformed by such "embodied" involvement in atrocity survivors' accounts (Frank 1995; Gunn 1997, 3)—the researcher who deposes atrocity must solicit the accounts of morally indefensible violence perpetrators. Campbell (2001) found in her study of rape sur-vivors that the interviewers "got through" unsettling accounts about rape by "checking out for a moment, filtering, selecting . . . regulating pain by limiting what you take in" (72–73). In fact, I actively engaged in this process while interviewing Brazilian torturers and assassins—shutting down emotionally during an interview in order to protect myself from what I was hearing. However, this is not without dilemmas of its own. Was I engaging in the same kind of numbing that had made it possible for violence workers to maim and kill their victims? Did such "checking out" make me into an emotionless machine capable of glossing over the objectionable content I was hearing?

A researcher's choices in studies of violence can create as many ethical and emotional problems as they resolve. Whether the researcher is male or female may not change the moral choices, but we suggest that gender may influence which kinds of moral choices surface and how they are experi-enced and handled. This question can only be answered by comparative reports from male and from other female researchers. Indeed, our com-parative analysis has raised many more questions than it has answered. We have discovered a number of gender-related problems and possibilities associated with women researching male-dominated police institutions, especially where penetrating secrecy is a necessary outcome of such research. We have argued that, in some cases, gender-related factors interacted in our cases with such associated status characteristics as age, professional status, nationality, and class/ethnicity, without being able to do more than speculate about the general consequences of such factors for all research processes and outcomes. Yet the very fact that some gender-associated and gender-interacting factors have been discovered in two women's studies of Latin American police institutions suggests the importance of exploring gendered research dynamics further.

A gender comparative study[7] might investigate whether male researchers have as many problems being taken seriously by male police interviewees as women researchers do. Perhaps young males who are not police themselves and who are unaffiliated with a university at the time of their research would experience many of the same problems as Marie-Louise Glebbeek. However, it is unlikely that many male police interviewees would construe an interview appointment as the male interviewer's desire to "date" them—a dynamic that very seriously complicated Glebbeek's research.

Perhaps the greatest impediment to both overcoming and examining gender dynamics in criminological research is that much published scholarship does not explicitly consider cross-gender research dynamics. However, as our research has illustrated, the gendered complications faced by women studying male-dominated and male-structured institutions need not keep a researcher from obtaining a wealth of useful information. Yet for such research to be successful the researcher must recognize the gendered stumbling blocks and develop conscious strategies for overcoming them.

NOTES

1. An earlier version of this article was published in *Theoretical Criminology*. Martha Huggins wishes to acknowledge Mika Haritos-Fatouros and Philip Zimbardo for their valuable contributions to *Violence Workers* (2002). Malcolm Willison's editorial comments on several versions of this article were invaluable. Suggested readings by Tulane Sociology Department colleague April Brayfield moved my thinking forward.

Marie-Louise Glebbeek wishes to thank her colleague Kees Koonings of the Department Cultural Anthropology of Utrecht University for reading and commenting on her work; she appreciated his informed comments.

2. The 1996 Peace Accord formally ended the thirty-six-year civil conflict and laid a foundation for extensive civil society reforms, including creating a single National Civilian Police, increasing community involvement in police recruitment, and creating a more multiethnic police force (Glebbeek 2001, 437–38). These proposed changes were potentially monumental in a country that had operated for almost forty years through a military-enforced national security doctrine.

3. While female recruits were included in Glebbeek's larger study, there were too few to include in this analysis.

4. Such units included the Social and Political Police (DOPS), Civil Police criminal investigations units (e.g., the DEIC in Sao Paulo), the Civil Police homicide and property crimes divisions, Civil and Militarized Police motorized patrols and SWAT and riot teams, and the Militarized Police intelligence division (P-2). Police were also sought from the special operations and intelligence squads that combined Civil Police, Militarized Police, and the military itself (e.g., GOE, OBAN, DOI/CODI).

5. Among the "violence worker" torturers and murderers, the largest subset—nine—still defined themselves within the police institution, even though in three of these cases they had long since retired from policing. Among the fourteen atrocity-perpetrating "violence worker" policemen, eight were no longer in the police force: Three had retired, one was in prison but had not been stripped of his police badge, three others were in prison and expelled from their force, and one, having been expelled from his police organization (but not in prison), was petitioning to reenter his police force. The other six atrocity perpetrators were still working policemen.

6. Huggins wishes to thank Tom McGee for suggesting this useful concept.

7. Such an anthology is exactly what Huggins and Glebbeek plan for the near future. If interested in participating, see the *Women Fielding Danger* Web site: www .womenfieldingdanger.com

REFERENCES

Becker, Howard S. (1967). "Whose Side Are We On?" *Social Problems* 14 (Winter), 239–47.

Bourdieu, Pierre. (1977). *Outline of a Theory of Practice*. Cambridge: Cambridge University Press.

Cain, Maureen. (1986). "Realism, Feminism, Methodology, and Law." *International Journal of the Sociology of Law* 14, no. 3/4, 255–67.

Campbell, Rebecca. (2001). *Emotionally Involved: The Impact of Researching Rape*. New York/London: Routledge.

Clendinnen, Inga. (1998). *Reading the Holocaust*. New York: Cambridge University Press.

Cohen, Stan. (1993). "Human Rights and Crimes of the State: The Culture of Denial." *Australian and New Zealand Journal of Criminology* 26 (July), 97–115.

Cotterill, Pamela. (1992). "Interviewing Women: Issues of Friendship, Vulnerability, and Power." *Women's Studies International Forum* 15, no. 5/6, 593–606.

Crelinsten, Ronald D. (1993). "The World of Torture: A Constructed Reality." Unpublished paper.

Cunningham-Burley, Sarah. (1984). "We Don't Talk about It . . . Issues of Gender and Method in the Portrayal of Grandfatherhood." *Sociology* 18, no. 3, 325–37.

Faraday, Annabel, and Kenneth Plummer. (1986). "Doing Life Histories." *Sociological Review* 27, no. 4, 773–98.

Frank, Arthur W. (1995). *The Wounded Storyteller: Body, Illness, and Ethics*. Chicago: University of Chicago Press.

Gelsthorpe, Lorraine. (1990). "Feminist Methodologies in Criminology: A New Approach or Old Wine in New Bottles?" In *Feminist Perspectives in Criminology*, edited by L. Gelsthorpe and A. Morris, 89–106. Buckingham, UK: Open University Press.

Gelsthorpe, Lorraine, and Allison Morris, eds. (1990). *Feminist Perspectives in Criminology*. Buckingham, UK: Open University Press.

Glebbeek, Marie-Louise. (2000). "The Police Reform and the Peace Process in Guatemala: The Fifth Promotion of the New National Civilian Police into Action." Paper presented at the Latin American Studies Association, Miami, FL, March 16–18.

———. (2001). "Police Reform and the Peace Process in Guatemala: The Fifth Promotion of the National Civilian Police." *Bulletin of Latin American Research* 20, no. 4, 431–53.

———. (2003). *In the Crossfire of Democracy: Police Reform and Police Practice in Post-Civil War Guatemala*. Amsterdam: Rosenberg Publishers.

Goffman, Erving. (1961). *Encounters*. Indianapolis: Bobbs-Merill.

Gunn, Janet Varner. (1997). "Autobiography in the 'Emergency Zone': Reading as Witnessing." Paper presented at the Modern Languages Association Conference, Toronto, ON, December 29.

Habenstein, Robert. (1970). "The Ways of Pathways." In *Pathways to Data: Field Methods for Studying Ongoing Social Organizations*, edited by Robert W. Habenstein. Chicago: Aldine.

Huggins, Martha K. (1998). *Political Policing: The United States and Latin America*. Durham, NC: Duke University Press.

———. (2000). "Legacies of Authoritarianism: Brazilian Torturers and Murderers' Reformulation of Memory." *Latin American Perspectives* 27, no. 2, 57–78.

Huggins, Martha K., Mika Haritos-Fatouros, and Philip Zimbardo. (2002). *Violence Workers: Torturers and Murderers Reconstruct Brazilian Atrocities*. Berkeley and Los Angeles: University of California Press.

Jaggar, Allison. (1989). "Love and Knowledge: Emotion in Feminist Epistemology." *Inquiry: An Interdisciplinary Journal of Philosophy* 32 (June).

Krieger, Susan. (1991). *Social Science and the Self: Personal Essays on an Art Form*. New Brunswick, NJ: Rutgers University Press.

McKee, Lorna, and Margaret O'Brien. (1983). "Interviewing Men: 'Taking Gender Seriously.'" In *The Public and the Private*, edited by Eva Gamarnikow, David Morgan, June Purvis, and Daphene Taylorson, 147–61. London: Heinemann.

Nordstrom, C., and A. Robben. (1995). *Fieldwork under Fire: Contemporary Studies of Violence and Survival*. Berkeley and Los Angeles: University of California Press.

Oakley, Ann. (1981). "Interviewing Women: A Contradiction in Terms." In *Doing Feminist Research*, edited by Helen Roberts, 30–61. London/Boston: Routledge & Kegan Paul.

Payne, Leigh. (2000). *Uncivil Movements: The Armed Right Wing and Democracy in Latin America*. Baltimore: Johns Hopkins University Press.

Phoenix, Ann. (1994). "Practising Feminist Research: The Intersection of Gender and 'Race' in the Research Process." In *Researching Women's Lives from a Feminist Perspective*, edited by Mary Maynard and June Purvis, 41–72. London: Taylor & Francis.

Rapoport, R., and R. Rapoport. (1976). *Dual Career Families Reexamined*. London: Martin Robertson.

Reay, Diane. (1996). "Insider Perspectives or Stealing the Words out of Women's Mouths: Interpretation in the Research Process." *Feminist Review* 53 (Summer), 57–73.

Reinharz, Shulamit. (1979). *On Becoming a Social Scientist*. New Brunswick, NJ: Transaction.

Robben, A. (1995). "The Politics of Truth and Emotion among Victims and Perpetrators of Violence." In *Fieldwork under Fire: Contemporary Studies of Violence and Survival*, edited by C. Nordstrom and A. Robben. Berkeley and Los Angeles: University of California Press.

Simmel, George. (1950). *The Sociology of George Simmel*. Glencoe, IL: Free Press.

Sluka, J. (1995). "Reflections on Managing Danger in Fieldwork. Dangerous Anthropology in Belfast." In *Fieldwork under Fire. Contemporary Studies of Violence and Survival*, edited by C. Nordstrom and A. Robben. Berkeley and Los Angeles: University of California Press.

Stanley, L., and S. Wise. (1983). *Breaking Out: Feminist Consciousness and Feminist Research*. London: Routledge & Kegan Paul.

Tefft, S. (1980a). "Secrecy, Disclosure and Social Theory." In *Secrecy: A Cross-Cultural Perspective*, edited by S. Tefft. New York: Human Sciences.

———. (1980b). "Secrecy as a Social and Political Process." In *Secrecy: A Cross-Cultural Perspective*, edited by S. Tefft. New York: Human Sciences.

Index

About the Editors and Contributors

Angela R. Demovic has a BA in psychology and English literature from Western Illinois University, and MA and PhD degrees in anthropology from Tulane University in New Orleans. Demovic is assistant professor in Wichita State University's Department of Geography and Anthropology, where she offers courses in anthropology and women and gender studies. With a research focus on the intersections of economics and gender, Demovic has conducted ethnographic research in Tanzania and New Orleans. She has also worked as an applied anthropologist, focusing on the ethical collection of oral histories for National Parks in Hawai'i.

Lynn Fredriksson, advocacy director for Africa (Amnesty International USA), is a doctoral candidate in political science at the University of Wisconsin–Madison. From 1997 to 2000, she coordinated the Washington office of the East Timor Action Network (ETAN). Since that time Fredriksson has been a consultant for human rights organizations in Africa and Southeast Asia, and for diaspora organizations working for human rights in Africa and the Middle East. Fredriksson has conducted fieldwork in numerous countries, including East Timor, Uganda, Rwanda, the Democratic Republic of Congo, Kenya, and Somaliland. Her dissertation examines nationalist self-determination claims in Africa. She is coauthor (with Tricia Redeker Hepner) of "Regional Politics, Human Rights and U.S. Policy in the Horn of Africa," *Africa Policy Journal* (Spring 2007).

Marie-Louise Glebbeek, assistant professor of cultural anthropology at the University of Utrecht in the Netherlands, studies police reform in post–civil war Guatemala, which resulted in her published PhD dissertation, *In the*

Crossfire of Democracy: Police Reform and Police Practice in Post-Civil War Guatemala (Rozenberg, 2003; Purdue University Press, 2004), and in an article, "Police Reform and the Peace Process in Guatemala: the Fifth Promotion of the National Civilian Police," *Bulletin of Latin American Research* (October, 2001, 20, 4). As coordinator of Utrecht University's undergraduate research project in Guatemala, Glebbeek advises the Guatemalan NGO Proyecto de Innovación Curricular Guatemala–Holanda on curriculum reform at the Guatemalan Police Academy. Her current research focuses on violence, crime, and citizens' security in postwar countries with fragile states.

Donna Goldstein, associate professor of anthropology at the University of Colorado–Boulder, has written extensively on the intersection of race, gender, poverty, and violence in Brazil. Her Margaret Mead Award–winning book, *Laughter Out of Place: Race, Class, Violence, and Sexuality in a Rio Shantytown* (University of California Press, 2003) presents a hard-hitting critique of urban poverty, drawing on more than a decade of experience in Brazil. Throughout her career Goldstein has worked toward a politically engaged global anthropology that investigates poverty, gender, race, and sexual inequality, as well as urban violence, HIV/AIDS, and human rights. Goldstein's current research focuses on the effects of pharmaceutical politics and the HIV/AIDS epidemic on local populations in Argentina, Mexico, and Brazil.

Martha K. Huggins, Charles A. and Leo M. Favrot Professor of Human Relations at Tulane University in New Orleans and Roger Thayer Stone Professor of Sociology Emerita at Union College in Schenectady, New York, has written three books on crime and social control in Brazil, edited one on vigilantism and the state in Latin America, and authored numerous academic articles on crime, social control, and human rights in Brazil. Huggins's latest book (with M. Haritos-Fatouros and P. Zimbardo), *Violence Workers: Torturers and Murderers Reconstruct Brazilian Atrocities* (University of California Press, 2002), published in Brazil as *Operarios de Violencia* (UNB, Brasília, Brazil 2006), has led to her subsequent work on institutionalized torture by the United States. Huggins's thirty-three years of field research in Brazil and twelve years of directing undergraduate students in field study there nurtured her interest in how other women negotiate field research.

Jennifer Bickham Mendez, associate professor of sociology at the College of William and Mary, focuses on gender and globalization and on Latino/a migration to the "Nuevo (New) South." Her book *From the Revolution to the Maquiladoras: Gender, Labor and Globalization in Nicaragua* (Duke University Press, 2005) chronicles the formation and political strategies of a Nicaraguan working women's organization in its 1990s struggles to improve conditions for women in Nicaraguan garment assembly factories of free trade zones. Her work has appeared in *Social Problems* and *Mobilization* and *Labor Studies*. Her current research focuses on Latino/a migration to Williamsburg, Virginia.

Lois Presser, associate professor of sociology at the University of Tennessee, earned her degrees from Cornell University, Yale University, and the University of Cincinnati. Presser studies the connections between discourse and crime, and the promises and problems of restorative justice. Her book, *Been a Heavy Life: Stories of Violent Men* (University of Illinois Press, 2008), explores how violent men construct themselves as decent, heroic, and masculine in the face of stigma and under circumstances of captivity. Her articles have appeared in journals of criminology and sociology, including *Signs*, *Social Problems*, and *Theoretical Criminology*. Currently she is developing a general theory of harm based on the narratives of individuals and groups.

Kat Rito has a BA in sociology and Latin American studies from Tulane University's Newcomb College (2004) and holds a degree from the Tulane University Law School (2007). Rito provided numerous pro bono services as a law student, including uniting families separated during the Hurricane Katrina evacuation of New Orleans, securing legal services and medical resources for Katina-displaced HIV/AIDS patients, and returning "Katrina pets" to their original owners. She now practices defense litigation in Lafayette, Louisiana, with an emphasis on civil rights, educational, public entity, and professional liability law.

Victoria Sanford, associate professor of anthropology at Lehman College and the Gradute Center, City University of New York, is an elected member of the Committee for Human Rights of the American Anthropological Association. Sanford is author of *Buried Secrets: Truth and Human Rights in Guatemala* (Palgrave-Macmillan, 2003), *Violencia y Genocidio en Guatemala* (F&G Editora, 2004), and *La Masacre de Panzós: Etnicidad, tierra y violencia en Guatemala* (in press), and coeditor (with Asale Angel-Ajani) of *Engaged Observer: Anthropology, Advocacy, and Activism* (Rutgers University Press, 2006) and of the Guatemalan Forensic Anthropology Foundation's report to the Commission for Historical Clarification (2000). After completing her upcoming *Morality and Survival: Child Soldiers and Displacement in Guatemala and Colombia*, Sanford will begin *The Land of Pale Hands—A Study of Feminicide, Social Cleansing and Impunity in Guatemala*.

Stephanie Schwandner-Sievers has conducted ethnographic fieldwork in Albania since 1992 and Kosovo since 2000. Her MA (1993) and forthcoming PhD are from Free University in Berlin, Germany. Now an Honorary

Research Associate with the School of Slavonic and East European Studies, University College, London, in the UK, Schwandner-Sievers was the first Nash Fellow in Albanian Studies (1997–2003). Since 2004 she has taught at the University of Bologna in Italy. Schwandner-Sievers has edited books and published academic articles on Albanian identity constructions, memory and violence, gender and social change, transnational crime, and victimization. As head of her own consultancy company, Anthropology Applied Ltd, Schwandner-Sievers has produced policy-related bottom-up studies, including the World Bank Report *Conflict and Change in Kosovo* (2000) and "'Gun Culture' in Kosovo," *Small Arms Survey 2005*.

Meera Sehgal, assistant professor of sociology and women's and gender studies at the University of Wisconsin–Madison, specializes in social movements, gender, and South Asia. Her research, based on extensive ethnographic fieldwork, focuses on the mobilization and participation of women in a religious right-wing movement in India. Originally from India, Sehgal employs a transnational feminist perspective in her teachings and research; she travels regularly to India for research and family. Sehgal teaches courses on South Asia, social movements, qualitative methods, postcolonial feminist theory, feminist approaches to research, and women's health in the United States.

Roschanack Shaery-Eisenlohr received her PhD from the University of Chicago (2005) and was a postdoctoral fellow in the Department of Asian and Near Eastern Languages and Literatures and International and Area Studies at Washington University in St. Louis, Missouri. She is now fellow at Leiden's (NL) International Institute for the Study of Islam in the Modern World. Her book *Shi'ite Lebanon: Transnational Religion and the Making of National Identities* is forthcoming (Columbia University Press). This book is on Lebanese Shi'ites' national identity production since the 1970s in light of their transnational ties to Iran.Shaery-Eisenlohr has published on Iranian-Lebanese Shi'ite relations in peer-reviewed Persian and English policy-oriented journals. Her new book project focuses on the politics of trauma therapy in postwar Lebanon.

Monique Skidmore, an anthropologist, has studied Burma since 1994 and is currently associate dean at the Australian National University in Canberra. Skidmore's books include *Myanmar: The State, Community, and the Environment* (with Trevor Wilson, Australian National University Press, 2008), *Karaoke Fascism: Burma and the Politics of Fear* (University of Pennsylvania Press, 2004), *Burma at the Turn of the Twenty-First Century* (University of Hawaii Press, 2005), *Women and the Contested State: Religion, Violence, and Agency in South and Southeast Asia* (with Patricia Lawrence,

University of Notre Dame Press, 2007). Skidmore's articles and books have been recognized by a Rockefeller Visiting Fellowship (2002–2003) at the University of Notre Dame's Kroc Institute, and her selection as a 2003–2007 Australian Research Council Scholar at the Australian National University's Center for Cross-Cultural Research.

Mangala Subramaniam, associate professor of sociology at Purdue University, was educated at Delhi University in India, the University of Pennsylvania, and the University of Connecticut. Among her many awards are a dissertation-writing fellowship at the United Nations University's Institute of Advanced Studies in Tokyo, Japan; the American Sociological Association/National Science Foundation grant for "cutting edge research" and research activities: Fund for the Advancement of the Discipline award. Subramaniam has published articles in *Critical Sociology*, *Mobilization*, and *Gender & Society*. Her latest book, *The Power of Women's Organizing: Gender, Caste, and Class in India* (Lexington, 2006), focuses on the women's movement in India with specific attention to *dalit* women's organizing. She is completing a volume on gendered dimensions of dowry and marriage among South Asians.

Jocelyn Viterna, assistant professor of sociology at Harvard University, received a BA in sociology and Latin American studies from Kansas State University (1995) and an MA (2000) and PhD (2003) in sociology from Indiana University Bloomington. She taught at Tulane University in New Orleans from 2003 to 2006 and was an Academy Scholar at Harvard's Weatherhead Center for International and Area Studies from 2006 until 2007, when she joined Harvard's Department of Sociology and Social Studies. Viterna's work has been published in the *American Journal of Sociology*, *Social Forces*, and the *Latin American Research Review*. She is working on a book from her dissertation, *When Women Wage War: Explaining the Personal and Political Consequences of Guerrilla Activism in El Salvador*.